The Archaeology of Value

Essays on prestige and the processes of valuation

Edited by

Douglass Bailey
with the assistance of Steve Mills

BAR International Series 730
1998

Published in 2019 by
BAR Publishing, Oxford

BAR International Series 730

The Archaeology of Value

ISBN 9780860549635 paperback
ISBN 9781407350516 e-book

DOI https://doi.org/10.30861/9780860549635

A catalogue record for this book is available from the British Library

This book is available at www.barpublishing.com

BAR Publishing is the trading name of British Archaeological Reports (Oxford) Ltd. British Archaeological Reports was first incorporated in 1974 to publish the BAR Series, International and British. In 1992 Hadrian Books Ltd became part of the BAR group. This volume was originally published by John and Erica Hedges in conjunction with British Archaeological Reports (Oxford) Ltd / Hadrian Books Ltd, the Series principal publisher, in 1998. This present volume is published by BAR Publishing, 2019.

BAR
PUBLISHING

BAR titles are available from:

BAR Publishing
122 Banbury Rd, Oxford, OX2 7BP, UK
EMAIL info@barpublishing.com
PHONE +44 (0)1865 310431
FAX +44 (0)1865 316916
www.barpublishing.com

Contents

Contributors

CAROLINA ANDERSSON
AND ANN-MARI HÅLLANS

Central Board of National Antiquities
Department of Archaeological Excavations
UV Stockholm
S 104 62 Stockholm

DOUGLASS W. BAILEY

School of History and Archaeology
University of Wales at Cardiff
P.O. Box 909
Cardiff CF1 3XU

JOHN CHAPMAN

Department of Archaeology
University of Durham
South Road
Durham DH1 3LE

ALEKSANDER PALAVESTRA

Institute for Balkan Studies
Knez Mihailova 35
Serbian Academy of Sciences and Arts
1100 Belgrade

MIKE PEARSON

Department of Theatre Studies
University of Aberystwyth
Aberystwyth
Ceredigion SY23 2AU

ANDRZEJ PYDYN

St. Cross College
University of Oxford
Oxford OX1 3OZ

FERNANDO QUESADA

Depto. de Prehistoria y Arqueologia
Universidad Autonoma de Madrid
28049 Madrid

NERISSA RUSSELL

Department of Anthropology
Mississippi State University
Mississippi 39762

ANTHONY SINCLAIR

University of Liverpool
William Hartley Building
Brownlow Street
Liverpool L69 3BX

ROBIN SKEATES

School of World Art Studies
and Museology
University of East Anglia
Norwich N4 7TJ

Acknowledgements

This book is the result of a day-long session held at the 1995 meeting of the European Association of Archaeologists which took place in Santiago de Compostela. With the exception of Russell's and Skeates', all of the chapters are rewritten and revised papers delivered in Compostela. I am grateful to the organising committee of the Santiago conference (especially Filipe Criado Boado) and to the members of the EAA who made the session a success.

The School of History and Archaeology of the University of Wales at Cardiff has supported the production of this volume in many ways. Travel and conference costs for the editor were provided by the school's Research Committee which also provided funding for preparing some of the artwork. In this respect, the editor is also grateful to Howard Mason and Ian Dennis who drew a number of illustrations and who oversaw the preparation of others. Geoff Boden provided much needed assistance with scanning images for Chapter 9 as well as general advice on the preparation of the manuscript. Problems with software were solved by Mark Hale of the Computing Centre in Cardiff and I am very grateful for Mark's help. I am also grateful to John Hedges at BAR who took on this book and produced it without delay. My greatest debt, however, lies with Steve Mills who carried out most of the work required to turn the manuscript into a publishable volume. Many thanks to him.

Finally, I would like to thank each of the contributors for patiently reworking and rewriting their chapters and for doing so quickly and without complaint. The result, I hope, is a coherent volume which brings together a diversity of perspectives on the archaeology of value, prestige and wealth.

DWB
Cardiff July 1998

Chapter 1

On being famous through time and across space

Douglass W. Bailey

Introduction

This chapter introduces the contributions to this book by suggesting that one of the fundamental principles of prestige, value and wealth is the ability to transcend time and space. This chapter looks at Nancy Munn's seminal work on value among the Gawa of the western Pacific, highlights her introduction of the mechanisms of extension, contraction, synchronisation and schismogenesis and asks the question, what is fame. The chapter then considers how each of the contributors to this book attacks the problem of an archaeology of prestige, value and wealth.

The Gawans and the kula

In 1973-5 and 1979-81 Nancy Munn lived among and studied the Gawa, a group who live in the northeast section of the Massim region of Papua New Guinea on a heavily forested atoll (Munn 1986). The atoll measures c. 7.6 sq. miles and which is populated by just over 500 people. The Gawans are an important link in the kula trade ring. The kula is a highly ritualised exchange of shell bracelets and necklaces along a ring of islands. The bracelets and necklaces are significant symbols of reciprocal relationships between the various trading partners. These formal reciprocal trading partnerships are maintained over long periods of time and connect the various island cultures of the Massim. The kula connects the Gawans with their proximate neighbouring groups as well as more distant contemporaries with whom the Gawans have no face-to-face contacts. For the Gawans the kula marks their widest regional network. Most importantly for Munn, the Gawans had become well-known for their ability to kula. Indeed they have become famous for it.

Munn wanted to know how the Gawans had become famous for their kula-ing. She suggested that at the base of the Gawan kula-fame is their ability to use hospitality and exchange to determine what activities happen where and when and with which people they happen. Munn proposed that the Gawans have a particular way in which they think in terms of time (past, present, future) and in terms of space (here, there, other places). This particular way of thinking, she suggested, is based on their conception of space-time. The Gawan mode of space-time is intersubjective (i.e., it is about the relationship between individuals and groups). It refers equally to the activities and processes which connect people as it does to the activities and processes which separate people. Munn was able to show that the Gawans think about their world in a variety of ways and that all of these ways can be defined in terms of time and space. Munn suggested that the fame of Gawans rests in the ways in which they manipulate ideas about their inter-subjective space-time. Most importantly, the Gawans characterise value in terms of different levels of spatio-temporal transformation. For the Gawans, the value of an act or an object is equal to its capacity to transform intersubjective space-time.

Extension, contraction, synchronisation, schismogenesis

Munn suggested that there are four principal ways in which the Gawans can transform intersubjective space-time and thus create or limit fame. The first mechanism for manipulating space-time is extension: the capacity of a thing or a person to go beyond the self. For the Gawans, the kula is a mechanism of extension: it is an exchange drama which transcends the actors and the immediate moment of the transaction. The kula extends intersubjective space-time by creating expectations for future exchanges and reciprocal returns of material between the participants. The relationships between individuals and groups and between islands therefore can be extended beyond the limits of the exchange event.

Munn argued that Gawans use garden stones to extend space-time in another way. Garden stones mark the limits of group ownership or of individual boundaries. The space-time of the garden is one of permanent storage or resource potential of the land. The stones function to define and express the permanence of the gardens: they assure renewal and long-term continuity. Garden stones thus extend the space-time of the garden beyond the immediacy of seasonal plantings and harvesting. The stones carry within themselves a synthesis of the past and future, held together, in the present.

For the Gawa then, the kula and the garden stones are key components of two, opposite conceptions of extending time-space: the stones are about immobility and internalised continuity in one place; the kula shells are about mobility and external release through the islands. Extension is a critical mechanism for creating fame because it allows a personal- or group-identity to move beyond the specific time and the restricted place of an event or a life.

Munn's second principal mechanism for manipulating fame by transforming intersubjective space-time is contraction. Munn defines contraction as the failure to expand space-time or the subversion of acts and processes which expand space-time. Amongst the Gawa, examples of contraction are activities which subvert the kula. For example, a precursor for kula exchanges is the provision of food hospitality to inter-island visitors. Food hospitality sets-up expectations of further food hospitality which may, in future, lead on to the more expansive kula shell exchange. The failure to offer food hospitality (or the consumption of food meant to be offered) is, therefore, an act of contraction. Other potential acts of contraction include the failure to remember reciprocal requirements or the death of an individual, which would contract space-time by focusing, through mourning, on the past without future potential. Contraction, therefore, is a critical component of fame in that it limits and prevents the movement of an individual- or group-identity beyond the specifics of the here and now.

The third mechanism for manipulating fame by transforming intersubjective space-time is synchronisation. This Munn defines as the co-ordination of acts to create a synchronous space-time which transcends the otherwise fragmented space-time of separate people in separate places. Synchronisation reinforces agreement, consensus and trust. Munn argues that the event of all Gawans sailing on the same kula trip at the same time is an example of synchronisation. Thus synchronisation can be a powerful amplifier to individual and, more especially, group fame.

The fourth mechanism for manipulating fame is schismogenesis. Munn defines schismogenesis as a lack of synchronisation: a form of disagreement which can break-down a project. Munn offers the failure to agree to sail at the same time as an example of schismogenesis. Schismogenesis, therefore, is a mechanism for fragmenting and reducing the power of acts of common expressions of individual or group fame.

Each of Munn's four mechanisms, therefore, contribute to the particular mode of Gawan time-space and to ways in which they promote or relegate positions of fame. Some mechanisms, such as extension and synchronisation are positive in character. Contraction and schismogenesis on the other hand are negative. Each mechanism, however, can be used to create or limit the fame of an individual by manipulating the interactive space-time of the Gawans and their near and distant exchange links.

Through the expectation of reciprocal transactions of food or shells, the kula establishes a temporal link between individuals. This link extends outside of the present, into the past and the future. Through acts of giving and travelling the kula establishes spatial links between people in different places. It is in the establishment of such links that fame emerges and spreads.

What is fame?

Munn argues that fame is an enhancement which transcends material, bodily being and which extends beyond the physical body, yet refers back to it. It is mobile. It circulates. It is a dimension of the person: a person's name travels apart from his or her presence. Munn shows how the kula is a process which transcends the simple act of exchange: it transcends and manipulates time and space. Through the kula the circulation and transaction of shells is converted into the oral circulation of the names of the shells and of the men linked to those shells. Thus names circulate via shells well beyond the possible physical travels of people: the kula extends the space-time of the individual and thus brings fame.

From Munn's analysis of the Gawa there emerge several important concepts which are applicable to the archaeological study of prestige. Perhaps most important is the attention which Munn directed at identifying the ways in which space-time can be manipulated and changed or maintained and confirmed. Thus an archaeology of prestige-fame must consider the potential of activities which extend, contract, synchronise and schismogenerate space-time.

Equally important is the light which Munn sheds on how different qualities and properties of things have different potencies for transforming interactive time and space. One of the key distinctions she notes is between consumables and durables. The durability of certain media allows occasional and non-repetitive acts to occur and to have lasting effect. With respect to increasing potencies for extending the space-time of one's fame or prestige, the giving of a perishable (e.g., the harvest via food hospitality) lays the groundwork for the kula exchange: in the latter, a man obtains a durable, named, artefact that works on a more extensive level of space-time and which eventually stimulates the circulation of the man's name. In a similar fashion the potency of the garden stones for expressing permanence and continuity (their heaviness and durability) makes them successful for marking the fixity of the internal structure of the garden.

Towards an archaeology of fame-prestige

An archaeological examination of fame, therefore, needs to consider objects and acts in terms of their potency for transforming time-space via the four mechanisms noted by Munn. Archaeological attention must focus on evaluating objects' and acts' durability or perishability and mobility or immobility. One advantage of examining the potential for fame in terms of space-time transcendence is that it forces investigation away from the assumptions of traditional approaches to value and prestige goods. Thus value is not inherent in an artefact because it is made of a non-local material or because it required great effort in its production or, even, because it was exchanged for something else. Value is created, maintained and manipulated. A second advantage of the space-time transcendence approach is that it opens interpretation to the reality of multiple, contemporary levels of prestige expression (e.g., the apparently opposite schemes of the garden stones and the kula shells which both exist within one group's conception of time and space).

Thus the whole adventure of investigating prestige in the archaeological record becomes detached from assumptions of inherent value and becomes linked to a study of the socio-political contexts of people and objects: the interactive space-time of prestige-fame. The target of investigation becomes the mechanisms through which fame can be manipulated. For Nancy Munn and the Gawa, the principal mechanisms are extension, contraction, synchronisation and schismogenesis. For other communities in other places and other times the shape and name of the mechanisms will, undoubtedly, be different. What will be the same however, (and this is the benefit of looking at Munn's study) is that people use mechanisms of some sort to manipulate identity over time and space. This is the thrust of this collection of essays: to move the study of value and prestige away from *a priori* assumption and towards a recognition of the context of value creation, maintenance, and disruption.

The structure of this book

In this book nine contributors investigate prestige-fame in a series of studies which range from the recent (post-medieval Sweden) to the early prehistoric (Palaeolithic Cantabria). Through this chronological depth and across the pan-European range, the contributors focus on a common theme: they each take a new perspective on value and prestige in the archaeological record. For some this entails a new look at a topic common to traditional studies of value and prestige. Thus Aleksander Palavestra looks at princely tombs in the late Bronze and early Iron Ages of the central Balkans, Fernando Quesada focuses on Iberian grave assemblages from the Iron Age and Mike Pearson examines early Bronze Age burials in lowland Britain. Similarly, Andrzej Pydyn investigates later prehistoric exchange in north-central Europe and Nerissa Russell attends to the value of cattle in the Neolithic Balkans. What is new about these investigations of traditionally value-laden categories of material culture or monumental landscapes is that each has taken a novel approach to the subject and each has picked apart (and in some cases turned on their heads) traditional ideas about prestige.

Equally thought provoking is the attention which the remainder of the contributors train onto elements of the archaeological record which are traditionally value-free. Thus Carolina Andersson and Ann-Mari Hållans, Mike Pearson and Anthony Sinclair promote new ideas about the values of the supposedly more mundane categories of material culture: Andersson and Hållans look at bulk-finds and refuse materials; Pearson considers objects in general; and Sinclair reworks traditional ideas about late Upper Palaeolithic stone tools. Similarly John Chapman pushes towards the values which are attributed to places in Neolithic Serbia.

There are two other big issues which almost all contributors address. The first is the processes through which value is created, manipulated or destroyed. Andersson and Hållans and Pydyn focus on consumption, acquisition and use; Pearson promotes performance; Pydyn unravels the ways in which value can change in the distance between export and import communities; and Sinclair sees value in the places and times of hunting and butchering animals. The second big issue is the dynamic nature of value and the reality of its multi-level character. Thus Palavestra draws a distinction between three levels of value of his princely tombs, Quesada suggests a distinction between qualitative and quantitative values within Iberian grave assemblages, and Pydyn differentiates relative and universal value-systems.

Most of the contributors met together for a day-long session at the inaugural meeting of the European Association of Archaeologists held at the end of 1995 in Santiago de Compostela in Spain. Two of the contributors (Russell and Skeates) was unable to attend and several of the Santiago participants choose not to examine the key issues and themes outlined above. All of the participants benefited from the opportunity to discuss their common interests in Santiago and the editor thanks the conference organisers for facilitating the meeting. All of the papers included in this volume are substantially re-written versions of the original presentations.

Chapter précis

Sinclair

In Chapter 2, Anthony Sinclair looks for value in hunter-gatherer societies of the later Upper Palaeolithic of south-west Europe. He suggests that we drop the factor of scarcity as the logic of value and look instead for the expression of values based on other premises. Sinclair chooses to focus on value based on skills and know-how as seen in the knowledge required and the technical skills necessary to produce particular stone tools. He argues that such value is associated with the performance of particular tasks and that it is these which are the subject of valuation.

Sinclair begins by questioning the relationship between material value and social status. He addresses Sahlins classic model identifying the original affluent society with the materially poorest hunter-gatherers. Sahlins' model was based, in part, on sharing and the high value which was placed on generosity. Sinclair suggests that archaeologists have been guilty of looking at the past in line with theories of value which were based on principles of material scarcity such as that developed by the economist John Kenneth Galbraith.

Sinclair argues that there is a cultural basis to the sharing model of Shalins and that, contrary to Sahlins assumptions, different hunter-gatherer groups behave differently. Indeed when distinctions between different (and within individual) hunter-gather groups are assessed (e.g., immediate return versus delayed return), it becomes evident that different systems of value have their own cultural values and their own cultural logic. Sinclair concludes his review of value in hunter-gatherer societies by setting the task for the remainder of his essay: to try and unlock the cultural logic of the later Upper Palaeolithic societies of southwestern Europe.

Sinclair begins by looking at the skills and knowledge which were valued and the ramifications of such valuations on other areas of life. He focuses on the Late Glacial Maximum and notes the trends in animal exploitation (e.g., the targeting of reindeer and red deer). Sinclair focuses attention on the distinctive stone tools made in western Europe at this time and directs particular emphasis to finely retouched bifaces (i.e., Solutrean points). He suggests that the bifaces were not just practical or utilitarian items but were symbolic of the hunting and processing of animals.

In unlocking the symbolism and use of the bifaces, Sinclair suggests that the sharing of meat after a kill created personal authority and prestige because of the reciprocal and dependency relations which were thus created. Ownership of a kill entailed not the right to keep it but the right to give it away and to create debt. Further study of the bifaces focuses on the techniques of bifacial thinning retouch which required progressively greater precision and of fine pressure flaking which required considerable physical strength. Adding these observations to ideas of emerging task-scapes in Late Glacial Maximum Europe leads Sinclair to argue that the events and places of hunting and butchering animals were events and places of high value. Similarly the times of hunting and butchering were also of high value. Sinclair concludes that, for the later Upper Palaeolithic Solutrean, value was differentially held and that particular places and times resonated with value based on tasks. Thus the hunter-gatherers of this time did not live in a time before differential value but within an alternative set of values which were not based on scarcity or accumulation.

Andersson and Hållans

In Chapter 3, Andersson and Hållans look at perceptions of status through patterns of consumer behaviour in the central Swedish town of Nyköping during the seventeenth century. Nyköping was one of Sweden's earliest towns and provides detailed evidence for the changes which occurred in Sweden in the Post-Medieval period. This study focuses on a particular slice of Nyköping's history: from the rebuilding of the town after the fire of 1665 until the destruction of the town during the final phase of the Great Northern War in 1719. Andersson and Hållans examine a well-documented town-block in Nyköping and focus their work at the level of the household.

They examine social differentiation among the households of a baker, a widow, a fisherman-boatman, a tanner and a turner. They note the distinction between the enfranchised master craftsmen (the baker, turner and tanner) and the disenfranchised (the boatman-fisherman and widow). A rental map of 1674 and other written sources provide detailed information about these households. Andersson and Hållans use the written sources to rank the households in order of social and economic status. The written records suggest that the households of the baker and turner had the highest economic status.

Archaeological investigations of the town-block allow Andersson and Hållans to qualify the information provided by the written sources. In order to shed light on social status, particular attention is directed to the bulk finds (tiles, ceramics and the houses themselves) and analysis centres on the artefacts usually described as waste (i.e., as found in the refuse layers).

Andersson and Hållans make an important contribution both to the investigation of value and to our understanding of post-medieval Sweden. They make a strong case for the role which consumption plays in communicating status and in regulating social interaction: consumer behaviour is the expression of social status. They confirm the importance of the processes of acquisition, use and disposal in the wider consideration of wealth, status and prestige. They argue forcefully that material culture must be interpreted and evaluated and not perceived as a direct reflection of human behaviour. Indeed, they propose that for seventeenth century Sweden, expressions of social and economic status are best understood as dramas where the home should be seen as the stage and the craftsmen as the actors. All of this is presented as part of the larger historical transition from a feudal society; a transition which challenged the old hierarchical order.

Pearson

In Chapter 4, the performance artist and scholar Mike Pearson investigates the process of valuation. Pearson approaches valuation from the basis of a 'theatre-archaeology' which he and others have been developing in recent years. Such an approach employs the terminology of the theatre and performance studies: audience, actors, props, staging, backdrop. Pearson offers the archaeologist an examination of contemporary theatrical theory and practice in an attempt to extend and elaborate the study of prehistoric funerary procedures.

Pearson introduces a glossary of terms: 'ostension' as a notion similar to that of showing and which implies two orders of participants (the watchers and the watched); 'performance' as a mode of communication and action distinct from the normal or everyday; 'omission' as the complexity of the real world as it is omitted in performance; 'kinesics' as communicative body movements; 'proxemics' as relative distances of body to body; 'haptics' as the touch of self and others; and 'scenario' in which activities may be choreographed or improvised.

Against this exciting new vocabulary, Pearson investigates the classic mortuary practice of early Bronze Age lowland Britain: the Beaker burial. Following John Barrett, Pearson argues that burial assemblages have more to do with the structure of the funeral than with the status of the individual. Grave-goods include three orders of material: that affixed to the corpse; that purposefully placed around the corpse; and the discarded paraphernalia of mourning. Pearson suggests that the funeral should be seen as a choreography and thus the absence of objects may reflect the nature of the funeral and not the poverty of the deceased.

Pearson asks the reader to see the deceased as a principal

performer, the grave as a perfect stage picture (a frozen moment), in an infinitely long performance. He asks us to consider four sets of relationships within any performance: performer to performer, performer to spectator (and vice-versa), and spectator to spectator. Furthermore Pearson suggests that performance is manifest in four axes: space, time, pattern and detail. Within all of this the body of the performer takes on great importance and consideration of location, costume, gesture, reach, posture take on new parameters.

Pearson gives equal attention to objects, those things which dominate so much traditional mortuary archaeology. For Pearson, it is via performance that objects become valued. Props are appropriated, found, and fabricated. Objects establish and identify location, period and character. Objects can be portative. They can be part of a kit. They can be accumulated and discarded. They can be *aide-memoire*, loci for nostalgia, replicas.

Pearson then turns back to the early Bronze Age burial and performance record. He focuses on the physical manipulation of bodies (mutilated, trussed, positioned), the preparation of bodies (undressing, redressing, decorating), the preparation of the ground and the positioning of the observer-participants. In all Pearson opens up new vistas of opportunity for observing the reality of early Bronze Age burial practice.

Russell

In Chapter 5, Nerissa Russell examines the place of living animals in human social systems. In particular she investigates the wealth potential of domesticated cattle in the southeast European Neolithic. She directs the reader's attention to the value of cattle as living domestic animals. Russell notes the position of cattle as slow-reproducing animals wrapped up in considerable costs and benefits. Cattle represent considerable investment, are harder to replace than other domesticates and are of a size which demands that consumption of a slaughtered individual stretch beyond the limits of a single household. Russell focuses on the value of cattle as wealth in Neolithic Europe.

Russell begins her study with ethnographic accounts of how cattle can function as wealth in living societies. Ethnography on herding is vast and although much of this work has concentrated on subsistence economics, Russell notes how some attention has been focused on the value of animals beyond protein and calories. Russell reviews the particular significance of animals as bridewealth and the mechanics of herding- and herding-societies. She notes that among pastoralists, wealth is almost always measured in livestock or cattle: household wealth is almost always defined in terms of the size of the household herds. Russell then investigates the possible factors which make cattle frequent measures of wealth in agricultural as well as in pastoral communities. The characteristics which make cattle good wealth also present potential problems (e.g., their mobility makes theft easier).

Russell then investigates the limitations of converting livestock such as cattle into real political power beyond the acquisition of 'big-man' prestige based on admiration, wealth and generosity. Russell turns to consider the links between cattle pastoralism and the emergence of social inequality.

Next the chapter considers the wide-spread custom of using cattle as bridewealth (the payment from the groom's side to the bride's side to seal a marriage). Russell notes the association of bridewealth with polygyny and the fact that wealth and women flow in opposite directions. Cattle are used as bridewealth because they maintain a fairly steady value. The use of cattle as bridewealth leads to the dispersal of cattle and the use of cattle in bridewealth substantially reduces risks to the maintenance of cattle herds. Indeed in some cases (e.g., among the Nuer and Dinka) the bridewealth system dictates herd management; in many cases in southern and East Africa cattle create and define social relationships. Russell then investigates the restrictions and potential for the expansion of hunter-gatherers to adopt herding. It appears that the adoption of herding may be more complex and difficult than is the shift to agriculture or sedentism. Bridewealth is one way in which hunter-gathers can be sucked into herding

Turning to cattle in Neolithic Europe, Russell combines her in-depth knowledge of the fauna from the late Neolithic site of Opovo in Serbia with the more general comparative data from across Europe. Russell addresses the question, did cattle function as wealth in Neolithic Europe or were they valued solely as a source of food and, perhaps, labour? Russell suggests patterns to be sought in a quest for evidence of the use of cattle as wealth: a decline in the size of individual cattle; the keeping of cattle in places not suitable for their keeping; the keeping of cattle relatively far from the settlement; and the prominent place of cattle in ritual and symbolism. Based on the evidence from Opovo Russell argues that cattle may have been kept more for wealth than for subsistence. Chief among the supporting evidence is that although the site is in a relatively poor habitat for cattle, cattle make up 50-60% of the domestic fauna. In addition it appears that the cattle were kept at some distance from the settlement Furthermore, evidence for symbolic use of cattle imagery at Opovo and at many other sites contemporary to Opovo adds support to the cattle as wealth model.

In concluding her study, Russell considers the implications of the cattle as wealth model. It appears highly likely that cattle were used as bridewealth in Neolithic Europe. Furthermore, Russell suggests that the dynamics of cattle wealth, and especially of brideweath, may offer new insights into the spread of Neolithic economies across Europe. Perhaps the indigenous hunter-gatherers were assimilated into agro-pastoral economies through a bridewealth system stimulated by the intruding agro-pastoralists' desire to marry hunter-gatherer women. Perhaps a knock-on of this was the continued adoption of the agro-pastoral economy.

Overall, Russell shows how the meaning and importance of what is traditionally considered an economic resource has powerful social under-currents which drive strategies of exploitation and management without concern for the primarily nutritional return.

Palavestra
In Chapter 6, Aleksander Palavestra addresses the late Bronze-early Iron Age phenomenon of rich princely tombs in the central Balkans. Palavestra investigates the use of these tombs within the contemporary cattle breeding communities. He argues that the burial mounds were symbols of chiefly power but were intended as more than mere expressions of individual wealth. Rather the tombs functioned on three distinct levels: ritual, territorial and tribal.

Palavestra places the tumuli into the contexts of early Iron Age seasonal cattle breeding movements and territories. He shows how the tumuli were erected in crucial places within the systems of cattle movements (under summer pastures, along communication lines). Palavestra shows how the princely tombs appear precisely in the areas where three large cultural complexes met (the Bosut-Basarabi, Glasinac and Donja Brnjica).

Palavestra provides the chronological and cultural background to the phenomenon of the princely tombs and discusses the changes which mark the disappearance of the tumuli in the end of the sixth and the beginning of the fifth centuries BC. Discussion includes the typology and chronology on the material from the tumuli as well as detailed presentations of the princely tombs of the necropolis at Pilatovići I, Atenica, Novi Pazar, Pečka Banja, and Lisijevo Polje. Attention is drawn to ritual elements of the burial contents (i.e., the sacrificial pits and their animal contents).

Palavestra then addresses a long-neglected aspect of the princely tomb phenomenon: the symbolic significance of tumuli location within their micro-regions. In this discussion the territorial level of tomb value is presented and common characteristics are noted (construction in river valleys; on flat terrain; with high visibility; in mountainous hinterlands; proximate to roads connecting valleys and uplands). Tumuli distribution is mapped with Thiessen polygons and inferences are drawn about borders of early Iron Age territories. Palavestra suggests that the princely tombs were the symbolic, ritual and political centres of larger territories.

The discussion then links these territories to communities or tribes. Palavestra argues that individual tribes controlled territories containing highland summer pastures, valley winter pastures, water supplies and communication routes. Tribes were nomadic and moved within each territory. The value of these territories and the potential socio-political stress caused by occasional climatic change are proposed as stimuli for the erection of tumuli as symbolic claims to territory. The tumuli thus served as markers of cattle-breeders territories.

Quesada
In Chapter 7, Fernando Quesada examines the changes in systems of wealth and prestige in high status burials of the Iberian Iron Age. He suggests that the significant change in mortuary behaviour which occurred at c. 425 BC is best understood in terms of a shift from the quality of grave-goods to the quantity of grave-goods.

Quesada suggests that during the Orientalizing Period wealth and status were displayed by the placement of chariots and imported goods into burials. Weapons were rare and more emphasis was placed in the quality of grave-goods than on the accumulation of goods. After 425, prestige display changed: weapons appeared and the accumulation of lower-quality imported goods was used to indicate wealth and status.

Quesada begins his study with a review of the Orientalizing Period and the Iron Age in the Iberian Peninsula. The influence of the Phoenician colonists from 800 BC is noted as a stimulus for the emergence of the Iron Age in western Andalusia at a time when most other regions of Iberia lagged behind. Foreign merchants and colonists brought in new technologies and luxurious and exotic objects which were quickly adopted by the local rulers as symbols of status. Additional intervention of Samian and Phokian Greek traders and colonists (c. 600 BC) added new elements to the indigenous repetoire. Quesada then traces parallel but different developments on the eastern seaboard of the Iberian Peninsula. Additional detail about developments after the sixth century (the early phases of the Iberian culture) is provided highlighting the intense contacts with Helladic, Semitic and Carthaginian influences.

Quesada then focuses his attention on the details of the burial traditions of the Orientalizing and Iberian Periods. First he presents the princely tombs of the Orientalizing Period. These consisted of impressive tumuli with a ritual set of grave-goods: jug-brazier-*thymiaterion*. The princely tombs are compared with the contemporary ordinary burials (the non-princely burials). Quesada presents examples from Las Cumbres, the south coastal area of Málaga-Almería, the Guadalquiver valley, and the northern periphery. Next Quesada presents the quality and variety of status expression in the princely burials. He focuses on details of the tumulus structure and the number and type of grave-goods.

Next Quesada turns to the changing pattern evident in the fifth century with the Iberian Culture. The changes are documented in new types of grave-goods, the use of monumental sculpture and a new military iconography, and new patterns in the use of wine. Each of these categories of mortuary behaviour are examined in detail. Quesada then turns the reader's attention to the classical Iberian Culture of the fourth century BC and focuses on the changes in the conception of power, in the social structure of cemeteries and in the composition of grave goods (including the use of imported pottery as an expression of wealth, the use of gold, and weapons as foundations of social power).

The study concludes by suggesting that the burial evidence supports the following long-term model for change in the regions considered. For the Orientalizing and early Iberian Periods the reader should think in terms of sacred monarchies with paternalistic functions. In the fifth century this pattern evolved into heroic monarchies which, in turn, disappeared at the end of the fifth century when warrior aristocracies appeared.

Pydyn

In Chapter 8, Andrzej Pydyn investigates the creation of different dimensions and systems of valuation in long-distance exchange during the late Bronze and early Iron Ages of central Europe. Pydyn examines the distinction between the creation of universal and relative values. He argues that the value of objects is a combination of shape, originality, artistry as well as the more traditional dimensions of prime- and added-value. Pydyn shows how some objects can take on several different values as they move into and out of different geographic, economic and social contexts.

In focusing on the late Bronze and early Iron Ages, Pydyn shows how different exchange systems created different value systems. In these different systems, different material objects expressed power and social positions. In this way the same object could have very different values in neighbouring and distant regions. Pydyn offers the example of the two separate exchange networks active in central Europe during Hallstatt B3 and C (i.e., the Urnfield and Nordic cultures). The social structures of local communities within both networks were based on the same principal but chose different objects to express their social structure. In the case of imported objects, decisions about value were made by the local importing communities.

Pydyn suggests that as prestige objects travel they change their value from economic and artistic to social. Within local circles of knowledge which unite producers and consumers, goods have one value; when they move out of these local circles they start to have a special value in symbolic or practical terms. Pydyn suggests that this is why long-distance trade will always have an important position in establishing, maintaining and changing social, political and economic power. Within this disjuncture between export and import communities, merchants could create value (Pydyn offers amber and shell as examples). Pydyn next turns to the value of bronze and bronze objects and suggests that a similar fragmentation of knowledge about the geographical origins and technological processes was a prime stimulus in the creation and manipulation of value.

Pydyn then considers the importance of shape in the creation and maintenance of value in bronze objects. Suggesting that bronze needed to be rendered into particular shapes to be valued, Pydyn notes the absence of ingots and the presence (even in hoards) of scrap bronzes cut into defined shapes. An example of this phenomenon in the Nordic zone is the bronze rings which appear never to have been used as ornaments and which may have been used to store a value of bronze.

Value creation is also found in the methods of transport of exchanged goods with boats playing an important role not only to confer value but also as valuable things in themselves. Boats and boat-shaped things (such as boat-graves) show the growth in economic, social and symbolic value of transportation. Horses and wheeled-vehicles take on a similar role in valuation during the same time (e.g., wagon-graves, horse inhumations).

Having dealt in detail with the different ways in which value was created in the late Bronze and early Iron Ages, Pydyn turns the reader's attention to the systems through which social and material values were maintained and changed. Pydyn focuses on the process of exclusion and consumption. The development of iron metallurgy is offered as an example: it was socially and culturally, but not technologically, limited in distribution. Iron technology was restricted because it could threaten existing systems of value and thus destabilise the power of existing elites.

Pydyn places the transition to the early Iron Age in the context of the shift in value systems: the replacement of prestige bronze objects by other goods of a high social value such as blue glass beads, cowrie shells and other products of Mediterranean origin. During the Bronze Age of northern Europe, elites had played an integrating role in communities; they had been an essential part of social structure; the position of a chieftain had to be maintained through the public consumption of objects of high value. In the Iron Age, many communities experienced a process of progressive individualisation of their members. In these communities, powerful individuals achieved their positions through continuous competition with other individuals. The production and consumption of iron was much more suitable for this new social situation than was bronze.

Chapman

In Chapter 8, John Chapman directs the reader's attention to the ways in which people attribute value to particular places. Chapman's article has two parts. In the first part he reviews recent work on place in social theory and material culture studies. In the second part he looks at the value of place at one site (Vinča) in the Balkan Neolithic.

Noting the general absence of discussions of the value of places, Chapman investigates the field of landscape in terms of objectification and valuation. He considers places as objectified and embodied spaces. From a review of recent research into material culture, Chapman presents a theoretical framework for analysing place-value. Chapman focuses first of Pierre Bourdieu's use of the concepts of habitus and field. Chapman notes that Bourdieu has privileged time over place and one particular kind of place over all others. Chapman next addresses the processes of embodiment and objectification (for the latter looking at the work of Danny Miller and Roy Wagner). Objectification is seen as the inculcation of value in persons and things. Chapman asks how is this achieved and thus turns to the process of presencing.

Chapman then asks the key question: what is a place? Part of the answer is presented in the concepts of the human geographer Yi-Fu Tuan and in Michael Mann's idea of an arena of social power. Additional discussion focuses on the concepts of materialisation and rhetoric in an investigation of the relationship between places, people and identity. Chapman concludes this wide assessment of the key concepts in the study of the valuation of space and place by considering ideas of place-value, place-myths and time-marks.

The second part of Chapman's contribution turns from the high-level theoretical concerns to the realities of the Serbian Neolithic and the classic site of Vinča-Belo Brdo. Chapman asks the question that no one has yet asked about the site: what was it about the place of the site which made it so important for its prehistoric occupants? Chapman lends his expert knowledge of the site to a presentation of its major components and the history of its prehistoric life. He suggests a three-part Vinča narrative of places in order to determine the site's place-value. Chapman details the development of Vinča from nascent pre-tell settlement to the emergence of cohesive, long-lasting communities. Thus Vinča developed from a ritual centre, to an important node in a network of inter-regional exchange links, and on to a place of monumental visibility. Chapman argues that the height of the tell settlement was perceived as a sign of deeper ancestry and that the dwellers of tells such as Vinča were at an ideological advantage over flat-site occupants. The tell became a time-mark in increasingly long-distance exchange networks.

Skeates

In Chapter 10, Robin Skeates takes a social perspective on Italian Neolithic painted pottery. He traces painted pottery's distinctiveness as a category as it changed over time and in relation to other categories of material culture.

Skeates begins by considering the recent life-history of Italian Neolithic painted pottery and argues that traditional strategies of museum display and interpretation have distanced this pottery from its original contexts. The use of pottery as a museum commodity or as a tool for building chronologies are noted as examples.

Next Skeates presents a social history of Neolithic painted pottery in the Abruzzo region of eastcentral Italy. He traces the appearance of pottery in the region and describes the significant changes in ceramic treatment. Special attention is focused on the increase in technologically and stylistically distinct categories of pottery and changes in the ways in which pots entered the archaeological record (e.g., in burials and in cave deposits). Skeates works at the local as well as the inter-regional scale and links the changes in ceramic tradition to a strengthening of long-distance social and exchange relations between Abruzzo and the south.

Attention to changes in the use of pottery on the local scale highlights increasingly distinctive painted finewares which may have been bound with processes of redefining the social identity of members of the community. Skeates presents a model for the later painted pottery (4700-4400 BC) in which production and use of regionally distinctive painted finewares enhanced the identity, legitimacy and cohesion of a newly established social group at a time of competition for resources between lowland communities. Further changes after 4400 BC centred on the increasing production of indistinguishable black- or red-burnished wares and a decrease in the production of fine yellow wares and the abandonment of trichrome painting. Changes are linked to stability in the inter-regional exchange networks.

Skeates concludes his study by arguing that potters participated in a widespread strategy to maintain and strengthen social access to increasingly important long-distance ceremonial exchange networks. They did this by masking traditional regional differences which were bound up with traditional forms of material culture and ritual practice and by emphasising similarities in the styles of finewares which were displayed, used and exchanged on public occasions. The value of Neolithic Italian painted pottery therefore rests in its role as an individual and inter-community negotiator.

* * *

As a collection then these contributions attack the archaeological understanding of value, prestige and wealth. They include both theoretical discussion of the concepts of valuation and prestige as well as detailed case studies which work these ideas through well documented material. Like value and valuation, the contributions display the breadth of the different processes of valuation: via consumption, acquisition, use, disposal, performance, long-distance exchange and exclusion. The enquiry ranges from the level of the household through the intra- and inter-regional. Attention focuses on a diversity of materials involved in valuation and bears witness to the importance of the objects which are regularly left out of discussions of wealth and prestige due to their supposed 'common' nature: bulk finds; daub for houses. Valuation appears (as Pydyn shows via scales in exchange networks, as Palavestra argues for three levels of meaning for tumuli and as Quesada reveals for the quality and the quantity of burial assemblages) in many dimensions within one and the same set of archaeological objects and site-plans. Thus perhaps the diversity which runs through this volume suggests that efforts to seek a single theory to explain valuation and prestige in archaeology is misguided. Perhaps it is best to follow Munn's lead and to work on the level of fundamental mechanisms which can be employed to manipulate the intersubjective space-time of people and of groups. Perhaps in this way a better understanding of prestige, wealth and value will emerge regardless of the context.

Bibliography

Munn, N. 1986. *The Fame of the Gawa. A Symbolic Study of Value Transformation in a Massim (Papua New Guinea) Society*. London: Duke University Press.

Chapter 2

The value of tasks in the late Upper Palaeolithic

Anthony Sinclair

Introduction

It seems clear, some would say, that archaeology has had remarkable success in looking for value in the archaeological record of the past. It has been able to point to the appearance of prestigious goods, whether in circulation or not, from the time of the Neolithic in various parts of the world. This supports models of social evolution, where technological development goes hand-in-hand with material gain and its flip-side social inequality.

A corollary of this, however, is that we have difficulty in looking for value before these times. Indeed we might even be tempted to argue, as Marx and Engels once did, that these earliest societies were the original egalitarian, or communist, societies. What do you value when you cannot easily hoard or keep the things which are scarce? How do you express value when you cannot own or keep to yourself the things that you might want to? Instead of arguing for such an early communist society, I suggest that the process of looking for value in hunter-gatherer societies in the past requires that one attempts to answer these questions. I shall do this by suggesting that one needs to drop the factor of scarcity as the logic of value, and instead look for the expression of values based on other premises. For the later Upper Palaeolithic in southwest Europe, I suggest that the values which one can see are based on skills and knowledge, something apparently open to all. This is expressed most clearly in the tools which are made. It is embodied in the knowledge required and the technical skills necessary to produce certain tools. In turn, these particular values are associated with the performance of particular tasks which are valued, tasks which are not necessarily open to all. Value always seems to be differential.

Following this logic through, it is but a short step to suggest that as tasks are performed at particular times and in particular places, so values, times and places resonate as one. This will be the second part to this piece. But let me begin with a short story. The story is set in the future, and just as the past is perhaps another country, so is the future.

'Consume, Consume'

The well known science-fiction writer Philip K. Dick wrote a short-story about the accumulation of material goods and value. He called it 'Consume, Consume' and set it on the Earth at a time when the greatest problem, scarce energy supplies, had been solved (Dick 1991). In this world, material production has been dramatically released from its check and the manufacturing economy rushes at full speed. To keep the economy working, however, consumption must equal production. So, it becomes the duty of all to consume as much as they can. Furthermore, these things must be consumed properly; that is they must be worn out. Not for these Earthlings the simpler option of burial of goods underground. Supply cannot be so easily limited.

It is in this context that I think Dick's ideas are most thought provoking. In his society material value and social status now stand in an inverse relationship to the accumulation of material goods, no matter what material they are made of. The richest people in society are now those with the least or, to be more precise, those who have earned the right to have the least. In this world of unlimited energy, unrestrained production and constrained consumption, people are allocated an amount of goods to consume each year, but consume properly. This might be a couple of cars, a computer, two robots and so on. The more you consume and the greater you exceed your allocation, the less, not more, you get next year.

The end result is that those with the highest social status have worked their way into a position in which they can possess very little. They live in what we might describe today as material poverty; but in a society where the satisfaction of material needs and wants is both easy and also compulsory. The absence of material goods is in fact not poverty, it is in fact prosperity, if that word can really be used in this context.

Of course Dick's story has a happy ending. Some bright person programmes the robots to consume material goods and to enjoy doing it. There is a wonderful scene in a cellar where robots in checked plus-fours merrily wear-out the year's supply of golf clubs. Soon everyone does it and all are reduced to a state of joyful material poverty.

Marshall Sahlins and the Zen road to affluence

Well so much for the future. Let us turn instead to the present, although in this case it is the ethnographic present. In some ways, Philip Dick's story is reminiscent of a famous article by Marshall Sahlins. Sahlins suggested that the poorest hunter-gatherer societies were in fact not poor at all. They were the original affluent society. They stood aside from our own problems and instead followed the Zen road to affluence (1972). Unable to carry much in the way of material goods around with them, they have evaded the frustrations of the materialist desire to accumulate by having just a few material wants which they can easily satisfy.

According to Sahlins, those material things which hunter-gatherers do have they pass on easily in a social environment characterised by generalised reciprocity. Such generalised reciprocity (or sharing) Sahlins argues, is part of their culture. It is the cultural ethos of sharing and minimal material wants that gives the economic system both its form and its social meaning: material wants have been contained and that which is valued most highly is generosity or sharing.

The interesting thing about hunter-gatherers is that what is scarce is very often food and yet food is also the thing that they share. Indeed, Hawkes (1993) has shown that the most successful hunters often give away all their food to people beyond their immediate family and kin. Moreover, they must allow other people to use the thing that they would like to own, the land upon which they get their food.

A natural logic of value

I have started with these accounts of the present and the future, because they raise certain questions about our own approach as archaeologists to the discussion and identification of value in the past. Long ago, the Keynesian economist, John Kenneth Galbraith argued in his book *The Affluent Society* (1962) that our sense of value (and with it affluence) was based on the principle of scarcity. When he wrote *The Affluent Society* he was attempting to argue that the poverty of 1950s and 1960s United States was a product not of real material impoverishment but rather of its appropriation and use in a world which still worked on a principle of scarcity. In other words, there was not enough to go around and what you had, you hung-on to. This principle provided the logic for hoarding and keeping things, which in another society might have been shared around, so allowing each to have enough.

Likewise, when looking for value in the archaeological record we have also followed this principle and we have looked for value as expressed in the context of material scarcity. We see value and wealth where we can see scarce goods. We suggest that like our own, the value and wealth of the earliest societies (i.e., the early Neolithic societies) are based on materials not easily acquired and in short supply. These are of course metals such as gold, silver or indeed other precious materials. When looking at times when the once precious and scarce metals become common, we interpret their hoards as attempts to maintain a sense of scarcity and thus retain their value, instead of looking for other logics that might explain the pattern.

So in the first example, Philip Dick's story seems to be about a world where the logic of scarcity does not hold. This, unfortunately, is not really true (which is a shame as I rather like the story). In the case of Philip Dick's future Earth, material goods are no longer scarce: what is scarce is the time which is free from consuming them. So it is free-time not material goods which is valuable and it is this which is gradually accumulated. It is this scarcity which is broken by getting the robots to spend their time consuming the goods and in so doing consume themselves. What might have been interesting would have been to have seen what happened when this process took off completely. How would value have been acquired?

As recognised by Galbraith, though, this wealth and value rests on the premise of scarcity, whether actual or not. But even scarcity is cultural and not natural. What happens if the logic is based on something different, perhaps sharing? Let us return to the happy and affluent hunters and gatherers. There are various ideas about the reason for their principle of sharing. Some have suggested that sharing is naturally necessary, others that it is a cultural pattern.

To biologically inspired anthropologists generosity and sharing have an evolutionary determinant. Sharing is not an ethos, it is a necessity. Hunter-gatherers are dependent upon what they can reap from the natural world, and when that world is uncertain they must adapt to cope with this uncertainty. Sharing is a coping mechanism and is therefore adaptive. Those who have, must share with those who do not because one day they, themselves, might be without and they will have to rely upon others to help them. This of course would be particularly the case in highly seasonal environments. In this schema of things, it is the rigours of nature which prevent hunters and gatherers from entering into the modern materialist frame of mind in which it is the hoarding and keeping of things which confer value. Furthermore, it is argued that the social prestige acquired from sharing is an evolutionary strategy designed by men, who appear to do most of this sharing, to win future mating opportunities and continue their genetic line.

If we look more closely, however, there is still a cultural logic at the base of sharing. When we look at what is shared it is often just meat. According to Lee's account of the attitudes of !Kung women, it is meat which is real food. It is also meat which is shared. Meat is of course the product of men's labour. It is meat which is shared publicly and which makes the relationships between people, even if it is the product of women's gathering that feeds them for most of the time, vital nutrients or not. Wealth and value in sharing are men's values and wealth.

In contrast to the biological anthropologist's natural logic, other anthropologists have fleshed out the cultural approach to sharing. Bird-David (1992) has written of sharing and giving as being metaphors for life. Hunter-gatherers share things because they have trust and confidence that things will be there for them if they need it. It is not so much fool-hardiness as almost faith.

In a slightly similar vein, Peterson (1993) has suggested that rather than talk of free-sharing one should talk of demand-sharing. Goods are demanded as much as they are shared. It is a way of keeping people in check and socially up to standard. These societies are not non-materialistic, they just seem to manage this desire in a particular manner. Thus, anthropologists are continually pestered to give money, food and material goods. Demand sharing is an assertive means to express the value of shared goods.

Sahlins tacitly assumes that all hunter-gatherer societies are the same. This work by Peterson and Bird-David begins to show that all hunter-gatherer societies are not necessarily the same. There are major differences. They have been described by Woodburn (1979; 1982) as the difference between immediate-return and delayed-return hunter-gatherers. It is the immediate- return hunter-gatherers who seem to be non-materialistic. These are the people with few material possessions. It is also these groups who are prepared to give away what they do have or to demand from others when they do not have. Delayed-return hunter-gatherers are very different. According to anthropologists such as Burch they are materialistic in outlook. They value things and have a sense of property, particularly land. But they also share out meat when necessary. Delayed-return groups in the sub-Arctic, for example, also value the individual. They stress the importance of individual knowledge and skill and seek to accumulate this for themselves and to encourage its accumulation in their children (Riddington 1982). According to Riddington, knowledge is power and for that reason its accumulation is valued. Immediate return hunter-gatherers and delayed return hunter-gatherers do not stand outside of a system of differential value; they express values in particular ways. Each has its own cultural logic, as well as its own benefit.

I have tried in this all too brief discussion to note some of the complex factors that give meaning and value to hunter-gatherer societies. There are profound factors which prevent the accumulation of material items and which bring about the passing-on of both material goods and also foodstuffs. But this does not result in society without a sense of differing values, both between things and between people. If we are looking for value in past hunter-gatherer societies we must try and unlock the cultural logic of value in these past societies, much as Dick does in his short story. I suggest that we might start by looking at the skills and knowledge which are valued and the ramifications of this on other areas of life.

The value of tasks in the later Upper Palaeolithic

The Last Glacial Maximum is an important period in Palaeolithic archaeology. It is the final cold episode of the last glacial stage and the first occasion in Europe when Anatomically Modern Humans (*Homo sapiens sapiens*) lived in such severe climatic conditions. In Western Europe this period is notable for its remarkably distinctive stone tools and possible changes in the subsistence economies. Researchers have noted that the major shift in subsistence strategies from an encounter-foraging pattern, where the animals hunted are those encountered, to a more deliberate and specialist hunting strategy, where herds of animals are targeted and hunted, in western Europe happens not with the arrival of Anatomically Modern Humans but at the Last Glacial Maximum (Clark and Straus 1983; Straus and Clark 1986; Mithen 1990; Straus 1986; 1987). This change might be likened to that between foragers and logistic-collectors set out by Binford (1980) where earlier Upper Palaeolithic gatherers and hunters are more similar to the forager model, whist later gatherers and hunters more closely match the logistic-collector model. The composition of the faunal assemblages from certain French sites, such as Laugerie-Haute, Badegoule and Sainte Eulalie IV (Boyle 1990: 321-2) indicate the targeting of reindeer, an interpretation supported by the location of the sites in likely migration corridors (White 1985: 135). Similar arguments have been made regarding the exploitation of red deer in Northern Spain (Straus 1983: 146).

The stone tool assemblages are distinctive due to the presence of a number of tools which have been finished by a fine bifacial retouch which covers the pieces and also thins them. These tools generally take the form of either shouldered-points or leaf-shaped points in France. In Spain there are both leaf-shaped points, shouldered-points, points with concave bases and tanged projectile-points. These artefacts have come to be known as Solutrean. As well as these tools there is a range of other types, made on either flake or blade blanks, which are more simply and sparsely retouched. For these tools, the retouching is confined to the edge of the pieces creating a working edge, whether that be in the form of a scraper-edge or a burin-point and so on.

There are of course differences in the types of tools made over such a large region, as well as in assemblage composition within smaller areas. For example there is a form of bifacially retouched point in the assemblages from Northern Spain which have a concave base. In southern Spain, there are much smaller bifacial points that are tanged and barbed. The renowned, large, bifacially retouched leaf-points are a southwestern French phenomenon. It has also been noted that there are differences in the shape of leaf-shaped points between areas in France (Smith 1973). Solutrean stone tool assemblages are, therefore, not uniform entities and there will be many interpretations, both practical and sociological, to account for the features noted above.

Straus (1990: 425) notes that the stone tools from this period can be divided into two; bifacial tools and a 'substrate' of other tools similar to those made at any other time during the Upper Palaeolithic. This substrate comprises tools made on flakes and blades, rectilinear or not, which can be classified as endscrapers, scrapers, burins, awls and pieces where one side has been continuously retouched. This bipartite separation reinforces the distinctiveness of the bifacial pieces, especially in the light of other tools made at this time.

Although the bifacial tools appear to be distinct, with the exception of perhaps the very large and rare examples, all of the stone implements made at this time were used, both the simple and common Upper Palaeolithic stone implements as well as the rare and distinctive bifacial tools. Smaller points seem to have been used as spear- or javelin-

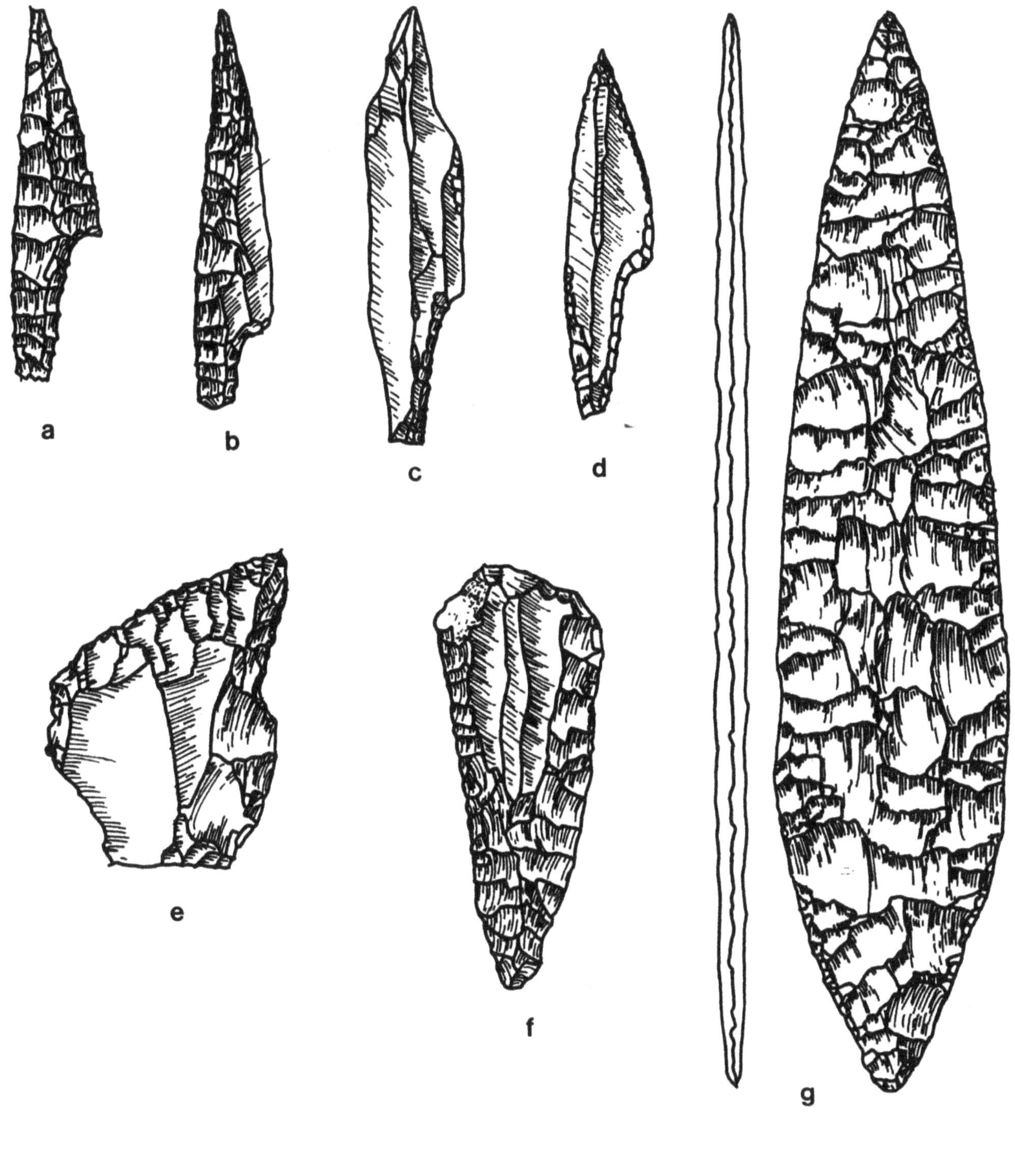

Figure 1 A selection of typical 'Solutrean' tools from sites in south-west France. These include shouldered points (a-d) and a classic leaf-shaped point (g). The two other tools, an inversely retouched scraper (e) and an endscraper (f), are included as examples of the use of Solutrean techniques of retouch beyond the classically recognised repertoire. The artefacts derive from the sites of Jean-Blancs, Laugerie-Haute and Pech-de-la-Boissière.

points. The uses of the larger bifacial points have been more difficult to determine but it seems possible and likely that these pieces had been used as knives (see discussion in Sinclair 1995).

Whilst clearly there are particular design requirements for these tools to be effective, it can be argued that the degree of bifacial retouching used in the making of these tools is not one of these requirements. Indeed if they had been more simply made the distinctive bifacial tools would not stand out from the other 'substrate' tools in these assemblages. Bifacial, thinning retouch draws attention to these tools in relation to the others. When these bifacial implements have been replicated it is clear that the manufacture of the bifacial tools takes significant lengths of time.

It might be appropriate to ask why these tools were just utilitarian items, 'tools', at all. Bone and antler points are significantly more robust when used in the same way and indeed points made from these materials are found in the same assemblages as the bifacial lithic points. It would perhaps make sense to suggest that the bifacially thinned pieces were not just practical or utilitarian items but were in fact also symbolic. If this is the case, what is this symbolism about?

In hunter-gatherer societies an association between the practical and the symbolic is commonplace. It is the practical tasks themselves which are meaningful and we must consider what this meaning might concern. The interpretations that can be ascribed to the way in which these bifacially retouched tools were practically used make it possible to draw a line around a series of activities, in particular the hunting of animals and the processing of their carcasses.

If this is the case, what is so important about these activities such that they would be a focus for the symbolic potential of material culture? Studies of modern hunter and gatherer societies have noted that these societies are not as egalitarian as has often been thought. 'Sharing' is also an important activity in this respect. It is a way of creating relationships of dependency within these societies. The giving of a gift entails the getting of a gift. The sharing of meat after a kill creates personal authority and prestige because by sharing the meat from the kill relations of reciprocity and dependency are created. The ownership of a kill is not the right to keep but the right to give away (Dowling 1968) and create debts. It is for this reason that Hawkes (1993: 341-2) has suggested that hunters are prepared to work hard to acquire game from which neither they nor their immediate family might energetically benefit.

Whilst it is possible to consider the meaning of tools made at this time purely in terms of the typological differences between artefacts and the contexts of their use and discard, this ignores one of the real advantages of working with stone tools: the accessibility of information regarding the actual making of these pieces. Such information is crucial when trying to analyse the relationship between structure and agency in the creation of meaning in lithic technology.

Societies may make and do many of the same things, but they will do so in particular ways. Leroi-Gourhan has stressed that there is a structure to the making of things. This structure is syntactic in that it involves sequences of decisions and operations, a chain of operations. Within the syntactic chain there are key moments when significant decisions are made which in a sense determine the next sequence of actions (Schlanger 1990). Stone tool assemblages from the last glacial maximum can be studied from this perspective.

The making of a stone tool (or more properly perhaps in the context of the Upper Palaeolithic, the stone component of a tool) entails a sequence of operations or episodes during which choices are made. In the making of a particular tool this sequence of operations may follow a distinct structure in which particular choices are necessarily made but there may also be moments when the structure is more free to allow the making of individual choices. It is such free choices that can be seen in the making of the bifacial tools.

It was noted above that the stone tool technology of France and the Iberian Peninsula at the time of the Last Glacial Maximum could be divided into a bifacial and a non-bifacial component and it was suggested that attention was being drawn symbolically to the activities for which these bifacial tools were used, activities associated with the killing of animals and the butchery of their carcasses. This, however, is a simplification. When the bifacial pieces are examined individually, there is an evident continuity in the degree of elaboration. Bifacial thinning retouch is differentially applied. Some pieces are slightly retouched, others are highly retouched with pieces displaying all states of retouch in between. This is especially the case among the shouldered-points, where the least retouched points are more similar to the substrate tools in that retouching is confined to the perimeter of the pieces creating the working edge and little else. In other cases, the shouldered pieces are completely retouched. Similar degrees of variation in the final retouch can be observed among the other bifacial tools. It is clear that there is considerable freedom of action in the elaboration of these tools. Although we might classify them as distinct types or sub-types they are in fact different finishing points along a continuous process. This suggests that it is not the type itself which is important or symbolic. It is the technique by which it is made (Sinclair 1995).

In his discussion of the cognitive basis of tool-use Wynn (1991) has drawn attention to the work of anthropologists concerning technological action which develops the twin concepts of constellations of knowledge (Dougherty and Keller 1982) and sequences of action in tool-use (Gatewood 1985). Associations of processes, materials, implements and desired ends are embedded within constellations of knowledge, which may be linked one with another by correspondence between particular features. Correspondence between constellations of knowledge provides an important key to understanding the craft products of hunters and gatherers. There is a saliency between the techniques employed in the making of things and those valued in the pursuit of other important activities. If we turn to the techniques in use at the time of the last glacial maximum, we must ask what were the salient characteristics of bifacial retouching techniques?

Most of the retouch procedures used at this time merely altered the perimeter of the piece. They were quick to carry out, and by focusing on the edge and its immediate vicinity there was a natural end to this process. There was no need for a particular order to the retouch blows and as a result there was little need for much strategic thinking ahead.

These techniques also relied upon direct percussion where the need for precise position of the retouch blow and physical strength is not so great. In contrast, bifacial thinning retouch entails a sequence of application of retouch blows that requires greater order and precision. This approach to retouching not only alters the perimeter of the piece but also the volume of the piece by thinning. As the sequence develops each blow requires progressively greater precision in its application. The final blows are especially difficult. Certain of the classic Solutrean pieces are finished using fine pressure-flaking. In contrast to direct percussion, pressure-flaking requires considerable physical strength. Pressure-flaking is more often applied to the smaller foliate- and shouldered-points. These are the pieces used for hunting equipment. The overriding characteristics of this process are care, order and thinking ahead as the risks of failure gradually increase. On certain pieces, the use of physical strength is also apparent. These are the skills, technical and knowledge based, which we might suggest are valuable at this time.

Taken together it is possible to suggest that these manufacturing skills are comparable to skills that would have been necessary in other aspects of the lives of hunters and gatherers at this time. Together they form a constellation of knowledge and skills. For example, the specialised subsistence economies that are apparent from this time (Straus 1986) must have embodied constellations of knowledge which focus on order, care and control over timing to ensure that people were properly prepared at the right time and in the right place for a successful hunt. Order, timing and perseverance would have been essential qualities for both individuals and groups. It is perhaps for these reasons that the bifacial retouching techniques so obvious at this time might have been salient to makers of stone tools and may have created a correspondence between constellations of knowledge exercised in tool production and subsistence. That these tools themselves were also actually used in these other activities must have further reinforced the correspondence between the skills between these two realms of life.

Valued tasks in time and space

In a recent article, Ingold (1993) suggested that people do not so much live on a landscape, but live within a taskscape. Taking his lead from Gibson (1979), Ingold suggested that people appropriate or perhaps perceive parts of a landscape as they are revealed or made relevant to them through their lives. This he terms a 'taskscape'. This taskscape is both spatial and temporal. Tasks are performed not only in space but also at particular times. These spatial and temporal dimensions of the taskscape are different according to the individual involved and the tasks that they do. The taskscape inevitably changes according to age and gender. People will acquire new taskscapes as they get older, much as they will lose others. For hunters and gatherers, Ingold suggested (1986) that their landscape was one of paths and places, not some abstract space, the sort of squared space that one rents these days for offices. Places are where tasks are performed. Paths lead to places as well as being 'taskspaces' in their own right, at times.

In many ways, this contrasts with Binford's approach to hunter-gatherer use of space. Binford suggests that to understand the use of space by hunter-gatherers we need to understand the degree of seasonality of the land. If the growing season is long, hunter-gatherers can move as a group from living-site to living-site. If the growing season is short, hunter-gatherers must move around, organising themselves into particular specialised work, or task, groups. He contrasts these two as the generalised landscape of the forager and the specialised landscape of the logistic-collector.

But of course these differences imply differences in the taskscape which might be roughly termed the difference between a generalised taskscape versus a specialised taskscape. The move to a logistically organised subsistence economy following the Last Glacial Maximum in south-west Europe suggests the appearance of a new taskscape with new places of value and new times of value. Working from the value-infused tools outwards, I would suggest that these places of value were the places where animals were hunted and the places where they were butchered perhaps both after death and also before consumption. We might turn our attention to the specialised hunting sites in the mountainous areas of northern Spain and the Pyrenees of the Basque region. We might also think of the hearth when meat was cut and shared out. The times of value would have been those seasonal and specific times during which these activities happened. The Autumn and the Spring would have been the times of the great migration of the reindeer in France. In Spain we might think of hunting ibex in the spring time and so forth.

Of course, these would have not been the only aspects of a taskscape at this time, but these places and times would have resonated with the values expressed in the material tools of the Solutrean of southwest Europe

Conclusions

I have suggested that value in later Upper Palaeolithic society was organised around knowledge and skills. These were the knowledge and skills associated with the tasks of the individual and group hunter, and the task of sharing. The values of this time acted as metaphors for living. People placed their trust in these values so that society would continue as they wished. I have also suggested that this knowledge and these skills were not necessarily possessed by all. Value, then as now, might have been differentially held. When we look around these tasks we need to recognise that they structured taskscapes in which particular places and specific times resonated with value. Hunter-gatherers of the later Upper Palaeolithic did not live in a time before differential value but in an alternative set of values, not based on scarcity and accumulation.

Bibliography

Binford, L. 1980. Willow smoke and dogs' tails: hunter-gatherer settlement systems and archaeological site formation. *American Antiquity* 45: 4-20.

Bird-David, N. 1992. Beyond "The Original Affluent Society": a culturalist reformulation. *Current Anthropology* 33: 25-47

Boyle, K. 1990. *Upper Palaeolithic Faunas of South-west France: A Zoogeographic Perspective*. Oxford: BAR.

Clark, G.A. and L.G. Straus 1983. Late Pleistocene hunter-gatherer adaptations in Cantabrian Spain. In *Hunter-gatherer Economy in Prehistory*, edited by G.N. Bailey, pp. 131-148. Cambridge: Cambridge University Press.

Dick, P.K. 1991. 'Consume, Consume!'. In P.K. Dick, *Beyond the Web. The Collected Short Stories. Volume 1*. London: Harper Collins.

Dougherty, J.W.D. and C.M. Keller 1982. Taskonomy: a practical approach to knowledge structures. *American Ethnologist* 5: 763-74.

Dowling, J. 1968. Individual ownership and sharing of game in hunting societies. *American Anthropologist* 70: 502-7

Galbraith, J.K. 1962. *The Affluent Society*. New York: Random House.

Gatewood, J. 1985. Actions speak louder than words. In *Directions in Cognitive Anthropology*, edited by J. Dougherty, pp. 123-156. Indiana: University of Illinois Press.

Gibson, J.J. 1979. *The Ecological Basis of Perception*. London: Houghton-Mifflin.

Hawkes, K. 1993. Why hunter-Gatherers work: an ancient version of the problem of ancient goods. *Current Anthropology* 34: 341-61.

Ingold, T. 1986. *The Appropriation of Nature*. Manchester: Manchester University Press.

Ingold, T. 1993. The temporality of the landscape. *World Archaeology* 25: 152-74.

Mithen, S. 1990. *Thoughtful Foragers: a Study of Prehistoric Decision Making*. Cambridge: Cambridge University Press.

Peterson, N. 1993. Demand sharing: reciprocity and the pressure for generosity amongst foragers. *American Anthropologist* 95(4): 860-74..

Riddington, R. 1982. Technology worldview in an adaptive strategy in a northern hunting society. *Canadian Review of Sociology and Anthropology* 19: 469-81.

Sahlins, M. 1972. *Stone Age Economics*. New York: Aldine.

Sinclair, A. 1995. The technique as a symbol in Late Glacial Europe. *World Archaeology* 27(1): 50-62.

Smith, P.E.L. 1973. Some thoughts on variations among certain Solutrean artefacts. In *Estudios Dedicados al Prof. Dr. Luis Pericot*, edited by J. de Montes. Barcelona.

Straus, L.G. 1983. *El Solutrense Vasco-Cantabrico: Una Nueva Perspectiva*. Madrid: Centro de Investigacíon y Museo de Altamira.

Straus, L.G. 1986. Cantabrian late Wurm adaptive systems. *Journal of Anthropological Archaeology* 5: 330-68.

Straus, L.G. 1987. Upper Palaeolithic ibex hunting in Southwest Europe. *Journal of Archaeological Science* 14: 163-78.

Straus, L.G. 1990. The original arms race: Iberian perspectives on the Solutrean phenomenon. In *Feuilles de Pierre*, edited by J. Kozłowski, pp. 425-447. Liege: ERAUL.

Straus, L.G. and G.A. Clark 1986. *La Riera: Stone Age Hunter-Gatherer Adaptations in Cantabrian Spain*. Tuscon: University of Arizona Press

White, R. 1985. *Upper Palaeolithic Land Use in the Perigord. A Topographic Approach to Subsistence and Settlement*. Oxford: BAR.

Woodburn, J. 1979. Minimal politics: the political organisation of the Hadza of Tanzania. In *Politics in Leadership: A Comparative Perspective*, edited by P. Cohen and W. Shack, pp. 244-266. Oxford: Clarendon Press.

Woodburn, J. 1982. Egalitarian societies. *Man* 17: 431-451.

Wynn, T. 1991. Tools, grammar and the archaeology of cognition. *Cambridge Archaeological Journal* 1: 191-206.

Chapter 3

Consumer behaviour in early modern times: show me your home and I will tell you who you are

Carolina Andersson and Ann-Mari Hållans[1]

Introduction

Consumption is a means of communication and an important part of social interaction. Material culture can be used to manifest and strengthen an existing social structure, but also to influence or change a relation by signalling an actual or fictitious social affiliation. By acquiring and using an object, the consumer both sends and receives social messages, which involve coding, deciphering, and identifying material culture. Material culture, however, should not be perceived as a direct reflection of human behaviour but must be interpreted and evaluated.

This article seeks to study consumer behaviour as a social strategy, with the household as the basic social unit. The analysis is based on seventeenth-century material from a block in the central Swedish town of Nyköping (Fig. 1). The households included in the analysis can be identified, mainly, as belonging to craftsmen. In the surviving written sources there is a hint of social differentiation between the craftsmens' households within the town-block.

The early modern period in Sweden was a time of social turbulence, which stimulated the burgher class to challenge the hierarchical social structures of the estates of the realm. The picture of the social topography of the town-block painted by the written sources served as the starting point for an archaeological study of consumer behaviour as an expression of social status. In this article, the home will be the stage and the town's craftsmen will play the leading roles.

Sweden in the seventeenth century

The early modern period gives us a unique opportunity to correlate written sources with archaeological remains and thus achieve greater nuances in our interpretation of seventeenth-century society.

There has long been a blind faith in the potential of written sources to give a complete picture of post-medieval society. It must be stressed that the seventeenth century was a period of great expansion in Swedish history, when the crown tried to expand its territories on the continent of Europe. As part of the endeavour to become a great power, it was important to create a powerful image both politically and culturally. These circumstances mean that the written source material is sometimes tendentious and hence difficult to interpret.

The spirit of the age as we tend to see it is coloured by the outlook on life held by the upper classes in society. The reasons for this are that it is mainly historians who have studied the period and that the written sources they use mainly reflect the social élite and their view of the lower classes (e.g., Englund 1989; Revera 1975).

The early modern period in Sweden is characterised by the growth of state power and the Reformation. This was a society in change, at the transition from a feudal to a capitalist order. During this epoch, there was a challenge to the old hierarchical order with its division of the population into four estates: nobles, clergy, burghers, and peasants. The period was one of great social mobility. The centrally steered nation needed a system of control and co-ordination in the form of a civil administration. This favoured the growth of a class of officials. It was primarily nobles who were recruited to these offices, but there were not enough nobles to meet the demand. This meant that members of the now economically strong burgher class had a chance to advance socially.

The growth of a new moneyed burgher-class threatened the hierarchical world-view of the nobility. The favourable development of the burgher class was a consequence of several factors. The world-wide system of trade that developed during the period stimulated the exchange of goods and ideas alike. Moreover, this flow of ideas encouraged the ongoing process of secularisation. The questioning of the old estate system led the aristocracy to use, more than ever before, symbols and external attributes to retain and reinforce their social position (Englund 1989: 70ff). This was expressed in unbridled luxury consumption which, contrary to the intentions of the nobility, ultimately benefited the economic position of the burghers.

The new ideas that began to spread in the early modern period included humanism. This engendered an ideal of education and culture which embraced both learning and behaviour. State officials had to have an education, so nobles and burghers alike sent their children to foreign universities. Yet the ideal of culture prescribed not just book learning but also correct behaviour. One manifestation of this moral upbringing is seen in the etiquette books. Great emphasis was placed on the behaviour of the individual in the company of other people (e.g., table manners and conversation). Together, the cultural ideal of humanism and the evangelical faith can be seen as an aspiration to refine both the inner and the outer life of the individual (Ariés 1989: 7).

The burgher class, which included both tradesmen and craftsmen, was not a homogeneous group. As in the nobility, there was a hierarchical structure within the group which stimulated continuous manifestations of deliberate

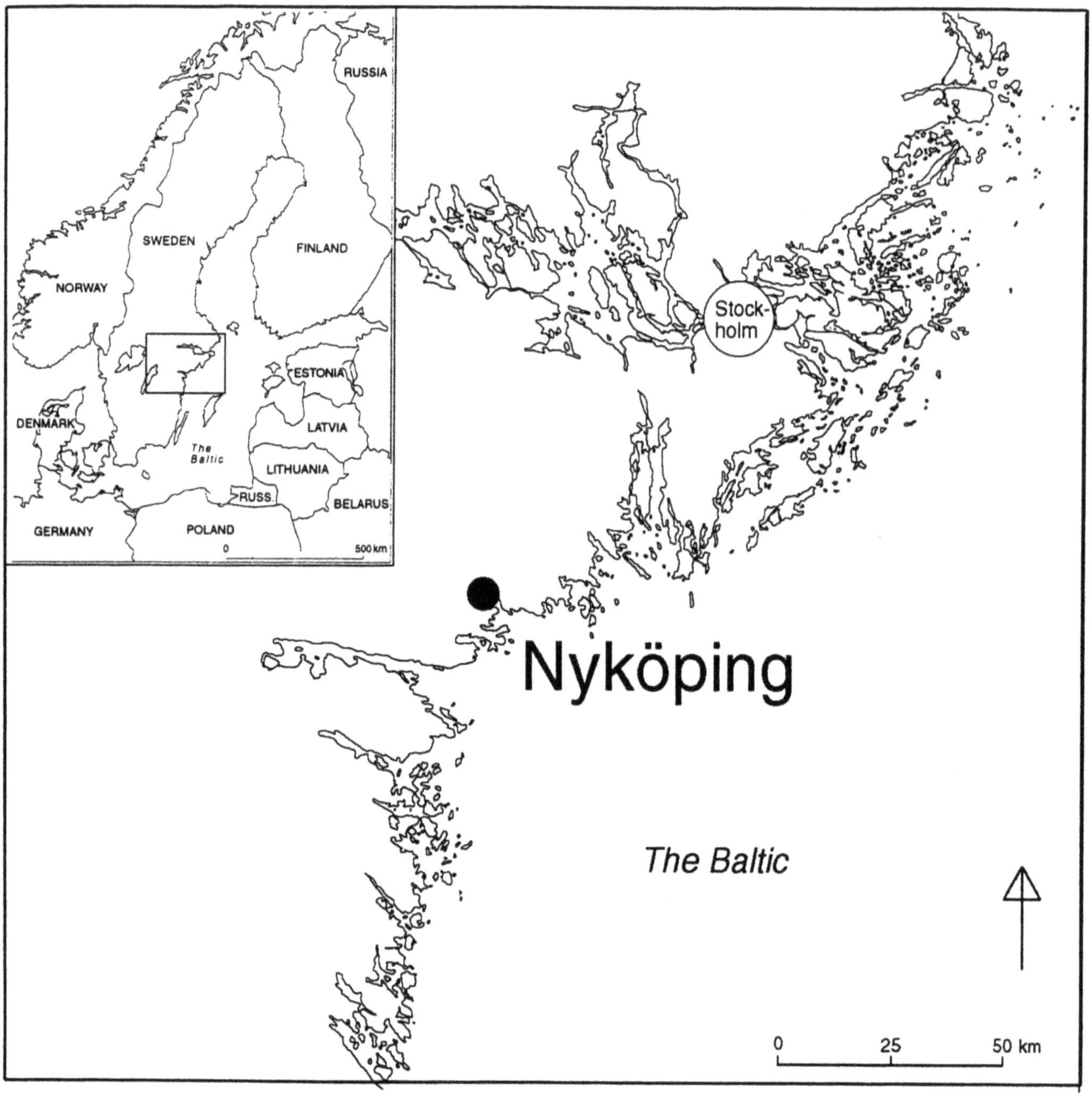

Figure 1 Sweden and the town of Nyköping.

consumption (Englund 1989: 40, 77). In this context, the-expression of social mobility.

Craftsmen in the town of Nyköping
The year 1987 saw the start of a rescue excavation in the town-block called Biografen at the western edge of Nyköping (Fig. 2). Nyköping is one of Sweden's earliest towns. It stands on a waterway, the Nyköping river, which flows into a sheltered bay of the Baltic Sea and thus held a strategic position for trade and the exchange of goods. In the Middle Ages the town of Nyköping grew up on both banks of the river. The development of the urban centre was closely connected with the activities in Nyköpingshus, a fortification founded at the beginning of the thirteenth century. In the following centuries the royal presence in the castle contributed to the prosperity of the town, which became an important port for overseas trade.

At the end of the sixteenth and the beginning of the seventeenth centuries, there was increased migration of craftsmen and merchants to the town. Nyköping was then the centre of the principality of Duke Karl, later King Karl IX. The presence of the court and the administration in the castle gave the merchants and craftsmen a better market for their goods. When Duke Karl became king in 1599, the town lost its position as an important centre of princely administration, and its trading and manufacturing role also diminished. But even in the 1680s, 4.5% of the country's exports, mainly iron and brass, went out through Nyköping (Petersson 1973: 346).

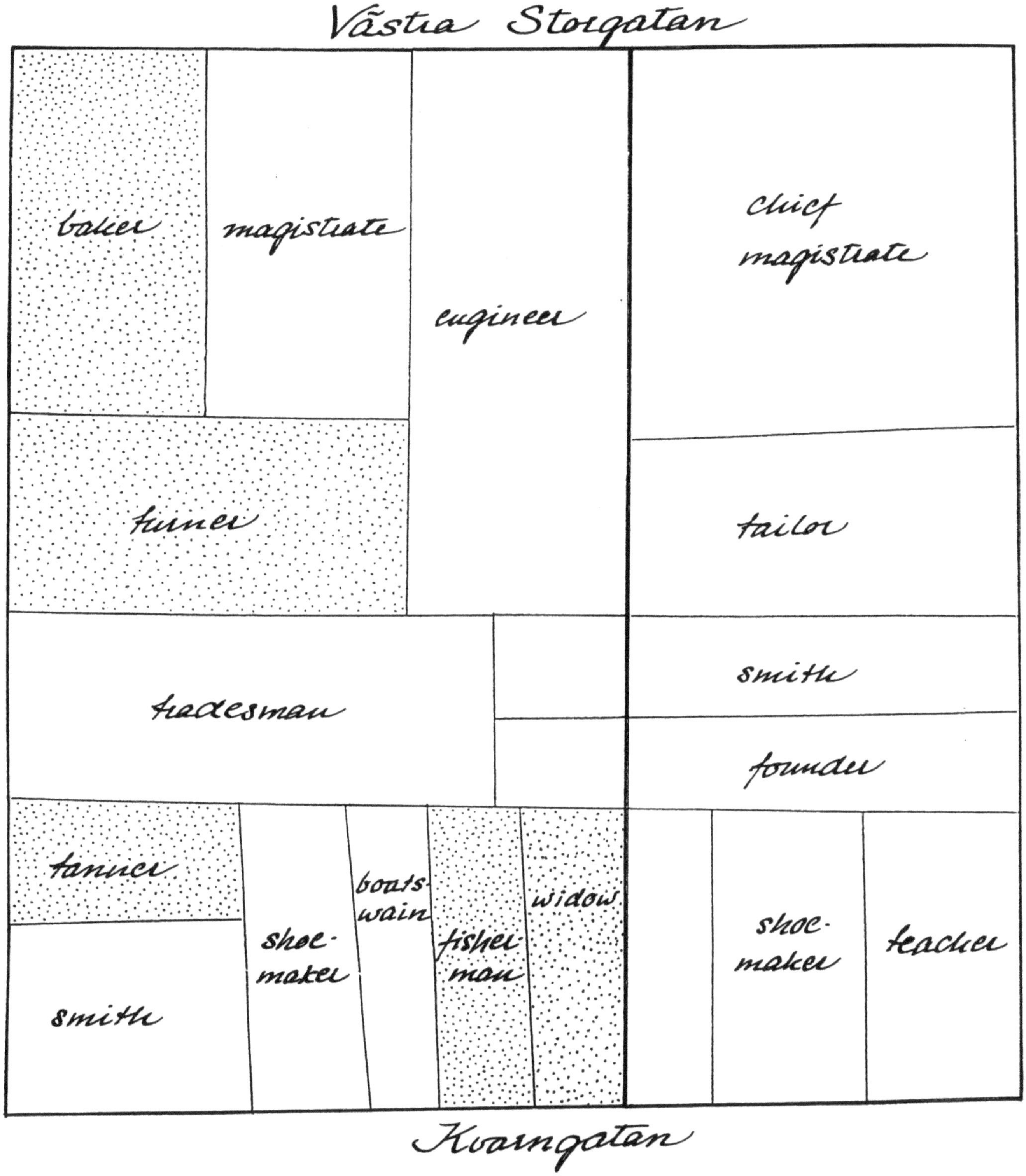

Figure 2 Rental map from 1674 showing the inhabitants and their occupations and the plots excavated in 1988 (shaded).

A rental map from 1674 shows that the excavation touched on eleven seventeenth-century plots. Of these, we chose to investigate five: numbers 1, 12, 13, 17, and 19 (Fig. 3). The choice of plots was partly dictated by their location in the town-block. The rental map shows that there was considerable variation in the size of the plots. The big plots lay beside the main street, Västra Storgatan, while the small ones were on the back street, Västra Kvarngatan.

For each of the excavated plots we chose one household as the analytical unit. A household consisted of those who stood in some relationship to the head of the household, such as wife and children, parents or other kin, servants, journeymen or lodgers (Hedlund 1980: 139). The selected households had all occupied the block at about the same time (Table 1).

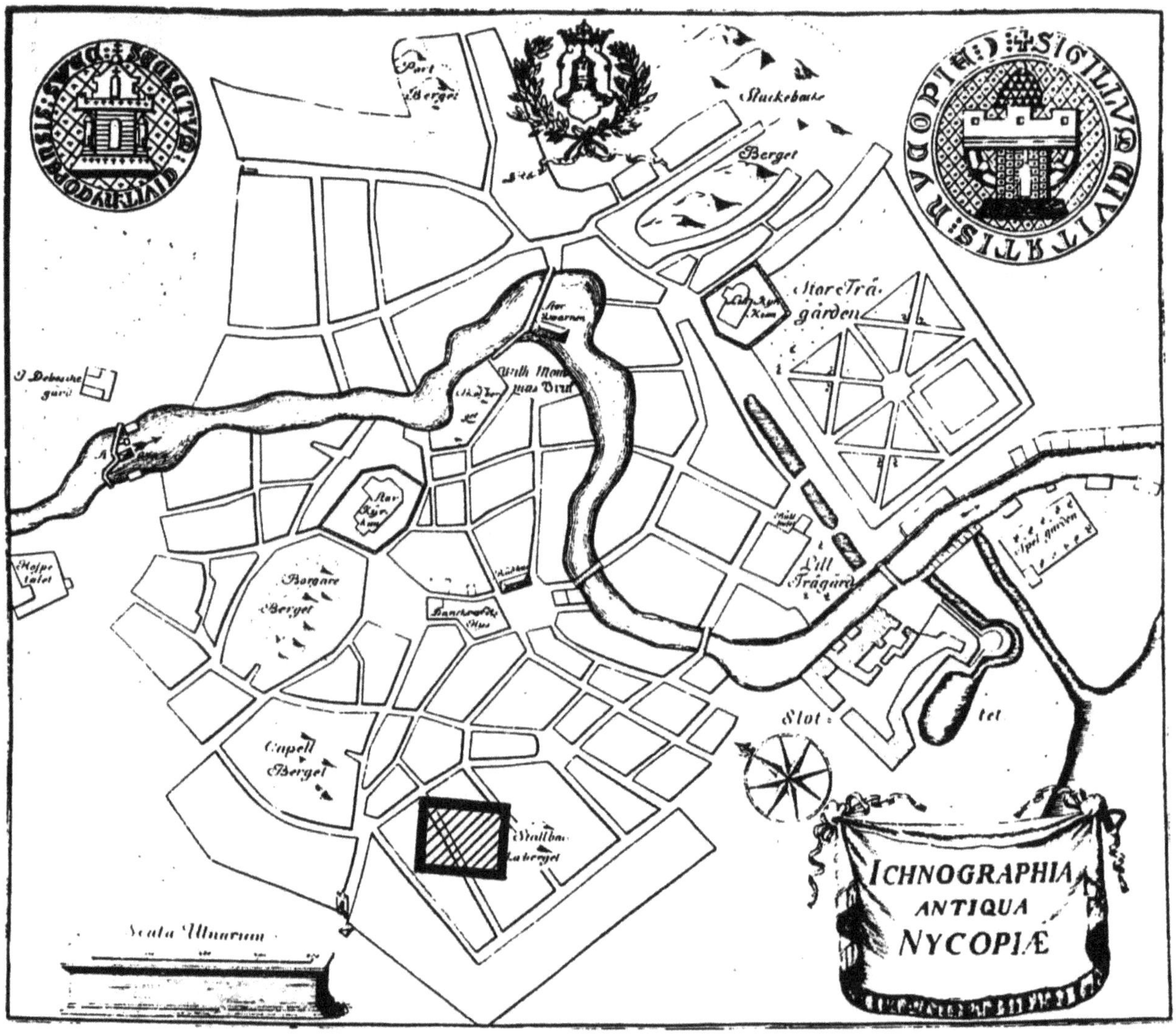

Figure 3 The earliest town map showing the town before the fire of 1665. The extract shows the Biografen block.

In Plots 1, 17, and 19 the heads of the households were craftsmen: baker, tanner and turner. They were master craftsmen and were enfranchised (i.e., they held the freedom to practise a craft and hence to own a workshop and employ labour). Besides these three craftsmen's households, there were two households with heads who were not enfranchised: a boatman-cum-fisherman (Plot 13) and a widow without any occupational designation (Plot 12).

The excavation of these plots uncovered the remains of the properties built by the craftsmen after the fire that ravaged the town in 1665. Catastrophic fires occurred regularly in Swedish towns. When fires began, the closely-packed wooden buildings had no hope of survival. Of all the fires in the history of Nyköping, that of 1665 is the best documented. Virtually all the town was reduced to ashes. The town soon recovered, and had largely been rebuilt nine years after the fire (Fig. 4). The newly-built town had a completely different appearance from the earlier one: it was changed from a town with an erratic pattern of streets and lanes (which had been allowed to follow the line of least resistance) to one with streets arranged at right angles and with regular town-blocks. The rapidity of the rebuilding of Nyköping was partly due to its being granted freedom from royal taxes for six years. This made it a favourable place in which to work and live. The demand for craftsmen was met by newcomers who were quickly enrolled in the town's guilds. Casche the baker may be an example of this. He moved from the town of his birth, Stralsund, to Stockholm, where he had applied, in vain, for franchise. In Nyköping, however, he received both enfranchisement and the title of master by marrying a baker's widow.

Plot	Household	Years of occupation
1	Staffan Cashe, baker	1675-1715
12	Nils Jonsson's widow	1668-no date
13	Johan Samuelsson, fisherman & boatman	1668-1717
17	Johan Andersson, tanner	1689-1719
19	Olof Olsson, turner	1687-1719

Table 1 The selected households and years of occupation.

Figure 4 . Nyköping in the 1660s. Print by Erik Dahlberg (graphic print from *Suecia Antiqua et Hodierna*).

The citizens of Nyköping had only fifty years in which to enjoy their new town. In 1719, during the final phase of the Great Northern War, the Russians harried the Baltic coast and Nyköping was one of the towns which was destroyed by fire. The craftsmen's houses in the block were totally destroyed. Compensation and a new remission of taxes, this time for eight years, allowed the craftsmen to rebuild their houses and resume their trades. In 1720 there were about 80 craftsmen in Nyköping; a decade later this number had risen to 116. Despite this, the population remained small, numbering roughly 2,000 in the middle of the century. Of these, about 24% were craftsmen distributed among 33 different crafts; only 7% were merchants and manufacturers (Petterson 1973: 354f, Table 4-5). It is clear that the urban economy was thus dominated by the group of craftsmen.

The archaeological excavation

The results of the excavation may be briefly described as follows: the surviving remains of buildings came from urban properties built after the fire of 1665. They had been rebuilt, partly, and extended until the fire of 1719. Unfortunately, the properties rebuilt after 1719 had been badly disturbed by later stone foundations and were therefore difficult to reconstruct (Andersson et al. 1990).

The excavation also generated a vast quantity of finds, about 13,000 objects in all, which were found in a complex stratigraphy consisting of a large number of units or layers. The largest category of artefacts was vessels of late redwares, faience, porcelain, and glass, which made up 46% of the total finds. Other large groups included manufacturing refuse (25%) and constructional details (17%).

The aim of the excavation was to shed light on consumer behaviour per individual household by integrating written sources and archaeological material. Consequently, it was crucial to be able to correlate the archaeological remains with the households described or mentioned in the written documents. This method, however, required exact determination of context and the dating of every separate stratigraphic unit. Since the present study is based partly on layer-related artefacts, it is important to clarify the source value of the layers that we have used: this means assessing the way the layers came about and any secondary influence.

The layers found during the excavation can be summed up as usage-layers, construction-layers, waste-layers, demolition-layers, and filling-layers. The usage-layers often lay on stone or wooden paving; they covered the whole area and were thin. The construction-layers and demolition-layers were directly related to the building and destruction of houses or other structures. The construction layers mainly consisted of wood chippings while the demolition-layers were dominated by fragments of brick and lime mortar. The filling-layers were often relatively thin layers of pure clay or sand lying, for example, under stone paving. Refuse-layers were very thick and rich in finds and were found in out-of-the-way parts of the plot. There were of course transitional forms of layers which were difficult to categorise in this way, but the aim was to try to understand the motives behind the creation of the layers and thus to determine the context of which the layer was part. The study deals only with artefacts which can be described as waste (i.e., objects found in refuse-layers). These objects are part of a consumption process which included acquisition, use, and disposal.

In this context it is particularly important to assess whether a layer was a primary or a secondary deposit. To be able to study consumer behaviour in relation to individual households, it must be possible to assign a layer to a specific household with high probability. A layer that is interpreted as a primary source must have a composition and context typical of the layer type and not appear as if it was a secondary addition.

With the aid of source-critical layer analysis and date-indicating finds such as clay pipes, coins, and faience, we have been able to attribute refuse-layers to the individual households which the written sources show to have occupied the plots. In other words, we think that we know with fair probability whose waste piles we have investigated 300 years later.

Waste is not an uncomplicated phenomenon, however; it involves many problems of source criticism. A fundamental question is whether the discarded object was what can be regarded as a non-artefact, that is, valueless waste, or if it was still part of a use cycle. Objects which can no longer be used for their original purpose can be sorted and collected for reuse in a different context. Examples of this are layers containing lots of potsherds which can be used as filling for streets. Such assemblages of pottery are thus not valueless. Instead they represent capital accumulation (Magnusson Staff et al. 1995: 49).

Another important aspect is people's attitudes to waste. Was waste a sanitary nuisance which had to be transported away? Was there deliberate waste management and, if so, how could it have been organised within a plot or a town? Legislation decreed that refuse had to be carted away, but it is not certain how far the law was observed. In addition, the removal of waste presupposes a certain degree of economic resources and may thus have been related to status.

The written sources

The registration of the inhabitants of Sweden began comparatively early. State officials, and particularly parish priests, provided information to the crown from an early date. Unfortunately, many town archives, of which the church documents made up a part, were destroyed by the numerous devastating fires. This was true of Nyköping. Its parish registers were destroyed by the fires of 1665 and 1719 and so it is difficult to obtain precise details about the people who lived in the town. However, the parish registers can be supplemented by the censuses of population in which were entered the names of everyone obliged to pay the poll-tax. However, they do have some shortcomings for they do not include all the inhabitants. Social groups such as aristocrats, priests, crown appointees and sailors were exempted from the tax, as were children, the elderly, and the sick (Lext 1968).

Rental lists and rental maps form another important source. They record the plot-owners who had to pay rent to the town for their plots. The earliest recorded rental (from 1668) gives the names and occupations of the owners of plots in the newly-built town-blocks. The rentals also record the size of the plots and whether they were freehold or owned by the town. The map of 1674 is based on the rental list of 1668.

While can obtain biographical information about the people who lived in Nyköping from the written sources, it is more difficult to find information about the layout of the urban plots. Nevertheless, inventories drawn up at an owner's death give details of personal property and, sometimes, even of their buildings.

Further information about the plots can be obtained from the Claim for Reparations of 1719. After the Russians burned Nyköping in that year, a list was drawn up of all inhabitants whose property had been destroyed.

Social status in the written record

The written sources imply that there were social differences between the households in the various plots in the block. The concept of status may refer to differences in access to material resources, income, wealth and security, or in good name, esteem, respect and reverence (Dahlström 1971: 11f). Since the various aspects of status are so closely associated, it is difficult to make a general distinction between economic and social status. In this study, however, we have chosen to place the emphasis on the social intentions of consumer behaviour.

Consumer behaviour is a meaning-bearing manifestation of will, influenced by many factors (Henry 1991: 5). Those which we have found to be important and verifiable through written sources are as follows: the time factor, access to a market, the composition of a household, the permanence of a household in a plot, the life-cycle of a household, and its social and economic status. It is easy to control for the time factor and access to a market as the selected households lived and worked at the same time and in the same town, even in the same block. We also have a basic knowledge of the lifetime of the household and, to a certain extent, its composition (mainly the adults and the servants). We lack information, however, about the true size of the household and its life-cycle, as there are no surviving parish registers.

The written sources enable us to rank the households in relative order of social and economic status.

Size and position of the plots

The rental lists and rental maps provide information about the size of the plots. Originally, the amount of rent was related to size but through time it came to be more symbolic and was unconnected with size (Hedlund 1980: 107). The large plots often lay in attractive positions (e.g., by a main street or a market place). The right to the tenancy of a large plot with its need for representative buildings and finer activities must certainly have commanded a certain social and economic status in the town.

Of the 17 plots in the block, one-third are big plots in the front part of the block while two-thirds are small plots at the back of the block. Plots 1 and 19 are examples of large plots and are on the main street, Västra Storgatan, at the front of the block. Plots 12 and 17 are small plots at the back of the block.

Buildings and personal property

After the fire of 1719 each fire-damaged property in the town put in a claim for damages to the municipal court. These claims provide an idea of the economic status of the households. The claims were divided between real estate and personal property. We can assume that the claims were probably in proportion to true value of the damaged property.

The larger claims for compensation coincide with the bigger plots in the block. Plot 1 filed the fourth largest claim, while Plot 19 had the sixth largest. The claims for Plots 12/13 and 17 were among the lowest in the block.

Inventories are another source of information about the value and make-up of personal property, although they can be very summary when treating single and cheap objects (Jarrick 1990: 216ff.). Only one of the selected households (that of the turner Lax) has a surviving inventory. It shows that most of the 'domestic equipment' was lost in the fire of 1719. Despite this, the inventory includes objects of silver and pewter and linen napkins and tablecloths (Inventory of Olof Lax 11/4 1720).

Employed labour

The employment of labour by a household implies a certain economic status. The number of employees was often only one per household, but there could be as many as three (Stadin 1979: 83ff). To have only one employee seldom involved an increase in production leading to the betterment of the economic situation of the craftsman (Hedlund 1980: 95f). Sometimes, the poll-tax returns include information about employed people (i.e., servants connected to a household). Mostly described as maids or hired-hands, they are sometimes also apprentices and journeymen.

The baker's and the turner's households were with employees. The baker had a servant boy and two or three maids, while the turner had a maid and a servant. Neither the tanner nor the widow employed any labour.

Trade of the master

Many investigations into conditions in the nineteenth and twentieth centuries have shown that the strongest indication of the social and economic status of a household is the trade or profession of its head or master (Spencer-Wood 1987).

It is difficult to say in general whether particular categories of crafts in the seventeenth century had a higher status than others. Studies of taxation registers from the sixteenth and seventeenth centuries show that some craftsmen (e.g., goldsmiths) were often taxed at a higher rate, whereas others (e. g., carpenters) were taxed considerably less. But there were often great discrepancies between craftsmen within the same category (Lindberg 1989: 59; Stadin 1979: 96; Hedlund 1980: 95).

Crucial factors in whether a craft was capital-intensive (thereby demanding steady and high profits) were production time, the extent of the permanent structures, and the price of the raw materials (Söderlund 1943: 207). Production time means the period between obtaining the raw materials and completing the finished product. The crafts in question here (baking, turning, and tanning) did not have the same need for investment. The baker mass-produced a cheap commodity and the size of bakeries varied (ibid., 185). Baking, like brewing, was often on a large-scale and therefore needed some capital investment, for example a large oven (ibid., 172). Tanning was also often large-scale. The tanneries had a long production time (up to one year) and tanning also needed capital investment in the form of raw materials and large permanent structures (ibid., 207). On the other hand, wood-turning needed little capital investment, only a lathe which the turner could make himself and a number of small tools. Nor was the raw material expensive (ibid., 225).

Lax the turner was both a master and a town councillor, which must have been a worthy post and which gave him high prestige in the town. There are, however, more problematic cases which are connected with trade or profession. For example, was the tanner low in the social order because his trade was foul-smelling? Was it respectable to be a boatman in the service of the crown even though the income was erratic and small?

Social ranking of the households

The relative order of household rank can be summarised as follows. The baker and the turner occupied large plots with a prominent position in the block. Judging from the claims for damages, their properties must have been large and in good condition. They seem also to have had flourishing economies as they employed a number of people. Yet another sign of the turner's status in the town is his position on the town-council. In contrast, the amount of compensation claimed for the tanner's property was small, which may be partly explained by the fact that the tanner was dead at the time of the fire. The plot may have been unoccupied or the business closed, both of which could have led to a decline in value. But craftsmen's widows could also inherit the franchise and continue the craft, so the above scenario need not be correct (Stadin 1979: 44). As there is no record of employees, the tannery was probably a small-scale operation. The boatman and the widow had very low reparation claims and therefore rank lowest on the list.

The written sources thus suggest that the households of the baker and turner had a higher economic status than those of the tanner and the widow. This picture can be qualified or perhaps reappraised when supplemented by archaeological source material. A combination of these different kinds of sources may enrich our knowledge of the social position of craftsmen in an age when an older hierarchical order was being threatened.

The home as a social stage

Material culture expresses an undercurrent of values and thoughts that in many cases are not expressed in words; they can be described as an expression of the spirit of the age. Matthew Johnson assigns an important role to the use and design of artefacts in the sixteenth century in a process of social change in and of everyday life. In this connection, the adoption of new phenomena and artefacts can be a way to signal social status (Johnson 1996: 192).

In the early modern period there was a gradual change in both the exterior and the interior of the home. The living-room, known as stuga or in bigger houses sal, was still the central place in the house. It was given a ceiling, and the open hearth was replaced by a fireplace with a chimney. The introduction of the ceiling meant that the house acquired an upper-storey. In its oldest form, this was used only for storage, but later it was divided into smaller rooms. The exterior of the dwelling was thus transformed into a two-storey house divided into several rooms (Fig. 5). The opening in the roof was the exterior light-source of the living-room. This disappeared with the introduction of the chimney stack and windows were inserted in the walls for light. These two new features changed the home environment radically giving bright rooms without smoke. The masonry chimney stack also made it possible to heat the adjacent bedroom by means of a tiled stove (Erixon 1947: 788; Werne 1993: 69-71, 211, 223).

The change in the home can be seen as an expression of ideals that have their origins in humanism. The home became inviting; people from outside the family could be invited in for trials of social strength. This provided an opportunity to show off one's furnishings and fine manners. The generous light from the windows allowed the guest to see all the decoration in the room. The closed chest formerly used for storage was replaced by an open dresser. Here, stored for all to see, were decorated earthenware vessels of all shapes (Rybczynski 1988: 81-82). The increasingly open forms of these vessels, such as dishes and bowls, exposed the colours and complex patterns of the pipeclay decoration. At meals these vessels had yet another opportunity to be viewed, by functioning as serving vessels. A meal

Figure 5 A lafted building under construction. A drawing by Lorenzo Magalotti in 1674 (from Sverige under år 1674).

thus became an exhibition of exquisite table manners expressing the inner refinement of the hosts (Elias 1989: 192ff.).

Social status expressed in material culture

The specific time when a home was clad in this new guise depended on the social stratum to which the household belonged. The ideas were first introduced in the upper classes, but it is uncertain when and to what extent these new fashions were adopted by the lower classes. However, the ideological meanings and connections of an artefact do not need to permeate or even be noticed by the household acquiring it. The archaeological source material should have the potential to shed light on this question. The material for analysis mainly comes from craftsmen's households and the categories of artefacts that they may have used to signal social status can be both social constructions and individual objects. It would be natural to study objects which can be considered exclusive, but this involves problems both with the concept of luxury and with the representativeness and interpretation of luxury phenomena. A crucial objection to the use of exclusive artefacts is that they only occur as isolated phenomena in the archaeological material. For this reason, in this analysis we want to test the potential of bulk-finds to shed light on social status. The analysis will therefore be based on houses, tiles, and ceramic vessels.

The exterior of the home

In the Middle Ages the dwelling-house was often located at the back of a long, narrow plot. In the early modern period, the plots changed their appearance, becoming more square. By the mid-eighteenth century the new arrangement of houses built in a square around a yard was fully developed, and the dwelling-house now lay on the street, with outbuildings of various kinds around the yard (Palmqvist 1989: 40).

It is impossible to study the exterior of the home unless the dwelling-house can be identified. The house structures that were found in the five plots were very fragmentary, consisting in principle solely of the foundation (i.e., the parts lying under the floor). Most foundations were built on stout wooden sills lying on rows of widely spaced stones. Besides the fragmentary state of the houses, identification was made difficult by the fact that the excavated plots were more or less destroyed by later, heavier house foundations. It was chiefly the front parts of the plots that had been destroyed by later interference.

The baker in Plot 1 had a square-built property with houses grouped around a courtyard. The house on the corner of Västra Storgatan has been identified as the dwelling-house. It was visible in the form of a drystone foundation consisting of two layers of stone. The stone frame was filled with a thick layer of pure clay except for the part containing the remains of a vaulted cellar. Judging by the sturdy foundation, the house must have had two storeys (Fig. 6). Above the foundation there were traces of interior walls dividing the ground floor into four rooms. In one of the rooms the base of a tiled stove was excavated.

It was more problematic to find the dwelling-house in the turner's plot (Plot 19) since the part of the plot facing the street had been destroyed by later house foundations. None of the surviving house structures which were also grouped around a yard and which were further in from the street appears to have been a dwelling-house. According to the inventory of the estate of Lax the turner, drawn up after his death in 1719, it is clear that there was a cellar in his plot. This may have been located in the large, stone-filled pit found on Bagaregatan. The location of the cellar and hence of the dwelling-house in the area right beside the street means that the plot had a similar arrangement to that of

Figure 6 Imaginative reconstruction of the Baker's Plot.

Plot 1.

Tanner Andersson's property in Plot 17 consisted of one house along Bagaregatan, another house along the northern boundary of the plot, a yard in the middle, and a smaller house at the very back of the plot. The houses along the plot boundary were the buildings used for the tanning operations, with a lime-house and a beam-house. The house structure by the street was rather anonymous since all that could be seen of it was an earth raft of sill-beams filled with clay. The foundation was rather large, however, and the position of the dwelling-houses in Plots 1 and 19 suggests that the tanner also had his dwelling-house along the street.

The two small plots on Kvarngatan (Plots 12 and 13) have a form reminiscent of the Medieval plot. These two plots were narrow and relatively deep, which means that the houses were placed in a row and not around a yard. The houses on the inner parts of the plots had the character of small sheds or workshops. It is probable that the dwelling-houses were also located by the street but that later disturbances have destroyed the front section of these plots.

This analysis of the households' plot arrangements shows that the new square-built town-yard had caught on, except among the households which according to the written sources had the lowest social status. On the other hand, the widow's and the fisherman's households, like the others, had adopted the changed placing of the dwelling in the area adjacent to the street. Because of the fragmentary appearance of the surviving house structures (and in many case the absence of any structures) it is difficult to study the exterior of the dwellings. However, the baker's house shows that the idea of a dwelling-house of two storeys divided into several rooms had been adopted at least by the craftsmen's households which the written sources show to have had a higher social status. In addition, there was a vaulted cellar under the house; the economic investment necessary for this must have been a signal of social status. We know nothing about the look of the turner's house, but the mention of a cellar in the estate inventory indicates that the turner had a dwelling similar to the baker's. The tanner had built his property according to the new ideal, but the dwelling-house can only have had one storey judging by the slender foundation structure.

The interior of the home

We have seen that the exterior of the households is difficult to reconstruct because of the fragmentary character of the structures. The new ideals of the age, however, greatly affected the interior of the house and both the furniture and the fixtures. To ascertain whether the households had adopted these new phenomena, in this part of the analysis we use the content of the refuse-layers identified in each plot. The difficulty of interpreting the stratigraphy in Plot 13, however, means that material from this plot has been excluded.

Tiled stoves and glazed windows

Archaeological excavations have shown that tiles and window glass began to appear in urban settings in the sixteenth and seventeenth centuries. As modern fashions these categories of find may be an expression of a change of attitude. The tiled stove and glazed windows meant a radical transformation of the atmosphere in the home. The interior milieu acquired heat and light which would have made it more inviting. Fragments of window glass and tiled stoves can show the extent to which the different households strove to acquire or incorporate a new ideal of home furnishing. In our analysis we have chosen to compare the amount of tiles in the refuse- and demolition-layers of the various households.

Figure 7 shows that the amount of tiles in proportion to the total quantity of finds was slightly higher in Plots 1 and 19. This may be a sign that the baker and the turner had assimilated the new ideals of the interior environment as a way to manifest their high social status.

Ceramic vessels

Ceramic vessels as a reflection of table manners may be an expression of changed forms of social intercourse. Whether positioned on the table or along the walls the vessels may have signalled social affiliation (Fig. 8).

The excavation of the Biografen block uncovered vessels of porcelain, faience, stoneware, redware, wood, and glass. In the following analysis we compare the proportion of indigenous redware to the amount of imported pottery types such as faience and stoneware. In addition, we relate the open and closed redware vessel shapes to each other. The analysis of the ceramic vessels follows up the hypothesis that table manners, as both mental and a physical expressions, may signal an ambition to change one's social position in a socially mobile age.

Redware

Redware occurs in several forms of vessel: dishes, bowls, pots, and pitchers. The open shapes, such as bowls and dishes, first began to appear in the sixteenth century when new table manners required new types of vessel. Laying the table with serving dishes and perhaps one place per person was a material expression of a new form of social intercourse. As serving vessels, dishes and bowls were supposed be an adornment to the table, they were often decorated. In addition, the open forms exposed the decoration, which meant that vessels of this type were more often decorated than were the closed forms. In a study of price data for different types of pottery, Miller has found that the decoration determined the price (Miller 1980; Spencer-Wood 1987). Decorating a vessel must have increased costs in the production phase, since it was time-consuming and moreover required specially trained labour. On this basis, we may assume that decorated ceramics were more expensive than undecorated.

In the relation between open and closed vessels, Figure 9 shows that open vessel forms are over-represented, except

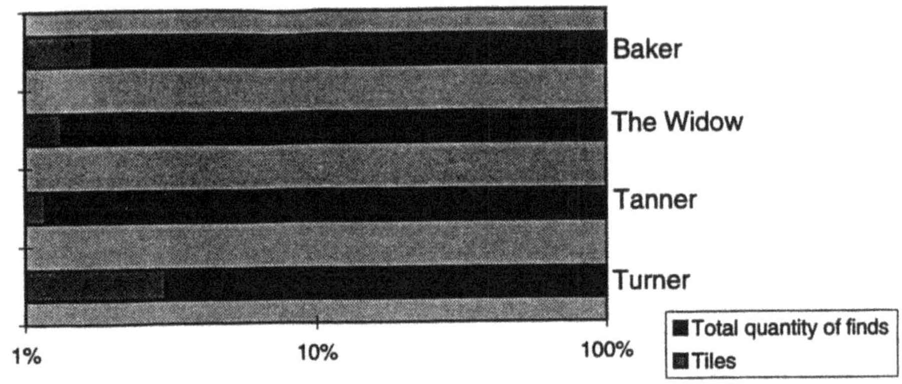

Figure 7 Relationship between tiles and total quantity of finds showing how the households strove to incorporate a new ideal of home furnishing.

Figure 8 'The wedding in Kana'. Painted tapestry by Johannes Nilsson 1797 (from Arcadius 1987).

in the tanner's household, where the proportion is relatively equal. The baker's household is distinguished by having the largest proportion of bowls and dishes, and is followed by the proportions in the turner's and the widow's households.

Vessels of faience and porcelain

As imported commodities, porcelain, faience, and stoneware were more expensive to buy than redware. In addition, faience involved the introduction of new forms of vessels intended for exclusive drinks such as coffee and tea.

The artefacts can represent everything on a sliding scale from life's necessities to unnecessary luxuries. Whether a phenomenon is to be described as necessary or unnecessary depends on the context in which it was intended to function. If we look at the concept of luxury and the way it was interpreted in the eighteenth century, we see that the official ordinances on luxury list a great many goods which were considered unnecessary at the time. In true mercantilist spirit, the aim of these ordinances was to curb imports in order to benefit the economy of the nation. In addition, the ordinances were issued at a time when the nobility felt that luxury should be confined to the social élite. At the same time, luxury was debated from the moral point of view as a sign of vanity, desire, and selfishness (Peterson 1984: 3ff). The ordinances list the goods that were considered unnecessary luxury, such as coffee, tobacco, silk, and porcelain. It is reasonable to assume that these listed-luxuries were strongly associated with status-related consumer behaviour, but that they account for only a very tiny proportion of the archaeological finds. It is often a question of isolated finds whose representativeness and source value may be difficult to ascertain. The excavation of the Biografen block yielded very small amounts of porcelain and faience. The two types of wares should be seen together as representatives of a more exclusive type of vessel than was the redware.

Figure 10 presents the relation of faience and stoneware to redware, showing that the baker's household appears to have had a slightly higher proportion of faience and stoneware than the other households in the block.

The analysis of phenomena from the home interiors shows that tiles and ceramic vessels such as redware dishes and bowls occur in all the households. The same distribution also applies to vessels of faience, porcelain, and stoneware. Between the households, however, there is a small quantitative difference in the occurrence of tiles, dishes and bowls of redware, and vessels of faience, porcelain, and stoneware. The baker's household also had the largest proportion of ceramic vessels of the types selected for the analysis, while the turner had the largest proportion of tiles. The

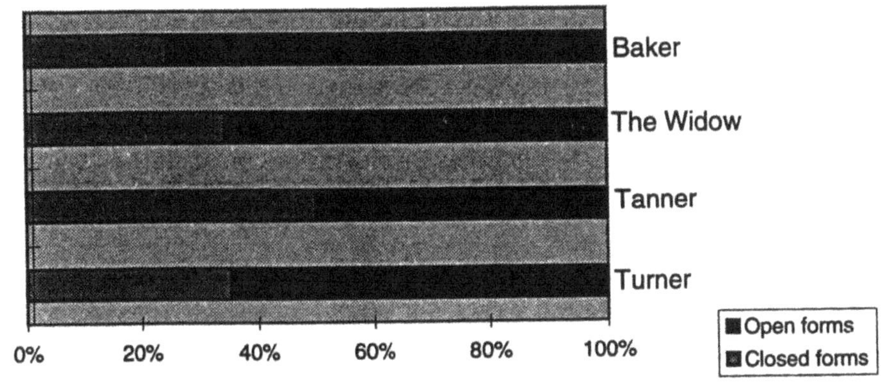

Figure 9 The relationship between open and closed vessel forms showing household consumption of redware.

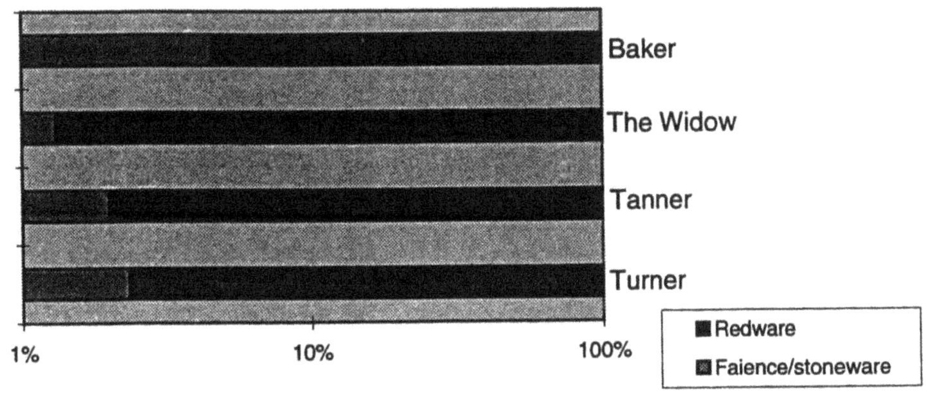

Figure 10 Relationship between faience and stoneware/ redware showing the household consumption of faience and stoneware.

households of the tanner and the widow both had a lower proportion of all these artefacts, but the differences between these households and those of the baker and the turner were marginal.

Evaluation

On the basis of this analysis, we may observe that the new ideals appear to have caught on in all the households. There are variations in the degree of acquisition, it is true; the turner and in particular the baker appear to have embraced the new ideas concerning both the exterior and the interior of the household.

Since the results of the analysis are not unequivocal, three hypothetical explanations are possible: 1) the material selected for analysis signals social status and thus the households had an equivalent social status; 2) the material selected for analysis does not signal social status and thus the households did not have an equivalent social status; 3) the material selected for analysis signals social status and thus the households did not have an equivalent social status.

The first hypothesis appears improbable since the written sources undoubtedly show economic differences (e.g., in their claims for compensation after the fire of 1719). The relatively large differences in the claims paint a picture of prosperous versus modest properties.

The second hypothesis, on the other hand, may be valid. The material selected for analysis occurs in all households and the differences in frequency are relatively marginal. This means that the households in general adopted the ideals of the times concerning the interior of the home. Most social intercourse between people probably still went on outside the sphere of the home. Consequently, there was neither a need for, nor perhaps even any awareness of, the possibility of using, for example, table manners to display where one belonged socially. Perhaps the exterior of the home was the household's social status signal – a large two-storey house speaks clearly for itself.

One question remaining to be answered, however, is to what extent economic resources furthered or hampered people's opportunities to realise the ideals completely. The small variations that can nevertheless be discerned in the analysis could be a sign of this.

The assumption in the hypothesis that the selected material does not signal social status may be further challenged on the basis of estate inventories from this time. The inventories suggest that categories of artefacts other than those selected were used to a greater extent to signal status (e.g., silver and pewter).

The third hypothesis is associated with refuse management and the attitude of the households to waste. Archaeological material being refuse or residues is more or less incomplete by its very nature. The possibilities and limitations of the material are also influenced by the town decrees about refuse management. In addition, we still have the question of whether every household deliberately sorted its waste.

The analysis should inspire the continued study of consumer behaviour on the basis of other bulk-finds and of individual, exclusive artefacts. In addition, other periods of time and other settings should be studied to shed further light on social strategies in the early modern period. To sum up, it can be said that the archaeological source material has problematized and qualified the picture painted by the written documents of the craftsmen's households in the block. The black-and-white picture has thus been enriched with grey scales.

Endnotes

1. Translation by Alan Crozier.

Bibliography

Andersson, C., A-M. Hållans and B. Persson 1990. *Biografen. Ett 1600-1700-talskvarter i Nyköping.* (Rapport UV 1990: 1). Stockholm: Riksantikvarieämbetet och Statens Historiska Museer.

Arcadius, K. 1987. Bröllopet i Kana - ett motiv, två målare. *Halland*, pp. 20-22.

Ariés, P. 1989. Introduction. In *A History of Private Life. Volume III. Passions of the Renaissance*, edited by R. Chartier, pp. 1-11. Cambridge, Mass.: Harvard University Press.

Dahlström, E. 1971. *Klasser och Samhällen. Teorier om Social Skiktning och Social Integration*. Stockholm: Prisma.

Elias, N. 1989. *Civilisationsteori. del 1: Sedernas historia.* Stockholm: Atlantis.

Englund, P. 1989. *Det Hotade Huset. Adliga Föreställningar om Samhället.* Stockholm: Atlantis.

Erixon, S. 1947. *Svensk Byggnadskultur*. Malmo: Aktiebolaget Bokverk.

Hedlund, R. 1980. *Västerås Befolkning vid Slutet av 1600-talet. En Socialhistorisk Studie.* Vasteras: Vasteras Kulturnamnd.

Henry, S. L. 1991. Consumers, commodities, and choices: a general model of consumer behavior. *Historical Archaeology* 25(2): 3-14.

Jarrick, A. 1990. Borgare, småfolk och böcker i 1700-talets Stockholm. *Historisk Tidskrift* 1990(2): 191-227.

Johnson, M. 1996. *The Archaeology of Capitalism*. Oxford: Blackwell.

Lext, G. 1968. *Mantal Skrivningen i Sverige före 1860.* Goteborg: Landsarkivet.

Lindberg, F. 1989. *Hantverk och Skråväsen under Medeltiden och Äldre Vasatid.* Stockholm: Prisma.

Magnussen Staff, B., G. Erikdotter and S. Larsson 1995. The street as monument. *Lund Archaeological Review* 1995: 35-52.

Miller, G. L. 1980. Classification and economic scaling of 19th century ceramics. *Historical Archaeology* 14: 1-41.

Palmqvist, L. 1989. Städernas hantverksgårdar. In *Hantverket i Sverig*, edited by B. Nystrom, A. Björnstad and B. Bursell, pp. 40-44. Stockholm: LTs Förlag.

Peterson, B. 1984. 'Yppighets Nytta och Torftighets Fägnad'. Pamflettdebatten om 1766 års överflödsförordning. *Historisk Tidsskrift* 1984(1):3-43.

Petterson, A-M. 1973. Nyköping under 1700-talet. In *Nyköpings Stads Historia II*, edited by S. Dahlgren, pp. 323-490. Nyköping: Almqvist Wiksell.

Revera, M. 1975. *Gods och gård 1650-1680. Magnus Gabriel De la Gardies godsbildning och godsdrift i Västergötland.* (Studia Historica Upsaliensia 70). Uppsala: Uppsala Universitet.

Rybczynski, W. 1988. *Hemmet. Boende och Trivsel Sett i Historiens Ljus).* Stockholm: Bonnier.

Spencer-Wood, S. M. 1987. Miller's indices and consumer-choice profiles: status-related behaviors and white ceramics. In *Consumer Choice in Historical Archaeology*, edited by S.M. Spencer, pp. 321-358. New York: Plenum.

Stadin, K. 1979. *Småstäder, Småborgare och Stora Samhällsförändringar. Borgarnas Sociala Struktur i Arboga, Enköping och Västervik under Perioden efter 1680.* (Studia Historica Upsaliensia 105). Upsalla: Uppsala Universitet.

Söderlund, E. 1943. *Stockholms Hantverkarklass 1720-1772. Sociala och Ekonomiska Förhållanden.* (Monografier utgivna av Stockholms kommunalförvaltning). Stockholm: Stockholms Kommunalförvaltring.

Werne, F. 1993. *Böndernas Bygge. Traditionellt Byggnadsskick på Landsbygden i Sverige.* Höganäs: Wilken.

Chapter 4

Performance as valuation: early Bronze Age burial as theatrical complexity

Mike Pearson

Is this a dagger which I see before me?
(Shakespeare, Macbeth II.i.33)

One of the principal ambitions of the interdisciplinary approach to performance and the past which we have termed 'theatre/archaeology' (Pearson and Thomas 1994) must surely be the discernment of performed behaviours in prehistory. Encouragingly, archaeologists are beginning to employ the terminology of theatre (staging, backdrop, audience) in other than metaphorical terms (e.g., social actors, academic audience) and to identify the occasions and locales where performance is more or less likely (Barrett 1994: 17-18). Barrett adds that 'The history of southern British mortuary rituals could now be seen as progressive attempts to make some of these rituals increasingly effective media for display. This would have demanded more than the simple use of exotica for burial with the corpse, requiring instead a more public staging of the ritual process.' (Barrett 1990: 186). Julian Thomas comes closest to distinguishing performative activities in his examination of early Bronze Age funerals. He suggests that '...the intended reading of the dead person was made by the audience within the temporarily restricted conditions of the funeral' with 'the large pit acting as a stage for its display' (Thomas 1991b: 34).

Both Barrett and Thomas employ the term display, a notion close to that of showing or ostension, 'the most basic instance of performance' (Eco 1977: 110). Both imply the presence of two orders of participant, the watchers and the (albeit dead!) watched, two orders fundamental to the contract of performance. If we accept these initial perceptions, then an examination of contemporary theatrical theory and practice might reveal a number of attributes to further extend and elaborate the description of prehistoric funerary procedures.

Early Bronze Age burial in lowland Britain

The early Bronze Age in lowland Britain is marked by changes in mortuary practice: the 'classic' Beaker-associated rite of burial involves the inhumation of a single individual. The accent changes from bones to bodies, from ancestral remains to a single episode of deposition, from tombs to graves, from recurrent ritual to funeral. However, the particulars of disposal vary widely: bodies are interred crouched, flexed or extended; lying to the left, to the right, on the back and even face down; partially covered, shrouded, wrapped; in wooden structures and in wicker, plank or log coffins; in graves or covered on the ground surface. Occasionally, they are accompanied by objects drawn from a standardised repertoire of daggers, knives, small tools and ornaments (Needham 1988: 245) although 'of 379 burials listed by Greenwell only 94 were accompanied by objects' (Ashbee 1960: 95). From time to time, the burials include an array of mace-heads, body ornaments, multiple bead necklaces which are made of stone, gold and rarer materials conventionally regarded as signs of wealth and prestige, a correlation being drawn between material value and social station. Whilst these objects are no longer viewed as 'for the use of the deceased in the echoing vaults of eternity' (Ashbee 1960: 69), they are regarded as symbolic of the social role of the deceased, as constituting indices of status, rank and occupation (Needham 1988: 245).

Yet far from simply marking the rank of the deceased and emphasising some newly established elite, these artefact assemblages are increasingly interpreted as 'the fortuitous outcomes of a reordered funerary ritual' (Barrett 1994: 63) and are seen as having more to do with the structure of the funeral than with the status of the individual (Barrett 1988: 130). They include three orders of material: that affixed to the corpse (dress, ornament, decoration); that purposefully placed around the corpse; and the discarded paraphernalia of mourning (Barrett et al. 1991: 139; Barrett 1994: 63). The archaeological record is constituted as the material residue of a series of acts within which the body is the principle referent (Mizoguchi 1993: 225). It is the mourners who are the active participants in a liminal period which includes preparation, transportation, positioning in the grave and covering (Barrett 1994: 116). The funeral may be seen as a choreography with and around the body and the creative and practical deployment and manipulation of a particular series of cultural resources (site, objects and even the corpse itself). The absence of objects may reflect the nature of the funeral, not the poverty of the deceased.

The twin procedures of body and grave preparation culminate in interment. The location, the nature and arrangement of the assemblage, the positioning and orientation of the body may tend towards display, towards the construction of an image in death (Barrett 1994: 115). The positioning of the body and objects suggest that it may have been on view. This may have involved the creation of a highly formalised, idealised and restricted identity in death, which has no connection with reality (Thomas 1991b: 35). The funeral is directed towards a moment of visual perfection.

I could regard the deceased as the principal performer in a sequence of events, public and private, more or less performed. I could see the grave as a composition of body and objects, a perfect stage picture, the final curtain perhaps. I could call this a frozen moment, in an infinitely long performance, for the archaeologist too looks at him. His folded body is a body we can look at. Here surely is an arrangement which can be, which is meant to be, looked at by others, kin and strangers. In a *tableau vivant* (sic) he performs his own ultimate rest. This is a body in repose, in the posture of enfolding another on a cold night, but perhaps also performing a quiescence it did not know in life. Here is the intimately familiar and infinitely other: partner, father, brother, son. The family face.

'I am the family face
Flesh perishes, I live on
Projecting trait and trace
Through time, to times anon.'
(Thomas Hardy 'Heredity' 1993)

'...the focus of signification must have been not the monument but the body itself' (Thomas 1991b: 34). And for some contemporary watchers that and that alone. For this performance, this terrible stillness, evokes the most extraordinary range of emotions, memories of the past, hopes and fears for the future. Of course, he did not do this himself. This arrangement is a collusion of 'how he would want to be remembered', 'how we want to remember him' and 'how things should be done', the correct way to go on. He follows direction so perfectly!

It is natural perhaps for us to concentrate on this 'moment', preserved as it is in the archaeological photograph and drawing, presenting itself on the stage of the page. Of course, this is actually a 'moment' of excavation, a pause to record the palimpsest of the residues of funerary procedures. At best it is a snap-shot (from a privileged viewpoint) of a process which may only have paused momentarily at this point. At worst, it is a construct, the conflation in time of a number of trajectories of activity. Whichever, can we ever reveal the sequences of performed behaviours of which these residues are part, that choreography of bodies which archaeology can barely observe? We can draw inspiration from anthropologist Linda Farnell's desire to perceive movement as a processual flow of events in space, to reveal the human body as a moving agent in a spatially organised world of meanings (Farnell 1994: 931-5). Only then she believes can we recover person and genuine authorship, suitable aspirations surely for an interpretive archaeology which seeks an understanding of what may have been possible within certain material conditions. But this, as we shall see later, will require modes of registration and specification adequate to the task. It will certainly necessitate the detailed case-by-case analysis of specific burials, a process which perhaps falls most readily within the domain of archaeologies of regional or local attention. For '...the circumstances of each burial may have varied quite as much as the status of the individual, even assuming this was fixed or clearly acknowledged in his or her lifetime anyway.' (Whittle 1988: 163).

Performance

Our address to early Bronze Age burials will require a more extended definition of what performance is, of what it could have been. It's an awkward word, performance: we take it to mean so many different things. It can be the operational function of script: 'the Royal Shakespeare Company's performance of King Lear'. It can be a concrete event in time, a particular occasion or real-time manifestation: 'last night's performance'. Or the dramatic construct or concept itself: 'Brith Gof's latest performance, 'Arturius Rex'. Or 'time-based' art: 'performance art'. It can be the activity of the individual; 'her performance as Lady Macbeth'. Or something to do with the degree of effort or quality of energy expended: 'the team's performance'. Its meaning is further complicated by its application in social theory. Goffman (1959) has made extensive use of theatrical terminology to describe the performance of everyday life. Finnegan (1992: 91) regards it as 'perhaps an element in every action' and Barrett adds, 'The practice of social life is thus lived out through time; it is performed' (1994: 29).

To avoid confusion therefore I take performance to be a mode of communication and action, distinct from the 'normal' or 'everyday', marked out by special types of behaviour and 'registers of artfulness'. It is most often, though by no means exclusively, manifest in scheduled events bound in time and space. These may be ordered, structured, programmed. They are recognised by a coordinated gathering of performers and spectators, as a heightened occasion, formally set apart from everyday life, with modifications of behaviour for all present. And they engender degrees of anticipation and expectation. Performance may be most apparent at the places set aside for its sole usage, places with formal spatial organisation.

Performance is not merely a set of operational devices and techniques for the staging and presentation of plays, the illustrative function of dramatic literature. In performance, we might distinguish between the dramatic text (i.e., that produced for the theatre – the play) and the performance text (i.e., that produced in the theatre, everything we see and hear before us) (Elam 1980: 3). The latter is not subservient to the former. It is possible to 'write' in the performance text, to devise, to create meaning, with techniques of staging, with the art of the performer. At its core may be complex sets of practices and procedures rather than the play script.

Performance is particular, but it is not unique. It shares characteristics with a nexus of other human activities including play, game, sport, ritual (cf. Schechner 1969). All are set in the non-productive sphere: they don't manufacture goods. Energy is expended for purposes other than profit. A special world is created which is under the control of the participants. This can be a fantasy world, a metaphorical world, a world with quite different rules and modes of behaviour. Yet it can be of vital importance for the participants as a forum for examining, challenging and transgressing the everyday, with real changes in status and extra-daily experiences: a place where identities are created, contested and changed. Significantly, these activities are not discrete. From moment to moment they may interpenetrate, forming new hybrids. We do after all commonly talk of play-acting, game-playing, ritual performance...

All these activities are bound by implicit or explicit rules in the form of contracts, mutual agreements, taboos and prohibitions which mark off the strip of behaviour, define the nature of the special world and ensure coherence, direction and momentum. They all include a dynamic interplay of strategy and tactics, of planning and improvisation. They have special ways of ordering time as in set-time when all the activity must be achieved within a given time, stimulating a certain dynamic. And they all assign an enhanced, even arbitrary, value to objects (toys, kit, props) beyond their material worth. They become the focus of attention around which activity is organised. A toy changes in the mind's eye of the child and subsequently in the nature and quality of the play which it engenders. In game and sport, objects become the locus of contest around which rules emerge to organise the activity, to give it purpose and pattern and to allow strategic planning and role specialisation.

Watchers and watched

The particular nature of performance is that it must be watched or witnessed for it to make sense. Of necessity, there are watchers and watched, what Foucault (1979: 202) calls the 'see/being seen dyad'. Performance thus resides in a complex set of contracts and transactional conventions between two orders of participant – watchers (spectators) and watched (performers) – and in four sets of relationship – performer to performer, performer to spectator and vice versa, spectator to spectator. This does not mean that performance need make a direct appeal to the outside, an overt acknowledgement of the presence of the watchers. But it does rely upon the shared competence of all the participants to identify and to mark off a strip of behaviour as being performative. The spectator needs cultural competence to interpret this partial assemblage of performers, activities and objects, which is characterised by omission and extra-daily juxtapositions, as a representation of the social whole. Significantly, each and all of these contracts is available for renegotiation.

Meaningfully constituted, performance is rich in signs: every aspect is susceptible to semanticization, of being read as 'present on purpose'. This richness of meanings is only partly controllable. For if the watchers are able to bracket-off performance as a separate network of meanings, then they will expect, search for, and generate, meaning in everything they see. Whatever passes the boundary and enters the theatrical space is declared significant. However utilitarian, prosaic or banal, nothing will be neutral or simply decorative. Although performance may have things to say (it is more or less suggestive or denotative) it is read and interpreted according to the expectation/experience/background of the watcher. It is equally connotative. However, in the range of its material resources and the actions of the performer performance is characterised by omission. The complexity of the real world, of the daily use of the body is omitted. Instead there is a process of selection, simplification and intensification of the limited repertoire of material and performative means. The theatrical sign is synechdochic. We constantly understand that the part we see on stage represents the whole elsewhere. Semiotic economy is an essential feature of performance. A limited repertoire of sign-vehicles generates a potentially unlimited range of cultural units, this generative capacity due to the connotative breadth of the repertoire. For the theatrical sign is polysemic, generating a shifting network of primary and secondary meanings.

Performance is a sophisticated network of contracts, signalling systems – kinesics (communicative body movements); proxemics (relative distances of body to body); haptics (touch of self and others) – and space/time manipulations. And it tends towards showing, towards ostension, rather than to describing. 'The showing is emphasised and made explicit through indices, verbal references and other direct foregrounding devices, all geared towards presenting the stage spectacle for what it basically is, a display' (Elam 1980: 30). We might regard performance as existing in the ground between omission and ostension.

Performance is manifest, beyond the written text, in four axes: space, time, pattern and detail. Theatrical material and meaning can be generated and deployed in each and all of these. For instance, the genesis, delineation and formalisation of the performance area, the placement and configuration of performers and spectators, architectural and scenographic enclosure and restriction may all affect the nature and quality of the activity and its reception. Different time-frames may be manifest by performers in sequence or in parallel affecting the expenditure of energy, the application and quality of effort and the dynamic graph of the event.

The exposition of performance may be other than the evolution of dramatic narrative. It may exist as an explicit scenario, game-plan, story-board in which activities may be choreographed or improvised. It may be constituted as a pattern of singular events; as a strategy in the form of rules, tasks, instructions or restrictions, spatial, temporal and physical; as a sequence or string of discrete occurrences of continuous or diverse mode, style or technique. We might also characterise it as an unfolding of a series of inciting incidents and their trajectories. These are changes of consequence, crises or innovations and may include ruptures: sudden shifts in direction, emphasis, orientation, They may be more apparent at thresholds, such as entrances and exits, which are then followed by a period of change, resolution or elaboration. There may also be irrevocable acts (irreversible changes), decay (such as the destruction of objects) and nodes, in which like and unlike phenomena are drawn together into images with complex and equivocal meaning.

Performance is revealed primarily in the body, in the pathology, of the performer (cf. Barba 1982). Simply, the body is held in a way different from that in everyday life. The performer may not be searching for a fictional character as prescribed in the dramatic text as role, but for a fictional body, a body for art. This body which is fully occupied, fully engaged, may be achieved through a number of techniques which include putting the balance in jeopardy, employing physical contradictions, one force pitted against another in an internal conflict (hard and soft, straight and curved, tense and relaxed) in a play of opposites which requires great energy and concentration to sustain and investing any action, any gesture, with more or less energy, over more or less time, than is required to complete the same action in everyday life. Here too there is omission, for only certain gestures are selected, simplified and re-energised. These body practices may be occasioned or enhanced by the material conditions of location and costume.

For the performer, the performance continuum may exist as a chain of physical orientations and engagements, as an interrupted practice of different modes of expression of varying types and intensities, as a discontinuous strip of energetic release and relaxation, as a kind of incoherent behaviour, as a sensual experience. As the work-place of the performer, the designed environment of performance may increase or decrease ergonomic problems, extending, limiting or compromising clearance, reach, posture and the ability to apply strength. The substance of performance may, from time to time, be no more than a pattern of ergonomic problems and their address. The methods and organisation of effort, the flexibility of response and use of tools by the performer may be as engaging for the spectator as the fate of fictional characters. But such patterns only gain coherence by the judicious use of dynamics: modulations of speed, intensity, rhythm, mounting tension, energy expenditure.

Performance may resemble a devised world, all the elements of which (site, environment, technology, spatial organisation, form and content, rules and behaviours) are conceived, organised and ultimately experienced by its orders of participant.

Variables of performance

What then are the variables around which performance organises its resources?

Status: the identification and definition of two orders of participant, watchers and watched; the spatial separation of the two orders; the demarcation of their separation; the moment-to-moment changes in status, from participant to watcher.

Space: the creation of sociopetal arenas in which participants are drawn together; the delineation and restriction of area through marking out, cordoning off, no-go areas; the preparation and elaboration of such areas through clearance and refinement.

Ostension: the modulation of techniques of access and availability and denial, of public and private, of 'on stage' and 'off stage'; the presence of devices of staging, utilising relative height or depth; the presence of devices of framing, to cut out visual irrelevance and focus attention; the utilisation of backdrops, to bracket visually the performance activity; the arrangement and composition of image and effect within such devices; the organisation of visibility and lines of sight, including distance and angle, to give a variety of watching experiences; the use of scale and shape to enhance visibility.

Time: the presence, from time to time, in sequence or in parallel of three orders of time manipulation (event time when the activity takes as long as it takes for completion; set time when all the activities has to be achieved within a given time and symbol time, when one span of time represents another).

Narrative: the presence of a prescribed scenario which can be subject to tactical operation and improvisation; the existence of the event as a punctuated sequence of inciting incidents and their trajectories including irrevocable acts which give the sequence its direction and momentum, re-engagements, crises, sequences of tension, relaxation and acceleration, changes of consequence and innovation, ruptures and sudden shifts in direction and emphasis; the constitution of the event as a series of 'stepping back to look' procedures which turn participants into watchers; the modulation of effects and images around notions of familiarity and unfamiliarity, convention and innovation.

Omission: the limitation and restriction of material resources.

Behaviour: the employment of modified or extra-daily behaviours and body orientations of all participants; the suspension of personal decorum; the experience of extra-daily phenomena and alteration of perceptions and life strategies; the presence of material conditions which affect clearance, reach, posture and the ability to apply strength, requiring ergonomic adjustment and tactical engagement; the use of all proxemic vectors - intimate, personal, social and public; proxemic and haptic invasion and transgression in all three sets of performance relationship; the presence of architectural and spatial configuration which make transgression more or less likely.

Choreography: the employment of strategic patterns of movement in time and space, of episodes, encounters and passings, of body orientations, of altered demeanours, of body to surface, to object, to environment engagements; the use of prescribed processes.

The performative nature of Early Bronze Age burials

Archaeologists do not observe the entire sequence of the funeral (Barrett 1988: 32; 1991: 121) and perhaps Grinsell was right to list 'funeral orations, the wearing of funerary disguise, funeral dances, wailing, lying in state' as customs seldom or never evidenced in the archaeological record even though 'there can be little doubt that they were all practised frequently' (Grinsell 1936: 40). However, if we envisage it as a manipulation of space, time and objects

(Barrett et al. 1991: 120), as the narrative sequence of a network of people moving through time from place to place (Barrett 1994: 73) or as a narrative sequence of disclosure, guiding interpretation (Thomas 1991b: 34), we might begin to think of the liminal period as a trajectory of activities susceptible to the sort of variables listed above which provide an alternative way of describing and illustrating the performative nature of early Bronze Age practices.

Seeing

The presence of the corpse institutes the see/being seen dyad. There is always the watched and there are others who may prepare, flex, decorate, tend and carry the body, who grieve and who officiate at the grave side, who kneel to place objects but who also continuously step back to look, who change status from participant to watcher. Although the dead body is an entirely subject body, it is the most evocative and immediate medium for symbolic association (Shanks and Tilley 1982: 134-5). It is a sign-vehicle: it is always an icon of the absent person, at once familiar and infinitely other. In the conventional sense, it does not 'gesture' the essential mode of ostending the body although it does adopt postures and positions (flexed and carried) it may never have achieved in life. It does engage in meaningful physical communicative acts with others, in the form of proxemics and haptics.

Bodies

Here are old bodies – 'The lesions are largely indicative of an elderly individual suffering gross osteoarthritis and degenerative conditions which must have severely restricted his mobility' making 'his survival into relatively old age unlikely without the respect and support of others' (Butterworth 1992); young bodies; injured bodies, such as the victims of unsuccessful trepanation at Amesbury and Crichel Down (Ashbee 1978); mutilated bodies, such as the girl with legs amputated (Green and Rollo-Smith 1984). But here too is a body which continues to shift its identity as it is manipulated, trussed before rigour mortis sets in (Simpson 1976); formed into a bundle (Robertson-Mackay 1980: 142), a portable artefact, 'a bundle of symbolic meanings' (Mizoguchi 1993: 224); positioned, hands folded in front of the shoulders (Smith and Simpson 1966), right arm over chest (Donaldson 1977), hand behind cranium; decorated, with earrings encasing the whole ear (Russell 1990), with beads decorating a male body (Russell 1990), with labial plugs (Ashbee 1960: 75); composed, with a beaker between the hands (Green and Rollo-Smith 1984), holding a flint knife (Halpin), the body determining the arrangement (Barrett 1994: 117); and in narrative moments, embracing another (Ashbee 1960), facing away from another (Donaldson 1977). Seen from a variety of shifting stances and viewpoints, more or less public, during laying out, whilst being carried to the grave, in the grave itself.

Placing

In the sequence of preparing body we can visage undressing, redressing, decorating, manipulating, binding and transportation. In the sequence of preparing place, we can envisage the selection of grave location, clearing the vicinity including burning, digging the grave - and scratching marks on the grave wall, 'the doodling of a bored individual awaiting the burial' (Green and Rollo-Smith 1984: 279), placing the upcast on the turf, marking out the barrow ditch and stripping the internal turf area (leaving a small area under the upcast). Subsequent to burial and infill may be the building of a turf mound, the digging of the ditch and the placing of a white capping over the turf mound (Robertson-Mackay 1980: 138). Or the building of fires (Green and Rollo-Smith 1984) and the trampling of infill. And then endless revisits to a place of remembrance. In chalk lands, the grave and upcast would create a white terminus for the cortege, a focus for the choreography; the stripping of turf would create a white and delineated arena for the performance, bringing the participants into stark relief, and altering the ergonomic engagement with surface, necessitating and prescribing changes in gait and deportment.

Both trajectories meet at the grave side. Here we might discern the body orientations, the proxemic and haptic invasions and ergonomic problems of manoeuvring the body into the grave (a process differing with the size of the pit and the nature of the mortuary structures) of the physical decorum necessary to position it, of the kneeling to place objects, of the composition of the body/object image. And then the discarding of the objects of the living, beakers, the head and hooves remains of cattle-skin capes, the leftovers of feasting objects left outside the coffin but within the pit (Thomas 1991a: 129). In distinguishing objects found within and those placed outside the coffin we distinguish different moments in the sequence (Barrett 1988: 32). And precise inciting and irrevocable incidents such as breaking objects and arranging them and upsetting, a beaker (Donaldson 1977).

Grave dimensions vary markedly from shallow pits, within which the folded body fits tightly, to deep trenches. Bodies are also left on the ground surface and in 'mortuary houses'. The size and shape of these arrangements affect access to watching, angles and perspectives of viewing (sight-lines) and the living-to-dead proxemics during viewing. Bodies on the surface are therefore available for public gaze whilst those in shallow pits may contrive an intimate regard of those standing at the grave's edge. And these periods may have been fleeting, prior to wrapping, covering, shrouding, the closing of the coffin. The concentric circles of temporary stakes (withdrawn before mound building) may evidence the spatial organisation of the watchers. They certainly create an inside and an outside, a no-go area to which access may be restricted. They certainly mirror the shape naturally adopted by a crowd whilst watching an event (the circle) whilst further delineating an arena for the cortege.

Staging

The body is variously 'staged', serving to disattend out-of-frame activities. In the grave the body may be framed by chalk blocks, set against backdrops of moss, reeds, rushes, straw and leaves (Ashbee 1960: 92-93) or resting on a hide or blanket (Thomas 1991b: 35). The presence of mortuary structures, biers and coffins may lift and define the body, aiding visibility and there is some suggestion of 'viewing platforms' (Parker Pearson 1993: 78). This may raise questions about sequences and time-scales, for some mortuary chambers do seem to have been reentered and semi-articulated bodies reordered (Russell 1990). Or perhaps they were transported close to disarticulation and interred in that state, for the grave goods remain intact and undisturbed. At Amesbury 51, the mortuary chamber may have been prefabricated, manoeuvred into a prepared pit, secured by back-filling, half buried but exposed and visible before the barrow was built (Ashbee 1978). Here the body may have been available for reviewing over a protracted period. It certainly was at Amesbury 71, where the grave was left open for a time beneath an awning and where the ridge of compacted chalk around the edge may evidence the trampling of repeated viewing, the odd excavated human remains representing relics brought to the edge (Christie 1967).

Time

We might suggest that the liminal period is in set time, the time during which the entire, articulated body maintains its integrity (Garwood 1991: 14), or a series of set times, such as binding the body before it stiffens. Activities at the grave side are in event time, the time necessary to create the perfected image of objects and body. However, the weathering of grave sides (Robertson-Mackay 1980: 140; Simpson 1976: 224) suggests a slippage from set to event, of preparations in expectation of a death or of an extension of mourning.

I could begin to elaborate a scenario instancing sight lines and backdrops, routes and locales, arrivals and passings, approaching and being approached, encounters and movements, episodes and disengagements, discontinuities of behaviour - fleeting modifications, changes in status watcher to watched, performance manifest for occasional periods of time. I could characterise it as a series of inciting moments: the moment of death, the commencement of laying-out, the placing in the grave....As the interplay of strategy and improvisation, between motivation, material conditions and execution (Barrett 1988: 36). I could envisage the existence of the event for the participants as a chain of physical orientations and engagements, as an interrupted practice of different modes of expression and demeanour, of varying types and intensities, switching from intimate to public, within a performance continuum, as a series of experiential changes. I could suggest how the bodies of watchers and watched might engage with surface and volume, object and setting, in extremis and in repose. Not to say this did happen but perhaps this could have happened.

Objects

One of the closest convergencies between performance and funeral is in the functioning of objects. Performance values objects: they so often enable it to operate. In performance, the properties (or props) may be appropriated from everyday life (found) or they may be specially made (fabricated). But whatever their origin or market value, once selected by, isolated and recontextualised in the activity, they become invested with a richness of denotative and connotative meanings which jostle to inform interpretation.

In performance, objects help establish and identify dramatic location, social situation, historical period and character identity, when they function as insignia or emblem, an index of gender, status, class or type. Portative objects may be belongings, mementoes (the relics of a lost life and evocative of times and places outside the present drama) or functional tools. They may stimulate action, individual and social, private and public. They help to advance the drama. And as tokens of material or symbolic exchange, they facilitate dramatic interaction. Further, the personal assemblage or kit of a character may enable her to survive, to get on, to function as a recognisable entity in this hypothetical world. However, this kit may only exist, be feasible, make sense, in such a world.

Objects standing for something else

Any object, whether typical, atypical, exemplary or even a replica of its type, once drawn into performance, comes to stand for the class of objects of which it is a member and suggestive for spectators of all others: evocative of similar objects, similar occasions, of other times and other places. Because as soon as the spectators enter the theatrical space they know they have to take the things they perceive for something else: for signs, for stand-ins, for present substitutes for an absent world. Indeed there may be no fixed representational relationships: constant transformations are achieved through the shifting interpretations of the spectator. Objects are equally connotative: they evoke other meanings for the spectators, arising from their culturally determined perceptions, personal, social and aesthetic. Certain objects may be specifically included for their generative potential (their connotative potency); their exotic versatility and flexibility. Examples such as flowers or bread seem particularly resonant. For they exist in other narratives, other systems of thought and are thus suggestive and equivocal. Flowers hint at weddings but also funerals, the entry of the victor and commemoration; Pilate lurks in the shadow of the surgeon washing his hands. And such meanings interpenetrate, one always present in the other. Performance works with these ambiguities: it is a location where everyday meanings are represented, contested and inverted. Performance thus resembles a 'scene of crime' where everything is potentially important.

Function and semblance

Objects achieve significance through their varying usage in performance. A found object may be chosen for its particular intrinsic qualities: its appearance, its patina, its texture, its feel, its size. It may need to be appropriate to a particular period or governing aesthetic concept or idiolect. It may also be selected for its ergonomic potential: its fit, balance, weight and dynamism in manipulation. German dramatist

Bertolt Brecht describes how actress Helene Weigel selected her props 'for age, function and beauty' (Brecht 1976: 427). The performance prop is always double: with the drama it is representational, assisting in the creation of fictional identities. But it is also one of the tools of the trade of the performer: it allows her to go to work, it is equally functional.

The objects of the kit of a character may be accumulated or discarded according to personal preference or for aesthetic or ergonomic reasons. For the performer, they are invested with significance over the period of rehearsal. They may function as an *aide-memoire* for that state of mind and body necessary to complete the performance. On an operational level, they become the locus of nostalgia, reliable old friends: they provide an orientation for the performer, performance after performance, through their familiarity and the superstitions this often engenders. In this, they may resemble fetishes: their loss in transit can cause personal and artistic crisis. And they serve as talismen, tying each performer back to the months of research and rehearsal and the gradual clarification of intent and meaning, some tangible proof of hours worked and of a process now made manifest and at risk in performance.

As an example of this interrelationship of the functional and the semiotic, take a pair of shoes. Of course, they are chosen for appearance and historical accuracy. But fit and feel are also important: they affect gait, deportment and balance. There is an old adage in theatre: to create a character, first you must get the shoes right. And when a performer chooses old shoes, dead men's shoes, then other stories (histories, fictions and speculations for performer and spectators alike) are always present.

If fabricated, the object may be a replica of its everyday equivalent, though made in different materials and to different dimensions. Fabricated objects are usually designed, conceived and constructed according to a governing artistic, stylistic or aesthetic concept, idiolect or tradition. This convention sets the parameters for the assemblage limiting, for instance, the taxonomy and principles of ordering, the range of materials and techniques of fabrication to be used and the hierarchies of scenic arrangement. It may exist as a pro-active strategy or as a list of prohibitions. On the Japanese Noh theatre stage the schematic *tsukurimono* are reduced to a simple bamboo frame (little more than an outline drawing, a blueprint) representing building, vehicle, tree. They are temporary, carried on and off as necessary, are merely suggestive of form. Although they condition the choreography about them and may be entered, they remain insubstantial, ghostly, unable to withstand weight or force. We understand their pecise nature through the words of the narrator which enable us to elaborate whatever image we desire, in the imagination. Here, space is left for the engagement of the spectator.

Performance need not be discrete. Any one performance may include objects as diverse as utilitarian tools, such as ladders, and works-of-art, such as David Hockney's opera settings. The inclusion of that which is truly of the everyday world and not conventionally regarded as theatrical, such as industrial equipment or medical apparatus, may serve to confound the expectations of the watchers, causing shock, surprise or delight and upsetting anticipated patterns of critical interpretation and evaluation. And whilst props are usually regarded as mobile and transformative, lifting the performer off the background, and the set as immobile, not all backgrounds are illusionary, suggestive of another place. They may provide a ground or field against which, or a frame within which, performers and their activities can be isolated and composed. And there may be an interplay of the fixed (that which is of the playhouse), the semi-fixed (that which is of the setting) and the informal (the portative).

Significantly, performance is characterised by the selection, and thus by the omission, of objects. The whole world is not there. Instead a few objects stand in for the whole. Proscenium-arch theatre conventionally works with illusion, the creation of three-dimensional space by two-dimensional means in a three-dimensional space. To serve such conventions, objects change their nature. They change in scale and form so as to enhance visibility: the distance of spectator from stage may necessitate only visual similitude. The effects are organised around principles such as *trompe l'oeil*. Interpretation necessitates competence on the part of the spectator to recognise this and a creative engagement to fill in the gaps, to create a mental construct from a limited range of illusionistic clues. They must take what they see for something else: this part represents the whole. But performance may be other than the reproduction of social reality. It may construct a separate reality internally coherent around its own implicit laws and conventions. Although it may include found objects, the placement, ratios and combinations of objects is governed by extra-daily principles.

Certain assemblages of objects may indicate other locations, contemporary or historical, real or fictive, domestic or public through a limited number of indices. A few beds and screens can suggest a hospital ward. Some objects may be absent: they may be mimed, talked about. And in the subjective-objective continuum of human and inanimate, the object may even stand in for the performer. The presence of his hat and cane will always suggest Charlie Chaplin to us.

The 'poor theatre' of Polish director Jerzy Grotowski is reliant upon the mutability, versatility and multivalence of a fixed repertoire of objects, their meanings revealed through redeployment and juxtaposition. Grotowski states: 'It is absolutely forbidden to introduce into the play anything which is not already there at the very beginning. A certain number of people and objects are gathered in the theatre. They must be sufficient to handle any of the play's situations. There are no 'sets' in the usual sense of the word. They have been reduced to the objects which are indispensable to the dramatic action.' (Grotowski 1969: 75).

This repertoire is re-addressed, revealing dense, complex

and contradictory metaphors and allegories, anachronisms and ambiguities through recurrent use, misuse and change in context. We might think of this as a kind of *bricolage*, an improvised response to an environment of limited resources, a way of making sense of this hypothetical world with the tools to hand and which draws 'like' and 'unlike' objects together into extra-daily juxtapositions, into images only possible in the special world. Indeed we might track an object through its transformations (its biography) as we would a character through her development. And all this generates a wealth of equivocal meaning.

'Each object has multiple uses. Worlds are created with very ordinary objects, as in children's play. By his controlled use of gesture the actor transforms the floor into the sea, a table into a confessional, a piece of iron into an animate partner.' (Grotowski 1969: 76).

'The bathtub is a very pedestrian bathtub; on the other hand it is symbolic bathtub: it represents all the bathtubs in which human bodies were processed for the making of soap and leather. Turned upside down, the same bathtub becomes the altar in front of which an inmate chants a prayer. Set in a high place, it becomes Jacob's nuptial bed.' (ibid.).

Assemblage

So, an assemblage of objects, characterised by omission, ostension and juxtaposition, comes to suggest a hypothetical world. Here, diverse objects without natural affinities of origin, provenance and type, can be drawn together in new hierarchical relationships. They may appear through accumulation, a gradual selection through trial and error or through imposition as part of a designed other world complete in all its parts. The range and configuration of objects may be conditioned by the context. The shape of the performance locale and the need for visibility may condition scale and degree of verisimilitude. Its by-laws, codified as prohibitions, may limit the types of object employed. And theatrical genre, such as realism or expressionism, or stylistic sub-code, such as the aesthetic choices of a particular school, company or director, may set further parameters.

Clearly, objects may function in similar ways within all the activities of the nexus. Their role in contemporary performance might thus help illuminate their functioning in past ritual. Above all, it may cause us to appreciate the multiple identity, meaning and value of things revealed as a net of semiotic and phenomenological complexity and not as a simple index of wealth and status and to think beyond the range and number of goods as constituting the sole axes of differentiation (Whittle 1988: 162). To understand their meaning we need to begin to penetrate the dynamics within which they existed (Graves-Brown 1995: 90). For whilst the notion of display might lead us to the semiotic importance of objects, their versatility might demand that we map their various positioning during the funeral trajectory and make some attempt to discern the separation of, and the movement between, the different moments of their functioning.

With the body in Bronze Age burials are a number of objects. As Thomas says, 'The grave assemblage can only thus be grasped as a unity by the onlooker because all the items concerned have some relation to the body.' (Thomas 1991b: 38). I could suggest that these objects function in all the ways I proposed in performance, in that field between omission and ostension. Here too we know that we have to take the things we perceive for something else: for signs, stand-ins, for present substitutes which represent an absent world. They are on display, transformed into components of communication. And they are polysemic functioning variously as icon, index, symbol – and all points in between!

These objects may be found or fabricated, like and unlike, selected for appearance, texture, personal preference. Here are insignia, talismen, mementoes, equipment...of the living (beakers, head and hooves capes) as well as of the dead (ornaments affixed to body and dress). They may be denotative perhaps, of gender, status, rank, profession, of the state of death itself. This may be reinforced by their placement and spatial relationship to the body and to each other, the corpse determining the arrangement. Objects may be included for aesthetic and decorative reasons. They may be practical tools or the fictive devices to establish a separate reality. Equally, the range and configuration may be conditioned by the context, by the need to be seen.

Of made objects, some axes are standard, some morphologically similar but of diminutive size and a few atypical, exhibiting, for instance, thinness (Needham 1988: 233). Such miniaturisation and change need not spring from economic determinism but from the demands of display. Indeed the manipulation of identity may be possible with grave-goods of low secular value (Rissman 1989: 217).

Yet for the watchers (kith, kin, colleagues, foes, the curious) these objects are also connotative. They will always be working with familiarity and difference. Here may be known objects, with individual or family significance (the broken belt-ring sewn onto the funeral dress: Robertson-Mackay 1980: 143). Here may be the meanings inscribed in one context contributing to the meanings which are available to be recalled in another (Barrett 1991: 3); new objects (arrowheads without micro-wear: Robertson-Mackay 1980) or new configurations signifying the changed status of the dead: the look of unfamiliar object against familiar body. And interpretation here is a matter of great complexity for there is flexibility and mobility in their meanings and perhaps semiotic ambiguity as everyday objects slip the threshold and are transformed into objects of performative communication. The reading of any one object may be within any and all of the four key moments in the working of artefacts: the representational, the decorative, the functional and the cognitive (together with the surrogate moments formed from their interaction). And this may alter according to change of context during the trajectory. And this is but one object. There are several others to be read singly, in various combinations and as a whole, their very portability adding to their shifting identities in situations intimate and

public. The small objects at Hemp Hill for instance may only have been seen by those attending the corpse (Barrett 1994: 65).
But everything is not here. The assemblage is characterised by omission. Halberds and spearheads are exceptional and axes are added to an established repertoire rather than supplanting it (Needham 1988). And after all, it's me who wears my uncle's gold watch, which was his uncle's before him, my father's gold ring. These few objects act as a kind of *aide-memoire*, a set of mnemonic devices, evoking memories of other times and places, of similar objects, similar occasions, innumerable mental constructs. Indeed the flexibility and versatility of what is after all a fairly limited repertoire, may leave more room for the engagement of the watchers.

Notions such as omission and Grotowski's poverty might find parallels in ritual economy, the ability of a rite to expand and contract in scale without any essential change in format or rationale (Metcalf 1981: 563-4). These burials are about the creation of identities. A 'poor' grave therefore might reflect an intimacy of interment, the deceased known to the mourners (the family face) without the need for further indexical referencing. There is more room here for interpretation, for different memories (Barrett 1994; Mizoguchi 1993: 225). One old man has his tools in a bag, his age and familiarity precluding the need to display his toolkit. For the watchers surely know what the bag contains! Even one object can have immense mnemonic potency. And at Bush Barrow, where the body is on the surface, in the public domain, the large number of objects (helmet, weapons, regalia) serve to denote identity or identities to the maximum number and variety of watchers. This is a kind of closure where the possibility of misreading is reduced (Thomas 1991b); the message is over-determined and controlled. No one is left in any doubt. Here the objects have denotative wealth as well as material value. But the reading of body and objects will still include the connotative and the aesthetic: objects are always full, detailed, powerful, expressive things. And they change!

Of course, this examination of the performance-like nature of early Bronze Age funerary rites may be little more than an extended metaphor. But it may provide the means to describe them as complex space/time manipulations. Archaeology rarely gets further than the under-problematised artist's impression (cf. Parker Pearson 1993: front cover); we at least need the scenario or storyboard, some representation of that complex interaction of place, people and objects which constitute its true assemblage. And this will not be easy. We might attempt to reconstruct the discrete narratives of watchers and watched (experiences, body orientations, perspectives) composed as a kind of script, as a work of informed fiction. But if we are to regard the human body as a moving agent in a series of deliberate choreographies, then our ability to perceive and discuss movement as a flow of events in space depends on having appropriate modes of registration. Whilst Farnell's espousal of the complex dance notation system of Rudolf Laban is far from convincing, requiring specialist skills to encode and decipher, it does highlight the potential uses of techniques of contemporary performance documentation (cf. Farnell 1994). A more feasible method of representation might spring from the diagrammatic programmes of architect Bernard Tschumi which attempt to illustrate the complex interpenetration of event and space (Tschumi 1994). These combinations of drawing, map, plan and photograph attempt to indicate the ways in which events may be reciprocal, indifferent or in conflict in their relationships with locations. They make no attempt to read off activity from a given physical setting. They remain equivocal. They illustrate what could (have) happened. And as such, they may be pertinent modes of representation of an interpretive archaeology: an attempt to make sense of things that were never that certain in the first place.

Bibliography

Ashbee, P. 1960. *The Bronze Age Round Barrow in Britain*. London: Phoenix House.

Ashbee, P. 1978. Amesbury barrow 51: excavations 1960. *Wiltshire Archaeological and Natural History Magazine* 70/71: 1-60.

Barba, E. 1982. Theatre Anthropology. *The Drama Review* T94: 5-32

Barrett, J.C. 1988. The living, the dead, and the ancestors: neolithic and early bronze age mortuary practices. In *The Archaeology of Context in the Neolithic and Bronze Age: Recent Trends*, edited by J.C. Barrett and I.A. Kinnes, pp. 30-41. Sheffield, J.R. Collis.

Barrett, J.C. 1990. The monumentality of death: the character of early bronze age mortuary mounds in southern Britain. *World Archaeology* 22: 179-189.

Barrett, J.C. 1991. Towards an archaeology of ritual. In *Sacred and Profane*, edited by P. Garwood, D. Jennings, R. Skeates and J. Toms, pp. 1-9. Oxford: Oxford University Committee for Archaeology.

Barrett, J.C. 1994. *Fragments From Antiquity*. Oxford: Blackwell.

Barrett, J.C., R.J. Bradley and M. Green 1991. *Landscape, Monuments and Society: The Prehistory of Cranbourne Chase*. Cambridge: Cambridge University Press.

Brecht, B. 1976. Weigel's Props. In *Poems 1913-1956* (edited by J. Willett and R. Manheim). London: Methuen.

Butterworth, C.A. 1992. Excavations at Norton Bavant

Borrow Pit, Wiltshire 1987. *Wiltshire Archaeological and Natural History Magazine* 85: 1-26.

Christie, P.M. 1967. A barrow cemetery of the second millennium BC in Wiltshire, England. *Proceedings of the Prehistoric Society* 33: 336-366.

Donaldson, P. 1977. The excavation of a multiple round barrow at Barnach, Cambridgeshire 1974-6. *Antiquaries Journal* 57: 197-231.

Eco, U. 1977. Semiotics of Theatrical Performance. *The Drama Review* T21: 107-17.

Elam, K. 1980. *The Semiotics of Theatre and Drama.* Methuen: London.

Farnell, B.M. 1994. Ethno-Graphics and The Moving Body. *Man* 29: 929-974.

Finnegan, R. 1992. *Oral Tradition and the Verbal Arts.* London: Routledge.

Foucault, M. 1979. *Discipline and Punish.* Harmondsworth: Penguin.

Garwood, P. 1991. Ritual tradition and the reconstitution of society. In *Sacred and Profane*, edited by P. Garwood, D. Jennings, R. Skeates and J. Toms, pp. 10-32. Oxford, Oxford University Committee for Archaeology.

Goffman, E. 1959. *The Presentation of Self in Everyday Life*. New York: Doubleday.

Graves-Brown, P.M. 1995 Fearful symmetry. *World Archaeology* 27(1): 88-99.

Green, C. and S. Rollo-Smith 1984. The excavation of eighteen round arrows near Shrewton, Wiltshire. *Proceedings of the Prehistoric Society* 50: 255-318.

Grinsell, L.V. 1936. *Ancient Burial Mounds of England.* London: Methuen.

Grotowski, J. 1969. *Towards a Poor Theatre.* Methuen: London.

Halpin, C. 1987. Irthingborough Bronze Age barrow excavation 1986. *Northamptonshire Archaeology* 21: 3-30.

Hardy, T. 1993. Heredity. *Collected Poems.* Harmondsworth: Penguin.

Metcalf, P. 1981. Meaning and Materialism: The Ritual Economy of Death. *Man* 16:563-592.

Mizoguchi, K. 1993. Time in the reproduction of mortuary practices. *World Archaeology* 25(2): 223-235.

Needham, S.P. 1988. Selective deposition in the British Bronze Age. *World Archaeology* 20(2):229-248.

Parker Pearson, M. 1993. *Bronze Age Britain.* London: Batsford/English Heritage.

Pearson, M. and J. Thomas 1994. Theatre/Archaeology. *The Drama Review* T144: 133-161.

Rissman, P. 1988. Public displays and private values: a guide to buried wealth in Harappan archaeology. *World Archaeology* 20(2): 209-228.

Robertson-Mackay, M.E. 1980. A 'head and hooves' burial beneath a round barrow, with other neolithic and bronze age sites, on Hemp Knoll, near Avebury, Wiltshire. *Proceedings of the Prehistoric Society* 46: 123-176.

Russell, A.D. 1990. Two beaker burials from Chilbolton, Hampshire. *Proceedings of the Prehistoric Society* 56: 153-172.

Schechner, R. 1969. *The Public Domain.* New York, Discus/Avon.

Shanks, M. and C. Tilley 1982. Ideology, symbolic power and ritual communication: a reinterpretation of Neolithic mortuary practice. In *Symbolic and Structural Archaeology*, edited by I. Hodder, pp. 129-154. Cambridge: Cambridge University Press.

Simpson, W.G. 1976. A Barrow Cemetery of the second millennium BC at Tallington, Lincolnshire. *Proceedings of the Prehistoric Society* 42: 215-239.

Smith, I.F. and D.D.A. Simpson 1966. Excavation of a round barrow on Overton Hill, N. Wiltshire. *Proceedings of the Prehistoric Society* 32: 122-155.

Thomas, J.S. 1991a. *Rethinking the Neolithic.* Cambridge: Cambridge University Press.

Thomas, J.S. 1991b. Reading the Body: Beaker funerary practice in Britain. In *Sacred and Profane*, edited by P. Garwood, D. Jennings, R. Skeates and J. Toms, pp. 33-42. Oxford: Oxford University Committee for Archaeology.

Tschumi, B. 1994. *The Manhattan Transcripts.* London: Academy Editions.

Whittle, A.W.R. 1988. *Problems in Neolithic Archaeology.* Cambridge: Cambridge University Press.

Chapter 5

Cattle as wealth in Neolithic Europe: where's the beef?

Nerissa Russell

Introduction

Interpretations of Neolithic faunal remains have been cast almost entirely in terms of the value of animal products, principally the nutritional value of their meat (Bogucki 1993 and Sherratt 1982 are notable exceptions). While I do not wish to deny the importance of meat in the diet, this approach has deflected attention from the value of living domestic animals: livestock. Indeed, the key conceptual switch involved in animal domestication is a shift in focus from the dead to the living animal (Meadow 1984: 310). For the most part, wild animals are considered a communal resource that can be appropriated only by killing them. Domestic animals, on the other hand, have owners who invest labour and other goods in their maintenance. Every slaughter diminishes the herd (Bogucki 1993; Ingold 1980: 87). As a result, it is by no means a foregone conclusion that domestic animals will be slaughtered as needed for protein and calories; rather, the costs (to herd maintenance and growth, meeting future needs, etc.) and benefits (meat and other slaughter products, prestige, meeting social and ritual obligations) will be carefully weighed when deciding whether to slaughter an animal and which one to choose. This is particularly true for large, slow-reproducing animals such as cattle. Such animals represent a greater investment and are harder to replace (Bogucki 1993: 497). In addition, their very size means that they cannot be consumed at the household level; they require either storage (not always feasible) or sharing with a larger group (Meadow 1984: 329). This may have advantages in terms of prestige or maintaining social ties, but it also means that in terms of subsistence, the owners are not able to reap the full benefit of their investment.

It is clear, then, that we must devote much more thought to the place of living animals in human social systems. In this paper, I focus on the value of animals, in particular cattle, as wealth in Neolithic Europe. I will begin by using ethnographic accounts to consider the ways in which cattle and other animals have functioned as wealth in living societies, and I will review some models that attribute a key role to animal wealth in the development of inequality. I will then explore some ways in which we can use archaeological data to investigate cattle as wealth in the past.

Ethnographic insights

There is a large literature on herding in the ethnographic present, much of which is derived from African pastoral societies, but some of which extends into Asia and northern Europe. Of course I can merely scratch the surface of this literature here, and I will for the most part pass over the richness of ethnographic detail concerning particular societies and concentrate on broader conclusions derived from comparative studies. As in archaeology, much of this work has been heavily concerned with subsistence economics. Unlike archaeology, however, those studying living groups have usually been forced to confront the fact that traditional herders tend not to behave rationally according to our capitalist understanding of rationality. Thus there has been much more consideration of the value of animals beyond protein and calories. I will summarise some of these conclusions in relation to the economics of herding, the particular significance of animals as bridewealth, and the mechanics of the expansion of herding ad herding societies.

The economics of herding

This discussion focuses on societies that derive a significant part of their subsistence from domestic animals. Pure pastoralists (those deriving their entire subsistence from animals) are extremely rare, however, and most of these groups depend to varying, and often substantial, extents on agricultural produce (either what they grow themselves or what they get in exchange for animals and animal products). Indeed, Ingold argues that what he terms 'carnivorous pastoralism' (living off the meat from a herd) is impossible with cattle (but is possible with reindeer). His reasoning is that cattle are too fierce to be herded unless they are tamed through extensive human contact and this requires a labour input that would limit the herd size to far less than that required to survive on meat alone (Ingold 1980: 242).

The only form of pure pastoralism that cattle herds can support is what Ingold calls 'milch pastoralism', in which the primary subsistence product is milk (although some meat and occasionally blood are also consumed). In East Africa, Dahl and Hjort (1976) have calculated that with traditional zebu cattle, a family of six would need a herd of 60 animals during the wet season and 600 during the dry season to subsist on milk alone. More realistically including meat and blood, the family would still need 64 cattle to subsist entirely from the herd (Hjort 1980: 136). In most groups, only the richest families can hope to maintain herds of this size. While it is difficult to meet total caloric needs with cattle products, these products (milk, meat, blood) are, of course, excellent sources of protein. A family can meet its protein needs with only 28 cattle, or 16 cattle and 40 goats, populations still larger than many agropastoral herds (Hjort 1980: 137). In fact, milk is the main cattle product consumed. Kenyan groups are estimated to eat about 10 kg. of meat per person per year (compared to 60 kg. of beef alone per person per year in the USA in 1976), and this is fairly typical for African pastoralists (Schneider 1980: 211). Average family herd size among East African groups ranges from about five to 25 (Dombrowski 1993: 27). Thus even the classic cattle pastoralists of East Africa, for whom cattle hold crucial economic, social, and symbolic importance, have relatively small household herds.

In seeking to understand why pastoralists do not maximise their output, risk is a factor that has received much attention. That is to say, pastoralists are considered to be maximising the long term (one or more generations) viability of the household (Mace and Houston 1989). Two main tactics (not mutually exclusive) have been proposed as part of herding strategies aimed at the reduction of risk: increasing herd size and maintaining species diversity. Maintaining herds larger than needed for immediate subsistence provides a buffer against loss, essentially banking surplus against future need (Dombrowski 1993). The chronic overgrazing in many pastoral areas is then seen as a classic case of the tragedy of the commons (Hardin 1968): while the size of the total cattle population increases the risk of catastrophe for all (as well as depressing the yield of cattle products per animal) any individual herder is more secure with the largest herd possible. Keeping small stock (sheep and goats) in addition to cattle or other large stock (e.g., camels) provides further insurance against disaster, as these species vary in their resistance to disease, drought, and other stresses (Mace and Houston 1989). Small stock have other advantages as well. They reproduce more quickly, so that either the flock can be built up fairly rapidly or a flock of a given size will sustain a higher level of meat off-take. In Africa, at least, the seasonality of their lactation is complementary to that of cattle, helping to maintain a good milk supply throughout the year. The various taxa have different grazing habits, so a combination will make the fullest use of pasture. In addition, their smaller size makes them more suited for use both for meat and as 'small change' in economic transactions, since a whole animal can be consumed within a single household, and its loss has less impact on the structure of the herd (Hjort 1980; Mace and Houston 1989).

In recent years, it has become evident that a pastoral group does not have a single herding strategy, but that each herder has his (usually) own strategy. In particular, the wealth of the household (i.e., herd size) has several important effects on herd management. First, in agro-pastoral groups the proportion of subsistence derived from cattle products is greater among wealthy households (Sutter 1987: 203). This is true almost by definition, since wealth among pastoralists is nearly always measured in livestock or cattle, even by outside researchers. It is also the condition to which most people in the society aspire, as the pastoral side of the economy is usually valued much more highly than the agricultural side (Kelly 1985). Second, Mace has demonstrated that the optimal species composition of the herd in terms of risk avoidance varies depending on the size of the herd. Since small stock are more sensitive to drought but reproduce faster, a household with a herd at or below the size needed to provide its subsistence is best off concentrating on small stock. If the herder succeeds in building the herd above this point before disaster strikes, he will then benefit from 'trading up' most of the small stock for large stock. The greater resistance of large stock is generally preferable, but they also come in large units that are too valuable to risk losing in a small herd, and to slow to rebuild when the herd size is dangerously small (Mace and Houston 1989).

Third, the age/sex composition of the herd is affected by wealth differences. Sutter notes among the Fulani that everyone wants to increase the size of the household herd and increase the amount of milk available. To achieve this, they prefer to sell non-productive animals (sterile heifers, old cows, excess males) to purchase grain, which is raised by all households, but seldom in sufficient quantity. The highest prices are fetched by males that have reached their full growth (four years). However, the rich have a much greater ability to achieve these goals with their larger herds. The poor through necessity often have to sell reproductive animals (prime females), thus lowering the productivity of the herd and worsening the situation; the rich can afford not to. As a result, prime-age males are found mostly in the large herds. The rate of removal of cattle from the herd (through sale, slaughter, or gift) is also much greater in small herds. This tends to enhance differences in cattle wealth, although this effect appears to have been less pronounced in the past (i.e., prior to extensive involvement in the market economy) when traditional forms of redistribution tended to even out herd sizes to a greater extent (Sutter 1987). Nevertheless, the constraints on the management of small as opposed to large herds are likely to have been similar. There is a similar distinction between rich and poor Maasai in the intensity of milking. While all Maasai derive about 60% of their calories by milk, and to some extent varying supplies are evened out by gifts of milk between households, those with smaller herds are forced to milk their herds much more intensively to achieve this. The result is that the calves in the smaller herds get less milk and grow more slowly, while the women of the poorer households work harder to extract every possible drop of milk and the men spend more time in labour-intensive cattle watering to increase milk production (Grandin 1988).

There is disagreement in the literature over whether the labour-requirements of herding are large or small. Labour-requirements may depend considerably on the local availability of pasture and water. In Africa, pastoral labour does seem (quite universally) to be valued above labour expended in agriculture. In any case, there are some key features of herding labour that need to be noted. One is that milch pastoralism requires substantially more labour than does carnivorous pastoralism. In order to reserve some of the milk for human consumption, cows must be separated from their calves for much of the time. Milking cows must also be kept close to home, while other cattle may be grazed further afield to permit a herd larger than the nearby pasture can support. Different taxa also often need to be herded separately due to their varying needs and habits and this require still more herding personnel (Dahl

1980). On the other hand, labour-requirements are related much more to the intrinsic structure of the herd than to its size; herders do realise economies of scale as the herd grows and poor herders may wish to combine their herds in order to manage them properly. Agriculture, on the other hand, has a much closer relationship between labour input and the amount harvested (Dahl 1980).

A gendered division of labour usually applies to herding, with herding tending to fall into the masculine sphere (although there is much variation). In much of southern Africa there is a very strong division between male pastoral labour and female agricultural labour, with corresponding opposed symbolic systems (Kuper 1982). Women are considered dangerous to cattle. Although agriculture contributes more to subsistence, 'pastoralism is more prestigious and ceremonially more important' (Kuper 1982: 11). In East Africa, it is more common that women are in charge of milking and caring for the milking cows and their calves while men and boys tend the fallow herd that grazes farther from home (Grandin 1988).

Cattle as wealth and capital

It is striking that economic studies of pastoralists virtually always define household wealth in terms of the size of the household herd of cattle or other livestock, thus tacitly or explicitly acknowledging that cattle (or other large stock) form the accepted standard of wealth in herding societies. Small stock are not regarded as wealth, nor is grain, although both have exchange value. In Africa, land is generally not seen as an aspect of household wealth, since it is owned by a clan or other corporate group with households holding only usufruct rights. In essence, the economy is denominated in cattle, with household wealth and the value of other goods measured in cattle much as we would measure them in dollars.

How did cattle come to hold this position? Tim Ingold (1980) considers the properties necessary for something to develop as a unit of wealth in the domestic mode of production which is characterised by underproduction (Sahlins 1972). Ingold (1980: 224-226) argues that in these circumstances, a unit of wealth must: supply subsistence products; reproduce itself in nature (otherwise it would have to be acquired through surplus production and be counter to the nature of the domestic mode of production); have a relatively low reproductive rate (K-selected), as the growth of r-selected populations is determined largely by the environment rather than the number of offspring (for this reason, grain cannot be a unit of wealth, as increased harvests are fairly directly proportional to increased labour input; once the limit of available household labour is reached, surplus grain cannot be used to increase the next harvest); the animal must be social so that it can be kept in groups; and it must be able to survive on wild resources without foddering and raising feed (otherwise, like plants, a proportional increase in labour input would be necessary to increase the flock), and this is likely to require that it also be mobile to be able to move to new pasture. These factors essentially limit units of wealth in the domestic mode of production to large, social ungulates kept in an extensive herding system. The same species kept as 'barnyard animals' requiring substantial feed and care would not work as wealth (Ingold 1980: 227).

Schneider (1979; 1980) argues that in traditional East African economies, cattle did (and to some extent still do) function quite literally as money, and that this had quite far-reaching social and political effects. Among the many items that once functioned as money in African economies (iron tools, shells, beads, etc.), cattle were pre-eminent because demand for them was always high and constancy of demand is the key to an item functioning as money. The demand for grain was high before harvest, but low to non-existent just after a good harvest, so it would be a poor choice of currency, and has never been reported as such. This steady demand causes 'cattle or other consumption goods ...[to be] inexorably transformed into something other than what they were designed for in the first place, so to speak' (Schneider 1979: 101). Cattle have the added advantage (compared to iron, shell, and so on) of multiplying when not used. Although it is ultimately based on their importance in subsistence, the function of cattle or other goods as wealth does conflict to some extent with their use in subsistence, since wealth accumulation will interfere with extracting maximum subsistence resources from the herd. 'When a good is valued sufficiently to take on monetary characteristics, no matter what the reason for this valuation, managers of that wealth will conduct management strategies differently than if it were merely a commodity, if the return for managing it as a financial asset is greater than managing it for other, subsistence, reasons' (Schneider 1979: 226). A further implication of the use of cattle as units of wealth is that they are valued for themselves, as units (living animals), not for (or in addition to) their use value as food sources. The quality of the cow is less important than the fact that it is one cow, 'just as Westerners value a dollar as a unit and ignore whether it is wrinkled or torn' (Schneider 1980: 217). In particular, large cattle will not be strongly valued over small ones and since more small cattle can be raised on the same amount of pasture the size will tend to drop.

When cattle take on monetary value, the tendency is to use them to store wealth.

If cattle are convertible into most other things of value (thus giving their producers the kind of economic freedom and multiple options we obtain with money) and if grain is not so easily convertible, then it follows that the prudent farmer, when he can, will convert his grain into livestock. And it also follows that the farmer (to some extent at least) is not producing grain in order to feed himself and his family but in order to obtain livestock, which in turn are not produced for food (Schneider 1979: 65).

Thus cattle come to function as wealth not only in primarily pastoral societies but also in those with substantial agricultural components. In many areas, there is a specialisation at the level of the household or the ethnic group in agriculture or pastoralism with extensive exchange of grain for cattle and their products (Kuper 1982). During droughts, grain becomes very valuable; those with larger harvests can easily acquire many cattle. However, the wealth value of cattle means that they will be kept wherever practicable, even on fertile land that would yield more food through agricultural use (Schneider 1979: 63). The monetary analogy should not be pushed too far, however. Cattle are not freely exchangeable in many societies. It is much easier to trade-up for cattle (often in the context of kin relationships) than it is to dispose of cattle (Goody 1973: 5).

The mobility of wealth in livestock means not only that they can be exchanged more easily than land, but also that they are especially vulnerable to theft. The amount of cattle raiding increases with the number of cattle per capita in the region (Schneider 1979: 89). Raiding is both a major risk to those with cattle, and an important way to build up herds for those without (Hakansson 1994). Thus pastoralists are usually renowned as warriors.

A key feature of wealth in livestock, especially in uncertain environments where there is always a substantial risk of losing most or all of the herd to drought, disease, or raiding, is that differences in wealth tend to be short-lived. 'The distribution of animal wealth over the population is not static but changes constantly with stochastic luck in breeding a good proportion of female calves, with managerial skills, with the social demands for stock, and with the vicissitudes of theft and disease' (Dahl 1980: 207). Since the cattle-poor can start with small stock and, with luck and good management, trade-up to cattle[1] just as the rich can be suddenly impoverished, it is difficult to consolidate wealth differences into lasting power. This seems to be most true where herders use redistributive tactics (described below) to help buffer against risk and deal with labour shortages rather than converting cattle into money (Schneider 1979). Those with large herds gain prestige, both due to admiration for their herd management skills and because of their wealth and generosity, so that they may be termed 'big-men', but cannot translate this into real political power (Dahl 1980; Schneider 1979).

The big-man's homestead was generous with food and therefore was a favourite meeting place. He had many wives who could brew much beer and cook food for many visitors. In addition to being generous with food, a big-man also lent cattle to those in need, for example, to pay blood wealth or contribute to someone's bridewealth. Furthermore, he sacrificed bulls on ritual and ceremonial occasions in the community, such as initiations, funerals, births, and marriages. By virtue of having the largest number of sons, a big-man also contributed the most to the defence of the local community, a service which made others indebted to him (Hakansson 1994: 261).

For cattle wealth to have this egalitarian effect, pastoralism must dominate the economy. Schneider (1979: 10) sets the cut-off point at a ratio of one cow or more per person. This is because in agricultural economies land is easily monopolised by the rich and powerful, fostering hierarchy. While this seems to hold in East Africa, it does not apply in southern Africa, where wealth in cattle is associated with highly stratified political systems (Kuper 1982). The difference may be that here cattle, like land, are in fact owned by the ruler who distributes them to his or her subjects but grants only usufruct rights (Kuper 1982: 15). Moreover, the 'equality' in East Africa holds only among men (the cattle owners) with women universally held in lower status (Schneider 1979: 210).

In southern Africa the granting of usufruct rights to livestock while retaining ownership occurs in a hierarchical context, but loans of this sort also occur in egalitarian contexts in East Africa and elsewhere. Indeed, they are seen as a major factor in maintaining equality because they allow those with few or no cattle to borrow animals and keep part of the offspring, thus gradually building up their own herd. The lender benefits by reducing risk through distributing his animals in different herds, by retaining ownership rights without investing labour, and by establishing and maintaining a relationship with the borrower (Schneider 1979). Schneider (1979: 94-95) lists some of the reasons which Turu herders give for loaning out animals: to guard against disease; to obtain the goodwill of a respected man; to lessen grazing pressure; to benefit from the borrower's herding skills; to help relatives; to ease one's own work burden; to hide one's own wealth, to provide milk for a daughter's children; to obtain a steer in exchange while retaining partial rights to a cow; in response to demands to be generous; to get rid of small stock that produce little manure; and to gain others' respect. Borrowers have a similar range of reasons (and most herders are both loaners and borrowers): to get milk for their family; to get manure for agriculture; to create a tie to a rich man; to appear more wealthy (nobody knows for sure if who really owns the animals), to replace animals loaned to others; as a favour to a friend who needs to disperse his cattle; to get a stud bull; and as a favour to a friend who has taken your loaned cow. Typically the borrower has the right to the milk and some of the calves of a loaned animal; the owner retains the right to slaughter or otherwise dispose of the animal, and receives some of the calves. As cattle circulate, the question of ownership can become quite complicated, with many people holding rights to a single animal, rights which are recognised in the distribution of meat if an animal is slaughtered. Meat is distributed according to these rights rather than, as among hunters, to all members of the community. As Ingold puts it, hunters share out meat, pastoralists have shares in animals (Ingold 1980: 173).

The stock loans or stock associations referred to above are one way to redistribute cattle, and are particularly common where labour is short, and thus especially in milch pastoralism. Another mechanism that permits the destitute to acquire livestock is the clientage relationship in which those without herds attach themselves to wealthy households, offering their labour in return for support and a few animals from which to build their own herd and eventual independence. While this is clearly an unequal relationship (because the client is taken into the household of the patron – often actually adopted – and is provided with his own means of production rather than kept permanently separated from them) this institution actually works to break down hierarchy in the long run (Ingold 1980: 233-234).

Finally, I must touch briefly on whether cattle, when they function as wealth, constitute capital. This has been treated in some detail by Ingold (1980: 228-234) and Hart and Sperling (1987) so I will not repeat their analysis here. It has often been observed (e.g., Paine 1971) that pastoralists' herds resemble capital in that a store of wealth (when herding labour is invested in it) yields a return in the natural increase. Moreover, there is considerable linguistic depth to this analogy: both 'capital' and 'cattle' (and also 'chattel') are derived from the Latin *capitalis*, meaning 'of the head' or 'primary'. 'Pecuniary' is derived from the Latin *pecus*, which meant 'money' but the primary meaning of which was 'flock' or 'herd'. If, like Paine (1971), one defines capital simply as wealth that generates more wealth, then certainly cattle qualify. With Ingold (1980), I prefer to use the term in the Marxist sense, referring to a specific set of social relations of production in which capital is used to control the means of production so that workers lacking those means must offer their labour for a wage that is always less than the actual value of the goods produced, with the difference forming the capitalist's profit (Marx 1936 [1890]). This is intrinsically a relationship of exploitation and quite different from the kinds of social relations described above. As Ingold (1980) demonstrates, when herders start to raise cattle for profit they become ranchers rather than pastoralists. Although pastoralists are often involved in market economies of one sort or another, they do not behave like capitalists. Rather, since their goal is to sell or barter as much as necessary for household subsistence while maintaining as much wealth as possible in their herds, they will sell more cattle when the price is low and fewer when it is high (Ingold 1980: 232).

Although cattle are not capital, the analogy does have some value. As a result of the way in which cattle do resemble capital (i.e., by increasing when not 'spent'), pastoralists do tend to resemble capitalists in some ways. They are individualistic, pragmatic, competitive, and strive to accumulate material wealth (Ingold 1980: 228). Where cattle are wealth, herders will expend much of their energy and thought in trying to build ever larger stores of that wealth.

Bridewealth

The most important use of cattle wealth and the one with the most profound social and economic consequences is bridewealth. Bridewealth is common world-wide in mixed pastoral/agricultural societies (Kuper 1982: 169). Bridewealth, a payment from the groom's side to the bride's side to seal a marriage, is not simply the opposite of dowry. Dowry is a payment from the bride's family that is used to endow the new family created by the marriage; it does not pass to the groom's family. Bridewealth is paid by the groom's family (or more rarely the groom himself) to the family of the bride and is not available to the new family. It is given in exchange for rights to the bride and especially to her children. These rights minimally include exclusive sexual access, usually also rights to the children (securing their transfer from the bride's to the groom's lineage), and may include rights to the product of the bride's labour and, in extreme cases, chattel rights over the bride. Most often, the primary purpose is to legitimise the children in the father's lineage. In Africa, cross-culturally the size of the payment correlates with the rights bestowed, so that bridewealth is low in matrilineal societies where the groom does not receive rights to the children. In its most classic form, the bridewealth received is in turn used to secure a new bride for the bride's father or brothers. Bridewealth is associated with polygyny. A key feature is that wealth and women flow in opposite directions (whereas in dowry they flow in the same direction). Dowry thus amounts to early inheritance, while bridewealth is a transaction between families. Very often, the bridewealth is just part of a long series of exchanges between the bride's and groom's families (Tambiah 1973).

Bridewealth consists of movable wealth, most often livestock, whereas dowry can be any kind of property, including land. As a result, dowry is associated with densely populated, complex societies where land is the limiting resource in building and maintaining wealth, while bridewealth is found in situations where land is plentiful and labour is the limiting factor. Bridewealth in livestock is heavily associated with patriliny, probably because groups with large herds tend to pay higher bridewealth, thus securing rights to children for the groom (Goody 1973). Actually, this seems to be less true in southern Africa, where higher bridewealth is actually paid where agriculture is more important, despite the fact that less cattle are available for payments. This is related to the strong gendered division of labour in this region, where women perform most agricultural labour; where this is important, a higher bridewealth must be paid to secure rights to the fruits of this labour (Kuper 1982: 158). In East Africa, the size of the bridewealth is determined in practice largely by the ability of the groom's family to pay (Goody 1973).

The essence of bridewealth is balance. Bridewealth is sometimes paid by the groom's father, sometimes by a variety of his relatives. On the receiving end, bridewealth will flow back to this same set of relatives. It will then flow out again, usually in short order, to provide a wife for one of the bride's male relatives. Bridewealth is thus a means of regulating marriages, not a way for the bride's father to increase his herds (Goody 1973: 5). The rate is usually fairly standard within a society and often across societies within a region, although it may vary through time, usually following the total cattle population in the society (Schneider 1979: 98). If some people start paying higher bridewealth, the standard will tend to inflate, because the father of the bride wants to ensure that the bridewealth he receives will suffice for him or his son to obtain a bride. To achieve this, it helps to use a form of payment that maintains a fairly steady value. As we have seen above, cattle in Africa fulfil this criterion, in large part because although they are used for subsistence in pastoral societies they are only rarely exchanged except as bridewealth (Goody 1973: 5). Careful studies make it clear that the value of cattle as wealth stems primarily from their use in bridewealth, rather than from their subsistence functions (Kuper 1982: 167). In primarily agricultural societies, cattle may be kept for little except bridewealth (Kuper 1982). 'If cattle transactions are largely confined to marriage, then the dependence of the groom on a similar transaction is overwhelming....The effect is to reinforce the authority of the father and emphasise the tie with the sister' (Goody 1973: 5).

Of course, for bridewealth to work properly, there must be a balanced sex-ratio. While this is true at the population level, it is often not true within a particular household. Polygyny will help to even things out through time, but a deficit in daughters can leave a son waiting a long time to get married. Bridewealth thus tends to make men marry later and women earlier, while dowry tends to delay women's marriage. A family with extra daughters simply reaps an increase in wealth that helps offset the lack of sons for support in old age, but a family with extra sons faces greater difficulty. In this instance, some of the sons may enter into alternative marriages or unions in societies where these are permitted (without the full rights conferred by bridewealth), or in the present may leave to engage in wage labour. Another approach is to borrow from distant relatives or non-kin, to build up wealth through increased cultivation or other means, or, in desperation, to mortgage a future daughter's bridewealth by promising her in marriage in exchange for a present bride (Goody 1973: 8-10).

The amount of the bridewealth tends to vary with the size of the cattle population because the groom's family usually pays the maximum bridewealth possible, leaving themselves with just enough cattle to survive. This is done because it confers prestige on the groom's family, it attests to the skills of the groom as a herder or cattle raider, and presumably because they are in danger of being outbid. This means that normally only one marriage can be made from a herd at a time. It also acts powerfully to keep wealth circulating, and tends to equalise cattle distributions over time, as the wealth of the bride's family is not an issue (this is not always true in southern Africa, however). In addition, it stimulates overproduction of cattle, since herds are regularly reduced to a minimum and need to build again to a level that can sustain another marriage (Goody 1973). Where grain is exchanged for cattle, it will also stimulate surplus grain production (Schneider 1979: 90). This generally upward pressure on bridewealth rates encourages cattle-raiding by those with smaller herds, often a much quicker and more effective way to build a herd than increasing production (Hakansson 1994). Although the general tendency of bridewealth is likely to be inflationary up to the limits of the available pasture on total herd size (depending somewhat on the details of the bridewealth payment; see below), it is important to note that large herds are not necessary for bridewealth. The Shona of Zimbabwe had an average of two cattle per household at the turn of the century, with a bridewealth rate of four cattle. As herds later increased to five cattle per household, bridewealth increased to 10 animals (Huffman 1990: 6).

Dombrowski (1993) argues that the dispersal of cattle accomplished by bridewealth also constitutes a way of reducing risk. Since bridewealth is, in the long run, a reciprocal system, giving cattle as bridewealth serves much the same purpose as stock loans in terms of preventing catastrophic loss from local factors while at the same time cementing social ties. Indeed, marriage is often conceptualised as a special form of stock association by pastoral groups (Schneider 1979: 197). It also has the effect of combining small individual herds into a regional macro-herd. Risks are particularly large for small herds. 'In cases of poor rainfall, a string of male calves, or the random death of one or more prime breeding cows, may doom a seemingly flourishing herd to rapid decline' (Dombrowski 1993: 43). Dombrowski's simulation shows that bridewealth substantially reduces these risks (without even counting the additional security provided by the social relationships thus maintained), and, moreover, that larger brideweath creates greater security because it requires drawing on a larger pool of kin and thus creates a larger network across which risk is spread. In mixed agricultural-pastoral economies where women are responsible for cultivation and men for herding, bridewealth may also reduce risk by balancing agriculture and herding in the household economy (Kuper 1982: 169).

There are several cases in Africa of neighbouring societies that specialise in agriculture or pastoralism. Each society depends on grain for a substantial part of their subsistence and cattle for bridewealth and often a significant part of subsistence as well. Often each society keeps some cattle and raises some grain, but one of these resources is not reliably produced in sufficient quantities, so that the two societies are linked closely in cattle for grain exchanges. While this is partly linked to environmental differences (insofar as a group chooses to specialise in agriculture or pastoralism according to which is best suited to their territory) in many cases it would be quite possible to produce more of the lesser resource, so that the specialisation is not entirely a matter of necessity (Hakansson 1994). 'The concentration on production of livestock led producers to grow insufficient grain to feed themselves and forced them into the market for grain. And the exchange of cattle necessitated by such thins as marriage and the need to obtain grain would have caused imbalances in some herds...requiring further exchanges with stock associates' (Schneider 1979: 92).

As noted above, the demand for cattle as bridewealth stimulates surplus production in both economies and encourages exchange and interdependence. In the case of the primarily agricultural Gusii, who exchange grain for cattle with the primarily pastoral Luo, not only has the need for bridewealth cattle maintained a high level of surplus grain production, it has also determined the settlement pattern. They have fertile land available above 6000 feet that is not used because the cooler temperatures would permit only two, instead of three harvests per year, sufficient for subsistence but not to support the level of exchange needed to supply bridewealth. Moreover, it would take them too far from their lowland exchange partners (Hakansson 1994: 270-271). 'Hence, the causality of the Gusii settlement pattern is not to be found in inexorable population growth and social or environmental circumscription..., but in political competition and the quest for cattle through which control of labour and land could be realised The demand for cattle was practically unlimited and therefore geared Gusii households towards production for exchange' (Hakansson 1994: 271).

Kelly's (1985) exemplary study of the Nuer and Dinka traces the profound effects that bridewealth can have on society. The Nuer and Dinka were once a single ethnic group. After their split, the Nuer eventually embarked on a major and rapid territorial expansion (fourfold, to 35,000 square miles, in about 70 years) halted only by the introduction of European cattle diseases, chiefly at the expense of the Dinka. Kelly attributes this expansion, and many features of Nuer and Dinka society, ultimately to differences in the structure of Nuer and Dinka bridewealth. To begin with, 'the bridewealth system largely dictates herd management practices' (Kelly 1985: 112). This applied both to the size of the herd and to its age/sex composition. Nuer bridewealth rates were approximately double those of the Dinka. Moreover, while Nuer bridewealth payments flowed one way, the Dinka have an unusual system in which the actual payment from the groom's to the bride's family is about the same amount as the Nuer, but a virtually immediate reciprocal payment of about half this amount is paid back from the bride's family to the groom. As the amount of the bridewealth rises above the minimum, the proportion returned in the reciprocal payment grows, so that the effective bridewealth rate grows much more slowly than among the Nuer.

Also, the Dinka bridewealth formula involves mostly female cattle, leaving them free to slaughter excess males, while the Nuer bridewealth involves a substantial proportion of males, so large numbers of unproductive animals (in subsistence terms) were maintained for this purpose. Since the groom's family wishes to pay the maximum possible bridewealth, and others will strive to match these payments, the Nuer system has a strong inflationary tendency that pushed the size of their herds to the limits of available grazing. 'Nuer bridewealth payments...exert a strong positive influence on the size of the cattle population rather than merely being responsive to it, as are those of the Dinka' (Kelly 1985: 141). But since polygyny was valued and individual households at any given time might need more cattle even though the total village herd was at maximal size, there was a constant incentive to raid the Dinka for cattle (worsening the cattle overpopulation) and to expand into Dinka territory. The Nuer were remarkaby successful in doing this, apparently because their kinship system, by emphasising patrilateral ties more than the Dinka's, allowed them to field much larger forces. This kinship difference, too, is traced back to the structure of the bridewealth, with matrilateral kin receiving a greater portion of the bridewealth among the Dinka. In a very real sense, cattle create and define social relationships in southern and East Africa, so that the Nuer-Dinka divergence with respect to the reciprocal payment did not simply reflect a change in the relative significance of matrilateral relations but indeed constituted such a change in and of itself. In short, cultural valuations of the relative importance of matrilateral and patrilateral relations in the fabric of social life were transformed by changes in the bridewealth system, since the bridewealth system represents a primary context in which kinship valuations are both encoded and experienced (Kelly 1985: 188).

Kelly emphasises that when subsistence and wealth goals conflicted, it was wealth that was privileged in herding decisions. The Nuer aspired to living solely off their flocks with no involvement in agriculture, but were prevented from achieving this as much by their bridewealth system as by the ecosystem.

Economic and social goals were partially consistent with respect to the accumulation of cattle, but diverged at the point when cattle were deployed in bridewealth or other social transactions. The same cows designated for eventual inclusion in a son's bridewealth payment also facilitated reduced agricultural production in the interim. However, the accumulation of bullocks and oxen for bridewealth purposes did not contribute to the Nuer objective of reducing their reliance on grain, since male animals held in reserve for future exchange provided neither milk nor meat. It is evident that bridewealth effectively organises economic production and that objectives inconsistent with bridewealth requirements are of secondary importance (Kelly 1985: 232).

The expansion of herding

Kelly (1985) has described the expansion of one agropastoral society at the expense of another. There are also some hints from the ethnographic record of how hunter-gatherers might adopt herding. First, it must be recognised that there are considerable impediments to the adoption of herding by hunter-gatherers. As I noted above, there is a fundamental conflict in the way that hunter-gatherers and herders regard animal resources. The necessity of sharing out meat (and indeed most possessions) makes it difficult to accumulate livestock or other wealth. This can be illustrated by the cases of two !Kung would-be herders who used different strategies to deal with this conflict, both ultimately unsuccessful. Debe started to build a herd of goats and cattle and began to prosper, but whenever hunting was poor his relatives would visit and pressure him to share so that he was obliged to slaughter most of his flock. After a few years he gave up. Bo recognised this problem and dealt with it by giving visiting friends and relatives a good meal and then sending them off. This preserved his herd, but destroyed him socially. He was renowned for his stinginess and accused of sorcery. Eventually he sold all his animals and moved away (Lee 1984: 137-138). Hesse (1984: 245) reports a similar story observed by John Yellen, in which the stingy !Kung herder could not find a wife for his son. For this and other reasons, the adoption of herding by hunter-gatherers will not be easy nor automatic (Smith 1990). '[T]he ethos of herding – with its 'future' orientation, social and symbolic relations with domestic stock, political alliances over the control of water and pasture, private and corporate ownership of stock, and so forth – has little ideological relevance in hunting society' (Smith 1990: 57).

Ten Raa (1986) argues on the basis of the experience of the Sandawe of East Africa that the transition to herding may be more difficult than that to agriculture or sedentism. The Sandawe seem to have acquired and lost cattle more than once in the last few centuries. They did not, however, adopt all aspects of the pastoral cultures that brought them cattle, and found it difficult to protect the cattle. They had previously received little attention from neighbouring warriors because they had few desirable possessions, and their main defensive tactic was to hide when outsiders entered their territory. Once they acquired cattle, however, they immediately became vulnerable to raiding, in which they suffered not only loss of cattle but substantial loss of life. 'As soon as they had acquired only one single head of cattle they needed to construct a kraal to defend it against animal predators. Nor could they defend it against human raiders: it is impossible to hide an ox in a rock crevice or behind a tree, and it is also impossible to silence it. The acquisition of even one single animal cost them, therefore, their mobility as well as their invisibility' (ten Raa 1986: 373). The situation was so desperate that ten Raa suggests that they were saved as an independent ethnic group only by the advent of colonial rule and the attendant suppression of cattle raiding.

The Sandawe acquired their cattle from displaced pastoralists pushed into their territory by other groups. These refugees offered cattle as bridewealth, in place of the traditional beehives and arrows (ten Raa 1986: 368). Cronk (1989) has documented how exactly the same situation caused the Mukogodo of Kenya to adopt pastoralism in as little as a decade (1925-1936). Pastoralist groups displaced by colonial appropriation of their land entered Mukogodo territory and offered livestock instead of beehives for bridewealth. The cattle were worth more in exchange and carried prestige value among the surrounding pastoral groups (who looked down on hunter-gatherers). Pastoralism may also have appealed to the fathers of out-marrying Mukogodo brides because, although they say they enjoyed the hunting lifestyle, adult men were largely responsible for subsistence (hunting and bee-keeping), whereas women and children perform most of the pastoral labour in this region. In any case, many fathers accepted, so that a large number of women married out, creating a severe shortage of wives for Mukogodo men, as their pastoralist neighbours insisted on cattle as bridewealth. As a result, the Mukogodo abandoned hunting and bee-keeping and the caves in which they had lived, and adopted not only cattle but also the Maasai language, economy, and most customs. Because of this near-total lifestyle change, the Mukogodo, unlike the Sandawe, became successful herders (although still poorer than other groups in the region), and have maintained their identity as a separate group, although at the cost of their distinct culture (Cronk 1989).

Clearly the need for bridewealth is one way that hunter-gatherers can be sucked into herding. Smith (1990) suggests that another way is through the clientage relationships described above. Among San hunter-gatherers of southern Africa, government schemes that give them cattle have not been very successful, because of the lack of fit between cattle ownership and San ideology, particularly the imperative to share. They prefer to herd cattle as clients of other pastoralists, despite the exploitative nature of the relationship, because this allows them to use cattle products without the troublesome implications of ownership. Smith suggests that the related agro-pastoral Khoikhoi may have begun as such clients, and then broken off from their masters at a point when they had adopted the ideology of herding but still maintained a sense of ethnic identity.

Cattle in Neolithic Europe

The European Neolithic encompasses a large span of time and space, so that I clearly cannot attempt anything approaching a comprehensive analysis of the role played by cattle here. Instead, building from the ethnographic insights I have just reviewed, I will frame some questions that seem to me worth exploring. I will try to point the way toward how these questions might be addressed using a combination of results from an in-depth study of one site (late Neolithic Opovo, Yugoslavia) and much more general comparative data from across Europe. I am fully aware that I am thus glossing over considerable variation among regions, among sites, and probably within sites, and can only offer the excuse that we must start somewhere.

Food or Fortune?

The most fundamental question is whether cattle did in fact function as wealth in Neolithic Europe, at least in some times and places, or whether they were valued solely as a source of food and perhaps labour. As we have seen above, based on modern societies, cattle are quite likely to take on the function of wealth in economies exhibiting the domestic mode of production (as is usually assumed for Neolithic Europe) where cattle make an important contribution to subsistence (Ingold 1980; Schneider 1979; 1980). Outside of the Mediterranean zone, cattle are almost always the most numerous domestic species and usually the most numerous of any species at European Neolithic sites, often overwhelmingly so (e.g., Bogucki 1988; Bökönyi 1974; Glass 1989; Greenfield 1986). Based on the ethnographic cases, there are several results of the use of cattle as wealth that we might see in the archaeological record: size of individual cattle may decline; cattle may be kept where it is not optimal in terms of subsistence to do o; cattle will be kept relatively far from the settlement rather than as 'family cows'; there will be a trend for individual households, perhaps reflected at the settlement level, to trade-up from small stock to cattle through time; and cattle will figure prominently in ritual and symbolism.

Cattle in Europe and elsewhere decreased in size from the time they were domesticated until deliberate breeding to increase size during the Roman period. Indeed, this size change is a major criterion for the recognition of domestic cattle, and the reasons for it are poorly understood. It is possible that the desire to maximise the number rather than the size of cattle due to their value as wealth contributed to this. On the other hand, this same size decrease has been observed in many taxa with domestication, including some, like dogs and cats, that are unlikely to have served as wealth. Horses, which very likely did function as wealth after their domestication, are one of the few taxa that do not decrease in size with domestication. So although the reduction in size does not conflict with the use of cattle as wealth, it cannot be seen as particularly convincing evidence for such use.

Turning to the specific case of Opovo, several lines of evidence suggest that cattle may have been kept more for wealth than subsistence at this site. Opovo is located on the southern edge of the Pannonian Plain, in a marshy area that, judging from the composition and individual size of the wild fauna, provided prime habitat for red deer and wild boar but relatively poor habitat for cattle (in contrast to the central part of the Pannonian Plain, where aurochs are large and abundant). Unusually for a Vinča culture site, the fauna is predominantly wild (ca. 70%), mostly red deer and wild boar. With an apparently bountiful supply of wild game, one might question why the Opovo dwellers would bother to keep domestic animals in difficult circumstances if their concern was with a supply of protein and calories. They did, however, raise cattle, sheep, goats, pigs, and dogs. While the wild fauna indicate that ecological conditions were excellent for pigs but poor for cattle, cattle form 50-60% of the domestic fauna throughout the occupation of the site, while pigs never exceed 15% (Russell 1993; in press). This pattern strongly implies that cattle had value beyond their dietary contribution.

There are also indications that cattle were kept in a relatively loose herding system away from the settlement at Opovo, while smaller stock were kept confined in the 'barnyard'. While the sample is too small to make much of, one sheep bone shows exostosis at the elbow, a pathology cited by Baker (1984) as indicating close confinement, while there are no such pathologies in the more numerous cattle bones (Russell 1993: 377). More convincingly, the size ranges of wild and domestic pigs show a very clear separation, indicating a lack of interbreeding that is quite remarkable given how easily pigs go feral, and in distinct contrast to historically known practices that leave pigs running loose much of the year. Since pig dentitions that retain the area of the canine can easily be sexed, it is certain that this size separation does indeed represent wild vs. domestic pigs rather than males vs. females. The Opovo cattle, on the other hand, do overlap with aurochs (wild cattle) in size. Two of the skulls have features that Bökönyi (1974) argues result from hybridisation of wild and domestic cattle (Russell 1993: 119). This pattern of pigs that separate easily into wild and domestic forms and cattle that do not seems to hold in Neolithic Switzerland as well (Sakellaridis 1979), although in Switzerland there is evidence of stalling and foddering of cattle (Sakellaridis 1979; Troels-Smith 1984). Since there is also some evidence that these Swiss cattle were milked (Sakellaridis 1979), it may be that only milking females were kept at the settlement while the other cattle were herded farther away. Nevertheless, in the more continental parts of Europe at least, foddering may have been necessary to get cattle through the winter, which would certainly have limited their accumulation.

At Opovo, sheep and goats decrease from 26% to 15% of the domestic fauna over the 100-200 years of occupation, while cattle increase from 52% to 61%. This may be the result of the foundation of the settlement by young households budding off from an established village. As the households built their herds through time, some at least were able to trade-up to more cattle.

Cattle hold great symbolic importance in those societies where they serve as wealth, and play key roles in many rituals. Cattle also seem to have been symbolically important in Neolithic Europe. While other animal images also appear, cattle, bulls, and their horns predominate in southeast Europe, where they appear as figurines, on pots, and as large and small ceramic 'horns of consecration' (Gimbutas 1982: 91-93). John Chapman (1981: 68) has suggested that the clay bucrania in the Vinča culture are associated with the houses of wealthy herders, and appear to be separate from the complex of female figurines. Perhaps the clearest instance of cattle wealth symbolism is found at the Eneolithic cemetery at Varna in Bulgaria where the numerous gold bucrania unite two forms of wealth (Gimbutas 1977; Renfrew 1986). In central and northwest Europe, the symbolic importance of cattle is manifest in the actual cattle remains found in ritual and mortuary contexts, sometimes as the debris from feasts, sometimes as burials of cattle or parts of cattle (often heads) either separately or as part of a human burial (Döhle and Stahlhofen 1985; Hodder 1990: 250; Thomas 1991: 23-25).

Thus while much remains to be done to fill out our picture of the uses of cattle beyond subsistence in Neolithic Europe and particularly to understand regional and temporal variation, there is enough evidence to suggest strongly that cattle were valued as wealth as well as calories. I will now consider some of the implications of this wealth value.

The valuation of cattle

As should be clear from the ethnographic discussion above, cattle take on value as wealth in part because of their subsistence value, although their simultaneous value as wealth and as food source prevent either value from being maximised. Bogucki (1993) has argued that cattle took on wealth value only after they were used for dairy and especially for traction, giving economic value to living animals.

Use in traction is only well-attested after ca. 3000 BC, although there have been some claims for earlier use of cattle to pull ploughs in southeast Europe (Chapman 1981; Mateescu 1975). Dairy use seems also to have intensified around this time, although it may have existed much earlier. Is wealth value for cattle limited to milch pastoralism? Animals in carnivorous pastoralist societies still have wealth value (Ingold 1980) and the very act of domestication implies a focus on the value of the living animal if only as a means to continue the herd (Meadow 1984). Ingold's (1980: 242) argument with respect to the impossibility of carnivorous pastoralism based on cattle is clearly not relevant here, since he is referring to the impossibility of a pure carnivorous pastoralism, while in Neolithic Europe herding occurred in the context of mixed economies where agriculture was very likely dominant in most cases. Still, to the extent that the animal can yield subsistence in products in life (secondary products: Sherratt 1983), the goals of subsistence and of wealth accumulation are less in conflict. Wealth accumulation will certainly be enhanced, cattle will probably be felt to have greater value, and the larger pools of wealth thus produced are likely to have a greater effect on society.

I cannot here give a full treatment of the use of cattle for dairy products in Neolithic Europe, but the identification of dairying is a vexatiously difficult problem. Bogucki (1984) offers ceramic sieves as evidence for cheese-making and hence milking of cattle in the Linear Pottery Culture, but for the most part arguments for and against dairy use are based on kill-off patterns. By analogy to modern dairy systems, most male cattle are expected to be slaughtered quite early, as they do not produce milk and are not needed for reproduction, and the calves compete with humans for milk (especially given the much lower milk production of early cattle compared to modern specialised dairy breeds). It is difficult to sex immature cattle bones, so in practice one seeks a pattern with a peak in kill-off in the infantile age range and another late in life, and an adult sex ratio heavily biased to females (the result of killing males off early).

On this basis, arguments have been made, although not universally accepted, for dairy use of cattle in central and northwest Europe in the Neolithic (Bogucki 1982; Legge 1981), but not in southeast Europe (Greenfield 1988). There are problems with this kill-off model, however. First, it has been suggested that early cattle, probably until much later than the Neolithic, would not let down their milk without the presence of their calf (Cranstone 1969; Entwistle and Grant 1989; McCormick 1992). McCormick (1992) has combined historical and archaeological data from early Christian Ireland to show that cattle were kept primarily for dairy purposes, calves were retained to permit let-down, and that this produced a kill-off pattern with few calves slaughtered under one year of age, most between one and two years, and an adult sex ratio of 70-80% females. On this basis he sees no sign of dairy economies in Britain before the late Iron Age. Interestingly, Opovo, with an adult sex ratio of about 70% females and kill-of peaking in the juvenile stage (1-3 years old), matches very well with McCormick's dairy pattern. A further complication, however, is that the ethnographic studies reviewed above, particularly Kelly's (1985), have shown that the age/sex structure of the herd is shaped not only by subsistence, but also by the wealth value of cattle, and particularly by the form of bridewealth requirements.

It seems very likely that cattle were used as bridewealth in Neolithic Europe. As noted above, cattle seem ideally suited to bridewealth payments. Bridewealth is associated with mixed agricultural/herding economies in situations where land is plentiful and labour is the limiting factor in production; this would seem to describe at least most of Neolithic Europe (Hodder 1984). With the relatively low population densities of the Neolithic, it is unlikely that wealth in land would have been of much importance, as it is in historically known European societies. Bridewealth would then be crucial in securing rights to the labour of women and their children. Since bridewealth in cattle is strongly associated with patriliny and patriarchy, one could see a development or intensification of bridewealth running from southeast to northwest and early to late as reflected in the female-centred symbolism of Neolithic southeast Europe (Gimbutas 1982; Hodder 1990) as opposed to the male-centred symbolism of the later Neolithic of northwest Europe (De Marrais et al. 1996: 21), often considered to have a more strongly pastoral economy than the rest of Neolithic Europe.

Bridewealth and the Neolithization of Europe

In closing, I would like to suggest that the dynamics of cattle wealth, and especially bridewealth, may shed some light on certain aspects of the spread of Neolithic economies across Europe. One of the great mysteries of this expansion is what happened to the Mesolithic hunter-gatherers who previously inhabited these territories. Although there are occasional places where there is some evidence for survival of hunter-gatherers in interaction with Neolithic farmers, for the most part they seem to fade away in the face of the advancing farmers (Price et al. 1995; Zvelebil and Rowley-Conwy 1984). The experience of East African hunter-gatherers described above suggests that Mesolithic groups may have been rapidly assimilated into agro-pastoral economies through the bridewealth system. Because of their need for labour and the prestige value of polygyny, the intruding agro-pastoralists might have been quite motivated to marry hunter-gatherer women. This would be still more true if those on the agricultural frontier tended to be young men, perhaps those lacking sisters to provide their bridewealth; hunter-gatherer brides may have come cheaper (Dennell 1985). As in Africa, the shortage of wives thus created for hunter-gatherer men could push them into the adoption of the agro-pastoral economy and culture in the space of a generation.

The Nuer conquest (Kelly 1985) could also be offered as a model for the expansion of the Linear Pottery cultures, notable for the extremely rapid spread of a remarkably uniform culture across a large area of Europe (Price et al. 1995). The hearthland of the Linear Pottery cultures is the

Carpathian Basin, a centre of cattle breeding and perhaps local domestication during the Neolithic (Bökönyi 1974). Sherratt (1982) has proposed that the evident prosperity of this region was based on the export of cattle to surrounding regions. I would suggest that the wealth of the region derived not so much from exchange but from the large herds of cattle themselves, although the two are certainly connected. Along with this abundance of cattle, and perhaps driving it, there may have developed a bridewealth system like that of the Nuer that valued ever greater bridewealth payments. Once the herds reached the carrying capacity of the pasture land in the Carpathian Basin, bridewealth could only be maintained through territorial expansion. Since the Linear Pottery groups expanded not into the land of competing agro-pastoralists, but into that of hunter-gatherers (probably no accident), the process of assimilation through bridewealth outlined above would make territorial expansion even easier, not even requiring much warfare, although herds could not be rapidly augmented through cattle raiding outside the group.

Conclusion

In the space available to me here, I have only been able to begin to sketch how cattle might have functioned as wealth in the European Neolithic. It is also clear that both data and models need to be developed much more fully than they are at present to address these kinds of questions adequately. I have limited myself to the European Neolithic because it is the area and period with which I am most familiar, and to provide some focus to the discussion. Certainly cattle would also have been important as wealth in later times and in other parts of the world, although differing social and economic contexts will affect the workings of that wealth. What I hope to have accomplished here is to demonstrate that thinking of cattle as wealth rather than simply a food resource has broad implications for our view of Neolithic society.

Endnotes

1. Schneider (1979: 100) describes how Gisu herders can work their way up from field rats to cattle: when they have twelve field rats they can trade them up for a hen; six hens can be exchanged for a goat; and finally three-four goats for a cow.

Bibliography

Baker, J. 1984. The study of animal diseases with regard to agricultural practices and man's attitudes to his animals. In *Animals and Archaeology. Volume 4. Husbandry in Europe*, edited by C. Grigson and J. Clutton-Brock, pp. 253-257. Oxford: BAR.

Bogucki, P.I. 1982. *Early Neolithic Subsistence and Settlement in the Polish Lowlands*. Oxford: BAR.

Bogucki, P.I. 1984. Linear Pottery ceramic sieves and their economic implications. *Oxford Journal of Archaeology* 3(1): 15-30.

Bogucki, P.I. 1988. *Forest Farmers and Stockherders: Early Agriculture and its Consequences in North-Central Europe*. Cambridge: Cambridge University Press.

Bogucki, P.I. 1993. Animal traction and household economies in Neolithic Europe. *Antiquity* 67: 492-503.

Bökönyi, S. 1974. *History of Domestic Mammals in Central and Eastern Europe*. (trans. Lili Halápy). Budapest: Akadémiai Kiadó.

Chapman, J.C. 1981. *The Vinča Culture of South-East Europe*. Oxford: BAR.

Cranstone, B.A.L. 1969. Animal husbandry: The evidence from ethnography. In *The Domestication and Exploitation of Plants and Animals*, edited by P.J. Ucko and G.W. Dimbleby, pp. 247-263. London: Duckworth.

Cronk, L. 1989. From hunters to herders: subsistence change as a reproductive strategy among the Mukogodo. *Current Anthropology* 30(2): 224-234.

Dahl, G. 1980. Production in pastoral societies. In *The Future of Pastoral Peoples, Nairobi, Kenya, 1980, (Commission on Nomadic Peoples, International Union of Anthropological and Ethnological Sciences)*, pp. 200-209. Nairobi.

Dahl, G. and A. Hjort 1976. *Having Herds: Pastoral Herd Growth and Household Economy*. (Stockholm Studies in Social Anthropology 2). Stockholm.

De Marrais, E., L.J. Castillo and T. Earle 1996. Ideology, materialization and power strategies. *Current Anthropology* 37(1): 151.

Dennell, R. 1985. The hunter-gatherer/agricultural frontier in prehistoric temperate Europe. In *The Archaeology of Frontiers and Boundaries*, edited by S. Green and S. Perlman, pp. 113-139. New York: Academic Press.

Döhle, H.-J. and H. Stahlhofen 1985. Neolithischen Rindergraber auf dem "Löwenberg" bei Derenburg, Kr. Wernigerode. *Jahresschrift für Mitteldeutsche Vorgeschichte* 68: 157-177.

Dombrowski, K. 1993. Some considerations for the understanding of small herd dynamics in East African arid zones: The long-term consequences of bridewealth exchange networks. *Human Ecology* 21(1): 23-50.

Entwistle, R. and A. Grant 1989. The evidence for cereal cultivation and animal husbandry in the southern British Neolithic and Bronze Age. In *The Beginnings of Agriculture*, edited by A. Milles, D. Williams and N. Gardner, pp. 203-215. Oxford: BAR.

Gimbutas, M. 1977. Gold treasure at Varna. *Archaeology* 30: 44-51.

Gimbutas, M. 1982. *The Goddesses and Gods of Old Europe 6500-3500 BC.* (Second edition). Berkeley: University of California Press.

Glass, M.F. 1989. *Animal Production Systems in Neolithic Central Europe.* Unpublished doctoral dissertation, University of Calgary.

Goody, J. 1973. Bridewealth and dowry in Africa and Eurasia. In *Bridewealth and Dowry.* (Cambridge Papers in Social Anthropology 7), edited by J. Goody and S.J. Tambiah, pp. 1-58. Cambridge: Cambridge University Press.

Grandin, B.E. 1988. Wealth and pastoral dairy production: A case study from Maasailand. *Human Ecology* 16(1): 1-21.

Greenfield, H.J. 1986 *The Paleoeconomy of the Central Balkans (Serbia): A Zooarchaeological Perspective on the Late Neolithic and Bronze Age (ca. 4500-1000 B.C.).* Oxford: BAR.

Greenfield, H.J. 1988 The origins of milk and wool production in the Old World. *Current Anthropology* 29 (4): 573-593.

Hakansson, N.T. 1994. Grain, cattle, and power: social processes of intensive cultivation and exchange in precolonial western Kenya. *Journal of Anthropological Research* 50(3): 249-276.

Hardin, G. 1968. The tragedy of the commons. *Science* 162: 1243-1248.

Hart, K. and L. Sperling 1987. Cattle as capital. *Ethnos* 52 (3-4): 324-338.

Hesse, B. 1984. These are our goats: The origins of herding in west central Iran. In *Animals and Archaeology: Volume 3. Early Herders and their Flocks*, edited by J. Clutton-Brock and C. Grigson, pp. 243-264. Oxford: BAR.

Hjort, A. 1980. Herds, trade, and grain: pastoralism in a regional perspective. In *The Future of Pastoral Peoples, Nairobi, Kenya, 1980, (Commission on Nomadic Peoples, International Union of Anthropological and Ethnological Sciences)*, pp. 135-143. Nairobi.

Hodder, I. 1984. Burials, houses, women and men in the European Neolithic. In *Ideology, Power and Prehistory*, edited by D. Miller and C. Tilley, pp. 51-68. Cambridge: Cambridge University Press.

Hodder, I. 1990. *The Domestication of Europe: Structure and Contingency in Neolithic Societies.* Oxford: Basil Blackwell.

Huffman, T.N. 1990. Broederstroom and the origins of cattle-keeping in southern Africa. *African Studies* 49 (2): 1-12.

Ingold, T. 1980. *Hunters, Pastoralists, and Ranchers: Reindeer Economies and their Transformations.* Cambridge: Cambridge University Press.

Kelly, R.C. 1985. *The Nuer Conquest: The Structure and Development of an Expansionist System.* Ann Arbor: University of Michigan Press.

Kuper, A. 1982. *Wives for Cattle: Bridewealth and Marriage in Southern Africa.* Boston: Routledge, Kegan Paul.

Lee, R.B. 1984. *The Dobe !Kung.* New York: Holt, Rinehart and Winston.

Legge, A.J. 1981. Aspects of cattle husbandry. In *Farming Practice in British Prehistory*, edited by R. Mercer, pp. 169-181. Edinburgh: Edinburgh University Press.

Mace, R. and A. Houston 1989. Pastoralist strategies for survival in unpredictable environments: A model of herd composition that maximises household viability. *Agricultural Systems* 31: 185-204.

Marx, K. 1936[1890] *Capital: A Critique of Political Economy.* New York: Random House.

Mateescu, C. 1975 Remarks on cattle breeding and agriculture in the Middle and Late Neolithic on the Lower Danube. *Dacia* 19: 13-18.

McCormick, F. 1992. Early faunal evidence for dairying. *Oxford Journal of Archaeology* 11(2): 201-209.

Meadow, R.H. 1984. Animal domestication in the Middle East: A view from the eastern margin. In *Animals and Archaeology: Volume 3. Early Herders and their Flocks*, edited by J. Clutton-Brock and C. Grigson, pp. 309-337. Oxford: BAR.

Paine, R. 1971. Animals as capital: comparisons among northern nomadic herders and hunters. *Anthropological Quarterly* 44(3): 157-172.

Price, T.D., A.B. Gebauer and L.H. Keeley 1995. The spread of farming into Europe north of the Alps.

In *Last Hunters–First Farmers: New Perspectives on the Prehistoric Transition to Agriculture*, edited by T.D. Price and A.B. Gebauer, pp. 95-126.

Renfrew, C. 1986. Varna and the emergence of wealth in prehistoric Europe. In *The Social Life of Things: Commodities in Cultural Perspective*, edited by A. Appadurai, pp. 141-168. Cambridge: Cambridge University Press.

Russell, N. 1993. *Hunting, Herding and Feasting: Human Use of Animals in Neolithic Southeast Europe*. Unpublished doctoral dissertation, University of California, Berkeley.

Russell, N. in press. Symbolic dimensions of animals and meat at Opovo, Yugoslavia. In *Material Symbols*, (Southern Illinois University, Center for Archaeological Investigations, Occasional Papers). edited by J. Robb. Carbondale: Southern Illinois University Press.

Sahlins, M. 1972. *Stone Age Economics*. Chicago: Aldine-Atherton.

Sakellaridis, M. 1979. *The Economic Exploitation of the Swiss Area in the Mesolithic and Neolithic Periods*. Oxford: BAR.

Schneider, H.K. 1979. *Livestock and Equality in East Africa: The Economic Basis for Social Structure*. Bloomington: Indiana University Press.

Schneider, H.K. 1980. Livestock as food and money. In *The Future of Pastoral Peoples, Nairobi, Kenya, 1980, (Commission on Nomadic Peoples, International Union of Anthropological and Ethnological Sciences)*, pp. 210-223. Nairobi.

Sherratt, A.G. 1982. Mobile resources: Settlement and exchange in early agricultural Europe. In *Ranking, Resource and Exchange: Aspects of the Archaeology of Early European Society*, edited by C. Renfrew and S. Shennan, pp. 13-26. Cambridge: Cambridge University Press.

Sherratt, A.G. 1983. The secondary exploitation of animals in the Old World. *World Archaeology* 15(1): 90-104.

Smith, A.B. 1990. On becoming herders: Khoikhoi and San ethnicity in southern Africa. *African Studies* 49(2): 51-73.

Sutter, J.W. 1987. Cattle and inequality: Herd size differences and pastoral production among the Fulani of northeastern Senegal. *Africa* 57(2): 196-218.

Tambiah, S.J. 1973. Dowry and bridewealth, and the property rights of women in South Asia. In *Bridewealth and Dowry*, (Cambridge Papers in Social Anthropology 7) edited by J. Goody and S. J. Tambiah, pp. 59-169. Cambridge: Cambridge University Press.

ten Raa, E. 1986. The acquisition of cattle by hunter-gatherers: A traumatic experience in cultural change. *Sprache und Geschichte in Afrika* 7(2): 361-374.

Thomas, J. 1991. *Rethinking the Neolithic*. Cambridge: Cambridge University Press.

Troels-Smith, J. 1984. Stall-feeding and field-manuring in Switzerland about 6000 years ago. *Tools and Tillage* 5(1): 13-25.

Zvelebil, M. and P. Rowley-Conwy 1984. Transition to farming in northern Europe: a hunter-gatherer perspective. *Norwegian Archaeological Review* 17: 104-128.

Chapter 6

Landmarks of power: princely tombs in the central Balkan Iron Age

Aleksandar Palavestra

Introduction

This paper deals with the princely tombs of the central Balkans as symbolic pivots of cattle-breading communities and their realm. The princely tombs of the central Balkans are extremely opulent graves placed under large mounds which are rich in luxurious offerings of both indigenous and foreign origin (gold, silver and amber, as well as symbols of power and prestige). Chronologically they date from the second half of the sixth century to the first decades of the fifth century BC. The mounds are noticeable and distinguished at great distance and were undoubtedly clear and intelligible symbols of the power of local chiefs. It is improbable that such symbolic occupation of a particular place was merely an expression of an individual's riches and vanity. It is more likely that there was a specific meaning ascribed to the place and which was explicit for the entire community.

As the pivots of social power, the princely tombs probably acted on three levels: ritual, territorial and tribal. Judging by the princely tombs there existed several centres of power in the central Balkans at the end of the sixth and the beginning of the fifth centuries. It is suggested that the princely tombs of the early Iron Age in the central Balkans (as the symbolic centres of power and the crux of wider interests of the communities) may best be considered from the angle of the cattle-breeding movements and their territories. This is due to the cattle-breeding character of the ancient populations and the geomorphological conditions favourable for a transhumant and nomadic economy. In this paper I propose the outlines of several areas for seasonal cattle-breeding; areas consisting of highland summer pastures, river valleys, lowlands for winter shelter, and natural communication routes suitable for cattle-breeding and trade. The princely tombs are situated at crucial places in these areas: under highland summer pastures, at winter pastures, along the communication lines (even by their intersections) and along the well trodden cattlemen's paths, the direction of which has long been determined by infrequent mountain saddles, ravines and river valleys.

The horizon of the princely tombs is the most prominent phenomenon of the early Iron Age in the central Balkans. The cultures of the indigenous communities which had formed as early as the late Bronze Age underwent a relatively peaceful and undisturbed development during the first phase of the early Iron Age. Even the impact of the Thraco-Cimmerians from the steppes (from the middle of the eighth century BC) did not affect the local population, which although adopting the novelties in iron-working metallurgy from the newcomers, remained fundamentally attached to the older cultural tradition. In the area of the central Balkans, three distinct cultural complexes may be delineated for the early Iron Age: the cultural complex of Bosut-Basarabi; the Iron Age Glasinac Culture; and the culture group of Donja Brnjica. In all three of these complexes, interior social movements and increasing power of the warrior class and tribal aristocracy are noticeable by the end of the seventh century and during the sixth century BC. These phenomena reached their climaxes by the end of the sixth century in the horizon of princely tombs.

It is interesting that princely tombs appeared precisely in the areas where these three large cultural complexes met, intertwined and, most surely, collided. In the bordering areas small local groups belonged to any of the three larger complexes and vigilantly guarded their pastures and controlled communication routes: thus the princely tombs may have conspicuously and symbolically marked their precious territories. Although it is possible to connect the three complexes to particular ethnic groups (which are certified by somewhat later written sources), the princely tombs themselves may hardly be associated with any of these culture groups. Nor may the ethnical affiliation of the individuals buried be easily determined. A uniform cultural model which was created by the prestige goods, luxurious imports, emulation and 'peer polity interaction' erased the local differences and individual characteristics of local groups and clans which may be inferred from the analysis of meagrely furnished graves and settlements.

Early Iron Age central Balkans

In order to shed more light on the princely grave phenomenon, it is necessary to outline the wider cultural pattern of the central Balkans during the early Iron Age. The Bosut-Basarabi cultural complex dates from the eighth century till the end of the sixth centuries BC and is connected to the wider region of the Danube valley. In the central Balkans it appears in a western (the Bosut) and an eastern (the Basarabi) variant. Bosut-Basarbi encompassed the areas of Srem, Šumadija, the Morava valley and eastern Serbia (where a separate form – the Zlot group – appeared). Along the Morava valley, the fortified hill-fort settlements and rich graves (with the characteristic massive silver belts of the so-called Mramorac type) testify to the rise of the warrior aristocracy from the eighth to the fifth centuries BC. As a distinct cultural phenomenon of the central Balkans and the Danube valley, the Basarabi pottery style is found across the entire region and rendered local cultures and ethnical groups into a relatively uniform autochthonous Iron Age cultural complex. Judging by somewhat later written sources, the Basarabi Culture encompassed the regions settled by the tribe of Triballoi. The presence of the

Bosut-Basarabi Culture in the western part of Serbia (the region where the princely tombs are situated) has not been attested, nor have the western boundaries of the territory of the Triballoi been fully established. At the end of the seventh century BC this territory witnessed the intrusion of the Glasinac tribes from the west which today is more or less certainly identified as the Autariatae.

The Glasinac Culture covered southeastern Bosnia, eastern Herzegovina, parts of southwestern Serbia and Metohia and Montenegro. As this cultural area borders upon the territory of the Mati Culture in northern Albania, the entire complex embraced several distinctive but closely connected cultures and thus is labelled the Glasinac-Mati Culture (i. e., the original area of Glasinac and the adjacent lands, southwestern Serbia, parts of Metohia and northern Montenegro, eastern Herzegovina, and northern and parts of central Albania). Chronologically the Glasinac Culture dates from 800 to 300 BC. The economy of the population was semi-nomadic cattle-breeding supplemented by armed raids, active and passive trade (i.e., control over communications and collection of duties), and well developed metalworking (bronze and iron jewellery and weapons). The settlements of the period, though insufficiently investigated, were of the hill-fort type and some of them served merely as refugia or fortified centres for an area of scattered hamlets of cattlemen.

The majority of information about this culture comes from the investigation of a large number of graves containing rich assemblages. More than a thousand mounds have been excavated in the original area of Glasinac. The dead were buried under mounds (tumuli), their bodies intact. In the second half of the sixth century, cremation became the dominant funerary rite.

If one accepts that at the beginning of the sixth century BC the Autariatae intruded into the territories of the Triballoi up to the Moravica River and the Maljen Mountain near Užička Požega (i.e., the intrusions of the Glasinac population towards the proponents of the Basarabi style) then one can assume that the territory of the Triballoi stretched all the way to the Kolubara River in the west (i.e., the territory corresponding to the spread of the Basarabi style).

In the lands south of the Zapadna Morava River at Kosovo, the Donja Brnjica culture communities lived, more or less undisturbed from the late Bronze Age. By the beginning of the seventh century, these communities had become jeopardised, a fact testified by changes including the appearance of fortified hill-fort settlements. Funerary rites were not changed, however, suggesting continuity in traditional culture despite the changed circumstances. The Donja Brnjica communities cremated their dead and deposited the ashes in urns or shallow pits within various types of stone constructions. Judging by the later written sources, the Donja Brnjica Culture populations (and their successors in the Iron Age at Kosovo) can be identified ethnically as the Dardanians. By the end of the seventh and the beginning of the sixth centuries BC the Dardanians were also exposed to pressures from the Autariatae and the Illyrian raids from northern Albania (Illyrii *proprie dicti*). The Autariatae penetration towards the plateau of Pešter (apparently in search of new, better pastures) came to a stop in the seventh century BC at the Golija Mountain; this attests to the ability of the Dardanians (perhaps as a tribal alliance) to resist the warrior tribes of Glasinac. During the sixth century BC the Dardanians put up similar resistance to the Illyrians *proprie dicti* along the border of Kosovo and Metohia and this offers a reliable proof of their vitality (Srejović 1981; Garašanin 1988; Palavestra 1984; Vasić 1990). Srejović summarised the ethno-cultural situation in the central Balkans at the time of the emergence of the princely tombs as follows: 'The territory of Serbia during the sixth century BC was for the most part peopled by the ancient, interrelated indigenous communities – the Dardanians (Kosovo and the area between the Ibar, Zapadna and Južna Morava River valleys), the Triballoi (Šumadija and eastern Serbia) and an offshoot of the Daco-Getae (Banat, Srem, Bačka), whereas only smaller areas were peopled by the Illyrian tribe – the Autariatan branch (the Drina and Lim river areas, from Povlen and Maljen to Pešter) and the Illyrians *proprie dicti* (southwestern Metohia). These boundaries did not considerably change until the end of the fourth century BC, that is until the arrival of the Celts into the Balkan Peninsula and the conflict between the ancient Balkan tribes on the one hand and the Macedonian state and the Hellenistic rulers on the other.' (Srejović 1981: 60-61).

Although no drastic changes in the ethno-cultural pattern of the central Balkans occurred in the end of the sixth and the beginning of the fifth centuries, a sudden disappearance of princely tombs is conspicuous. Their disappearance suggests the dissolution of the system of power and authority the foremost exponent of which had been the princely tombs. Rich graves were much scarcer after the beginning of the fifth century and their construction and offerings were incomparably poorer to the ones from the end of the sixth century. The reasons for this social crisis and the abrupt dissolution of the traditional system of power are not at all clear. Although abundant, the archaeological material of the early Iron Age in the central Balkans does not provide sufficient data for an in-depth analysis of social structure, stratification and relations. This is due primarily to the absence of systematically explored settlements, as well as to the impossibility of relating finds from burials with settlements. Furthermore, the relative absence of larger cemeteries containing burials with a wealth of grave goods (such as those in the western Balkans and in west central Europe) has limited the study of social structure. Therefore, the archaeological material at our disposal for attempting to construct a model of the early Iron Age society in the central Balkans is limited to the princely tombs. The study of the princely tombs offers at least partial answers to a number of important questions. The tombs contain a great quantity of archaeological material. Although not forming a statistical sample, the material enables insight into the character of the archaeological material of the central Balkan Iron Age. This material is a good starting point for comparative, typological and chronological analyses. Despite the fact that preliminary reports of some graves of this horizon remain unpublished (even a few decades after their discovery) a substantial number of studies address the situation. The importance of the phenomenon has been emphasised in its wider European framework (Palavestra 1984; 1988; Vasić 1987). Comparative grave analysis has been performed (Palavestra 1984; B. Jovanović 1979; Čović 1979). There have been attempts at solving the problems of imported material (Parović-Pešikan 1960, 1988; Čović 1983; Vasić 1986; Babić 1990). The relation between the graves and trade-routes (Palavestra 1989; 1994b) and some ritual and cult aspects of the princely tombs have been discussed (Stipčević 1984; Čače 1985). Also there is a number of publications on individual graves (e.g., the monograph on Atenica: Đuknić and Jovanović 1966) and various archaeological reports, some of which are very thorough and others concise (Mano-Zisi and Popović 1969b; M. Zotović 1984; 1985; Srejović and Marković 1981; Srejović and Vukadin 1988).

Judging by the tomb construction and grave goods Pilatovići, Atenica, Novi Pazar and Pečka Banja may be considered as the clearest representatives of princely tombs in the central Balkans. A number of related burials (albeit with poorer grave goods) belong to the same horizon and are rightly considered to belong to the class of princely tombs in the main due to the frequent inclusion of luxurious imported goods: the graves at Lisijevo Polje, Kruševica, Mrčajevci and (to a certain extent) some tombs at Glasinac and Romaja.

Pilatovići

The Pilatovići Iron Age necropolis is several kilometres east of Požega. About 80 grave assemblages were recorded under a number of mounds. While several graves contained cremations the majority of graves were inhumations placed in stone constructions. In some instances large circles surround the central part of a mound. The majority of graves contained modest offerings, but some yielded fine bronze jewellery, amber beads and weapons thus indicating a somewhat greater esteem for the deceased. The largest mound (set apart from the others) was a princely tomb and consisted of the central, stone burial construction and two peripheral graves. The mound was enclosed by a regular circular drywall. In the central grave the remains of a pyre were mixed with the offerings which were also damaged by fire. The warrior equipment (curved knives and swords, as well as shield- and armour-parts) and the grandeur of the construction vouch for the fact that this must have been a princely tomb. The most interesting piece, a scarab, most probably reached Pilatovići, along with the other imported goods, from southern Italy.

In the peripheral Grave No. 2 a female skeleton was found (princess) with markedly rich offerings: golden wire spirals for hair braids; a rich necklace of amber, bronze and pottery beads; golden saltaleons; several bronze fibulae; and fragments of a bronze astraghal belt. Most of the amber beads were amorphous, but the execution of several of the shaped ones points to southern Italian workshops. The set of bronze vessels of Graeco-Italic origin (a large bowl and two phialae, one with ribbed recipient and the other of the mesomphalos-type) also points to connections with the Greek trading centres, probably reached via the Adriatic ports. This kind of wine-drinking set must have contained more vessels (e.g., a krater, hydria). The existence of such a vessel at Pilatovići is suggested by a bronze statuette of lying lion, an ornament which was characteristic for the rims of Greek kraters and cauldrons of the end of the sixth century. Very similar lions decorate the bronze cauldron from Hochdorf in Germany which is dated only a few decades after the Pilatovići graves.

In the peripheral child's grave, amber beads and Scythian arrowheads were found (i.e., parts of the regular repertoire of child burials in princely tombs of the Iron Ages central Balkans). The comparison of the princely mound with the other graves of the necropolis of Pilatovići proved that the woman's grave fits with the general type of female burials of the area (i.e., jewellery and other numerous offerings). The male burials at Pilatovići were also inhumations, but were poorer and mainly contained weapons, bronze pins and fibulae. A similar repertoire was found in the central burial of the princely tomb; the fact that the deceased was cremated (a special, privileged rite) marks his special character. The exclusiveness of the grave is further emphasised by its position in the centre of the mound: in the other mounds at Pilatovići the central area was reserved for sacrificial and funerary rituals and was not occupied by a grave. The material from Pilatovići is partially published. It is dated to the sixth century BC, the princely grave being more closely dated into the second half of the century (Zotović 1985: 80-100; Palavestra 1984: 23, 57-58).

Atenica

Atenica is located near Čačak. Two large mounds were identified and explored (Fig. 1). Under the Mound I two graves (one central and one peripheral) were found under stone constructions. The graves were enclosed by a ring of stone and pebbles. In the graves were found the ashes of the cremated deceased. The pyre was found by the peripheral circle. The offerings were mixed with the remains of the pyre, scattered between the stones of the construction. In Mound II, which was larger, only one grave was found. It was placed centrally and beside it was a sacrificial construction and a pyre. A supporting wall of stone enclosed the grave. Before the funeral, the surface was levelled, and a dog, two boars and three aurochs were sacrificed. The surface was levelled again and the other funerary constructions were then built: the pyre lined with stone slabs beside the grave; the sacrificial stone and pebble construction; and the central grave with the supporting wall. The sacrificial construction, bordered by stones, consisted of three rectangular areas which had 22 regularly placed sacrificial pits. The grave itself was built of stone and the offerings were mixed with soil and placed among the remains of the pyre scattered between the stone layers. The offerings in all three graves were luxurious and the mounds from Atenica are rightfully denoted as princely burials. Beside the so-called grave of the princess in Mound I was found the rem-

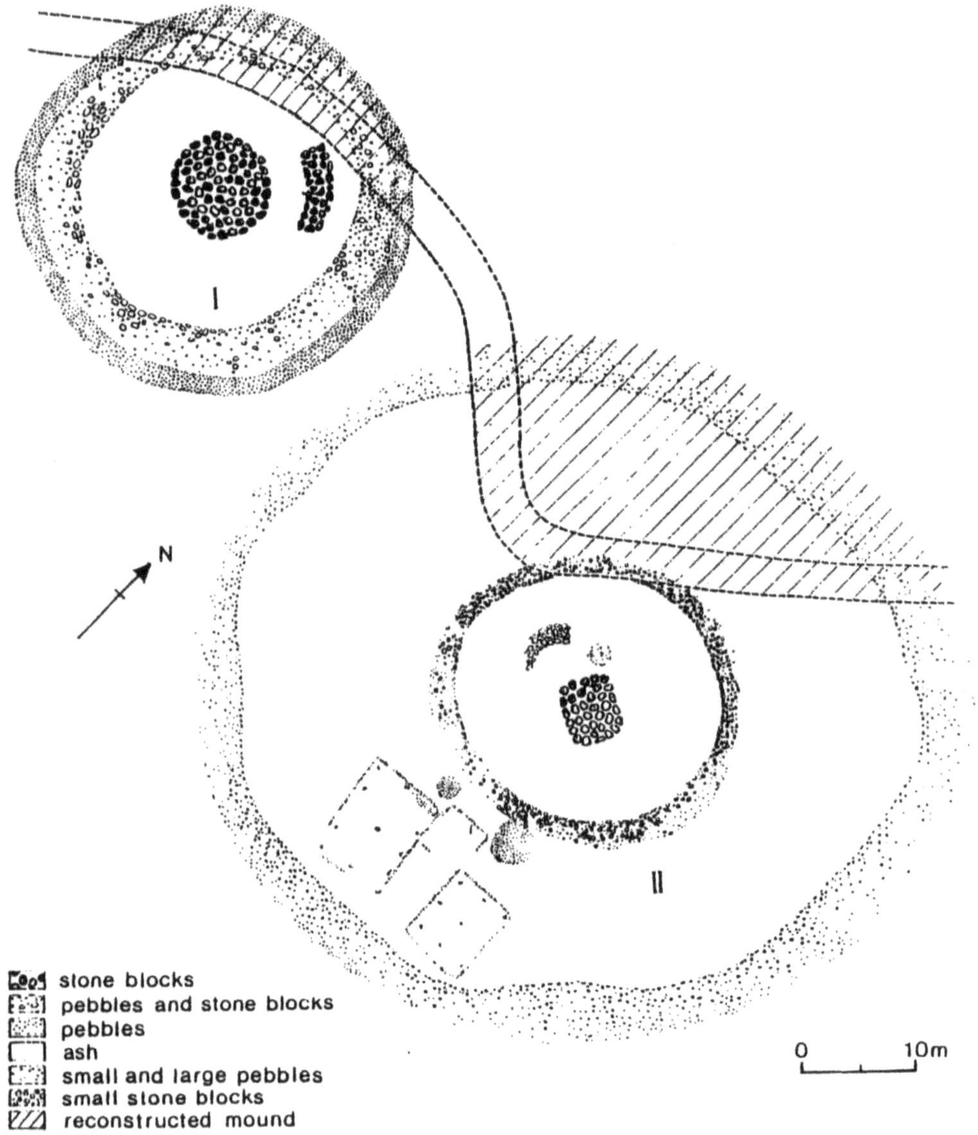

Figure 1 Groundplan of Atenica burial mounds (after Đuknić and B. Jovanović).

nants of a two-wheeled chariot burnt during the funerary rite. The remains from Mound II, where the prince was buried, include a four-wheeled vehicle. Golden and silver appliqués of different shapes (bees, swastika, triangles, rhombuses, circles) were found among the grave offerings (Fig. 2). A plaque of gilded silver representing a boar and executed in the Archaic Greek style must have decorated a piece of armour and was a part of the luxurious imports. Parts of a rich necklace of golden tubes and discs and a large quantity of amber- and glass-beads were also found. Some of the amber was amorphous, but there were also pieces of Archaic execution (lion and ram's heads, birds, ribbed fruits, masks). Supplied as Greek imports (obviously from the same source, Greek colonies in south Italy, in the Adriatic and Ionian Sea) this style is characteristic of the princely tombs of the central Balkans. The graves also contained Greek bronze vessels, badly damaged by the cremation fire. The handles of two cauldrons and the fragments of the base and the rim of a larger vessel (a krater or hydria) were found. Among the carved bone objects a box indicates an Etruscan component among the imports. The pottery was both of domestic and imported origin. Both offensive and defensive warrior equipment was found (swords, daggers, Scythian arrowheads, parts of shields and armour, buckles, etc.) as were pieces of horse equipment. Based on the grave offerings, the central grave of the Mound I contained a woman (the princess) and the peripheral grave a child. In Mound II was buried the prince himself. The graves are dated to the end of the sixth century and the beginning of the fifth century BC (Đuknić and Jovanović 1966; B. Jovanović 1979: 63-71; Palavestra 1984; Čače 1986; Vasić 1986).

Novi Pazar

The opulent princely tomb (known as the find from Novi Pazar) was found in the foundations of the Church of St. Peter at Ras, about two kilometres from Novi Pazar. During reconstruction of the church, Iron Age bronze vessels and jewellery were found under the foundations. Two consecutively built tumuli were identified under the church and were dated to the Bronze and the early Iron Ages. The younger mound contained the remnants of a very rich princely burial.

A large number of offerings was found in and around a wooden chest. The chest itself was found under stone slabs. The luxurious objects include: two massive golden belts of the Mramorac type; six golden disc pectoralae; and three

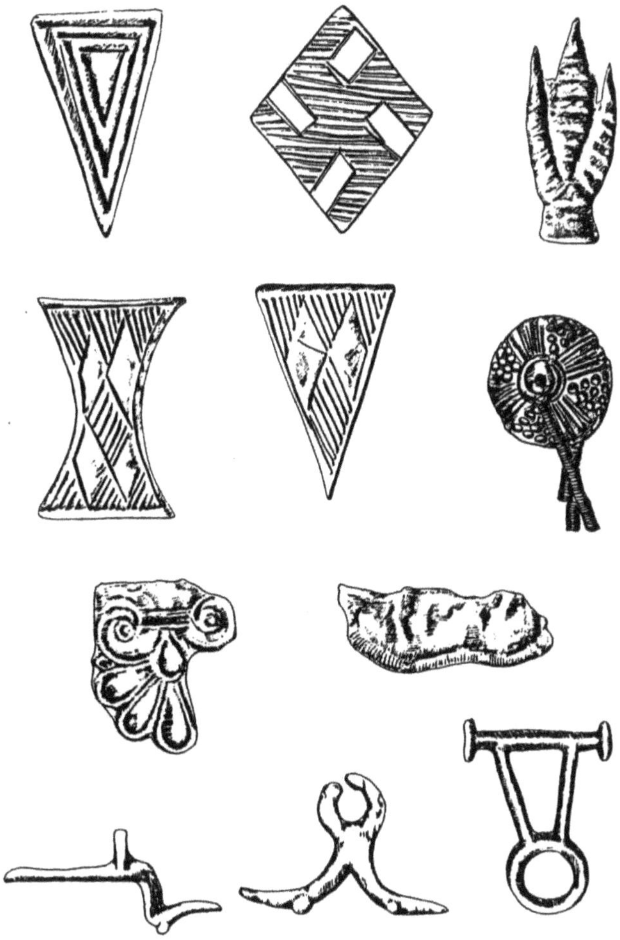

Figure 2 Bronze, silver and gold plaques and jewellery from Atenica.

Figure 3 Gold fittings for armour, plaques and jewellery from Novi Pazar.

golden mithre. In fact three sets of ornamental chest and abdominal armour were found, as was a large quantity of golden appliqués (triangles, rectangles, swastikas, rhombuses, circles and buttons) (Fig. 3). Among the numerous ornaments and jewellery were four silver omega-type double pins, a golden pin with loop-head, two pairs of golden fibulae with rectangular plate, five silver fibulae of the same type, golden earrings shaped like the Mramorac-type belts, four golden rings with filigree and granulation, golden biconical beads, silver bracelets with snake heads, and glass-ribbed beads (Fig. 4). Also found was a large number of amber beads, ranging from amorphous and crudely modelled ones to the finely exercised figurines of the Archaic style (ram's head, birds, masks, acorn, etc.) (Fig. 5). Attention is drawn to the statuettes of korai, as well as the two larger amber plaques of uncertain function but which were decorated on both sides with incised Greek mythological scenes. Luxurious imported vessels consist of a black-figure olpe with a representation of Dionysus, a black-figure skyphos with a dog, a bronze hydria with a kouros handle, a bronze vessel with lion's paws on its base, a silver phialae and a bronze infundibulum-strainer (Figs. 6-7). The amber and the bronze vessels were imported from the Greek manufacturing and trading centres, most probably located in south Italy (Figs. 8-9). The remains of the deceased were not found at Novi Pazar and thus it is not clear whether the finds from the chest are the grave itself or whether they are a part of a deposit belonging to an undetected grave. The mound had the peripheral stone ring and central grave construction which are characteristic of the princely tombs of the central Balkans. The grave goods are dated into the end of the sixth century and the beginning of the fifth century BC (Mano-Zisi and Popović 1969a; 1969b; Palavestra 1984).

Pečka Banja

Pečka Banja is located in Metohia on the north fringe of the Beli Drim valley. The remains of two graves under a mound were found during construction work. The central grave construction was preserved under the mound but as the grave goods had been disturbed the precise relations and grave assemblages could not be determined. The grave construction was founded on stone slabs and built in stone in an irregular rectangle about 2 m long. Based on the grave offerings, two grave assemblages were defined (a male and a female burial) although no traces of cremation or of inhumation were discovered. The male burial contained silver jewellery (a ring of Mramorac type, a double saltaleon with a loop), three bronze helmets of the Graeco-Illyrian type, a necklace of amorphous amber beads, glass beads, snail shells, three bronze fibulae, twelve large bronze buttons (four of which were dressed in silver foil)

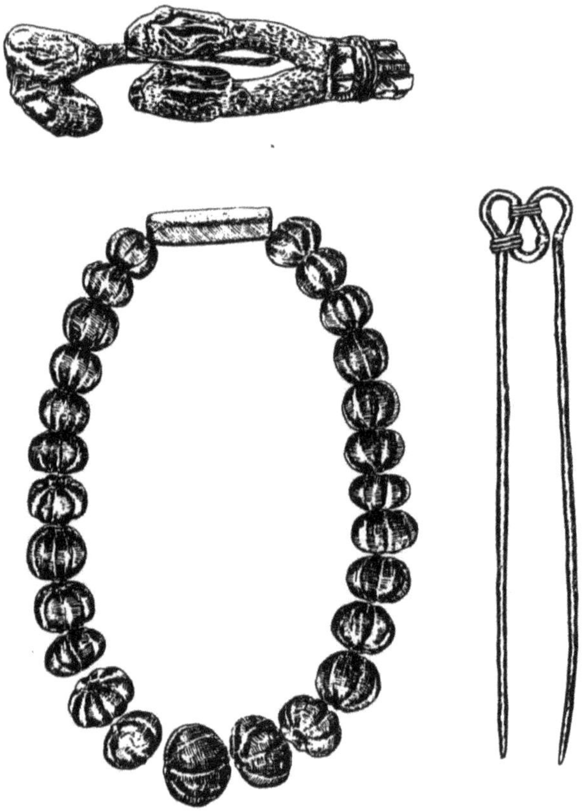

Figure 4 Silver bracelet and omega pin and glass bead necklace from Novi Pazar.

Figure 5 Carved amber beads and figures from Novi Pazar and Atenica.

and iron spears. The female grave contained a set of silver jewellery for a very gracile adult or a young girl. The set consisted of a pair of bracelets of Mramorac type, a pair of fibulae with rectangular plate, a pair of bracelets with snake heads, a ring, omega-pins and saltaleons, some Scythian arrowheads and a large amount of amber, both amorphous as well as shaped. Among the finds not associated with either grave is a bronze ornament with a palmette which was probably a part of horse gear. A separate group of finds consists of pottery: imported Greek black-figure vessels (an olpe, two large and one small skyphoi) and numerous locally manufactured vessels. The finds from Pečka Banja date to the end of the sixth and the beginning of the fifth centuries BC but have not been completely published (Palavestra 1984; Jeftović 1990: 185-187).

Lisijevo Polje
Lisijevo Polje is located near the village of Donje Luge, close to Berane in Montenegro. At Lisijevo Polje a small mound (5 m in diameter and 0.80 m in height) was accidentally opened and the remains of a skeleton and rich grave offerings were discovered. Beside the investigated mound were several similar ones which have not been excavated. A considerable amount of Glasinac type bronze jewellery was found as was a pair of broad bronze bracelets (probably belonging to an older grave), several bronze ornaments for clothing (fibulae, pectoral, pendants), some pottery, a pair of iron spears and a large amount of amber. Analysis of the material documented the existence of two burials: one a male and the other a female. The pre-eminent place among the finds is held by four amber plaques with incised figural motifs: a larger trapezoid plaque with a relief of a rider on a galloping horse accompanied with a hound; a pendant (a head with visible Archaic smile); and plaques representing a hare and a boar. Both technically and artistically, the plaques are superbly executed and may be listed among the most beautiful pieces manufactured in the workshops of south Italy. The finds date to the end of the sixth and the beginning of the fifth centuries BC (Srejović and Marković 1981).

Interpretation

One aspect of princely tombs which has never been discussed is the symbolic position of tombs within their microregions and their relation with the wider geographic areas. Graves (particularly monumental ones) although built for the deceased have exceptional importance for the living members of a community. An individual's leadership within larger social groups (such as those established in prehistoric Europe after the 'agricultural revolution')

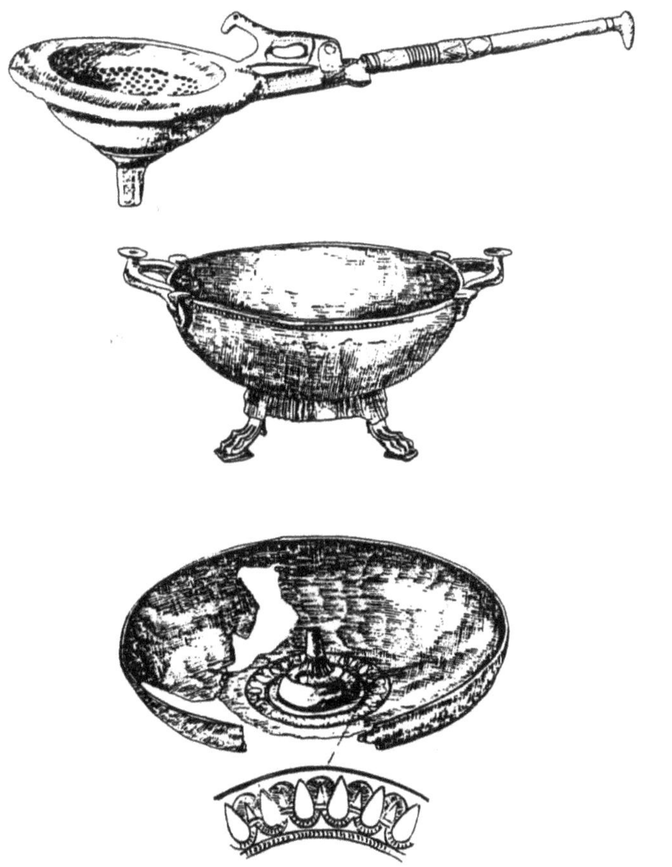

Figure 6 Bronze strainer and vessel and silver phiale from Novi Pazar.

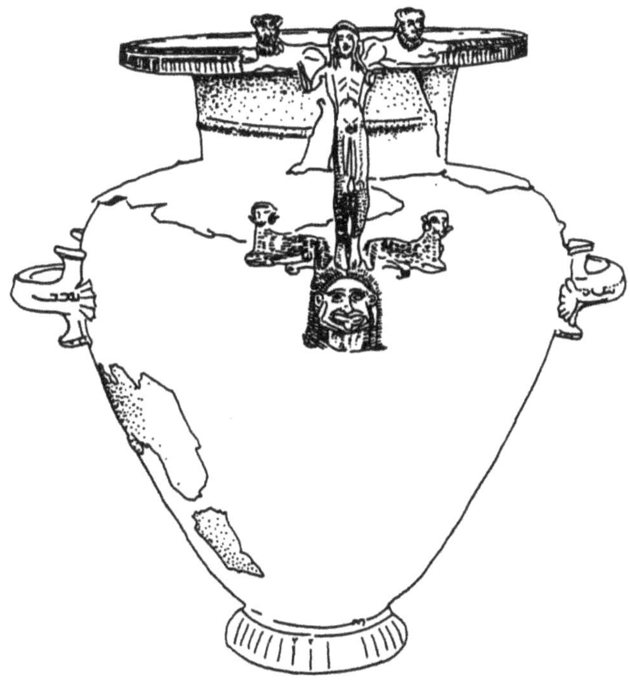

Figure 7 Bronze hydria from Novi Pazar.

needed to be recurrently confirmed by external insignia. Constant confirmation of leadership via the leader's personal contacts with the community members, although adequate for smaller groups and generally characteristic of primates, was impossible within complex social structures (Fleming 1973: 188).

According to some interpretations monumental megalithic tombs of the Neolithic and Bronze Ages of western Europe played their decisive role in maintaining the social structure on three levels. The first was the ritual level, on which the religious rites at the grave directed the entire community's attention to prominent individuals, regardless of whether the latter were chiefs, priests or both. On the second level, the tombs designated the centres which determined and directed the allegiance of an individual to his group in terms of territory, thus enforcing the centripetal tendencies in the community. This last aspect was particularly important for those communities which claimed certain territory even if, due to extensive agriculture or to nomadic migrations, they did not inhabit it continually. Finally, burials of the prominent individuals pointed out the power of living leaders, especially if their power was the result of kinship with the deceased or was inherited in some other way (Fleming 1973: 189-190).

In the early Iron Age of western and central Europe, princely tombs were a cultural phenomenon similar to the contemporary princely tombs of the Balkan Peninsula (Palavestra 1988) and had a clear territorial and regional significance. The term *Fürstengräberkreis* was proposed in order to denote the territorial surroundings of a princely tomb both in geographical, and in socio-political sense (Champion 1994: 146). In addition to the fact that their huge mounds are easily perceptible, prominent overground symbols (such as the stone stelae and monuments in Hirschlanden) confirm the importance of these tombs as clear and vivid signposts. (Zürn 1970; Mohen 1987: 45-46) One can only imagine how many monuments made of perishable wood must have marked and decorated the mighty princely tombs throughout Europe and the Balkan Peninsula (Bittel 1981: 92). The existence of ritual 'quadrate enclosures' (*Viereckschanze*) in the vicinity of the mounds confirmed a wider social and ritual dimension of princely tombs in central Europe (Bittel 1981). In western and central Europe however, the territorial spheres of the princely tombs were closely connected with the settlements as regional centres (*Fürstenzitze*) which were very important focal points of power and influence within a territory. The relationship between inner social structure and regional matters, based on the study of princely centres and tombs has been discussed in a number of studies (Frankenstein and

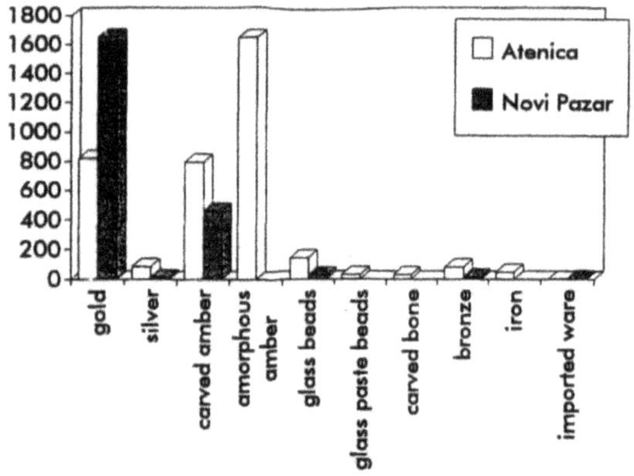

Figure 8: Comparison of finds from Atenica and Novi Pazar.

material	Atenica	Novi Pazar	Total
gold	823	1654	2477
silver	85	12	97
carved amber	797	459	1256
amorphous amber	1647		1647
glass beads	144	26	170
glass paste beads	28		28
carved bone	28		28
bronze	80	14	94
iron	46		46
imported ware	1	2	3
total	3679	2167	5846

Figure 9: Comparison of total number of finds from Atenica and Novi Pazar.

Rowlands 1978; Champion 1994).

For the princely tombs of the central Balkan region a somewhat different cultural model has recently been proposed. The absence of big 'central' settlements as regional economic, trading and ritual centres and the distribution of princely tombs along major communications suggested that society was based on seasonal cattle-breeding and on the control over pastoral and trade routes (Palavestra 1989; 1993: 281-288; 1994b). Nomadic and transhumant cattle-breeding (with its variants and regional differences)[1] could be documented in the Balkans from the beginning of the Eneolithic period (Grašanin 1977; 1994). This branch of economy, dominant in the Balkans and the Mediterranean (Braudel 1990: 85-102) from prehistory to the present left indelible marks in the culture, life-style and customs of the population of the region. The early Iron Age population of the central Balkans practised cattle-breeding. Classical written sources have confirmed this fact. A well known speech quoted by Arrian which Alexander the Great delivered to the Macedonians depicts the contemporary Balkan population concisely and vividly: 'Philip found you living as poor nomads, dressed mostly in hides, grazing your scarce herds, and fighting over them without much success, with Illyrians, Triballoi and Thracians' (Papazoglu 1969: 16). Other sources also argue that the palaeo-Balkan population was very mobile (due to nomadic and semi-nomadic cattle-breeding) and was often in conflict over herds or the salt-licks which were so important for the cattle (Papazoglu 1969: 361-364).

Many forms of ancient Balkan pastoral life and economy have remained almost unchanged for centuries. Perhaps one of the reasons for this was the limited choice of cultural models; the societies of transhumant and nomadic cattle-breeders were similarly shaped based on their economic structure. On the other hand, the conservatism and traditionalism of these communities helped to preserve for centuries their institutions (i.e., legal standards, rituals, costume, housing, exploitation of pasture-land, patriarchal-tribal societal structure). A good example is the custom common among palaeo-Balkan populations (as well as among the farmers of the Medieval period) of allocating pasture-land to community members every eight years (Suić 1967: 103-104; Pašalić 1967: 115-116; Čače 1979: 118-119).

Abundant ethnographic and historical material and literature about Balkan pastoralists in the Middle Ages and the modern epoch provide sufficient data for hypothesising about palaeo-Balkan cattle-breeders (Čubrilović 1976; Antonijević 1982). Isolated as they are, relicts of the ancient life in the Balkan Peninsula cannot serve as analogies in the interpretation of archaeological data. However, if set into a firmer methodological framework (as suggested by modern Balkanology) ample ethnographical and historical data on cattle-breeding in the Balkans offer a solid basis for establishing an archaeological model which is subject to further examination and thus to verification or refutation (Hodder 1982). In a methodological sense, this balkanological framework includes both the archaeological implications of 'long-term history' as proposed by Fernand Braudel and the Annales historiographical school as well as the anthropo-geographical dimension of J. Cvijić's balkanology (Hodder 1987; Bintliff 1991; Novaković 1992; Palavestra 1994a). In the discussion about the problems of the central Balkan Iron Age and especially about the princely tombs it was this methodological approach that paved the way for the establishment of specific archaeological models (Bankoff and Palavestra 1986; Palavestra 1989; 1993; 1994b).

The princely tombs of the early Iron Age are located in parts of the central Balkans famous for centuries for the intensive transhumant and nomadic cattle-breeding (Cvijić 1922; Ršumović 1976). Bearing in mind the fact that the princely tombs all appeared within a rather narrow span of time (from the last decades of the sixth to the first decades of the fifth centuries BC) a major concentration of power over the same period in the same relatively limited space must be assumed. This would suggest that several centres of power existed in the region delimited by the Drina River in the west, the Ibar River in the east, the Zapadna Morava River in the north and the Beli Drim and Erenik Rivers in the south. Some of the wealthier graves of the Glasinac complex, situated either in the culture's home area on the left bank of the Drina, or in Herzegovina and in the Zeta River valley, could also be included as related phenomena and comparative material (Palavestra 1984: 60-65). Regarding the pastoralist character of the palaeo-Balkan population and the region's specific geomorphology (for transhumant and nomadic cattle-breeding) the princely tombs of the early Iron Age in the central Balkans may be viewed from the aspect of nomadic migrations and territories as symbolic strongholds of power and centres of communities. In order to establish a better basis for the hypothesis that the princely tombs were landmarks of cattle-breeders' territories (i.e., the territories for seasonal pasturing controlled by a certain group) it is necessary to provide a more thorough insight into the particular positions of the graves.

Positions of the tombs

The monumental tomb in Pilatovići (dated to the second half of the sixth century BC and thus the earliest of the princely tombs) is located near Užička Požega , south of the Zapadna Morava River, on the right bank of the Moravica River, in the vicinity of its confluence with the Zapadna Morava. The tomb situated in the river valley (at 310 m a.s. l.), while the necropolis with mounds (dated to the early Iron Age) is located 500 m to the south. Mt. Krstac, a branch of the Stari Vlah Mountain range which descends towards the Morava River valley, raises above the princely tomb (Zotović 1985: 80-83).

Two princely mounds in Atenica are located in the south-eastern suburbs of Čačak, on the right bank of the Zapadna Morava (at 237 m a.s.l.). The slopes of Mt. Jelica (also a part of the Stari Vlah Mountain range) rise to the south-west. Although only 23 kilometres from Pilatovići (as the crow flies) these sites are clearly separated by Mt. Jelica and the Ovčar-Kablar Gorge and sit in two distinctive micro-regions (Đuknić and Jovanović 1966).

Novi Pazar is situated on a natural elevation on the right bank of the Deževska River which dominates the river valleys near the river's confluence with the Raška (500 m a.s. l.). Across the Raška, the slopes of the Golija Mountain range rise toward the northwest, while Mt. Rogozna rises in the southeast and east (Mano-Zisi and Popović 1969a; 1969b).

The princely mound of Pečka Banja is located in Metochia on the left bank of the Beli Brim River at 500 m a.s.l. in the northern fringes of the Beli Drim river valley. The slopes of the high Rusulija and Mokra Gora Mountains rise to the north and the fertile valley of the Beli Drim spreads southwards. The place is the crossroads of two routes, one leading from the mountainous region of Rožaje to Metohia and the other going through the Gorge of Rugovo (Palavestra 1984: 58-60; Jeftović 1990: 185-187).

The grave at Lisijevo Polje was discovered near Berane, in the Lim River valley, on the river's right bank (c. 670 m a. s.l.). The Lim valley and Lisijevo Polje are surrounded by high mountains, with the highest peaks on Bjelasica in the west and Mokra Planina in the southeast. Lisijevo Polje, too, is located on the crossroads of routes leading through mountains, gorges and river valleys (Srejović and Marković 1981).

It is not difficult to derive common characteristics shared by all princely tombs. They were all built in river valleys and on flat terrain or smooth slopes (the latter enhancing their visibility). All of the tombs have mountainous hinterlands suitable for cattle-breeding and all are located along the routes which run between the mountains and the valleys, routes that were used for centuries for trade and seasonal pastoral migrations. It was easy to control trade and other movements from these positions (Palavestra 1989) and to demonstrate the excellence of the graves to all travellers. It is not unusual to find graves along roads and there is also evidence that burial along herders' routes was a custom highly praised among Balkan cattle-breeders, a custom aimed at enabling the deceased 'to watch over' his herds (Antonijević 1982: 133).

It is noteworthy that contemporary rich graves (although obviously of lower-ranking individuals) were discovered in the neighbourhood of some of the above-mentioned princely graves. Hallstatt necropolises were discovered near Pilatovići: Uzići, Ražana, Godljevo, Kriva Reka (Zotović 1985). At the Guševac site in Mrčajevci (Palavestra 1984: 68; 1994b: 147) and at Ljuljaci (Srejović 1990) not far from Atenica, there are also a few rich graves with mounds. At Novopazarska Banja, near Novi Pazar, an Iron Age necropolis has been excavated (A. Jovanović 1995: 31-40), and another luxurious find, a few decades younger than the grave near St. Peter's church, was discovered 25 km north of Novi Pazar in the village Kruševica (Srejović and Vukadin 1988). Necropolises with mounds, such as Dojevići or Glogovik on Mt. Golija have also been excavated (Letica 1979; 1982). A similar situation exists at Pečka Banja with the Boka necropolis and some other graves from the Iron Age found in its vicinity (Tasić 1979). These finds may document a stratified social structure, but it would be necessary to perform a comparative analysis of all the graves, (a task which is beyond the range of this study) before any conclusions could be drawn.

The territorial distribution of the princely tombs could depict the hypothetical borders of the early Iron Age regional groups in the central Balkans (particularly in the light of the 'stock-breeders hypothesis'). If the princely tombs are regarded as hypothetical, symbolic centres of territories, the boundaries of these territories could be partly reconstructed in schematic form by means of Thiessen (or Dirchlet) polygons. This method is frequently used in geography as an instrument of territorial analysis but has also been present in archaeology for decades. In archaeology, it is important to make sure that the sites which represent the centres of the polygons are contemporary and are of similar importance, size or both (Clarke 1971: 509-510; Hodder and Orton 1989: 59-60). Thiessen polygons were used to determine 'individual territories' around the large Neolithic mounds in southern England in order to emphasise social, ritual and territorial aspects of these graves (Renfrew 1973: 544-547). Although its use in archaeology was criticised for its abstractness and schematism (Braithwaite 1984: 96) this model can be applied in determining (at least roughly) the spheres of influence and control of a certain group.

I have used the Thiessen polygon method in an attempt to draw hypothetical territorial borders the centres of which could be the princely tombs of the central Balkan early Iron Age (Fig. 10). This archaeological model has also incorporated neighbouring regions (the Glasinac area) and the 'warrior's' mound near Romaja in Metohia. The princely tombs at Glasinac suggest a somewhat different social structure from the one represented by the princely tombs east of the Drina River (Čović 1979; Palavestra 1984: 60-64). The cultural model of the warrior's graves at Romaja differs significantly from that for the burials in Novi Pazar or Pečka Banja. The issue of complicated comparisons and interpretations of funerary rites and social structures of the Iron Age societies in the Balkan Peninsula cannot be raised in this paper. Within this model, the sites of Glasinac and Romaja were merely representatives of the regions and spheres of influence bordering upon the princely tombs areas of the central Balkans. The map shows that the Thiessen polygon model for the princely tombs of the central Balkans is not complete and that only hypothetical borders (rather than entire enclosed polygons) were depicted. The

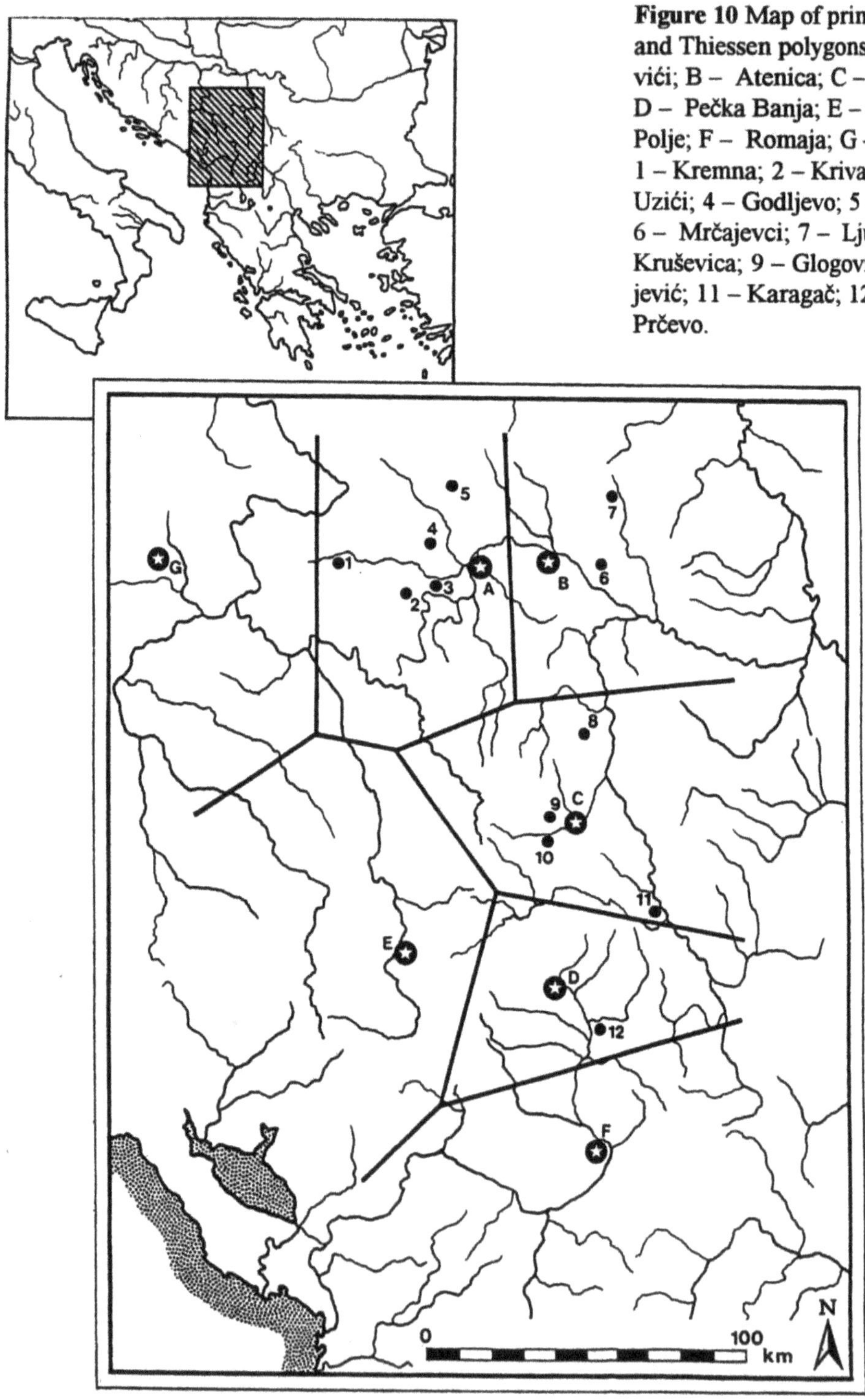

Figure 10 Map of principal sites and Thiessen polygons. A – Pilatovići; B – Atenica; C – Novi Pazar; D – Pečka Banja; E – Lisijevo Polje; F – Romaja; G – Glasinac; 1 – Kremna; 2 – Kriva Reka; 3 – Uzići; 4 – Godljevo; 5 – Ražana; 6 – Mrčajevci; 7 – Ljuljaci; 8 – Kruševica; 9 – Glogovik; 10 – Dojević; 11 – Karagač; 12 – Boka-Prčevo.

reason for this is the limited number of princely tombs and the lack of accessible archaeological data. Hypothetical as they are, these borders suggest the existence of enclosed territories with the princely tombs as their symbolic, ritual and perhaps political centres.

Therefore, the site of Pilatovići may have been the centre of the territory which covered the Zlatar and Zlatibor Mountains, the Zapadna Morava and Moravica River valleys, and, perhaps, the slopes of the Povlen and Maljen Mountains in the north across the Morava. The sphere of influence of Atenica stretched over Mt. Jelica, the Zapadna Morava valley and the slopes of the mountains of the Šumadija region north of the Zapadna Morava valley. The territory of the Novi Pazar princely tomb covered the Golija, Rogozna and Kopaonik Mountains and the Novi Pazar valley (the only lowlands in the region) as well as the gorges of the Ibar, Raška and Deževa Rivers. The territory 'controlled' from Pečka Banja extended over the eastern slopes of the Prokletije, Rusulija and Mokra Gora Mountains, the Gorge of Rugovo and the northern part of Metohia. The site of Lisijevo Polje (settled in the Berane basin in the Ibar River valley) was in the centre of the region bordered by the Bjelasica, Crni Vrh, Jadovnik and Giljeva Mountains.

Stock-breeding

All these regions, particularly the highlands, are well-known for their intensive transhumant and nomadic cattle-breeding. It is not necessary to quote vast geographic, ethnographic and historical literature to confirm this. However, it is interesting that J. Cvijić, when listing these mountains as highly appropriate for stock-grazing noted, said that 'the richest and finest pastures in the peninsula are located on the southern and western slopes of Mt. Rusulija, between Peć and Rožaje (Cvijić 1922: 85-86): this is exactly above Pečka Banja. Above the Atenica site, the highest point of Mt. Jelica is called Ovčar (*ovčar* = a shepherd) and although the mountain is no longer famous for cattle-breeding this may point to the cattle-breeding history of this region. The toponym of Pilatovići also implies the same origin since it was derived from the name of a seasonal station belonging to the Vlach fraternity of Pilatovac or Pilatovići referred to in the medieval sources (Filipović 1963: 62, 64).

As stated above, the princely tombs are located in lowlands beneath high mountain pastures on the age-old cattle-breeders' routes as conditioned by rare mountain passes, gorges and river valleys. Lowlands and river valleys with their mild climate were as important for the nomadic and transhumant cattle-breeding as were the mountains. They were the regions of wintertime pastures without which live-stock-breeding in the Balkans would have been impossible.

Data on seasonal cattle-breeding in the Balkans clearly show the importance attached to the territory controlled by a community (i.e., either a fraternity, a *katun*, or a tribe)[2]. Battles had been fought over pastures and livestock-breeders' routes and the duty of each community member was to defend the territory once it was occupied. For a community, boundaries of the occupied territories and pastures were marked with 'their dead' (i.e., their graves and monuments) (Lutovac 1976: 25). Seasonal movements between winter and summer pastures were strictly regulated by the 'mountain regime' (i.e., the customs of traditional law which meticulously regulated relations among cattle-breeders, their departure into the mountain (*izdig*), their return to the lowlands (*zdig*), the roads, the use of pasture and water, the habitations, etc.) (Čubrilović 1976; Krstic' 1979). For the Balkan cattle-breeder, an ideally conceived territory contains summer pastures in the highlands, winter pastures in the valleys, an abundance of water and convenient roads which are easy to control and defend. Livestock-breeders and their herds migrated constantly during the year between the 'upper' and 'lower' mountains on the one hand and the winter stations in the lowlands on the other (Lutovac 1976: 26-27). Although other nomadic movements also took place in the Balkans, seasonal movements mostly occurred within such territorial entities (Dunare 1976; Ršumović 1976; Lutovac 1976). If, due to the geomorphological character of the terrain or bad weather, a community had been prevented from performing the annual cycle in its own territory, it would have been forced to move further with its herds. The crossing of other tribes' territories was strictly regulated by the standards of customary law and must have tested such standards (Čubrilović 1976). This was especially the case with winter stations which, as they were harder to find in the mountainous regions, were extremely valuable. Records show that due to the severe climate cattle-breeders have migrated all the way from Vasojevići (Montenegro), or from the Tara Mountain, to the Zapadna Morava valley and the vicinity of Čačak (near Atenica) (Lutovac 1976: 32-33). The control of winter pastures was very important and even more profitable than agriculture, a fact to which documents from the period of the Turkish occupation attest (Antonijević 1982: 41-42).

The Balkan cattle-breeders of the Iron Age must have controlled their territories with equal care. Scarce winter pastures, river valleys, basins, crossroads of pastoralists' routes and particularly 'neuralgic spots' had to be protected with extreme 'jealousy'. It was to symbolically lay claim to a territory that the mounds of the princely tombs were erected in such locations. According to one of the hypotheses, the big prehistoric mounds of the Wessex culture in the south of England also had marked cattle-breeders' territory (Fleming 1971; 1973: 580-581). Extremely opulent 'princely' tombs at Altai (contemporary with the Balkan princely tombs) also seem to have been the landmarks of cattle-breeders' territories. According to the excavators (Polosmak 1994) the recently discovered and extremely well-preserved Ukoka mound (Altai) was the landmark of winter pastures which belonged to the plateau's semi-nomadic inhabitants. It has also been noted that during the conquest of Thrace Darius erected stone mounds in order to claim newly occupied territories (Theodossiev 1995: 383). The Thracian Odrisian rulers also built big mounds as landmarks of the regions they controlled and as frontiers with neighbouring tribes (Topalov 1994: 133). It is also likely that the princely tombs of the central Balkan early Iron Age played the role of symbolic spiritual *stožer* or strongholds of cattle-breeders' communities.[3]

Thiessen polygons suggest hypothetical borders of these territories. A few regions famous for their seasonal cattle-breeding (with high-summer pastures, wintertime river valleys and basins and with routes suitable for seasonal migrations and trade) were delineated. The princely tombs were located on the dominant points of such regions (i.e., on winter pastures by the communications, even on the cross-roads). Moreover, settlements existed in the vicinity of some of these rich graves. This could be the case not far from the Novi Pazar grave at the site of Postenje where rich Iron Age material has been recovered (Jeftović 1990: 209). The existence of permanent settlements in the vicinity of winter pastures would fit in with the transhumant tradition (Vlahović 1976: 42).

Conclusions

It is most likely that the princely tombs, as centres of social power, probably functioned on all the three above-mentioned levels: ritual, territorial and tribal. (Fleming 1973: 189). The ritual level, on which the attention of the community was directed to the leader both in cult and religious aspects, has been confirmed in the case of the Balkan princely tombs. During the burial in Atenica, complex sacrificial rites were carried out. Six animals (three aurochs, two boars and a dog) were sacrificed on the previously prepared base of the mound. The rite is associated with Indo-European triadic sacrifices, similar to the Roman suovetaurilia (Čače 1985). According to S. Čače, the elaborate sacrificial structure within the mound (which was also used for other sacrificial rituals), the spatial orientation to the North and the South, and the symbolism of numbers stand as evidence of a complex theology and suggest that the deceased may have been the 'king' in the archaic sense of the term which also meant the chief priest (Čače 1985).

On the second, territorial, level the mounds functioned as symbolic centres of cattle-breeding regions. They were located on winter pasture-lands in the valleys where all the livestock-breeders of the region congregated during the winter season. It was probably the right place and time for the enhancement of cohesive and centripetal trends in a mobile community which was otherwise dispersed over the vast area of summer pastures. Monumental mounds such as Pilatovići and Atenica could hardly have been built during summer, when almost entire populations had left the valleys with their herds. The winter season was the perfect time for engaging extra labourers in the construction of the big mounds. This hypothesis could be confirmed or refuted by pollen analysis which, unfortunately, is yet to be performed. These mounds may have also been the secondary burials of chieftains who died in the mountains during the summer or who were killed on the battlefield. The custom of performing secondary or repeated burials is common among Balkan livestock-breeders even in modern epoch (Antonijević 1982: 135). The mounds also served as focal points for territorial loyalty of various groups (fraternity, *katun* or some other social structure) which subsequently grew into more compound social structures (tribe, the tribal alliances, etc.). A similar process of evolution of cattle-breeders' communities into tribes occurred in the Medieval period and is documented in written sources (Đurđev 1963: 165-166).

The third, clan level, cannot be considered apart from the territorial and ritual levels. The true significance of the family or the clan can be deduced from the examples of family burials in Pilatovići, Atenica and Pečka Banja. According to some explanations, the princely tombs even document the divinization and heroization of the deceased (Stipčević 1984; Čače 1985). Kinship with the former ruler and his family could certainly have enhanced the power of a new ruler. The clan structure of the society and presence of prominent individuals as leaders are characteristics of Balkan cattle-breeders. In the Middle Ages, the leader in the Balkans had great authority among his fellowmen, no matter what his title was: *katunar*, *čelnik*, *ćehaja*, *celingas* (all meaning the leader) or even *knez* (the prince). The leadership over a *katun* was often inherited which led to the establishment of prominent families (although leadership was sometimes less traditionally based) (Filipović 1963: 81-91; Antonijević 1982: 48). In the light of the princely tombs, there is no doubt that leadership implied a religious dimension. Whether the deceased was the 'archaic king-priest' or not, such a dimension must have heightened the position of his clan.

The princely tombs of the central Balkan early Iron Age might have been important symbolic, cult and social centres of the cattle-breeders' territories. Cattle-breeding communities in general (i.e., not only those of the Balkan Peninsula) are conservative and retain ancient relicts and obsolete social institutions. Archaeological models can, therefore, be easily built on the basis of ethnographic and historical data. (Gibson 1988). They can be tested and modified in comparison with the archaeological material. The princely tombs of the Iron Age reflect the social structure and territorial organisation similar, but not identical to, those of the Balkan cattle-breeders of the historical periods. These prehistoric graves point to a considerably greater social power of the deceased, probably based on the ritual role of the archaic 'king-priest'. The chronological horizon of the princely tombs is rather limited: they all emerge simultaneously, at the peak of the power and wealth of a clan society. Their sudden disappearance, however, suggests that the princely tombs, as an external manifestation of power, were the agonising endeavour of an archaic social structure and the last effort of a hierarchy trying to remain in power. Archaeological data show that this effort failed and that after the 'princely tomb' horizon the societal systems in the Balkans, as well as in Europe, changed.

Endnotes

1. In nomadic cattle-breeding the entire population migrates with the herd; in transhumant cattle-breeding only the herders migrate. There are many variants of these two basic types (Braudel 1990: 85-102; Dunare 1976).

2. *katun*: a cattle-breeder's mountain settlement and a also a form of social organisation.

3. *stožer:* a communal and indivisible piece of land belonging to the entire commune or fraternity of the Dinaric region (Cvijić 1922: 275).

Bibliography

Antonijević, D. 1982. *Obredi i Običaji Balkanskih Stočara.* Beograd: Balkanološki Institut SANU.

Babić, S. 1990. Graeco-Barbarian Contacts in the Early Iron Age Central Balkans. *Balcanica* 21: 168-183.

Bankoff, A. and A. Palavestra 1986. Prehistoric settlements in the Ribarska Reka microregion near Kruševac. *Balcanica* 16-17: 17-41.

Bintliff, J. 1991. The contribution of an Annaliste/structural history approach to archaeology. In *The Annales School and Archaeology*, edited by J. Bintliff, pp. 1-33. Leicester: Leicester University Press.

Bittel, K. 1981. Religion und Kult. In *Die Kelten in Baden Würtenberg*, edited by K. Bittel, W. Kimmig and S. Sciek, pp. 85-117. Stuttgart.

Braithwaite, M. 1984. Ritual and prestige in the prehistory of Wessex c. 2,200-1,400 BC: A new dimension to the archaeological evidence. In *Ideology, Power and Prehistory*, edited by D. Miller and C. Tilley, pp. 93-110. Cambridge: Cambridge University Press.

Braudel, F. 1990. *The Mediterranean and the Mediterranean World in the Age of Philip II.* London: Fontana Press.

Champion, S. 1994. Regional studies; a question of scale. In *Europe in the First Millennium B.C.*, edited by K. Kristiansen and J. Jensen, pp. 145-150. Sheffield: J.Collis.

Clarke, D. 1971. *Analytical Archaeology.* London: Methuen.

Cvijić, J. 1922. *Balkansko Poluostrvo.* Beograd: Državna Štamparija Kraljevine Srba, Hrvata i Slovenaca.

Čače, S. 1979. Prilozi proučavanju političkog uređenja naroda sjeverozapadnog Ilirika. *Radovi Filozofskog Fakulteta u Zadru* 18: 43-125.

Čače, S. 1985. Obredi uz kneževski grob u Atenici i tragovi arhaičnog kraljevstva u Iliriku. *Radovi Filozofskog Fakulteta u Zadru* 24(2): 13-32.

Čović, B. 1979. Kneževski grobovi glasinačkog područja. In *Sahranjivanje kod Ilira*, edited by M. Garašanin, pp. 143-169. Beograd: Srpska Akademija Nauka i Umetnosti.

Čović, B. 1983. Importation of bronze vessels in the western Balkans (7th to 5th Century). In *L'Adriatico tar Medriteraneo e Penisole Balcanica nell'Antchita*, pp. 147-154. Taranto.

Čubrilović, V. (ed.) 1976. *Odredbe Pozitivnog Zakonodavstva i Običajnog Prava o Sezonskim Kretanjima Stočara u Jugoistočnoj Evropi kroz Vekove.* Beograd: Balkanološki Institut SANU.

Dunare, N. 1976.Typologie pastorale traditionnelle Sud-Est Européenne. In *Odredbe Pozitivnog Zakonodavstva i Običajnog Prava o Sezonskim Kretanjima Stočara u Jugoistočnoj Evropi kroz Vekove*, edited by V. Čubrilović, pp. 189-212. Beograd: Balkanološki Institut SANU.

Đuknić, M. and B. Jovanović 1966. *Ilirska Kneževska Nekropola u Atenici.* Čačak: Narodni Muzej Čačak.

Đurđev, B. 1963. Teritorijalizacija katunske organizacije do kraja XV veka. In *Simpozijum o Srednjovjekovnom Katunu*, edited by M. Filipović, pp. 143-169. Sarajevo: Naučno Društvo SR Bosne i Hercegovine.

Filipović, M. 1963. Struktura i organizacija srednjovekovnih katuna. In *Simpozijum o Sednjovjekovnom Katunu*, edited by M. Filipović, pp. 45-112. Sarajevo: Naučno Društvo SR Bosne i Hercegovine.

Fleming, A. 1971. Models for the development of the Wessex culture. In *The Explanation of Culture change: Models in Prehistory*, edited by C. Renfrew, pp. 571-585. London: Duckworth.

Fleming, A. 1973. Tombs for the living. *Man* 8(2): 177-193.

Frankenstein, S. and M. Rowlands 1978. The internal structure and regional context of Early Iron Age society in south-west Germany. *Bulletin of the Institute of Archaeology, University of London* 15: 73-112.

Garašanin, M. 1977. Zur Frage der Transhumanz in der dinarischen Bronzezeit. *Balcanica* 8: 37-42.

Garašanin, M. 1988. Formation et origines des Illyriens. In *Les Illyriens et les Albanais*, edited by M. Garašanin, pp. 81-144. Beograd: Srpska Akademija Nauka i Umetnosti.

Garašanin, M. 1994. Pastoralisme semi-nomade et nomade dans la Péninsule balkanique à l'Énéolithique et au début de l'Age du Bronze. *Balcanica* 25(1): 7-18.

Gibson, D. 1988. Agro-pastoralosm and Regional Social Organization in Early Ireland. In *Tribe and Polity in Late Prehistoric Europe*, edited by D.B. Gibson and M.N. Gaselowitz, pp. 41-68. New York.

Hodder, I. 1982. *The Present Past*. London: Batsford.

Hodder, I. 1987. The contribution of the long term. In *Archaeology as Long-term History*, edited by I. Hodder, pp. 1-18. Cambridge: Cambridge University Press.

Hodder, I. and Orton, C. 1989. *Spatial Analysis in Archaeology*. Cambridge: Cambridge University Press.

Jeftović, J. (ed.) 1990. *Gospodari Srebra. Gvozdeno Doba na tlu Srbije*. Beograd: Narodni Muzej Beograd.

Jovanović, A. 1995. Arheološka istraživanja u Novopazarskoj banji. *Novopazarski Zbornik* 19: 31-68.

Jovanović, B. 1979. Atenica i kneževski grobovi na Glasincu. In *Sahranjivanje kod Ilira*, edited by M. Garašanin, pp. 63-71. Beograd: Srpska Akademija Nauka i Umetnosti.

Krstić, Đ. 1979. *Pravni Običaji kod Kuča*. Beograd: Balkanološki Institut SANU.

Letica, Z. 1979. Ilirski grobovi u Dojevićiu. In *Sahranjivanje kod Ilira,* edited by M. Garašanin, pp. 73-78. Beograd: Srpska Akademija Nauka i Umetnosti.

Letica, Z. 1982. Pešter u bronzano i gvozdeno doba. *Starinar* 32: 9-17.

Lutovac, M. 1976. Stočarska kretanja u planinama Crnogorskih Brda i narodne regule pri korišćenju pašnjaka. In *Odredbe Pozitivnog Zakonodavstva i Običajnog Prava o Sezonskim Kretanjima Stočara u Jugoistočnoj Evropi kroz Vekove*, edited by V. Čubrilović, pp. 23-40. Beograd: Balkanološki Institut SANU.

Mano-Zisi, Đ. and Lj. Popović 1969a. Der Fund von Novi Pazar (Srebien). *Bericht der Römish-Germanischen Kommission des Deutschen Archäologischen Instituts* 50: 191-208.

Mano-Zisi, Đ. and Lj. Popović 1969b. *Novi Pazar - Ilirsko-grčki Nalaz*. Beograd: Narodni Muzej Beograd.

Mohen, J-P. 1987. Hirschlanden. In *Trésors des Princes Celtes*, edited by J-P. Mohen, A. Duval and C Eluère, pp. 45-46. Paris: Editions de la Réunion des Musées Nationaux.

Novaković, P. 1992. Po Marxu in pred Braudelom: Geografska šola Jovana Cvijća in arheologija. *Arheo* 15: 8-28.

Pašalić, E. 1967. Problemi ekonomskog razvitka u unutrašnjosti rimske provincije Dalmacije. In *Simpozijum o Ilirima u Antičko Doba*, edited by A. Benac, pp. 111-138. Sarajevo: Centar za Balkanološka Ispitivanja Akademije Nauka i Umjetnosti Bosne i Hercegovine.

Palavestra, A. 1984. *Kneževski Grobovi Starijeg Gvozdenog Doba na Centralnom Balkanu*. Beograd: Balkanološki Institut SANU.

Palavestra, A. 1988. The typological similarities of early Iron Age 'princely burials' of the Balkans and central Europe. *Balcanica* 18-19: 83-88.

Palavestra, A. 1989. Modeli trgovine i društvene strukture na centralnom Balkanu gvozdenog doba. *Balcanica* 20: 191-209.

Palavestra, A. 1993. *Praistorijski Ćilibar na Centralnom i Zapadnom Balkanu*. Beograd: Balkanološki Institut SANU.

Palavestra, A. 1994a. Balkanology, archaeology and long-term history. *Balcanica* 25(1): 83-98.

Palavestra, A. 1994b. Prehistoric trade and a cultural model for princely tombs in the central Balkans. In *Europe in the First Millennium B.C.*, edited by K. Kristiansen and J. Jensen, pp. 45-56. Sheffield: J.Collis.

Papazoglu, F. 1969. *Srednjobalkanska Plemena u Predrimsko Doba*. Sarajevo: Centar za Balkanološka Ispitivanja Akademije Nauka i Umjetnosti Bosne i Hercegovine.

Parović-Pešikan, M. 1960. O karakteru gr~kog materijala na Glasincu i putevima njegovog prodiranja. *Starinar* 11: 21-45.

Polosmak, N. 1994. Siberian mummy unearthed. *National Geographic Magazine* (October) 1994: 80-103.

Ršumović, R. 1976. Geografski uslovi i njihova uloga u evoluciji stočarskih kretanja u Jugoslaviji. In *Odredbe Pozitivnog Zakonodavstva i Običajnog Prava o Sezonskim Kretanjima Stočara u Jugois-*

točnoj Evropi kroz Vekove, edited by V. Čubrilović, pp. 159-176. Beograd: Balkanološki Institut SANU.

Renfrew, C. 1973. Monuments, mobilization and social organization in neolithic Wessex. In *The Explanation of Culture Change: Models in Prehistory*, edited by C. Renfrew, pp. 539-558. London: Duckworth.

Srejović, D. 1981. Kulture gvozdenog doba, In *Istorija Srpskog Naroda I*, edited by S. Ćirković, pp. 54-65. Beograd: Srpska Književna Zadruga.

Srejović, D. 1990. Tribalski grobovi u Ljuljacima. *Starinar* 40-41: 141-153.

Srejović, D. and Č. Marković 1981. A find from Lisijevo Polje near Ivangrad (Montenegro). *Archaeologia Iugoslavica* 20-21: 70-79.

Srejović, D. and O. Vukadin 1988. Blago iz Kruševice. *Raška Baština* 3: 7-14.

Stipčević, A. 1984. Kult heroiziranog pokojnika u ilirskoj religiji. In *Duhovna Kultura Ilira*, edited by A. Benac, pp. 215-221. Sarajevo: Centar za Balkanološka Ispitivanja Akademije Nauka i Umjetnosti Bosne i Hercegovine.

Suić, M. 1967. Nekoliko etnoloških podataka o antičkim Ilirima u djelima grčkih i rimskih pisaca. In *Simpozijum o Ilirima u Antičko Doba*, edited by A. Benac, pp. 99-110. Sarajevo: Centar za Balkanološka Ispitivanja Akademije Nauka i Umjetnosti Bosne i Hercegovine.

Tasić, N. 1979. Sahranjivanje na nekropoli Boka u Prčevu kod Kline (Kosovo). In *Sahranjivanje kod Ilira*, edited by M. Garašanin, pp. 89-100. Beograd: Srpska Akademija Nauka i Umetnosti.

Theodossiev, N. 1995. The sacred mountain of the ancient Thracianas. *Thracia* 11: 371-384.

Topalov, S. 1994. *The Odrisian Kingdom from the late 5th to the mid 4th c. BC. Contribution to the Study of its Coinage and History*. Sofia: Agato.

Vasić, R. 1986. Prilozi proučavanju Atenice. *Zbornik Radova Narodnog Muzeja u Čačku* 16: 5-21.

Vasić, R. 1987. Kneževski grobovi iz Novog Pazara i Atenice. In *Praistorija Jugoslavenskih Zemalja V*, edited by A. Benac, pp. 644-650. Sarajevo: Centar za Balkanološka Ispitivanja Akademije Nauka i Umjetnosti Bosne i Hercegovine.

Vasić, R. 1990. Gvozdeno doba u Srbiji. In *Gospodari Srebra. Gvozdeno Doba na Tlu Srbije*, edited by J. Jevtović pp. 15-22. Beograd: Narodni Muzej Beograd.

Vlahović, P. 1976. Katuni i sezonska kretanja stočara u jugozapadnoj Srbiji u prvoj polovini XX veka. In *Odredbe Pozitivnog Zakonodavstva i Običajnog Prava o Sezonskim Kretanjima Stočara u Jugoistočnoj Evropi kroz Vekove*, edited by V. Čubrilović, pp. 41-48. Beograd: Balkanološki Institut SANU.

Zotović, M. 1984. Nekropola u Pilatovići ima kod Požega i neke karakteristike u načinu sahranjivanja pokojnika. In *Sahranjivanje kod Ilira*, edited by M. Garašanin, pp. 31-48. Beograd: Srpska Akademija Nauka i Umetnosti.

Zotović, M. 1985. *Arheološki i Etnički Problemi Bronzanog i Gvozdenog Doba Zapadne Srbije*. Beograd: Savez Arheoloških Društava Jugoslavije.

Zürn, H. 1970. *Hallstattforschungen in Nordwürtemberg*. Stuttgart.

Chapter 7

From quality to quantity: wealth, status and prestige in the Iberian Iron Age[1]

Fernando Quesada

Summary

During the Orientalizing Period in southern Iberia, both wealth and status were displayed in funerary contexts by the deposition of symbols of excellence, such as chariots or imported goods, which were not available to lower status groups. However, weapons were conspicuously rare among grave-goods, and the concept of quality seems to have been more important than the mere accumulation of objects.

Both characteristics seem to have changed after about 425 BC. Weapons appear to take precedence over any other category of objects as symbols of status and/or wealth. At the same time, the old concept of quality was largely abandoned and the accumulation of lower-quality imported goods (such as Attic black-glaze pottery in relatively large quantities) was used to indicate wealth and/or status.

In this paper I aim to show that while the quantitative assessment of wealth is a good (but incomplete and ambiguous) indicator of status in Iberian cemeteries, it is probably not so useful for the earlier, Orientalizing burial sites, where the type and symbolic nature of objects, more than mere quantity, was of paramount importance.

Introduction: Orientalizing Period and Iron Age in the Iberian Peninsula[2]

During the first decades of the eighth century BC the indigenous communities in the southern areas of the Iberian Peninsula saw their pattern of development altered as the result of new and intense foreign influences. Western Andalusia, where the Tartessian late Bronze Age Culture was already thriving, felt the cultural impact of Phoenician colonists from at least c. 800 BC. The colonists were mainly interested in the rich silver ores of Huelva[3], but also in the exploitation of fertile lands. Due to this added impetus, this area entered the Iron Age at a time when most other regions of Iberia lagged behind. The Phoenicians brought with them new technologies (such as the potter's wheel, iron metallurgy and more complex urban patterns) but for a long time these probably only affected the way of life of the ruling elites. The pre-existing local aristocracies were in fact reinforced, as the newcomers used them as a means of indirectly controlling inland mining areas, masking the unequal character of this kind of 'trade' (González Wagner 1993: 105). These foreign merchants and colonists brought with them (as part of their trade) not only new technologies, but also luxurious and exotic objects which were quickly adopted by the local rulers as convenient symbols of status and excellence. At the same time, these imported goods stimulated the development of local prestige industries, mainly bronzework, jewellery and pottery, by a process of emulation. The extent to which all these changes affected the lower-status groups is still very much debated, but most scholars tend to accept that only the material culture and, perhaps, the ideology and way of life of the ruling elites were significantly altered (a convenient summary of current trends is Belén Deamos1994).

What had started during the Bronze Age as sporadic trade contacts (a 'pre-colonisation' phenomenon; see Almagro Gorbea 1989) developed into 'colonisation' which affected mainly the area of Gadir (modern Cádiz), the lower Guadalquivir valley, and the coast of Málaga-Granada-Almería. The cultural process thus evolved during the seventh and early part of the sixth centuries BC into what is known as the Orientalizing phase of the Tartessian Culture. During the seventh century BC the mining operations in Huelva reached industrial proportions, and the Orientalizing influences spread along the main axes of communications: eastward along the Guadalquivir valley into the rich mining region of Cástulo in Jaén; and northwards into Extremadura, reaching the Guadiana and later the Tagus River, along what was subsequently called the 'Via de la Plata'. Simultaneously, Phoenician trade progressed to the north by sea along the coast of Portugal (Arruda 1995; Aubet 1994) but also extended in eastern Spain. There is ample proof of Phoenician settlers in native settlements such as Peña Negra de Crevillente in Alicante (Gonzalez Prats 1986; 1991), and the Phoenician foundation of Ebussus (modern Ibiza) is no longer in doubt today (Ramón 1994). Even further north, at the mouth of the Ebro River and in the Gulf of Lion, there is increasing evidence of a thriving Phoenician trade (Sanmarti 1991; Aubet 1993a).

Around 600 BC this panorama changed again with the increasing intervention of new traders and colonists, this time Samian (the first) and later Phokaian Greeks. Even if the only genuinely Greek settlements were built far to the north (e.g., Emporion and Massalia) Greek merchants also traded in the south, even reaching the Tartessian nucleus of Huelva: the well known story about Kolaios of Samos (Hdt IV: 152) seems to have been vindicated by recent discoveries of significant quantities of Greek pottery in different parts of Huelva (Fernández Jurado et al. 1988-89). This Greek commerce added new types of exotica (very different in style from the Semitic imports) to the indigenous repertoire. In all, foreign trade (Semitic and Hellenic) made a significant contribution to the range of products and objects by which local aristocracies displayed their prestige and status to their own people.

The pattern of development along the Mediterranean seaboard of the Iberian Peninsula during the seventh and early sixth centuries BC followed parallel but different lines. The disparities lie not only in the different backgrounds (the late Bronze Age cultural traditions of the different areas) but also in the type and degree of the foreign influences: the Phoenician colonisation and intense trade in the south decreases as one goes north, while the later Greek influence goes in the opposite direction. In Catalonia and northern Levant in particular, the background of the late Bronze Age was heavily influenced by the incidence of the Urnfield elements present in northern Spain from much earlier (Bronze Age) dates. The term 'First Iron Age' is usually reserved in Peninsular archaeology for those areas in Catalonia, the Ebro Valley and Valencia whose background is not Tartessian, and where the origins of the Iron Age are to be found around 700 BC in a different process. The late Bronze Age Urnfield background was first modified by new north-Pyrenean influences of the so-called Iron Age Urnfields, and also by Phoenician and later Greek imports and techniques, including iron-working.

All these phenomena explain the wide variability to be found in the different areas, although some features are common to the whole Mediterranean and Andalusian coast (e.g., the appearance of wheel-made pottery fired in an oxidising atmosphere and painted with reddish, linear motifs).

By the end of the sixth century BC, and probably as a result of a complex set of economic factors, the once dynamic and powerful Tartessian Culture faded away. Its place was taken in western Andalusia by the Tudetanian Culture, less 'glamorous' and less spectacular than the preceding phase from the point of view of material culture, and whose links with the Orientalizing Period are hotly debated (from 'clear continuity' to 'total rejection' of earlier social, ritual and economic patterns). By then, a new cultural horizon was already flourishing in eastern Andalusia and southeast of the peninsula. During the sixth century BC the combination of a set of different cultural stimuli had given birth, in areas peripheral to the Tartessian centre, to a second Iron Age complex, the so-called Iberian Culture. These influences can be synthesised by the combination of a number of factors: the cultural substratum of each region and its geo-economic conditions; the intensity of Urnfield influences (decreasing as one goes south and almost non-existent south of Valencia); the intensity of Tartessian Orientalizing influence (strongest in western Andalusia and southern Extremadura); the kind and intensity of Phoenician (later Carthaginian) colonisation or trading; and the kind and intensity of Greek colonisation or trade. The varying degree in which these factors combined in the different areas explains the wide variation that can be seen in the different regions of the Iberian Culture.

Although the early phases of the Iberian Culture can be dated to the sixth century BC, it was not until c. 500 BC that the Iberian cultural complex was fully formed. From then onwards it evolved, not in comparative isolation as was previously thought, but forming part (as its extreme far west) of the Mediterranean trading network, with intense contacts both with Hellenic influences (mainly through Emporion and Massalia) and Semitic ones (through the old city of Gadir and the Carthaginians, in some ways heirs to the Phoenicians). By the mid-fourth century BC the peninsula had entered fully into the 'Big Game', the fight for power in the central and western Mediterranean between the superpowers of the time, Carthage and Rome; in doing so it became first a logistic hinterland for the Carthaginians (a source of silver and mercenaries) and later, during the Second Punic War, a battlefield. But after the Carthaginians were forcibly expelled by the Romans, the newcomers were not prepared to leave: they had come to stay and this fact sealed the fate of the evolution of the Iberian Culture, which slowly faded into something different, in a slow process called 'Romanisation'.

Burial traditions during the Orientalizing and Iberian Periods

In the following pages I shall discuss the evolution of one aspect of funerary customs in Southern Iberia over a five-century period (early seventh to mid-third centuries BC): the way rulers and aristocrats expressed status, wealth and prestige in burial rites (Fig. 1). To do so I shall divide this period in three parts: the Tartessian Orientalizing, early Iberian and middle Iberian. Each period is heir to the preceding one and the cremation rite is common to all but changes in display are evident. I must first warn the reader of an apparent flaw in the argument which may be misleading: I shall be comparing the grave-goods of the Orientalizing Period in the southwest with those of the Iberian Culture in the southeast. The reason for this is simple and complex at the same time: the Turdetanians, for some unknown reason (and the current debate is really too intricate to be summarised here[4]) did not bury their dead in formal cemeteries, or if they did, these have yet to be found. It is thus not really possible to compare the earlier Orientalizing and later Turdetanian burial practices in the southwest. Although it may seem at first glance that my approach means comparing the evolution of patterns in different (and thus not really comparable areas), I believe this not to be so. In fact, the Iberian Culture is the clear successor to the Tartessian in many respects and if the most dynamic area in Iberia during the seventh-sixth centuries BC was Tartessos, the Iberian societies of the fifth and fourth centuries in the southeast certainly exerted a similar primacy. In fact, what I shall be doing is comparing the way in which the Orientalizing princes and Iberian aristocrats expressed status and wealth in their burials (and they were respectively the leaders of the most dynamic societies in southern Iberia, each in their own times).

It may thus be useful to summarise briefly the main elements in burial traditions which will be discussed, and perhaps the best way to do this is in a Table (Fig. 2). It will be realised that while the deeper elements of ritual remain constant (e.g., use of monumental grave markers, expression of status through display of material elements in

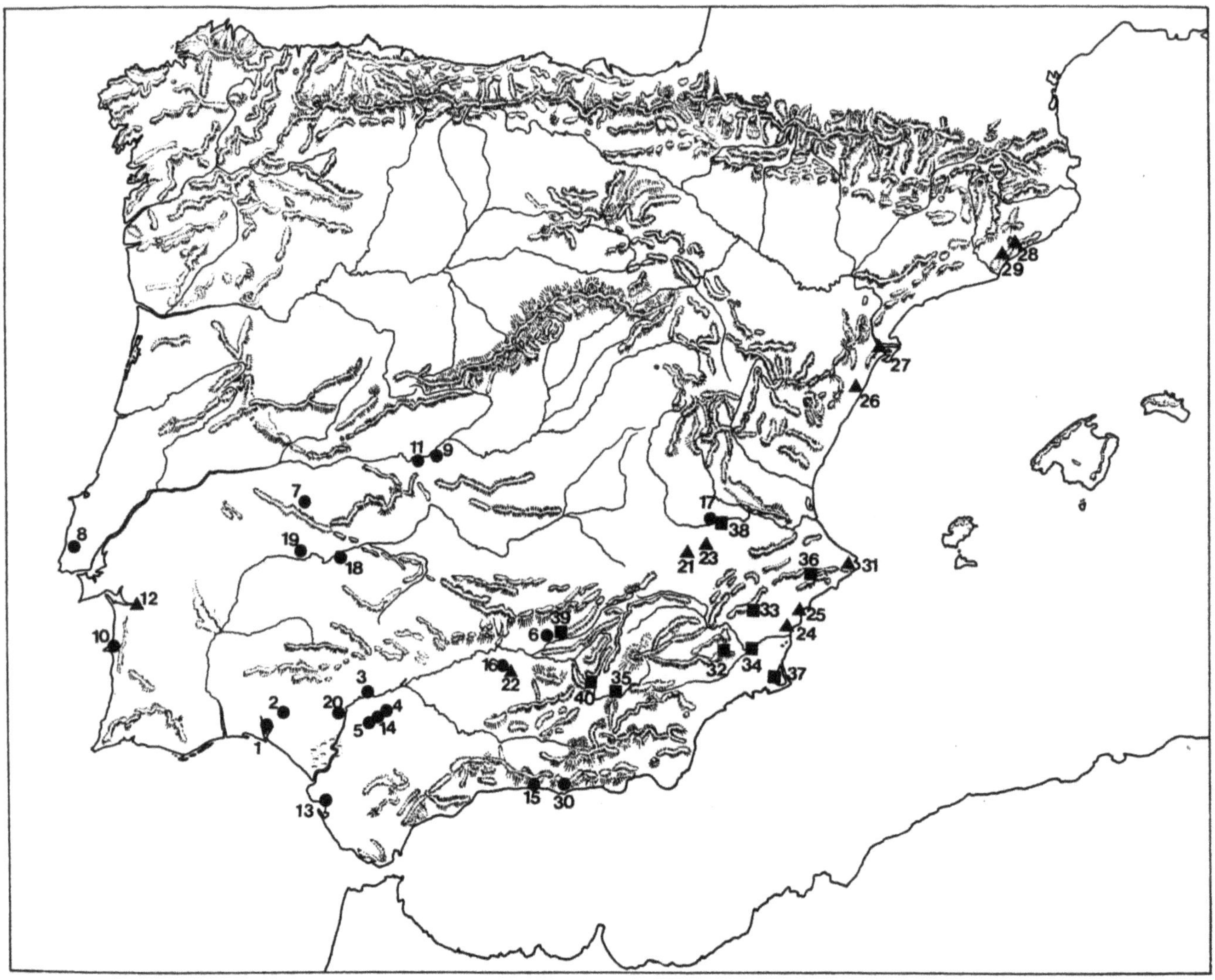

Figure 1 Iberia. Sites mentioned in the text: 1 La Joya (Huelva); 2 Niebla (Huelva); 3 Setefilla (Seville); 4 Cañada de Ruiz Sánchez (Seville); 5 Acebuchal (Seville); 6 Cástulo (Jaén); 7 La Aliseda (Cáceres); 8 Torres Vedras (Lisboa, Portugal); 9 Belvis de la Jara (Toledo); 10 Gaio (Sines, Portugal); 11 Las Fraguas (Toledo); 12 Alcacer do Sal; 13 Las Cumbres (Cádiz); 14 Cruz del Negro (Seville); 15 Frigiliana (Málaga); 16 Cerrillo Blanco de Porcuna (Jaén); 17 Casa del Monte (Albacete); 18 Medellín (Badajoz); 19 Aljucén (Badajoz); 20 El Carambolo (Seville); 21 Pozo Moro (Albacete); 22 Porcuna (Jaén); 23 Los Villares (Albacete); 24 Cabezo Lucero (Alicante); 25 El Molar (Alicante); 26 La Solivella (Castellón); 27 Mianes (Tarragona); 28 Llinars del Vallés (Barcelona); 29 Granja Soley (Barcelona); 30 Almuñécar (Granada); 31 Alt de Benimaquía (Alicante); 32 Cigarralejo (Murcia); 33 Coimbra (Murcia); 34 Cabecico del Tesoro (Murcia); 35 Baza (Granada); 36 La Serreta (Alicante); 37 Los Nietos (Murcia); 38 Casa del Monte (Albacete); 39 Estacar de Robarinas (Jaén); 40 Castellones de Ceal (Jaén).
Circles: Orientalizing. **Triangles**: Early Iberian. **Squares**: Middle Iberian.

grave-goods), the mechanisms vary. Monumental sculpture, for example, was not used (as far as we know) by the Tartessian princes, but was conspicuously employed by earlier Iberian aristocrats and less so by later warrior aristocrats. Weapons are much commoner in the latter period, while the use of evidently ritual bronze vessels became rarer. Three burials from different periods have been chosen as examples of the type of burial and grave-goods: Burial 17 at La Joya (Huelva) for the Orientalizing Period (c. 600 BC) (Figs 3-5); the monument at Pozo Moro (Albacete) for the early Iberian (c. 500 BC) (Fig. 6); and Grave 200 at El Cigarralejo (Murcia) for the middle Iberian (c. 375 BC) (Figs 7-9). I shall now examine in some detail the archaeological evidence in chronological order.

Princely tombs during the Orientalizing Period

Princely tombs as evidence of conspicuous display and consumption

As noted above, the pre-existing Tartessian aristocracies saw their power reinforced, rather than diminished, by the colonial phenomenon after c. 800 BC. The newcomers were glad to trade with these rulers who mined, processed and transported the precious metals and other raw materials to the coast for them, saving effort and streamlining the process (Aubet 1990). In exchange for these bulky raw materials, the Phoenicians and later the Greeks traded high value prestige goods, such as elaborate bronzework, jewellery, ivories, oil, wine, etc. One of the main results of this

	Orientalizing (7th-6th centuries BC)	Early Iberian (c. 500-400 BC)	Middle Iberian (c. 400-325 BC)
Burial Rite	Cremation. Inhumation sometimes. (La Joya, Cerillo Blanco)	Cremation.	Cremation.
Typical superstructure in important buildings	Earth tumulus	Turriform monuments, pillar stelae, low built platforms (tumuli).	Square stone or mud brick platforms (tumuli).
Use of sculpture	No	Yes, very elaborate. (Pozo Moro, Porcuna).	Rare, simplified.
Accumulation of objects	No accumulation by type or material but many different objects.	No. Grave goods limited in number of objects but significant by type.	Accumulation of many objects of the same type and shape.
Ritual objects	Standard ritual set of bronze vessels	Perfume, libation and drinking set (Pozo Moro).	No standardized sets. Bronze vessels rare.
Chariots/wagons	Elaborate burial hearse (La Joya).	?	No. Rarely, heavy iron-felloed wagon wheels.
Weapons	Rare but in evidence in many 'princely' graves.	Very rare.	Very common in all categories of burial including poorer ones. Duplication of swords and shields rare but known.
Imported pottery	Foreign amphorae. Rarely, good quality Greek pottery (e.g. Medellin lip cup).	A few chosen luxury items.	Attic black glaze of indifferent quality. Some Red Figure. Mainly drinking vessels. Up to seven vases of the same shape in same burial.
Jewellery	Frequent.	Rare ?	Rare. Only small pendants etc.
Use of wine	Imported. Restricted to elites.	Local and possibly imported. Restricted to elite and retainers?	Local. Redistribution to lower status groups.
Typical examples	La Joya 18 (Garrido 1978).	Pozo Moro (Almagro Gorbea 1983).	Cigarralejo 200 & 277 (Cuadrado 1987). Cabecico (Quesada 1989)

Figure 2 Summary of main elements in 'princely' and 'aristocratic' tombs (seventh-fourth centuries BC).

trade was to reinforce the ascendancy of local princes over the lower groups of the indigenous populations, by means of the anthropologically well-known systems of ostentation, display and redistribution.

Using valuables for funerary rites is one of the best documented forms of conspicuous display and consumption and therefore of gaining prestige. It thus comes as no surprise to find what one would expect: during the seventh and sixth centuries BC a comparatively small number of tombs can properly be defined as 'princely', not only because of their more or less impressive tumuli, but also on the basis of their grave-goods.

There are some princely tombs in the Tartessian nucleus and of a few others on the periphery. They can be conveniently synthesised in Figure 2 (more detailed descriptions in Aubet 1984; Ruiz Delgado 1989). Some of the excavator's dates may have been altered after later research. It should be noted that many other isolated discoveries (mainly bronze vessels) may come from plundered and/or destroyed graves containing the ritual-set (jug-brazier-*thymiaterion*) characteristic of the burials of the elite (see below).

Many of these graves were buried under big tumuli, but it is really the grave-goods and not the superstructure[5] that makes a burial 'princely' during the Orientalizing Period. Most of them contained a great number of objects, but I will show that in fact it is not the quantity but their variety and quality that renders these burials really exceptional. However, this can only be assessed by first comparing these tombs with ordinary burials dated to the Orientalizing Period, both in Huelva and in other areas (see Fig. 10).

Non-princely burials

Las Cumbres (Puerto de Sta, María, Cádiz). The big Tumulus 1 (22 m in diameter) in the cemetery of Las Cumbres near El Puerto de Santa María, Cadiz (Ruiz Mata 1989) is particularly interesting as a case-study because among its 63 shallow pit-burials there are some dated to the early part of the eighth century BC that show no traces of Oriental influence, while others, dated to the second half of the century, contain Oriental elements such as wheel-made cinerary urns or iron knives among their grave-goods. This veritable cemetery under a single mound is perhaps the first known funerary assemblage that can be classified as Orientalizing. Most graves contain only pottery (urn, cups, dishes) while only half of the burials contain a bronze object (belt buckles). Other items such as bronze vessels, chariot harnesses, silver and other luxury products are absent. Only the richest burial, some distance away under a subsidiary mound (Grave 24), contains a wide variety of artefacts (pottery vessels, two alabastra, a belt buckle, some silver, gold and faience beads); but even though it is clearly the grave of an important individual, the grave-goods bear no comparison with the later 'princely' graves listed above (see Figs 10-11).

South coastal area (Málaga-Almería). As for coastal re-

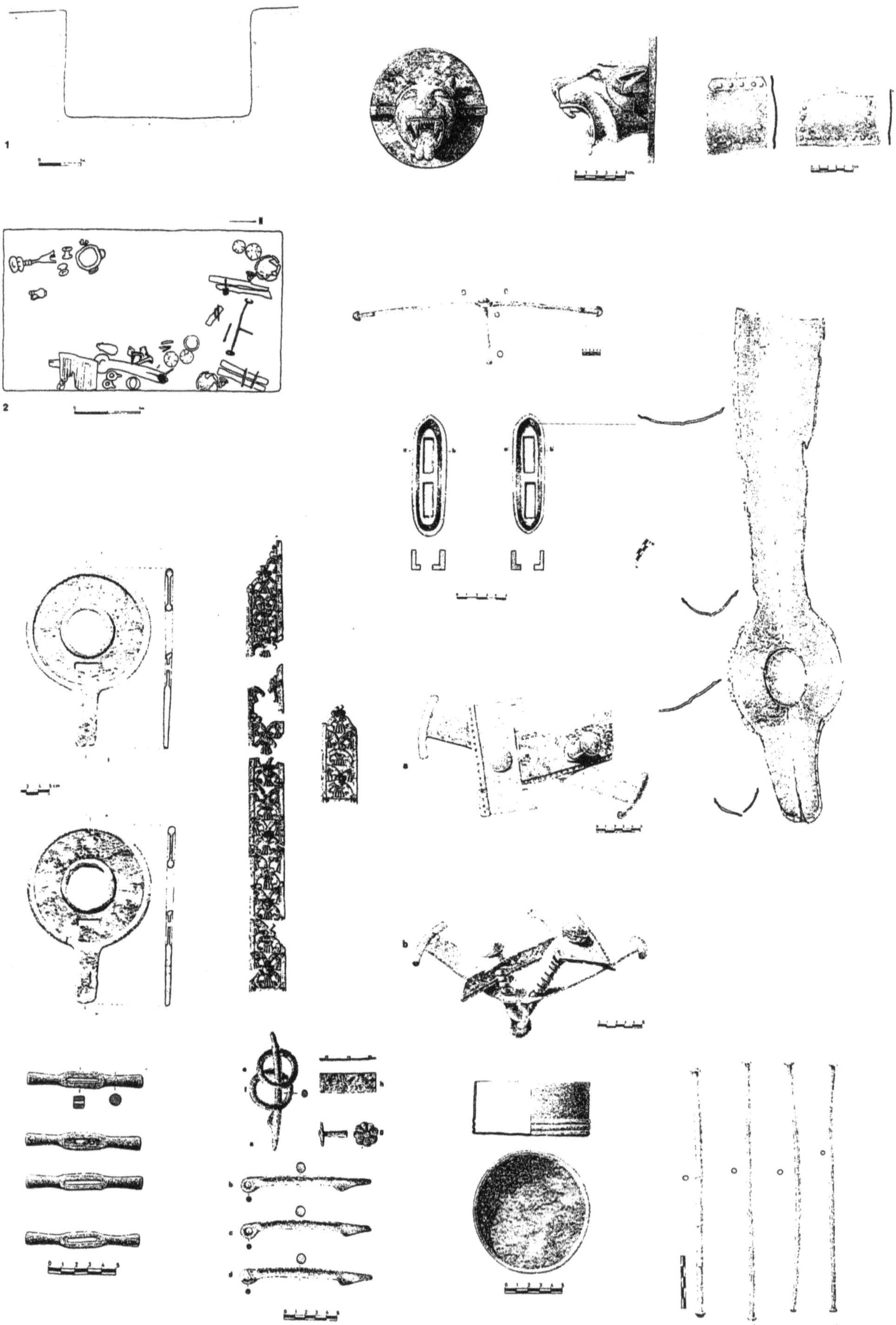

Figure 3 Orientalizing Period. Burial 17 at La Joya, Huelva (c. 600 BC).

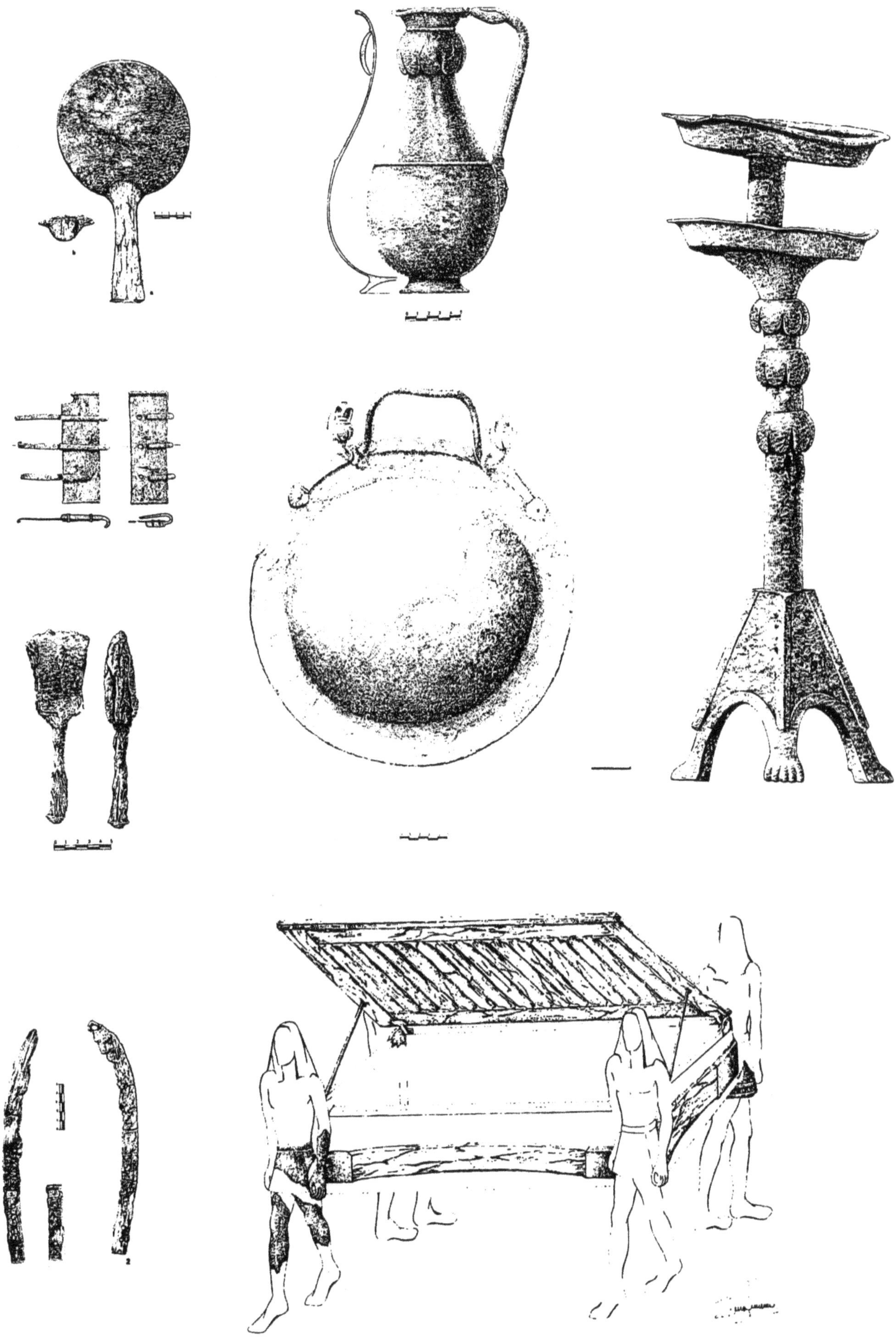

Figure 4 Orientalizing Period. Burial 17 at La Joya, Huelva (c. 600 BC).

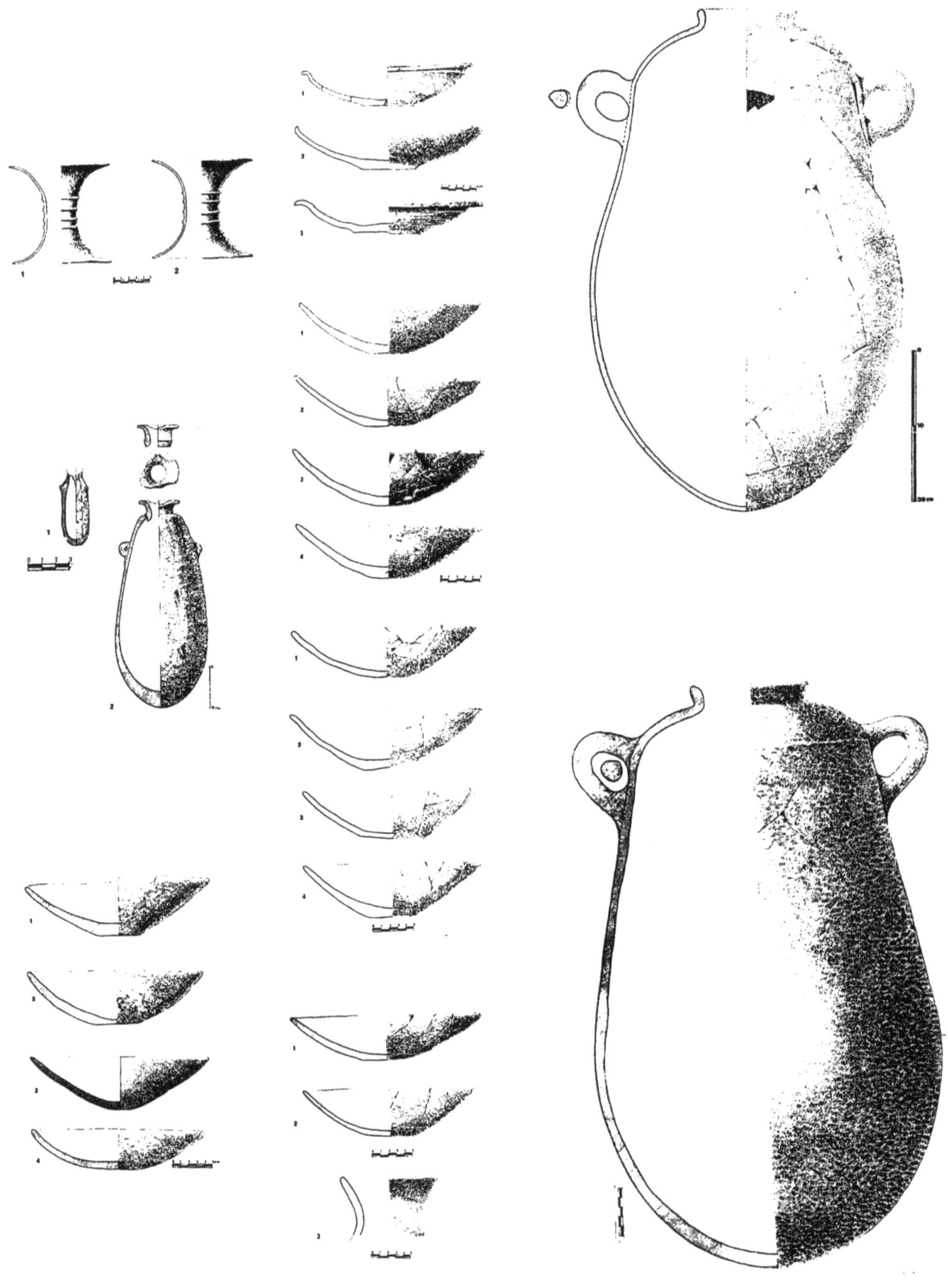

Figure 5 Orientalizing Period. Burial 17 at La Joya, Huelva (c. 600 BC).

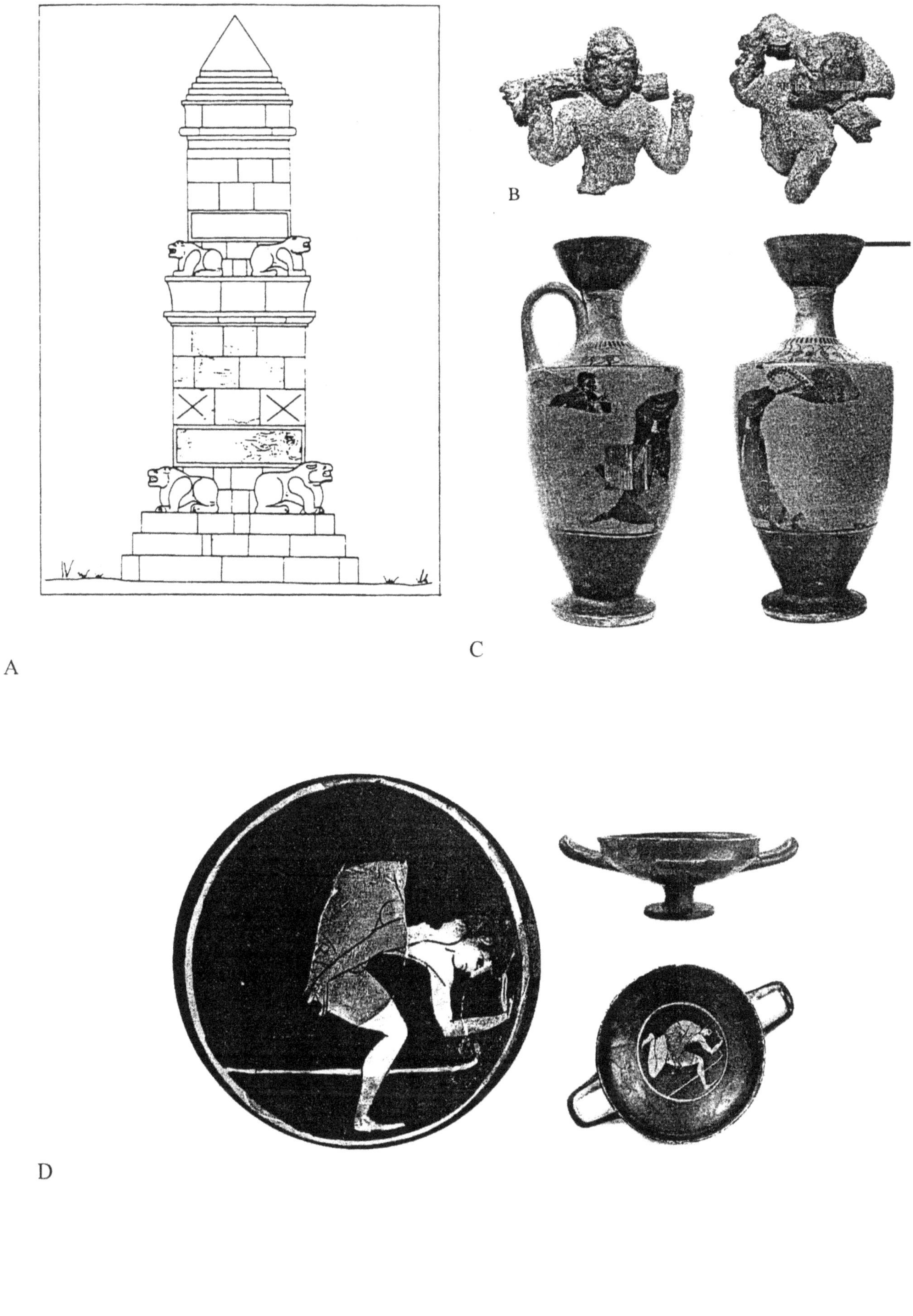

Figure 6 Early Iberian monument at Pozo Moro (Albacete). c. 500 BC. The illustrated grave-goods are only a small part of the contents of this burial which were largely destroyed by cremation.

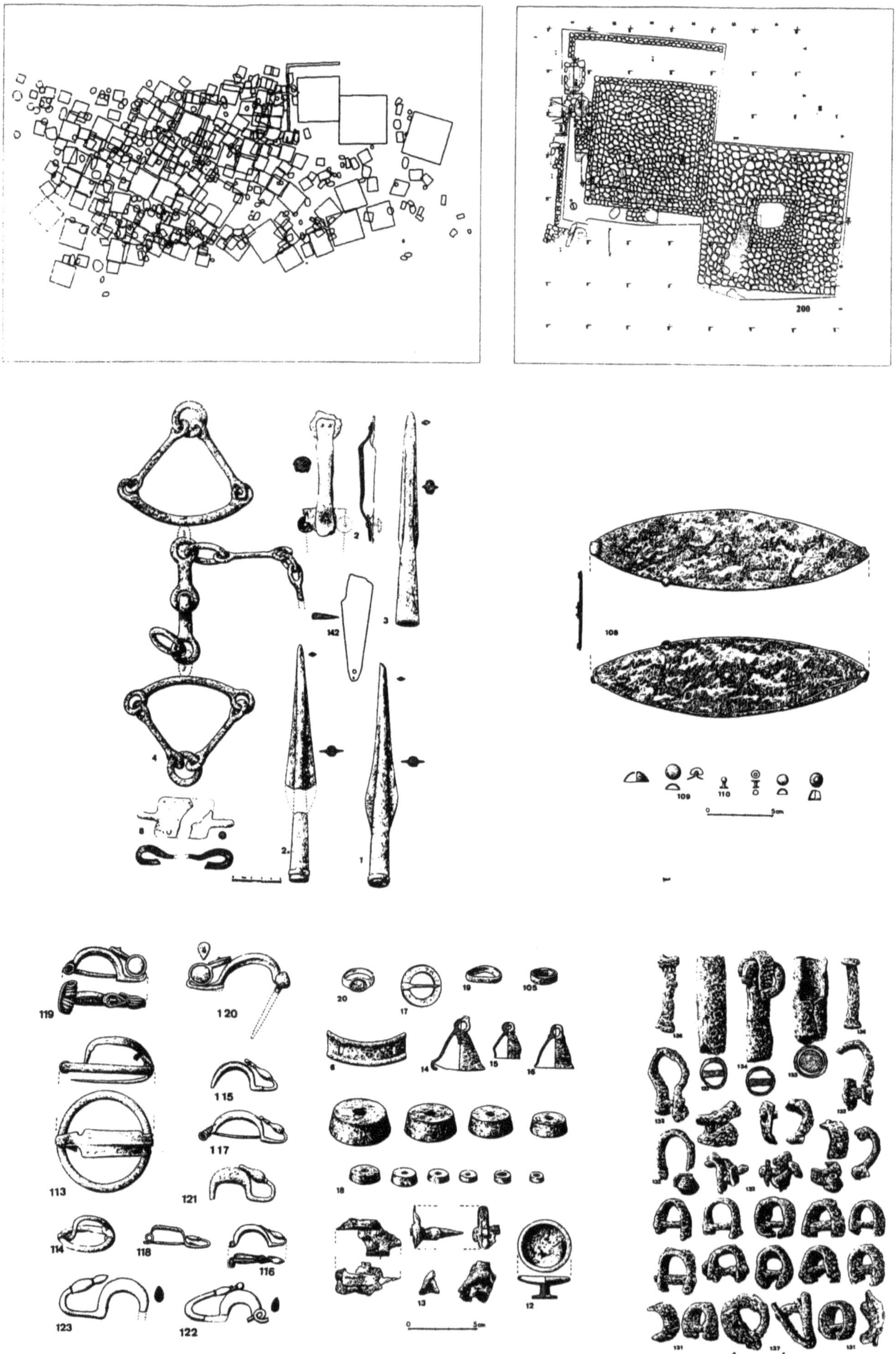

Figure 7 Middle Iberian. Burial 200 at El Cigarralejo (Murcia). c. 375 BC.

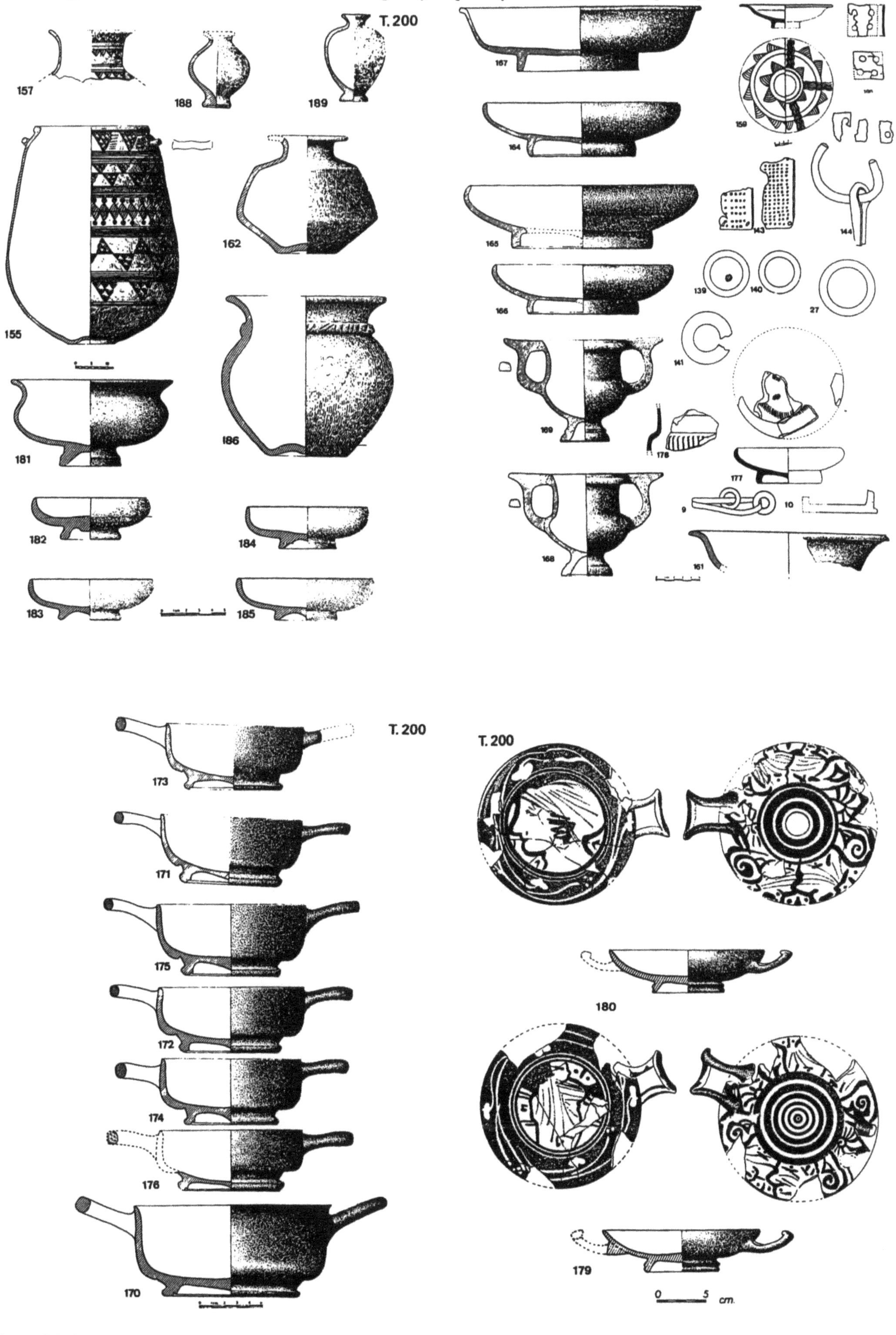

Figure 8 Middle Iberian. Burial 200 at El Cigarralejo (Murcia). c. 375 BC.

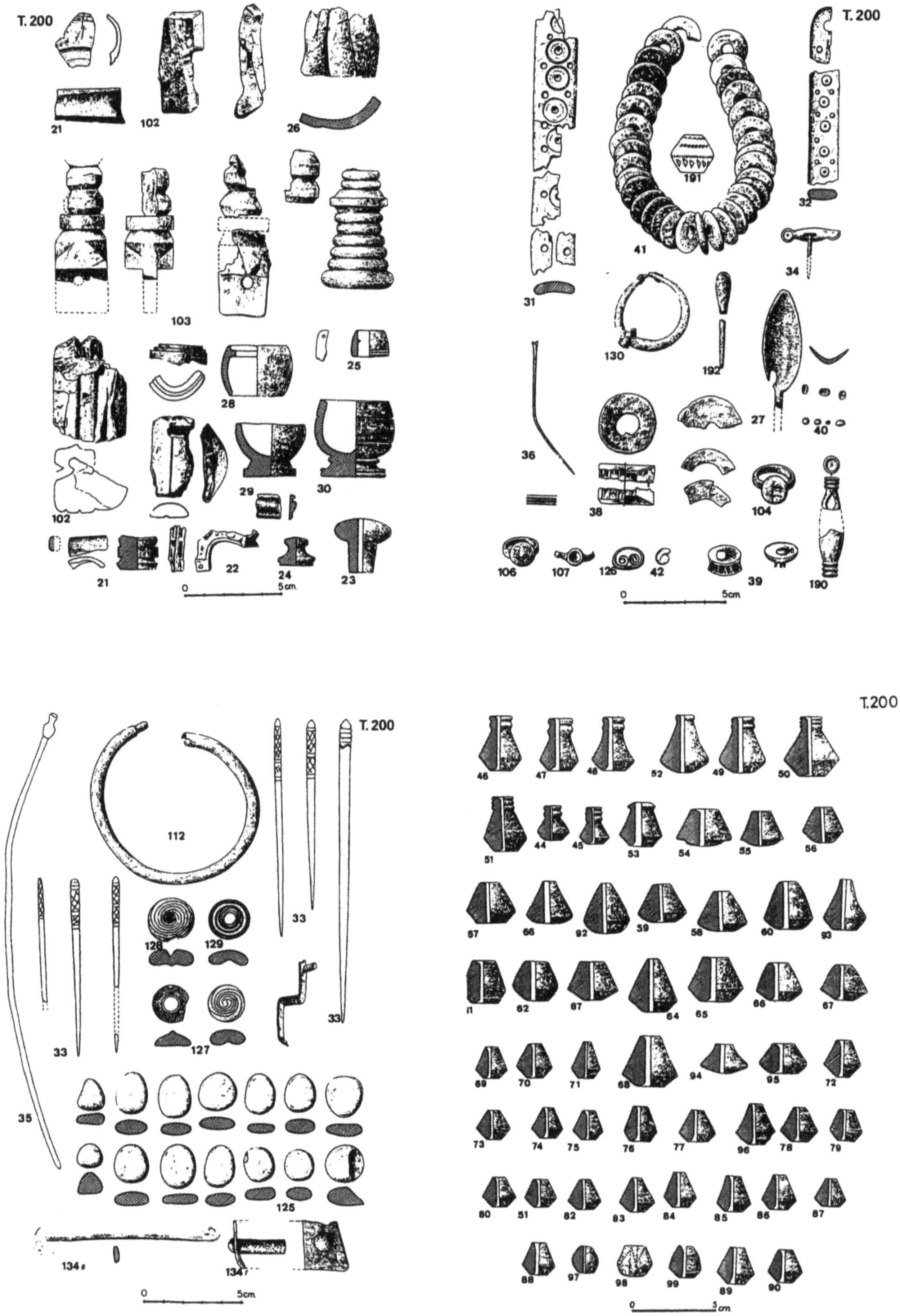

Figure 9 Middle Iberian. Burial 200 at El Cigarralejo (Murcia). c. 375 BC.

10 a Orientalizing Period. Typical examples of common burials.
(Collective under big tumulus or under small mound, low to moderate quantity and variety of grave goods, few imported objects, few metal objects).

Burial	Urn	Local pottery	Imported pottery	Alabastra	Iron knive	Bronze belt buckle/ brooch or bracelet	Gold/ silver	Faience beads	Ostrich egg	Weapons	Bronze vessels	Other	Date (centuries)	Notes	References
Las Cumbres 58	1	1	1										mid 8th		Ruiz Mata and Perez 1989
Cruz del Negro 7	1			1									7th-6th		Maier 1992
Cruz del Negro 18		1			1	2				1			7th-6th		Maier 1992
Setefilla A 14	1				1							1 bronze pin	7th-6th		Aubet 1975
Setefilla A 27	1	2				1						1 bronze tweezers	7th-6th		Aubet 1975
Cerrillo Blanco 9					1								mid 7th-end 6th	Inhumation	Torrecillas 1985
Cerrillo Blanco 18													mid 7th-end 6th	Inhumation	Torrecillas 1985
Frigiliana 7	1		1					1					6th		Arribas and Wilkins 1971
Frigiliana 8		1				2				2-3			6th	Richest in site	Arribas and Wilkins 1971
Boliche 13													7th-6th	No grave goods	Osuna and Remesal 1981
Boliche 47									1				7th-6th		Osuna and Remesal 1981
Aljucen 1	1	1											early 6th		Enriquez and Dominguez 1991

10 b Orientalizing Period. Some examples of important and 'princely' burials.
(Big mounds, built stone chambers, many objects of different materials and functions, bronze vessels as ritual sets, exotic materials, imported perishable commodities, rarely hearse and weapons).

Burial	Urn	Local pottery	Imported pottery	Alabastra	Iron knive	Bronze belt buckle/ brooch or bracelet	Gold/ silver	Faience beads	Ostrich egg	Weapons	Bronze vessels	Other	Date (centuries)	Notes	References
Las Cumbres 24	2	3	1	2		1	3	1				1	end 8th	Under separate mound	Ruiz Mata and Perez 1989
La Joya 17		17	3	2	1	1	2			1?	3	Funerary chariot, horse bit (x2), mirror, ivory casket	first half 7th	Chariot very elaborate with bronze fittings	Garrido and Orta 1978
El Palmaron			>1			2	2 dish	>1		4	2-3	'Stone axes', pebbles, other metals, lost	early 6th	Partly plundered	Belen 1995
Castulo	2	5-6			1	1 belt buckle	1 dish 1 ring			4-6	2	Melted bronze	7th-6th	Destroyed	Blanco 1963 Blazquez and Valiente 1982

10 c Iberian Period. Examples of 'princely' and aristocratic burials.
Monuments (Pozo Moro) or big square tumuli (Cigarralejo). Two different approaches to 'status' are in evidence.

Burial	Urn	Local pottery	Imported pottery	Alabastra	Iron knive	Bronze belt buckle/ brooch or bracelet	Gold/ silver	Faience beads	Ostrich egg	Weapons	Bronze vessels	Other	Date (centuries)	Notes	References
Pozo Moro		2				bronze objects	>1 Au >1 Ag				1	Big turriform monument with complex sculptured iconographic program mythological reliefs and lions in corner-stones). Iron, bronze and bone remains.	c. 500 BC	Many more grave goods destroyed by fire	Almagro-Gorbea 1983
Cigarralejo 277		19	>21			6	4	>15		18	1	Horse bit, spurs, bone pyxis, many wooden boxes, 28 bone needles, 9 spindle whorls, faience flask, bronze lion.	c. 375 BC	Probably double burial	Cuadrado 1987

Figure 10 Main differences between 'common' and 'princely' burials during the Orientalizing Period seventh-sixth centuries BC and Iberian Period fifth-fourth centuries BC.

Area		Cemetery/Grave	Chronology	Main References
Core	Huelva	La Joya 17. Dug in 1970.	c. 700/650 BC (Fdez. Jurado 1988-89)	Garrido and Orta 1978
		La Joya 9. Dug in 1967.	c. 700/650 BC (Fdez. Jurado 1988-89)	Garrido and Orta 1970
		La Joya 18. Dug in 1970.	c. 600 BC (Aubet 1984)	Garrido and Orta 1978
		La Joya 5. Dug in 1967.	c. 590 BC (Fdez. Jurado 1988-89)	Garrido and Orta 1970
	Niebla (Huelva)	El Palmaron (tumulus and built chamber). Looted c. 1934.	c. 635-550 BC	García Bellido 1966; V. Pingel 1975; Belen 1995
	Setefilla (Lora del Rio, Sevilla)	Túmulo H (over built chamber). 'Explored' in 1927.	c. 650-550 BC	Bonsor and Thouvenot 1928
		Túmulo A (over built chamber). 'Explored' in 1927, dug in 1973.	c. 650-575 BC (Aubet)	Aubet 1975
	Carmona (Sevilla)	Cañada de Ruiz Sánchez (tumulus). 'Dug' in 1895.	c. 650 BC	Bonsor 1899
		Acebuchal. Tumulus G (over built chamber). 'Dug' in 1896.	c. 600 BC	Bonsor 1899
Periphery (east)	Linares (Jaen)	Cástulo. Finca Torrubia. Casual find 1962. Pit with stone slab?	c. 700/650 BC (Blázquez and Valiente; Ruiz Gálvez). 6th century BC (Blanco 1963)	Blanco 1963; Blázquez and Valiente 1982; Bandera and Ferrer (1995)
		Cástulo. Los Higuerones. Tumulus A. Pit. Looted. Remains of offerings.	c. 7th century BC	Blázquez 1975; Blázquez and Valiente 1982
Periphery (north)	Aliseda (Caceres)	Aliseda treasure. Probably burial chamber and tumulus.	c. 625/600 BC (Almagro-Gorbea 1977)	Blanco 1956; Blázquez 1975; Almagro-Gorbea 1977
	T. Vedras (Lisboa)	Only remains of grave goods.	c. 650/600 BC	García y Bellido (1970)
	Belvis de la Jara (Toledo)	El Carpio. Pit. Dug1984.	c. 650 BC (Pereira 1989)	Pereira and Alvaro 1986; Pereira 1989
	Gaio (Sines)	Tumulus. Golden treasure.	7th-6th centuries BC	García y Bellido 1970
	Las Fraguas (Toledo)	Bronze objects.	7th century BC	Fernández Miranda and Pereira 1992
Dubious	Alcacer Do Sal (Tagus)	Grave 98. Remains of a chariot.	6th century BC?	Schüle 1969: taf 107; Stary 1989

Figure 11 'Princely' graves during the Orientalizing Period.

gions further east, two examples may suffice. In Frigiliana (Málaga), close to the colonial Phoenician settlements, an indigenous cemetery (which is not colonial as previously had been thought) shows the same pattern of simple pit-tombs under small mounds with rather simple grave-goods (only one tomb containing a badly corroded set of iron weapons (Arribas and Wilkins 1969). The Orientalizing site at Boliche, near Villaricos in Almería is another example of a seventh-sixth century cemetery and contained 51 burials. It was excavated by L. Siret at the turn of this century and has been recently re-examined (Osuna and Remesal 1981). All burials are simple, usually containing just one or two pottery vessels, and occasionally an ostrich egg, bronze bracelets and golden or faience beads.

Guadalquivir valley. It is difficult to assess the composition of grave-goods in many Tartessian cemeteries in the area of Seville, as many of them were excavated by Bonsor c. 1895-1905 and by Bonsor and Thouvenot in 1926-27. Most burials were never published in detail and only recent and painstaking research into Bonsor's papers (Maier 1992) is throwing some light on the details of these Orientalizing sites. For example, burials at La Cruz del Negro (Carmona, Sevilla) are always very simple, consisting of a cinerary urn, perhaps one or two pottery vessels, and very occasionally a bronze belt buckle or fibula or ivory comb. Only exceptionally (in three out of thirty-five burials) does one find a single small bronze or iron spear-head. No tumuli were in evidence.[6] A convenient summary of the cemeteries in the area of Los Alcores (Seville) can be found in Ruiz Delgado (1989: 248 ff.). The grave-goods they contain are also simple. The pattern is very much the same in the earlier burials under Mound A in Setefilla (Carmona) (Aubet 1975) and in the assemblage of simple burials under a single big mound (Tumulus B) (Aubet 1978).

The Orientalizing Period in the inland peripheral areas to the east (along the Guadalquivir valley) is not well known yet. Along with some impressive finds at Castulo which was one of the most important sites in Andalusia and which continued to be so during the Iberian Period (for example the grave-goods published by Blanco 1963), there is some evidence from the cemetery at Cerrillo Blanco (Porcuna). Its grave-goods are similar to those in burials in the Lower Guadalquivir; a few fibulae, bronze belt-buckles and iron curved knives are the modest indicators of wealth in the 24 inhumations (Torrecillas 1985). The recently published Orientalizing burial from Casa del Monte in the province of Albacete further east (López Precioso 1994) contains just a wheel-made urn, a covered dish and a Bencarron brooch of Andalusian type, all of which can be dated to the second half of the sixth century BC, a period which in this region can be considered as transitional between the Orientalizing and the Iberian Periods.

Northern periphery. Looking now at the northern periphery of Tartessos, the Orientalizing cemeteries show a similar panorama. Apart from a few, apparently isolated and poorly known 'princely' tombs (e.g., at La Aliseda, Las Fraguas, El Carpio or Torres Vedras, all of which are known through casual finds or looted materials), the excavated cemeteries do not contain exceptional burials. This is the case of Medellín (Almagro-Gorbea 1977: 287 ff.; 1991a; 1991b) and Aljucén (Enríquez 1991; Enríquez and Domínguez 1991) both of which are in the province of Badajoz. The assemblage of grave-goods usually consists of an urn, one or two cups or dishes and the occasional iron knife, bronze bracelet, belt buckle or brooch.

Quality and variety as an expression of status in princely burials

In marked contrast with this widespread pattern of simple Orientalizing pit-burials with a moderate quantity and variety of grave-goods (few pieces, not many different materials, few really luxurious imported objects) 'princely' burials, both in the central 'core' area and in the periphery, can only be described as impressive.

They can be briefly characterised by: 1) imposing but simple tumular structures (although this is not an exclusive characteristic); 2) many artefacts as grave-goods; 3) these artefacts reflect many different categories of material, shape and function, but only pottery dishes are usually found in great number (Fig. 5); 4) some objects (bronze jugs and dishes or *braserillos*, Fig. 4) are a recurrent assemblage with probably ritual significance; 5) imported objects of rare materials and/or beautiful workmanship are the norm rather than the exception. Many of them are single pieces, and chariots are very rare (Fig. 4); 6) weapons are very rare indeed; and 7) high status was also shown by perishable commodities, such as imported wine (Fig. 5) or oil. The contrast with non-princely burials is clearly shown in Fig. 10. I will now examine these points in some detail.

1) Tumular structures. Some of these tombs were visually imposing, consisting of great earth tumuli which covered masonry burial chambers. But this is not always so: some of the richest assemblages were found in tombs, such as those from La Joya or Castulo, which apparently were not covered by mounds. Erosion however has played a big role at Huelva and there is very little information about the tomb from Castulo. Thus it cannot be discounted that all these burials were also tumuli of great size, as some new mounds found in Huelva after 1979 could prove (Garrido and Orta 1989: 36). If not all princely burials were tumuli, then conversely, some big mounds did not cover princely graves.

2) Number of artefacts. The number of objects varies greatly. Most well-known 'princely' tombs contain well over the two-to-five objects typical of most Orientalizing common burials, reaching around fifty in La Joya 9, or around forty in Aliseda. However, I do not believe this is the most significant factor.

3) Categories of raw materials. Most of these tombs contain artefacts made of a combination of at least six different categories of material. These include pottery (wheel- and hand-made, local and imported), bronze vessels, bronze ornaments, precious metal vessels and ornaments, iron knives and very occasionally weapons, alabaster/glass vessels, ivory caskets, and combs (which were usually decorated). Occasionally, paste scarabs and amber beads also appear. The objects made from these materials may be imported or local productions, but are nearly always of high quality workmanship.

This variety is in itself a proof of wealth, especially when imported items are involved; it is even more significant, however, that the objects made in these materials cover a wide range of functions. They include containers of perishable food, such as wine or oil (both imported in this period), commodities which were probably distributed (in Homeric fashion) during redistribution banquets and feasts-of-merit to the equals and immediate retainers of these princes. Also present are: personal adornments identifying owners as members of an exclusive elite (bronze ornaments, jewellery); very exceptional symbols of rank and power (chariots, occasionally bronze or iron weapons); symbols of a sacred or ritual conception of power (sets of bronze vessels); and symbols of control over a new technology (iron knives with silver and ivory ornamentation).

Figure 12 shows a simplified picture of the different categories of objects found in grave-goods at La Joya in Huelva (for example, 'bronze' includes bronze vessels, *thymiateria*, belt buckles, fibulae, etc.). Even within these simplified categories it can be easily seen that the richest tombs (Numbers 5, 9, 17, 18) contain between five and seven categories of raw material, while other poorer and simpler burials contain only between one and four. It can be added that La Joya is not, perhaps, a good example of differences in status, as even its commoners' burials are very rich in comparison (as has already been seen) with other examples in the inner areas.

For yet another test one can chose the inner area of Tartessos Tumulus H at Setefilla (already looted in the Middle Ages) which contained at least six categories of raw materials with which artefacts had been made: pottery, ivory, gold, amber, bronze, and bone (Bonsor and Thouvenot 1928: 23-25). Aliseda (Almagro-Gorbea 1977) and Cás-

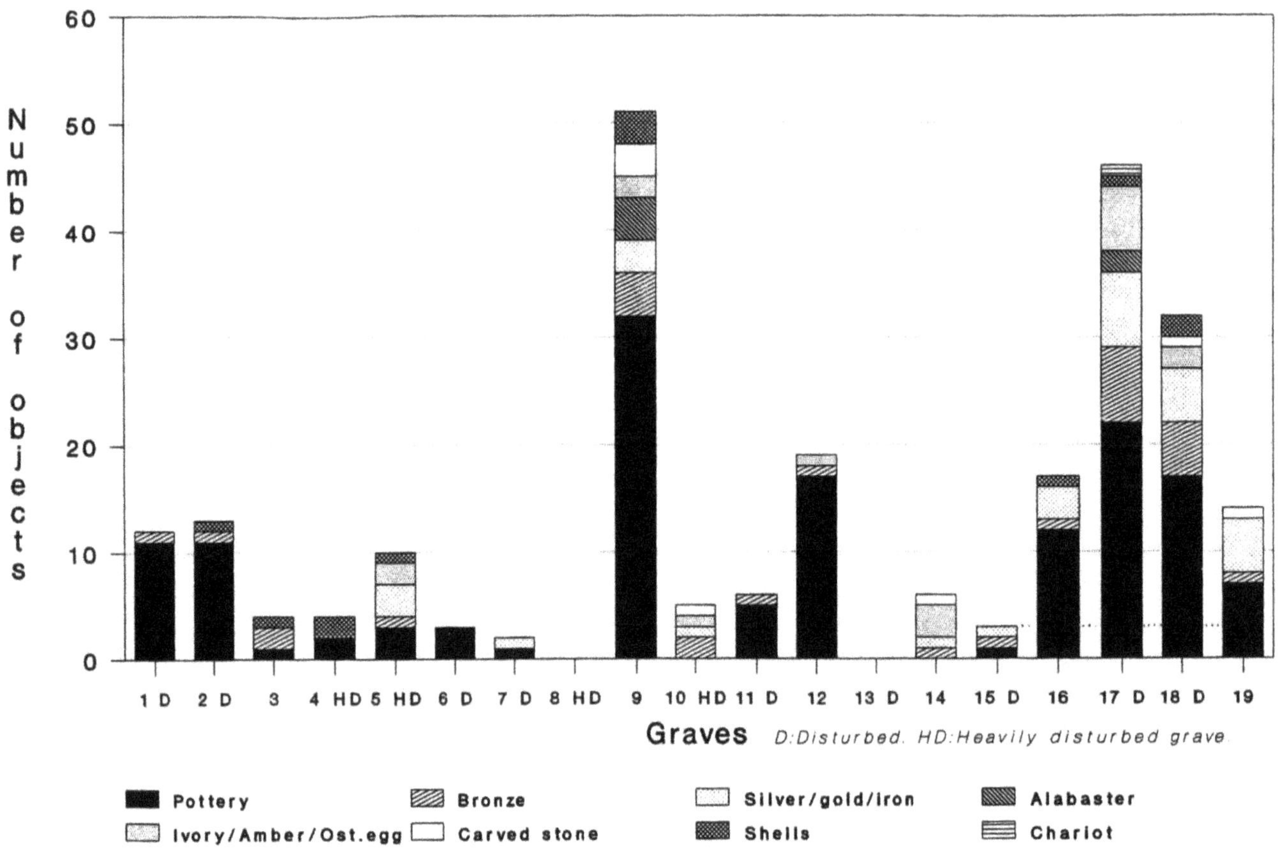

Figure 12 Cemetery at La Joya (Huelva). Composition and wealth of grave-goods according to number and type of objects.

tulo (Blanco 1963) are also good examples of this variety of raw materials and types of objects in the inner periphery, while the (admittedly more modest) burial at El Carpio in Toledo (Pereira 1989), sets the pattern for the outer periphery.

4) Recurrent ritual assemblages. It was mentioned in the previous paragraph that a common recurrence in princely burials is the so-called set of ritual objects (e.g., Aubet 1984: 451; Almagro-Gorbea 1990: 107; Fernández Miranda and Pereira 1992: Fig. 9), usually comprising a bronze jug, a bronze or silver 'brazier' or dish, an incense-burner (*thymiaterion*) and perhaps an iron knife (Fig. 4). In fact, the first two elements are nearly always found in association and they have come to be considered a kind of indicator of a princely grave even if nothing but some scattered elements remain of a looted burial (see Table in Fernández Miranda and Pereira 1992: 85). These vessels are exclusive to the elite burials and are widely considered to reflect the assimilation of purely Oriental funerary customs involving libation rites, the use of incense and food sacrifices, although many of the objects themselves are usually considered to be of local manufacture. Recently it has been proposed, following the ideas of J. Alvar and C. González Wagner, that *thymiateria* may have been part of the grave-goods and rituals of Semitic colonists and not necessarily of local dignitaries (Bandera and Ferrer 1994a: 60; 1994b: 54-55), but this hypothesis is not easy to reconcile with the (in my opinion) unquestionably indigenous nature of burials such as those at Castulo, Setefilla or even La Joya, and with the virtual absence of these very items in Phoenician burials in Iberia (Marín Ceballos 1988: 47).

In all, this association of bronze vessels with a ritual function is a qualitative indicator of status, far more so than the accumulation of many pottery dishes or even ornaments. However, the question of the degree to which these elements prove the adoption by local elites of a foreign ritual system or even religion, or only the modification of these Oriental rituals (libation, perfumes, sacrifice) to suit pre-existing local customs, or even the straightforward adoption of luxury items without their original meaning (on these issues see González Wagner 1992; Belén Deamos 1994: 506 ff.) remains open to debate.

The high statistical correlation of princely burials with this ritual-set may be related to a particular conception of power in which the sacred element was prominent, perhaps more so than in any other item.

5) Imported objects of exceptional workmanship. Apart from the ritual-set mentioned above, another characteristic feature of princely graves (compared with more 'common' graves) during the Orientalizing Period, is the systematic deposition of imported objects of exquisite workmanship, which are not found in other burials. They appear in addition to the more frequent, precious elements such as ivory combs, ostrich eggs, belt buckles, brooches and other items also found in simpler burials.

A good example of this kind of precious item is the ivory casket from Tomb 17 at La Joya in Huelva (Garrido and Orta 1978). Its four legs are carved in the shape of walking human figures in Egyptianizing style, while the hinges are of cast silver (Fig. 4). Other examples are large oval dishes in bronze with incised decoration (La Joya 16), alabaster containers of Egyptianizing style (La Joya 9), jewellery of the highest quality (Aliseda), translucent glass vessels with decorative 'nonsense' Egyptian hieroglyphic inscriptions (Aliseda), silver dishes (El Palmarón, Aliseda, Castulo), and bronze vessels with anthropomorphic figures (Castulo). Even the comparatively modest burial at El Carpio in Toledo contains elements that can be considered exceptional in the context of the Meseta or central plateau of Spain.[7]

But of course the most prominent symbol of status in Orientalizing graves are chariots, which so far have only been attested in serious archaeological contexts at La Joya. Light chariots of the Aegean type were known during the Bronze Age, Geometric Period of Tartessos as the carved images on the so-called Estelas del Suroeste clearly show (Quesada 1995a; in English see Piggott 1983: 131-133). These earlier, light war chariots have however, nothing in common with the Orientalizing Period vehicles from Graves 17 and 18 at La Joya. In Grave 17, in particular, the remains point to a rectangular hearse and not to a light war chariot (Fig. 3). The bronze terrets, delicate bronze ornaments, and elaborate axle-caps modelled as lions' heads prove that these were funeral wagons similar to those found in the royal cemetery at Salamis in Cyprus and not the war vehicles of bellicose chiefs (see also Aubet 1984: 451). Other tombs may have contained chariots, but as most of them have not been excavated in controlled condition, it is now impossible to tell. Some elements of other Orientalizing chariots however (notably terrets) have been found and are in private collections in Andalusia (e.g., Ferrer and Mancebo 1991). These ornamented hearses were probably the most exclusive element in the grave-goods of the greatest chiefs, princes or kings.

6) Weapon rarity. Perhaps unexpectedly, weapons are very rare among the grave-goods of the Orientalizing Period (see e.g., Maier 1992). However, they are not completely absent (as has sometimes been stated) in princely graves of the period. There were sets of iron weapons in some princely and even rich burials: a sword and spears) with spear-butts at El Palmaron and La Joya 16; a sword of a very interesting type at Finca Torrubia in Castulo; only a pair (probably) of spears at Cañada de Ruiz Sánchez (see references in Fig. 11). Other burials in this status group did not contain weapons but have usually been assumed (e.g., Aliseda) or have been proved by osteological analysis (El Carpio) to be feminine. Thus, although the percentage of princely burials with weapons is low it is not negligible. The really important point however, is that weapons are not a core element in the composition of grave-goods in the sense (detailed above) that the ritual-set is. Moreover, the composition of these grave-goods seems to indicate that the idea of a warrior aristocracy was not central to the conception of power during the Orientalizing Age, but that the ritual aspects were more important. Of course, iron (as a new material) is nearly always present in these burials in the form of curved knives; but these should not be regarded as weapons, but simply as instruments, very probably used in association with sacrificial rituals (involving drinking, libations and food) common throughout the Mediterranean Basin. Therefore, iron knives should not be associated with the weapon sets, but with the bronze ritual assemblages (see above point 4).

The fact that war (or at least the possibility of it) was well known and feared by Tartessian rulers is clear from the evidence in settlements. Sophisticated fortifications with massive stone walls and square bastions were known during the eighth century BC (e.g., Torre de Doña Blanca, Cádiz: Ruiz Mata 1993: 490-493; Tejada la Vieja, Huelva: García Sanz 1987: 103-104) and became common in the seventh century, both in the central and peripheral areas of Tartessos (Puente Tablas, Torreparedones, Ategua; see respectively Ruiz Rodríguez et al. 1991: 114; Cunliffe et al. 1993: 522; Blanco 1983).[8] During the sixth century BC fortifications were the norm in *oppida* (e.g., Cerro de las Cabezas, Fuente Tójar; Vaquerizo et al. 1992: 180-181). This being the case, the scarcity of weapons in burials acquires a new significance: even if fortifications were largely symbolic or of deterrent value, they were prominent in daily life. The fact that weapons are so scarce in burials (and in particular in princely burials) means that even if they were known and used, weapons did not have the symbolic and conceptual pre-eminence that they would acquire later, (i.e., from the fourth century onwards).[9]

6) High-status perishables. A further element that marked status in princely burials are the imported amphorae of Phoenician (or later) Greek types which are also present in settlements such as Huelva or El Carambolo. They are proof of the small-scale consumption of imported wine by local elites during the eighth-seventh centuries BC. Wine was a rare commodity during this period and was not produced locally until some decades later about the end of the seventh or early sixth century BC. During the Orientalizing phase it was probably reserved for consumption by indigenous elites and their immediate followers and would not have been distributed to lower status groups (Aubet 1984: 451; Quesada 1994a: 115).[10]

A controversial (and unconfirmed) possibility exists that human sacrifices were deposited around some burials during the seventh century BC. This possibility was raised by Bonsor at Acebuchal (Bonsor 1899: 294) where he found a cemetery containing inhumations in contorted positions, which he interpreted as human sacrifices, stoned to death ('*lapidados*'). This same hypothesis has been recently put forward by J.P. Garrido to explain inhumations of some individuals, apparently tied and surrounded by stones, near

Grave 17 at La Joya in Huelva (Garrido 1989: 32). This theory, however, must still be treated with reserve (Ruiz Delgado 1989: 262).

Changing patterns: the fifth century

The conceptions of power detailed above and their expression in the material remains of funerary rites take a different form during the fifth century after the disappearance around 500 BC of the archaeological horizon called 'Tartessos'. There are very few (if any) funerary remains in the southwest that can be dated to the fifth century BC. We must, therefore, turn our attention to the southeast, especially to Albacete and the high Guadalquivir Valley where the Iberian Culture was emerging and where new patterns of funerary ritual and new systems of displaying power were being developed.

These new patterns can be summarised with three points: 1) new types of grave-goods, deposited to show a still qualitative conception of power, status and wealth; 2) use of monumental sculpture and of a new, military iconography; and 3) new patterns in the use of wine.

Grave-goods, the rise of Greek imports and the perpetuation of tradition

Around 500 BC a local ruler was buried in what is now called Pozo Moro (Albacete) beside a very important trade route which was later called Via Heraklea (Almagro-Gorbea 1983: 182). The cremation of the grave-goods together with the body leaves us with little to study but their remains are enough to provide a few guidelines (Fig. 6). There are remains of objects made of different raw materials (at least pottery, gold, silver, bronze, iron and bone; see Almagro-Gorbea 1983: 184 ff.). However, there are no iron fragments which can be identified as weapons, although the remains are in very poor condition. One still finds the same sort of ritual-set described above for the Orientalizing Period, but with a different emphasis: the bronze jug is now of Greek and not of Oriental type and manufacture (Fig. 6b), and the bronze brazier has been replaced by an Attic kylix of the Pithos Painter group (Fig. 6d). Finally, this philohellenic prince was buried with an Attic lekythos (Fig. 6c) instead of alabaster perfume pots. In all, it seems that Greek influence was beginning to supersede the earlier, Orientalizing (Semitic) tradition. Finally, the burial I have described was placed under a turriform funerary monument of imposing size and decoration of which more will be said later.

Even if new materials of Greek origin were finding their way into Iberian burials all over the Iberian southeast,[11] Orientalizing-Tartessian traditions were still present. For example, in Tumulus Grave 20 at Galera in Granada (dated to the second half of the fifth century by the remains of a Greek *mesomphalos phiale*), an alabaster statuette in the shape of an enthroned fertility goddess of Syrian type was buried generations after it was made (i.e., the piece can be confidently dated on stylistic grounds to the seventh century BC; Blázquez 1975: 187-192; Olmos and Shefton 1991: 301ff.; Almagro-Gorbea 1992: 42). This survival of outstanding objects (even if they can be considered merely as heirlooms) points to the survival and understanding of rituals and traditions closely connected with power and status display.

In my opinion, these and other evidence show that while a new culture (based on the local substratum and on strong Punic and Greek influences) was developing in the southeast, the Orientalizing or Tartessian heritage also determined the shape of this new culture and, furthermore, that some links with the traditional conceptions of power still persisted.

Weapons

There are not many burials clearly datable to the fifth century BC in the southeast and very few of them contain weapons. Thus it seems that in this respect the pattern is similar to that of the sixth century: the most important burials often, but by no means always, contain weapons among the grave-goods deposited with the ashes of the deceased. For example, very few burials in the earlier levels at Los Villares (Albacete) contain weapons: probably none in the sixth century graves (Blánquez 1992: 247-253) and only a very few in the fifth century ones (e.g., Grave 18; see below). At Cabezo Lucero (Alicante) (one of the earliest Iberian cemeteries in Alicante and the one with the highest percentage of warrior burials) about 47% of the burials dated to the later fifth century contain weapons; this figure rises to 65% in the fourth century BC. On the whole, early (sixth-fifth centuries BC) coastal sites along the Mediterranean seaboard of the peninsula have a far higher proportion of warrior burials than do the inland and western areas which were more influenced by the Orientalizing tradition. Thus, the sites at El Molar (Alicante) or even further north at La Solivella (Castellón), Mianes (Tarragona), Llinars del Valles, Granja Soley (Barcelona) and many others are all small cemeteries or even isolated burials which contain a high proportion of weapons, including straight iron swords of north-Pyrenean type, bronze greaves and disc-breastplates (Quesada 1997). In all, the proportion of weapons in burials grew steadily during the fifth century; a pattern that can be connected with the growth of a new, militaristic monumental iconography.

The use of sculpture as an expression of old and new ideologies

There is a major break with the past in the new types of funerary monuments now to be found all over the Iberian area. Instead of the low round mounds of the Orientalizing Period, one now finds towering monuments of dressed masonry, decorated with reliefs or free-standing sculpture. These monuments have undoubtedly an Oriental origin as some examples of monumental funerary sculpture from the Phoenician colony at Almuñecar in the province of Granada prove (Almagro-Gorbea 1983: 230-231, 269-270). The first and best known of these turriform monuments is Pozo Moro, the reliefs of which are of clear Oriental (north-Syrian) influence and seem on stylistic grounds much earlier that the date of c. 500 BC assigned to the monument based on the above mentioned grave-goods as datum point. This fact has led some scholars (Bendala Galan 1987: 239 ff.) to hypothesise that the monument itself might be earlier (seventh century BC?) than the subsequent burial (c. 500 BC). Be that as it may, the fact remains that the mythological reliefs at Pozo Moro do not have many military connotations and the religious and ritual iconographic evidence suggests that the concept of power reflected by these images is more Orientalizing than Iberian, and thus would be a bit 'backwards' if the monument was to be dated to c. 500 BC.

In fact, only ten years after the princely burial at Pozo Moro (using the now accepted chronology; e.g. Blánquez 1992), a completely new form of art (in style and concept) emerged in Porcuna (Jaén) where a complex monument with many nearly life-size, free-standing sculptures was built c. 490 BC (Negueruela 1990). Its style has even been described as Phokaian (Blázquez and González 1985) although it is now generally agreed that it was the work of local artisans (even if they were acquainted with the current Ionian Greek styles). It is generally believed that it formed part of a funerary monument, but this cannot be proved as the monument was destroyed in antiquity, perhaps not long after its completion. However, it seems certain that the monument embodied some kind of heroic significance. There are at least two series of sculptures, the best preserved of which displays a series of fights, with one side clearly gaining the upper hand. Weapons, horse harnesses and wounds are clearly represented with a deep sense of *akribeia*. It is evident that not only the style but also the ideology reflected in these groups is profoundly different from that shown in the reliefs at Pozo Moro; the emphasis has shifted from a mythological and ritual world (in which the sacred content of power was emphasised) to a more warlike ideology. A concept of funerary heroization probably underlies both iconographic programs, although they are undoubtedly different in character.

These two are not the only monuments to be found in Iberian cemeteries during the later part of the sixth and fifth centuries BC: a catalogue would also document Greek-type archaic stelae with sphinxes (and also lions, bulls and fantastic animals) on top of different kinds of monuments (see the most complete, if slightly outdated, catalogue in Almagro-Gorbea 1983). This multitude of sculptures, standing against the aniconic tradition of Tartessian tumuli, shows not only a different tradition of external markers for burials, but also a new and more structured society in which different levels of rank probably had access to different types of monument ranging from the royal towers to the low mounds. At Los Villares in Albacete for example, two funerary monuments (dated to the beginning and end of the fifth century BC respectively) consist of a low, square platform acting as a tumulus on which a smaller than life-size stone equestrian sculpture was erected (Blánquez 1992). In both cases the riders are unarmed (they are not fighting warriors as in Porcuna) and again one is reminded that the main symbols of power are not weapons. In these funerary monuments, one probably has the evidence of a class of Iberian *hippeis* of rank lower than that of the true princes or monarchs buried at Pozo Moro and, perhaps, at Porcuna. The first of these burials Tumulus 18 (c. 490 BC, or about the same time as Porcuna), contains, among the grave-goods, an iron spearhead and its butt; one of the first sets of weapons documented in a properly Iberian burial. However, this can hardly be compared with the much more complex panoplies deposited even in poor burials during the fourth century BC (see below). The second burial at Los Villares (dated to c. 410 BC) did not contain a single weapon; however, a big assemblage of around fifty Attic vases was left as an offering deposit near the urn.

Changing patterns in the social uses of wine

As the site at Alt de Benimaquia (Alicante) has proved beyond doubt (Gomez Bellard et al. 1993), there is clear evidence of the local production of wine by the beginning of the sixth century. However, the production of local wines remained the privilege of the local aristocracies during the sixth and fifth centuries BC and the processes of production and storage were restricted to small, fortified settlements, where they could be strictly controlled. This pattern quickly spread to inland areas such as Albacete where the later small site at La Quejola can hardly be described as a settlement as most of the buildings were used to store wine amphorae (Blánquez 1993). I believe that while the wine service buried at Pozo Moro (Attic cup and bronze jug) still reflected the restricted and restrictive use of imported wine by the ruling elites c. 500 BC, local production (and therefore the increased availability of wine) meant a radical change. From the sixth century onwards wine was probably redistributed by the aristocracies to wider (and lower) social groups at events such as funerary ceremonies and on more mundane occasions such as feasts-of-merit and other community banquets (Quesada 1994a: 115-117). In this particular aspect in a way quality was giving way to quantity as well.

The 'classical' Iberian culture in the fourth century BC

During the so-called 'classical' or 'middle' period of the Iberian Culture in the fourth century BC (Ibérico Pleno), many changes took place in the conception of power, in the social structure of cemeteries and in the composition of grave-goods; so much so that in some respects the burials of the fifth century can be shown to be nearer in 'spirit' (whatever that is taken to mean) to the Orientalizing Period than to the later phase. These changes can be summarised as follows: princely tombs in the sense of the earlier periods came to an end; the earlier wagon graves did not have any real successors; the composition of grave-goods in burials changed (weapons became the main symbol of power and, indirectly, of wealth); and other expressions of status in cemeteries, such as the deposition of gold or ritual-sets, became less conspicuous.

Princely burials during the fourth century BC: a misleading term?

It was Dr. E. Cuadrado who coined the term 'princely graves' to refer to fourth century burials when he published Burials 200 and 277 at El Cigarralejo (Murcia) (Cuadrado 1968). The expression stuck and has been used ever since. Both burials date to the first half of the fourth century BC and consist of low square platforms of undressed stone. They are big (about 7.0 m square as against the usual 1.0-1.5 m square platforms of common burials) but not essentially different because the burials underneath (placed in oval pits) follow the usual pattern of the site. They are undoubtedly the burials of the local rulers from the early part of the fourth century BC, as their dominant position in the cemetery area (Quesada et al. 1995), the size of the tumuli, and the wealth of the grave-goods clearly prove. What is not really evident to us, however, is that the term princely can be deemed appropriate in this and other similar cases.

Although the grave-goods in these burials are impressive and although a 'wealth-units' method of quantifying wealth shows a great difference in wealth between these burials and the rest (see Quesada 1994b Fig. 4 for a graphic layout), I am not so sure that the term 'princes' rather than 'warrior aristocrats' is *le mot juste*. On the one hand, the grave-goods are not conceptually or qualitatively different from many other different sets from the same site and among which there are many differences in wealth. On the other hand, even if the tumuli are by far the biggest, they lack the princely distinction of Pozo Moro, Porcuna or other earlier monuments. In fact, the whole cemetery has a certain rural or local feel to it (even if the more cosmopolitan examples: Ilici in Alicante, or Cástulo in Jaen are not nearly as well-known). The same can be said of Burial 70 at Coimbra del Barranco Ancho in Murcia which is the best candidate for a princely (female) burial at that site (Iniesta et al. 1987), or of Burial 400 at Cabecico del Tesoro also in Murcia (Quesada 1989a).

Wagon graves?

There were no wagon graves in Iberia during the fourth century BC in the European La Tène or even in the Orientalizing Peninsular sense of the term. The *wagengräber* cited by Stary (1989) as belonging to his second phase (Cabecico del Tesoro, Baza, etc.) do not really exist. True, there are some heavy, iron-felloe wheels to be found in some tombs belonging to this period, but they cannot be compared with the princely Salamis type graves and complete chariots from La Joya. Among the late wagon graves, Grave 397 at El Cabecico (Stary 1989: 182; Fernández Miranda and Olmos 1986: 88) certainly does not qualify: a small unclassified piece of iron (which was probably meant to hold together two pieces of wood, and which was found in an otherwise very unexceptional grave) does not make for a wagon grave let alone a princely one. If any grave in this important site should be labelled princely, it would be Grave 400. It contains iron disc-breastplates, a set of offensive and other defensive weapons and belt-buckles with engraved silver decoration but no remains of a chariot (Quesada 1989a: volume 2). Also, there is no reason to consider that the possible chariot or wagon from Alcacer do Sal (near Lisbon, Portugal) belongs to a grave that should be dated to the fourth or even to the fifth century BC. Even if the scanty remains belonged to such a grave (Schüle 1969: taf. 107; Olmos and Fernández Miranda 1986: 87), the grave itself may have been much earlier as proof exists of six-century, Orientalizing levels in the site (Paixao 1983). Most other wheels dating to the fourth-second centuries BC come from settlements or from simple burials. Moreover, they are of a heavy type with much iron construction in them, typical of normal, everyday wagons and not of light, war chariots or elaborate funerary hearses. It is probable that sometimes (i.e., rarely) wheels were deposited in burials as *pars pro toto* and even that these wheels symbolised rites of transition and passage; but these features do not make for princely tombs.

Imported pottery as an expression of wealth and conspicuous consumption

During the fourth century BC another change in the composition of grave-goods (already visible in earlier sites such as Los Villares in Albacete) became evident. Attic black-glaze pottery (on the whole of a lower quality than in the earlier periods) became very common in burials both in Andalusia and the southeast (e.g., Cabrera 1994) while the productions from other workshops disappeared (e.g., in the southeast; Sala 1991).

The new repertoire of shapes in native sites is rather limited in comparison with, for example, the Greek colony of Emporion and consists mainly of open forms such as Lamboglia shapes 21, 22, 23 (Sánchez 1992; Rouillard 1991). The rare late-fifth century products of good quality, such as the cup from Lorca (García Cano 1989-90) tend to disappear. Attic red-figure ware is also frequent but the pieces are usually of abysmal quality (e.g., Retorted Painter). It has often been said that red-figure ware is more common in the more urban Andalusia while black-glaze is typical of the southeast. I believe this not to be the case and that if patterns are apparently different, then this is really only because of the earlier excavations in Andalusia, when black-glaze was simply not studied. Where modern excavations have taken place in Jaén or Granada the proportion of simple black-glaze is much greater.

A visible tendency towards the accumulation of Attic pottery in burials as an expression of wealth is also evident in well excavated sites such as Cigarralejo (Murcia), Coimbra (Murcia) or Cabezo Lucero (Alicante). Perhaps the best examples are the already mentioned princely tombs at Cigarralejo (200 and 277), and Grave 70 at Coimbra. While the ruler at Pozo Moro was buried c. 500 BC with a few selected Greek imports of clear and coherent ritual significance, the local aristocrats of the fourth century chose to be buried with up to 16 Greek vases of only four different shapes (including seven *bolsals*) (Figs 7-9; Cigarralejo Grave 200; see Cuadrado 1987: 370) which were clearly trade lots and not ritual-sets and thus which show wealth by accumulation.

It has sometimes been stated that the frequent occurrence of Attic pottery in Iberian burials implied a high degree of Hellenisation. I believe this is simply an oversimplification. While the selection of objects at Pozo Moro or the perfume pots from Los Villares may imply a certain knowledge of the ritual significance of each vessel, the accumulation of Attic pottery of generally open, drinking shapes, combined with the absence of perfume pots or jugs in fourth century sites, implies a different approach, in which the expression of status through foreign wealth was clearly more important than the understanding and adoption of foreign uses. The pattern of distribution of imported vessels in lower-wealth and therefore lower-status burials seems to confirm this idea: the range of shapes is more or less the same (with certain exceptions mainly in Andalusia) but the number of vases diminishes dramatically (see Quesada 1994b: Fig. 4; Santos Velasco 1994: 71-72). The use of black-glaze or red-figure ware and even the occasional occurrence of the odd shape (e.g., García Cano 1985-86) does not show any knowledge of Greek burial rites or ideas about death and does not imply Hellenisation in the full sense of the term. True, there is an abundance of wine-mixing and wine-drinking Greek vases (Santos Velasco 1991: 252; Olmos and Sanchez 1995; Blánquez 1995) but this need not imply the custom of symposia or of funerary *deipna* in the Greek sense of the term. In fact, wine was known and produced in Iberia before Greek colonisation. If there were social and funerary customs associated with the conspicuous consumption of wine and beer, then this has more to do with very old local customs than with superficial Hellenisation (see Quesada 1994a: 118-119). For example, as Olmos and Sanchez have pointed out when writing about kraterae, 'in the Iberian world the Greek collective vessel is transformed into an individual one' (1995: 124). Nothing can be further away from the concept of Hellenisation.

On the uses of gold

Another interesting pattern in Iberian burials is the extreme scarcity of jewellery or artefacts made of precious materials (particularly gold) even in otherwise very rich graves. This problem has been recently (and, in my opinion, satisfactorily) resolved by Chapa and Pereira (1991). These scholars believe that although objects (jewellery and vessels) made of gold were frequent among the Iberians (and many literary sources testify to this) they were not usually deposited as grave-goods because they were of the highest value and therefore linked to inheritance and the idea of transmission of power. Thus, the high intrinsic value of gold was replaced in burials by the accumulation of other objects as an expression of wealth: pottery (and especially imported pottery) and weapons.

Weapons: the foundations of power

The abundance of weapons in Iberian burials is arguably the best indicator of the profound changes that took place between the Orientalizing/early Iberian Period and the later phase. As we have already seen, from the last decades of the fifth century BC (c. 425-410 BC) onwards the percentage of burials with weapons rose sharply. Perhaps the site at Cabezo Lucero in Alicante (Aranegui et al. 1993) is the best example of the dramatic rise in the number of weapons from c. 425 BC. During the fourth century BC this pattern became the norm. A normal figure of burials with weapons is between 25-45% in the southeast Iberian cemeteries (see Fig. 13): e.g., Cabecico del Tesoro (Quesada 1989a) or Cigarralejo (Cuadrado 1989).

Thus, while weapons were rare during the Orientalizing and early Iberian Period[12] (and mostly limited to princely or very rich burials) during the Iberico Pleno in the fourth century BC the right (or custom) of carrying weapons into the grave became much more extended and included wider (i.e., lower) segments of the population. Another significant fact is that weapons are now often found grouped into coherent panoplies: the simpler ones consist of *falcata* sword, round shield and two spears; the complex ones may also contain a helmet, *soliferreum* and dagger.[13] However, it is not uncommon that the concept of wealth through accumulation, which was observed when discussing Attic pottery and other grave-goods, should also lead to the stockpiling of weapons: it is thus possible to find three or more spearheads, two swords and even, very occasionally, two shields in a particular burial, therefore disturbing the original functional or coherent panoplies.

On the one hand, therefore, the richer Iberian burials had a distinct military appearance during the fourth century BC as complex sets of weapons (often decorated with silver inlay motifs) make-up a considerable part of the grave-goods. On the other hand, weapons also became common in poorer burials.

In fact, it has been proven that burials in all wealth groups contained weapons, but that although nearly all of the very rich burials contain them, only a small proportion of the poorer groups had weapons and these were usually simple panoplies without daggers, helmets and other elements of the richer assemblages (see Quesada 1994b: Fig. 5). However, it can also be proved that burials with weapons are, on the whole, considerably richer than those without them; this is the case even if the weapons themselves are not taken into account when calculating the figures for wealth deposited in the different categories of burials.[14] In a society which had become much more involved with weapons, it seems that these differences in wealth must also mean differences in social status, an idea confirmed by the fact that the pattern of deposition of weapons tends to coincide with that of imported Attic pottery, the other great indicator of status and wealth (see Quesada 1989a; 1994b; Santos Velasco 1994 and especially 1989: 83-85).

From sacred monarchies to warrior aristocracies?

The pattern of facts described above fits well with the theory put forward by M. Almagro-Gorbea (1992). Almagro has developed a model of evolution of the concept of power during the Iron Age with which I generally agree. This scholar believes that during the Orientalizing and early Iberian Period (roughly eighth-sixth centuries BC) one

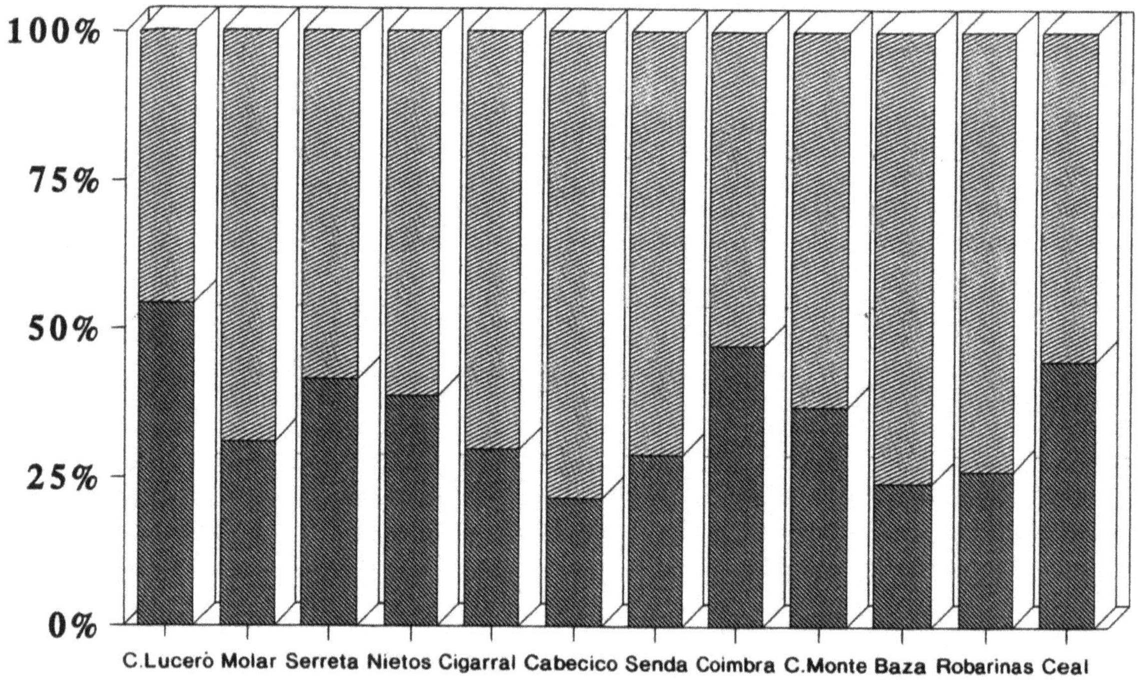

	C.Lucerò	Molar	Serreta	Nietos	Cigarral	Cabecico	Senda	Coimbra	C.Monte	Baza	Robarinas	Ceal
G. without weapons	43	178	31	19	383	472	32	38	24	135	31	21
Graves with weapons	51	80	22	12	162	129	13	34	14	43	11	17

Graves with weapons   G. without weapons

Figure 13 Iberian cemeteries in Andalusia and the southeast. Percentage of burials containing weapons.

should think in terms of 'sacred monarchies' with a nutritious function. During the fifth century this pattern would have evolved into different, 'heroic monarchies', which in turn disappeared by the end of the fifth century when 'warrior aristocracies' appeared.

I find the observed development of burial rites quite compatible with this idea. During the Orientalizing Period the Tartessian rulers were buried with rich grave-goods, conspicuously ritual in nature, including the ritual-set of bronze and silver vessels (*thymiateria*, libation jugs and dishes) iron knives and sometimes elaborate hearses. During the fifth century (early Iberian), the evidence from Pozo Moro and other sites shows that while a new culture based on the local substratum and on strong Punic and Greek influences was developing in the southeast (the Orientalizing or Tartessian heritage was also crucial in the shaping of this new culture) and that some links with the traditional conceptions of power still persisted: weapons were still rare in grave-goods and the reliefs at Pozo Moro are of a mythological nature. There are, however, signs of a more heroic understanding of power, as reflected in the same monument at Pozo Moro or in the complex fighting scenes at Porcuna. The composition of grave-goods shows increasing signs of Greek influence as do many funerary monuments crowned with sphinxes in the Greek style. At Los Villares in Albacete one can probably find evidence of a class of Iberian *hippeis* of lower rank than the princes or monarchs buried at Pozo Moro or (perhaps) Porcuna. The first of these burials (dated to c. 490 BC) contains an iron spearhead and its butt, one of the first sets of weapons documented in a genuinely Iberian burial. This, however, can hardly be compared with the much more complex panoplies deposited during the fourth century BC.

During the middle Iberian (roughly, fourth and third centuries BC), the standardised ritual-set disappeared from burials, although some of its elements, modified and simplified, remained in use, such as the bronze braziers or dishes of Iberian type (Type 2 in the classification of Cuadrado 1966). On the other hand, the complex bronze incense burners made of many different composite elements (including hathoric figures; Fig. 4) disappeared after the late sixth or early fifth century (Bandera and Ferrer 1994a: 53). The main indicator of wealth, and also probably of status, was now the accumulation of objects and this is clear from the large sets of Attic black-glaze pottery: at this time one should not expect to find a bronze jug or a good quality drinking cup such as those at Pozo Moro; rather one should expect drinking cups and plates of indifferent quality in sometimes large numbers (Fig. 8). Weapons (complete panoplies) became very common in all ranks of the segment of society represented in the formal burials of Iberian cemeteries and can nearly always be found in the richer burials. In all, the symbolic and social importance of weapons in Iberian funerary rites of the fourth century BC seems to reflect a new concept of power closely linked to military prowess which was different in character from that of previous societies. These aristocracies showed this in their grave-goods not only by the abundance of weapons but also by the accumulation of artefacts which differed more in number than in kind from those of poorer groups, who in many cases appear to have been their military retainers (see also Ruiz and Molinos 1993: 227).

Endnotes

1. This paper has been prepared within the framework of Research Projects PB 94/0189 and PB 97/0057.

2. Bibliography in English covering the Orientalizing Period and the Iberian Culture is not extensive, but fortunately we can now cite a few recent and useful summaries. For the Phoenician colonisation in the Peninsula the English translation of the work by M.E. Aubet (1993a; 1993b) is probably the best choice, although it has been superseded by an updated edition in Spanish which includes new and important discoveries on the Atlantic coasts of Portugal (Aubet 1994). The Greek presence in the Iberian Peninsula is more than adequately covered by A. Domínguez Monedero (1991). There is a (somewhat outdated) survey of the material culture of the Orientalizing Period in Chamorro (1987). The book by T. Judice Gamito on Tartessos is controversial (Judice Gamito 1988; see review by González Wagner, 1990 and answer by the author 1992). A brief but systematic and updated review of the cultural phases in the different regions of Iberia (including inland areas), during the first millennium BC, is that by M. Almagro-Gorbea and G. Ruiz Zapatero (1992), while Harrison's book, aimed more at the layman, can still be useful for English-speaking readers (Harrison 1988). On the complex matter of the relationships between Iberia and the Mediterranean throughout this very extended period the most recent summary is Cunliffe (1993). The Proceedings of the British Academy seminar edited by Cunliffe and S. Keay are an up-to-date, scholarly approach to many points of detail (Cunliffe and Keay 1995). All these works provide extensive bibliographies.

3. On the subject of mining and metallurgic importance of the Huelva region, a good summary will be found in Ruiz Mata (1989).

4. For example see Escacena (1989) and Bendala (1991).

5. See for example the non-princely mounds at Setafilla in Seville ('B') or Torre de Doña Blanca in Cadiz.

6. I do not really believe that La Cruz del Negro or some other sites in the area of Seville can be considered Phoenician or 'Semitic' as has been suggested. The elements of the discussion have been summarised recently by M. Belén Deamos (1994: 508-510).

7. The facts that the anthropological analysis of the burial at El Carpio (Toledo) has shown the burial to be that of a young woman and a newborn baby (Pereira 1989: 396) and that the jewels at Aliseda look feminine (which is by no means certain) have led M. Ruiz Galvez (1992: 238) to put forward the interesting hypothesis that the rich Orientalizing grave-goods, located so far from the Tartessian core area, may in fact have been the dowries of Tartessian princesses married to local lords. These dynastic marriages would have been part of a system of alliances to ensure peaceful trade and communications.

8. Contra Carrilero 1992: 126.

9. Of course, many weapons have been found underwater in the Ría del Huelva, but they are much earlier, perhaps dating to the mid-ninth or even tenth century BC when other pre-colonial conditions were applicable. On the other hand, at least two Greek helmets of Corinthian-type of Orientalizing date have been found underwater near Huelva (mid-sixth century BC) and Jerez de la Frontera (beginning of the seventh century BC) (Olmos 1988). They are probably votive offerings made either by foreign sailors or by local rulers. No other examples of this date have been found inland, in burials or elsewhere.

10. Phoenicians used wine as a first-class trading product not only in Tartessos but also along the Mediterranean coast as far north as the Ebro during the seventh century as the discoveries at Aldovesta show (see Quesada 1994a: 110 with further references).

11. On Greek imports during the sixth century BC: in general - Rouillard 1991; for Murcia - García Cano and Page 1991: 228; for Alicante - Sala 1991; for Andalusia - Cabrera 1994 (with a marked decrease in imports during the second half of the century).

12. This applies to the Iberian sites in Andalusia and the southeast. In Valencia and Catalonia the Iberian burials dated to the sixth-fifth centuries BC contain complex sets of aristocratic weapons, including bronze greaves. These burials show intense northern influence.

13. I have also argued elsewhere that the use of the bow in warfare was considered improper, as arrows were held to be effeminate and cowardly weapons not worthy of real warriors. This ideology would explain the almost complete absence of arrowheads in Iberian burials when they were relatively common during the Orientalizing Period in the more Semitic areas of the southwest (although they only appear in settlements and not in cemeteries; see Quesada 1989b; 1997).

14. For example, at El Cabecico (Murcia), burials containing weapons have a wealth index of 16.9 wealth units as against only 9.0 for the whole site and 5.3 for those burials without weapons. Just in case weapons had been overvalued, a new test was performed in which the value assigned to weapons was not taken into account. Burials with weapons were found to have a mean value of 10.3 wealth units, while the mean value of the 566 burials with grave-goods in the site was 8.5, and of those without weapons was still 5.3 (see Quesada 1989a, volume 1: 176 ff. for details and volume 2: 120-121 for a summary in English. On the complex matter of relationship between wealth and status in fourth century sites see also Quesada 1994b: 454 ff.).

Bibliography

Almagro-Gorbea, M. 1977. *El Bronce Final y el Periodo Orientalizante en Extremadura*. (Bibliotheca Praehistorica Hispana, Madrid: 14). Madrid: Consejo Superior de Investigaciones Científicas.

Almagro-Gorbea, M. 1983. Pozo Moro. El monumento orientalizante, su contexto socio-cultural y sus paralelos en la arquitectura funeraria ibérica. *Madrider Mitteilungen* 24: 177-293.

Almagro-Gorbea, M. 1989. Arqueología e Historia Antigua: el proceso protoorientalizante y el inicio de los contactos de Tartessos con el Levante Mediterráneo. *Gerión, Anejos II. Heomenaje al Prof. S. Montero,* pp. 277-288. Madrid: Ediciones de la Universidad Compultense.

Almagro-Gorbea, M. 1990. El periodo Orientalizante en Extremadura. In *La Cultura Tartésica y Extremadura* (Cuadernos Emeritenses 2), pp. 85-125. Mérida: Museo Nacional de Arte Romano.

Almagro-Gorbea, M. 1991a. La necrópolis de Medellín. *Extremadura Arqueológica* 2: 159-173.

Almagro-Gorbea, M. 1991b. La necrópolis de Medellín. Influencia fenicia en los rituales funerarios tartésicos. In *I-IV Jornadas de Arqueología Fenicio-púnica.*, pp. 233-252. Eivissa: Museo Arqueológico de Eivissa.

Almagro-Gorbea, M. 1992. Las necrópolis ibéricas en su contexto mediterráneo. In *Congreso de Arqueología Ibérica: las Necrópolis,* (serie Varia), edited by J. Blánquez Pérez and V. Antona del Val, pp. 37-75. Madrid: Dpto. de Prehistoria y Arqueología de la UAM.

Almagro-Gorbea, M. and G. Ruiz Zapatero 1992. Palaeoethnology of Iberian Peninsula: state of knowledge and future perspectives. *Paleoetnología de la Península Ibérica, Complutum* 2-3: 501-517.

Aranegui, C., A. Jodin, E. Llobregat, P. Rouillard and J. Uroz 1993. *La Nécropole Ibérique de Cabezo Lucero (Guardamar del Segura, Alicante).* Madrid-Alicante: École des Hautes Études Hispaniques, Instituto de Cultura Juan Gil-Albert.

Arribas, A., and J. Wilkins 1971 La necrópolis fenicia del Cortijo de las Sombras (Frigiliana). *Pyrenae* 5: 185-244.

Arruda, M.A. 1994. *Orientalismo e Orientalizante. Génese e Aplicaçtao dos Conceitos na Idade do Ferro do Centro-Sul de Portugal.* Lisboa.

Aubet, M.E. 1975. *La Necrópolis de Setefilla en Lora del Río (Sevilla).* Barcelona: Consejo Superior de Investigaciones Cientificas y Universidad de Barcelona.

Aubet, M.E 1978. *La Necrópolis de Setefilla en Lora del Río (Carmona). El túmulo B.* Barcelona: Consejo Superior de Investigaciones Cientificas y Universidad de Barcelona.

Aubet, M.E 1984. La aristocracia ibérica durante el periodo orientalizante. *Opus* 3: 445-468.

Aubet, M.E 1990. El impacto fenicio en Tartessos: las esferas de interacción. In *La Cultura Tartésica y Extremadura,* (Cuadernos Emeritenses 2), pp. 29-44. Mérida: Museo Nacional de Arte Romano.

Aubet, M.E 1993a. *The Poenicians and the West. Politics, Colonies and Trade.* Cambridge: Cambridge University Press.

Aubet, M.E 1993b. El comerç fenici i les comunitats del ferro a Catalunya. *Laietani* 8: 23-40.

Aubet, M.E 1994. *Tiro y las Colonias Fenicias de Occidente.* Barcelona: Crítica.

Bandera, M.L. and E. Ferrer 1994a. Thymiateria orientalizantes en bronce. In *Nuevas Aportaciones y Consideraciones. Homenaje al Prof. Presedo, edited by P. Sáez and S. Ordóñez,* pp. 43-60. Sevilla: Universidad de Sevilla.

Bandera, M.L. and E. Ferrer 1994b. El timiaterio orientalizante de Villagarcía de la Torre (Badajoz). *Archivo Español de Arqueología* 67: 41-61.

Bandera, M.L. and E. Ferrer 1995. Reconstrucción del Ajuar de una tumba de Cástulo: ¿Indicios de mestizaje? *Kolaios* 4: 53-65.

Belén Deamos, M. 1994. Fenicios en Andalucía Occidental. Diez años de investigación (1980-1990). *Hispania Antiqua* 18: 495-518.

Belén Deamos, M. 1995. El yacimiento tartésico de Niebla (Huelva). In *Tartessos, 50. Años Después*, pp. 359-379. Jerez de la Frontera: Ayuntamiento de Jerez.

Bendala, M. 1987. Arte ibérico. *Historia General de España y América. Tomo I.2*, pp. 223-250. Madrid: Rialp.

Bendala, M. 1991. La problemática de las necrópolis tartésicas. *Congreso de Arqueología Ibérica. Las Necrópolis*, (serie Varia), edited by J. Blanquez Perez and V. Antona del Val, pp. 27-36. Madrid: Dpto. de Prehistoria y Arqueología de la UAM.

Blanco, A. 1956. Orientalia. *Archivo Español de Arqueología* 29: 3-51.

Blanco, A. 1963. El ajuar de una tumba de Cástulo. *Archivo Español de Arqueología* 36: 40-69.

Blánquez, J. 1992a. Nuevas consideraciones en torno a la escultura ibérica. *Cuadernos de Prehistoria y Arqueología de la Universidad Autónoma de Madrid* 19: 121-143.

Blánquez, J. 1992b. Las necrópolis ibéricas en el Sureste de la Meseta. *Congreso de Arqueología Ibérica: las Necrópolis*, (serie Varia), edited by J. Blánquez Pérez and V. Antona del Val, pp. 235-278. Madrid: Dpto. De Prehistoria y Arqueología de la UAM.

Blánquez, J. 1993. El poblado ibérico de la Quéjola. *Patina* 6: 99-108.

Blánquez, J. 1995. El vino en los rituales funerarios ibéricos. In *Arqueología del Vino. Los Orígenes del Vino en Occidente*, edited by S. Celestino, pp. 213-240. Jerez de la Frontera: Consejo Regulador de las Denominaciones de Origen.

Blánquez, J.M. 1975. *Tartessos y los Orígenes de la Colonización Fenicia en Occidente*. Salamanca: Universidad de Salamanca.

Blánquez, J.M. and J. González Navarrete 1985. The Phokaian sculpture of Obulco in Southern Spain. *American Journal of Archaeology* 89 (1): 61-65.

Blánquez, J.M. and S. Valiente 1982. El poblado de La Muela y la fase orientalizante en Cástulo, (Jaén). Phönizier im Westen. *Madrider Beiträge* 8: 407-428.

Cabrera, P. 1994. La presencia griega en Andalucía (siglos VI-IV a.C.). In *La Andalucía Ibero-turdetana. Actas de la Jornadas*, (Huelva Arqueológica 14), edited by J. Fernánzez, P. Rufete and C. García, pp. 367-390. Huelva: Diputación Provincial.

Carrilero, M. 1992. El proceso de transformación de las sociedades indígenas de la periferia tartésica. In *La Colonización Fenicia en el sur de la Península Ibérica. 100 Años de Investigación. Almeria*, pp. 117-142. Almería: Instituto de Estudios Almerienses.

Chamorro, J.G. 1987. Survey of archaeological research on Tartessos. *American Journal of Archaeology* 91 (2): 197-232.

Chapa, T. and J. Pereira 1991. El oro como elemento de prestigio social en época ibérica. *Archivo Español de Arqueología* 64: 23-35.

Cuadrado, E. 1966. *Repertorio de los Recipientes Rituales Metálicos con 'Asas de Manos' de la Península Ibérica*. (Trabajos de Prehistoria Monografías 21). Madrid: Consejo Superior de Investigaciones Científicas.

Cuadrado, E. 1968. Tumbas principescas de El Cigarralejo. *Madrider Mitteilungen 9*: 148-186.

Cuadrado, E. 1987. *La Necrópolis Ibérica de El Cigarralejo, Mula, Murcia*. (Bibliotheca Praehistorica Hispana 23). Madrid: Consejo Superior de Investigaciones Científicas.

Cuadrado, E. 1989. La *Panoplia Ibérica de El Cigarralejo*. Murcia: Editora Regional.

Cunliffe, B. 1993. Core-periphery relationships: Iberia and the Mediterranean. In *Centre and Periphery in the Hellenistic World*, edited by P. Bilde, T. Engberg-Pedersen, L. Haanestad, J. Zahle, K. Randsborg (eds), pp. 53-85. Aarhus: Aarhus University Press.

Cunliffe, B., M.C. Fernández Castro, C. Poole, P. Davenport, I. Brook, S. Pressey, J.A. Morena and B. Torres 1993. Torreparedones, poblado fortificado en altura y su contexto en la Campiña de Córdoba. In *Investigaciones Arqueológicas en Andalucía 1985-1992*, pp. 519-528. Huelva: Junta de Andalucía.

Cunliffe, B. and S. Keay (eds) 1995. *Social Complexity and the Development of Towns in Iberia*. Oxford: Oxford University Press.

Domínguez Monedero, A. 1991. New perspectives on the Greek presence in the Iberian Peninsula. In *Proceedings of the First International Congress on the Hellenic Diaspora. Volume I*, pp. 109-161. Amsterdam: Gieben.

Enríquez, J.J. 1991. Los restos de la necrópolis de la desembocadura del río Aljucén dentro del contexto Orientalizante extremeño. *Extremadura Arqueológica* 2: 175-183.

Enriquez, J.J. and C. Domínguez 1991. Restos de una necrópolis orientalizante en la desembocadura del río Aljucén (Mérida, Badajoz). *Saguntum* 24: 35-52.

Escacena, J.L. 1989. Los turdetanos o la recuperación de la identidad perdida. In *Tartessos*, edited by M.E. Aubet, pp. 433-476. Sabadell: Ausa.

Fernández Jurado, J., P. Rufete, C. García Sanz, P. Cabrera, J.A. Correa, M. Cereijo, D. Paton, R. Moreno, A. Aguilar, F. Hernández 1988-89. Tartessos y Huelva. *Huelva Arqueológica* 10-11: 1-3.

Fernández Miranda, M. and J. Pereira 1992. Indigenismo y orientalización en la tierra de Talavera. In *Actas de las Primeras Jornadas de Arqueologia de Talavera de la Reina y sus Tierras*, pp. 57-94. Talavera de La Reina: Comunidad de Castilla-La Mancha.

Ferrer, E. and J. Mancebo 1991. Nuevos elementos de carros orientalizantes en la Alta Andalucía. *Cuadernos de Prehistoria y Arqueología de la Universidad Autónoma de Madrid* 18: 113-148.

García y Bellido, A. 1970. Algunas novedades sobre la arqueología púnico-tartesia. *Archivo Español de Arqueología* 43: 3-49.

García Cano, J.M. 1985-86. Una sepultura singular de 'El Cabecico del Tesoro'. *Boletín de la Asociación Española de Amigos de la Arqueologia* 22: 22-27.

García Cano, J.M. 1989-90. Una *kylix* de la 'clase delicada' procedente de Lorca (Murcia). *Anales de Prehistoria y Arqueologia de la Universidad de Murcia* 5-6: 95-100.

García Cano, J.M. and V. Page 1991. Panorama actual de las crámicas griegas en Murcia. *Huelva Arqueológica* 13(1): 219-239.

García Sanz, C. 1987. Excavacion de la muralla de Tejada. Tejada la Vieja: una ciudad protohistórica. *Huelva Arqueologica* 9: 93-105.

Garrido, J.P. 1970. *Excavaciones en la necrópolis de 'La Joya', Huelva (1ª y 2ª campañas)*. (Excavaciones Arqueológicas en España 71). Madrid: Ministerio de Cultura.

Garrido, J.P. and E.M. Orta 1978. *Excavaciones en la necrópolis de 'La Joya', Huelva. II.* (Excavaciones Arqueológicas en España 96). Madrid: Ministerio de Cultura.

Garrido, J.P.and E.M. Orta 1989. *La Necrópolis y el Hábitat Orientalizante de Huelva*. Huelva: Junta de Andalucía.

Gómez Bellard, C., P. Guerin and G. Pérez Jordá 1993. Témoinage d'une production de vin dans l'Espagne prerromaine. In *La Production du Vin et de l'Huile en Méditerranée* (Bulletin Correspondence Hellenique, Supplement 26), edited by M.C. Amouretti and P. Brun, pp., 379-395. Paris.

González Prats, A. 1986. Las importaciones y la presencia fenicias en la Sierra de Crevillente (Alicante). In *Los Fenicios en la Península Ibérica. Vol. II.* edited by M.E. Aubet, pp. 279-302. Sabadell: Ausa.

González Prats, A. 1991. La presencia fenicia en el Levante Peninsular y su influencia en las comunidades indígenas. *I-IV Jornadas de Arqueologia Fenicio-Púnica*, pp. 109-118. Eivissa: Museo Arqueologico de Eivissa.

González Wagner, C. 1990. Review of Judice Gamito 1988. *Trabajos de Prehistoria* 47: 399-406.

González Wagner, C. 1992. Tartessos en la historiografía: una revisión crítica. La colonización fenicia en el sur de la Península Ibérica. In *100 años de Investigación*, pp. 81-115. Almería: Instituto de Estudios Almerienses.

González Wagner, C. 1993. Las estructuras del mundo tartésico. In *Los Enigmas de Tarteso*, edited by J. Alvar and J.M. Blázquez, pp. 103-114. Madrid: Cátedra.

Harrison, R.J. 1988. *Spain at the Dawn of History. Iberians, Phoenicians and Greeks.* London: Thames and Hudson.

Inesta, A., V. Page and J.M. García Cano 1987. *Excavaciones Arqueológicas en Coimbra del Barranco Ancho. Sepultura 70 de la Necrópolis del Poblado.* Murcia: Editora Regional.

Judice Gamito, T. 1988. *Social Complexity in Southwest Iberia 800-300 BC. The Case of Tartessos.* Oxford: BAR.

Judice Gamito, T. 1992. Answer to review by González Wagner of Judice Gamito 1988. *Trabajos de Prehistoria* 49: 415-418.

López Precioso, F.J. 1994. El enterramiento orientalizante de la Casa del Monte (La Recueja, Albacete). *Al Basit* 35: 51-61.

Maier, J. 1992. La necrópolis de la 'Cruz del Negro' (Carmona, Sevilla): excavaciones de 1900 a 1905. *Cuadernos de Prehistoria y Arqueología de la Universidad Autónoma de Madrid* 19: 95-141.

Marín Ceballos, M.C. 1988. La colonización fenicia de la Península Ibérica en época arcaica. Problemas y evidencias. In *Actas del I Coloquio de Historia Antigua de Anda lucia.I*, pp. 19-47. Córdoba: Caja Sur.

Negueruela, I. 1990. *Los Monumentos Escultóricos Ibéricos del Cerrillo Blanco de Porcuna (Jaén)*. Madrid: Ministerio de Cultura.

Olmos, R. 1988. El casco griego de Huelva. *Clásicos de la Arqueología de Huelva* 1: 37-79.

Olmos, R. and M. Fernández Miranda 1986. *Las Ruedas de Toya y el Origen del Carro en la Península Ibérica*. Madrid: Ministerio de Cultura.

Olmos, R. and C. Sánchez 1995. Usos e ideología del vino en las imágenes de la Hispania prerromana. In *Arqueología del Vino: los Orígenes del Vino en Occidente*, edited by S. Celestino, pp. 105-136. Jerez de la Frontera: Consejo Regulador de las Denominaciones de Origen.

Olmos, R. and B.B. Shefton 1991. Apuntes ibéricos. Relaciones de la élite ibérica y el Mediterráneo en los siglos V y IV a.C. *Trabajos de Prehistoria* 48: 299-308.

Osuna, M. and J. Remesal 1981. La necrópolis de Boliche (Villaricos, Almería). *Archivo de Prehistoria Levantina* 16: 373-411.

Paixao, A.C. 1983. Uma nova sepultura com escaravelho da necropolis protohistórica do Senhor dos Martires (Alcacer do Sal). *O Arqueólogo Portugues* 4 (1): 273-286.

Pereira, J. 1989. Nuevos datos para la valoración del hinterland tartesico. El enterramiento de la Casa del Carpio (Belvis de la Jara, Toledo). In *Tartessos*, edited by M.E. Aubet, pp. 395-409. Sabadell: Ausa.

Pereira, J. and E. Alvaro 1986. Aportes orientalizantes en el Valle del Tajo. *Revista de Arqueología* 62: 29-39.

Piggott, S. 1983. *The Earliest Wheeled Transport. From the Atlantic Coast to the Caspian Sea*. London: Thames and Hudson.

Pingel, V. 1975. Zur vorgeschichte von Niebla (Prov. Huelva). *Madrider Mitteilungen* 16: 111-136.

Quesada, F. 1989a. *Armamento, Guerra y Sociedad en la Necrópolis Ibérica de 'El Cabecico del Tesoro' (Mula, Murcia, España)*. Oxford: BAR.

Quesada, F. 1989b. La utilización del arco y las flechas en la Cultura ibérica. *Trabajos de Prehistoria* 46: 161-201.

Quesada, F. 1994a. Vino, aristócratas, tumbas y guerreros en la cultura ibérica (ss. V-II a.C). *Verdolay* 6: 99-124.

Quesada, F. 1994b Riqueza y jerarquización social en las necrópolis ibéricas: los ajuares. In *Homenaje al Prof. J. M. Blázquez*, (volume 2), edited by J. Alvar, pp. 447-466. Madrid: Ediciones Clásicas.

Quesada, F. 1995a. Datos para una filiación egea de los carros grabados en las 'Estelas del Suroeste'. Actas del V Congreso internacional de Estelas funerarias (Soria1993). *Soria* 1: 179-187.

Quesada, F. 1995b. Arte y poder en el mundo ibérico. In *Arte y Poder en el Mundo Antiguo*, edited by J. Domínguez Monedero and C. Sánchez, pp. 203-248. Madrid: Ediciones Clásicas.

Quesada, F. 1997. *El Armamento Ibérico. Análisis Tipológico, Geográfico, Funcional y Simbólico de las Armas de la Edad del Hierro Peninsular.* (Monographies Instrumentum 3). Montagnac: Editions Monique Mergoil.

Quesada, F., J. Baena and C. Blasco 1995. An application of GIS to intra-site spatial analysis: the Iberian Iron Age cemetery at El Cigarralejo (Murcia, Spain). In *Computer Applications and Quantitative Methods in Archaeology*, pp. 137-146. Oxford: BAR.

Ramón, J. 1994. El nacimiento de la ciudad fenicia de la Bahía de Ibiza. El mundo púnico. In *Historia, Sociedad y Cultura*, edited by A. González Blanco, J.L. Cunchillos and M. Molina, pp. 325-371. Murcia: Editora Regional de Murcia.

Rouillard, P. 1991. *Les Grecs et la Peninsule Ibèrique du VIIIe au IVe Siècle avant Jésus-Christ*. Paris: Centre Pierre Paris.

Ruiz Delgado, M.M. 1989. Las necrópolis tartésicas: prestigio, poder y jerarquías. In *Tartessos*, edited by M.E. Aubet, pp. 247-286. Sabadell: Ausa.

Ruiz Mata, D. 1989. Huelva: un foco temprano de actividad metalúrgica durante el Bronce Final. In *Tartessos*, edited by M.E. Aubet, pp. 209-243. Sabadell: Ausa.

Ruiz Mata, D. 1993. La colonización fenicia en la Bahía de Cádiz a través del Castillo de Doña Blanca. Puerto de Santa María. In *Investigaciones Arqueológicas en Andalucía 1985-1992*, pp. 489-496. Huelva: Junta de Andalucía.

Ruiz Mata, D. and C. Pérez 1989. El túmulo 1 de la necrópolis de 'Las Cumbres' (Puerto de Santa María, Cádiz). In *Tartessos*, edited by M.E. Aubet, pp. 287-295. Sabadell: Ausa.

Ruiz Rodríguez, A. and M. Molinos 1993. *Los Iberos. Análisis Arqueológico de un Proceso Histórico*. Barcelona: Crítica.

Ruiz Rodríguez, A., M. Molinos and C. Choclán 1991. Fortificaciones ibéricas en la Alta Andalucía. Fortificacions. In *Simposi Internacional d'Arqueología Ibèrica*, pp. 109-126. Manresa: Societat Catalana d'Arqueología y Centre d'Estudis del Bagés.

Sala, F. 1991. La cerámica de importación de los siglos VI-IV a.C. en Alicante y su repercusión en el mundo indígena. *Huelva Arqueológica* 13(1) *(Iberos y Griegos: Lecuras Desde la Diversidad)*: 277-296.

Sanmartí, J. 1991. El comercio fenicio y púnico arcaico en Cataluña. *I-IV Jornadas de Arqueología fenicio-púnica.*: 119-136. Eivissa: Museo Arqueológico de Eivissa.

Santos Velasco, J.A. 1989. Análisis social de la necrópolis ibérica de El Cigarralejo y otros contextos funerarios de su entorno. *Archivo Español de Arqueología* 62: 71-100.

Santos Velasco, J.A. 1991. Importaciones de barniz negro en la cuenca media del Segura. *Huelva Arqueológica* 13(1) *(Iberos y Griegos: Lecturas Desde la Diversidad)*: 243-261.

Santos Velasco, J.A. 1994. *Cambios Sociales y Culturales en Época Ibérica: el Caso del Sureste*. Madrid: Cran.

Stary, P.F. 1989. Eisenzeitliche wagengräber auf der Iberischen Halbinsel. *Madrider Mitteilungen* 30: 151-183.

Torrecillas, F. 1985. *La Necrópolis de Época Tartésica del 'Cerrillo Blanco' (Porcuna, Jaén)*. Jaén: Diputacion Provincial.

Vaquerizo, D., J.F. Murillo and F. Quesada 1992. Excavación arqueológica con sondeos estratigráficos en Cerro de las Cabezas (Fuente Tójar, Córdoba). Campaña de 1991. Avance a su estudio. *Anales de Arqueología Cordobesa* 3: 171-197.

Chapter 8

Universal or relative? Social, economic and symbolic values in central Europe in the transition from the Bronze Age to the Iron Age

Andrzej Pydyn

Introduction

In this paper I discuss some aspects of value and the processes in the creation of universal and relative values in relation to long-distance exchange in late European prehistory. Value, like prestige and power, belongs to those categories which are very difficult to define but which at the same time all of us recognise. People value different things: material objects, power, freedom, friendship, love and knowledge. On the one hand there is no more subjective judgement than the judgement of value. Consciously or not, we are always making decisions about the value of different things and very often we mix separate categories of value. On the other hand, values can have an absolute or universal character and very often they form the basis for social communications and social relations. They have a universal and integrating character in a given society. On the basis of value systems, we create categories which help us define the material and ideological world. Here it might be useful to quote Frederick George Bailey from his book *Gifts and Poison*: 'Communities and societies are made up of people but we only recognise them as a community or as a society, because people who belong share some ideas about how things are and how things should be: they have a common set of categories with which they 'word' the social and the natural world around them and they share a definition of the good things and the bad things in life. From this point of view a community is a set of shared values and categories' (Bailey 1971: 9).

In this paper I will not propound either relative or absolute interpretations of value. In all societies some values have a static and others a dynamic character; moreover, the same things can have a relative economic value and an absolute social value.

In the last two centuries the term value has been used in different contexts by archaeologists, sociologists, philosophers and economists, but it is possible to differentiate two general meanings of this term. In the first, value is connected with morality, ethics, welfare and social relations. The second meaning of the term value is related to economics and to the material world. Twentieth century interpretations have brought many different approaches towards value. Marx and his extreme followers have given an economic value to everything. Post-modern thinkers have tried to stop societies from making any judgement of value. It could be suggested that economists and literary critiques have discussed different kinds of value, yet one has to remember that an economy is part of a culture and can be analysed only in this context. Furthermore, the world of material things and economic values is directly connected with the world of social structures and social values.

A specific character of archaeological data forces us to analyse social relations and social values in relation to material objects and their economic value. A study of exchange and trade, particularly in archaeological contexts, is a study of the relationship between human beings and material objects. On the one hand, material things have their own lives, their own biographies, they are made, used and then abandoned (Kopytoff 1986); on the other, they create and preserve social relations. Material objects can be exchanged for other objects, services, prestige, or directly for power.

From relative to universal: a process of creation of values

One of the most interesting problems associated with values is the method of their creation. What is the relationship between an economic value and a social value? Why do some objects, in a specific geographical and political environment, move from a stage of having a relative value to a stage where their value is socially accepted and unquestionable? At the same time other objects will always have only economic value. Most Bronze Age specialists will agree that the value of bronze objects known from the region north of the Alps and the Carpathian Mountains could not be directly associated with their economic value. Even in the areas of intensive metal production (e.g., the Carpathian Basin or the Alps region), the value of metal objects was not a simple sum of a prime value and an added value. Instead, as I will argue below, the value of different types of objects was also related to their shape, originality and to their artistic value. All products of high prestige value had to be socially recognisable but at the same time they had to be very closely related to an owner. As has already been pointed out by Renfrew (1986: 157), it is difficult to accept Marx's opinion that nothing can have value without being an object of utility (Marx 1970: 48). It is particularly true for pre-capitalist societies, whose utilitarian character was geared to obtain goods, which then could be exchanged for prestige and power, while the objects themselves could have a very limited practical use.

A description of value presented by Simmel has a much more universal character, since in his opinion value is not an inherent property of objects but is a judgement made about them by subjects (Simmel 1978: 73). It is particularly true for an exchange value, where there is no connection between producers and customers. In an archaeological context, prestige goods first of all have an exchange value; this value usually increased together with the distance which separates producers and customers.

High labour in production and the prime values of objects significantly increase their likely exchange value. For instance, impressive swords and vessels could be exchanged primarily because of their economic and aesthetic values. As these objects travelled from the centres of their production they began to have a new social value. In return, demands for specific products increased their social value in the original centres of their production, and it is clear that metallurgical activities began to be the subject of social distribution. Furthermore, if prestige goods were made of rare materials, this would not necessary directly have increased their value; instead it would have made access to them even more restricted.

A practical or use value of prestige products was not their most important value. Many swords and other weapons were made not to fight but to be presented. Many ornaments, particularly those known from the Nordic world were too big, too small or too heavy to be worn on a regular basis. Even more, some of these products were excluded from practical use (e.g., the Mälar axes, which were broadly distributed between central Sweden and the regions of the middle Kamei and Volga Rivers, in the period from Bronze IV to VI (in the Montelian chronology). According to Patrushev (1971), the Mälar axes were used only as weapons or more likely (in my opinion) as prestige objects and thus would have stood in contrast to local axes which were used as every-day tools. This might suggest that these foreign objects, distributed through the process of long-distance exchange, had a predominantly prestige and symbolic value.

Different exchange systems known from central Europe in the late Bronze Age and the early Iron Age created different value systems. In these systems, power and social positions were expressed by different material things which did not have the same value in other regions. A very good example of this process is known from central Europe during Hallstatt B3 and C (in Reinecke's chronology) (Fig. 1). As the result of strong competition between different groups of the Urnfield culture (including the Lusatian culture) and the Nordic culture, at least two separate exchange networks appeared. Through these networks bronzes and other prestige items were distributed between the Alpine region and the area of the Baltic Sea. Via the western routes, bronze objects (e.g., vase-headed pins, ribbed arm-rings and swords of Weltenburg and Möringen types) were distributed from the Alps through southern and central Germany, the area of the Billendorf group to Mecklenburg (Seddin), Jutland and southern Scandinavia. At the same time eastern routes (which connected the north Adriatic region, the eastern Alps, the area of the Bylany Culture with Silesia, Kujavia – Biskupin – and Pomeranian) were used to distribute other types of prestige objects such as spectacle-shaped fibulae (*Brillenfibeln*).

Distribution patterns of these artefacts not only suggest possible patterns of interregional contacts but also mark regions where similar systems of value developed. Social structures of local communities which were incorporated

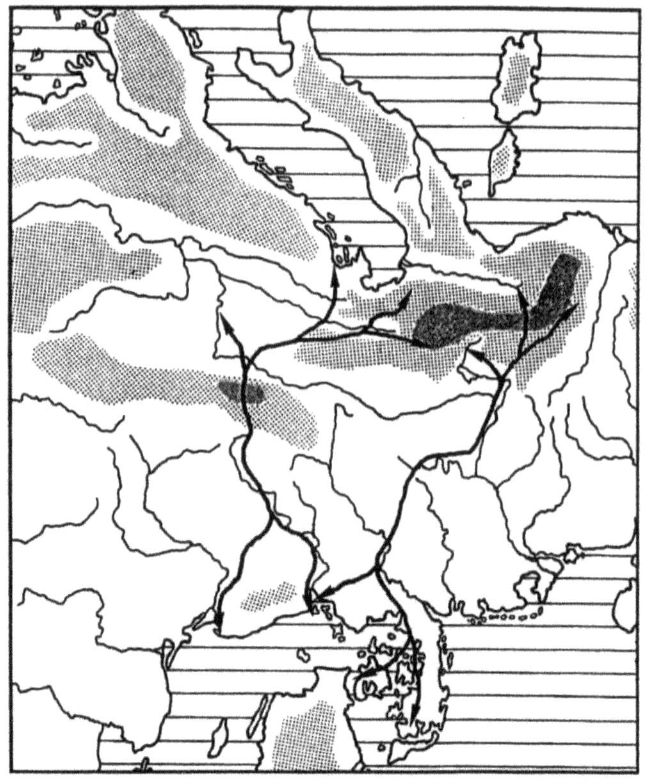

Figure 1 Networks of long-distance contacts between the southern and northern regions of central Europe, in the Hallstatt B_3 and the first part of the Hallstatt C period.

into these two exchange networks were based on the same principle (i.e., prestige goods economy). However, they chose different material objects to express their social structures. Probably, it would be more correct to say that these social structures had manifestations in different archaeological materials.

In both, exchange networks or imports (in other words commodities) which changed their social or economic context achieved a high prestige and symbolic value. An import is a material object or idea which moves out of its original cultural universe (in which practical (technical) and symbolic – religious – knowledge united producers and customers) and which thus is redefined in a new universe for practical and ideological reasons.

One of the most important questions is: when do material things begin to have this important and powerful social value? This value does not necessarily have to be related to a distance, an authenticity or even a prime value. A social value of imports is not associated with place of origin or with the societies in which they were produced; the social value is created within a community which adopts and uses foreign products. A local community decides which products are valuable and which ones are valuables. Within a local society some rules are made which allow some objects to have a negotiable value and to be freely traded; other rules restrict the open exchange of objects of a high social value. Of course cross-cultural contacts influenced local systems of value, particularly in situations when a majority of high prestige objects was obtained through external trade.

Objects of a high prestige value travelled in one direction from more advanced cultural and technological centres; but what was the value of products which moved in an opposite way? Sherratt (1993: 4) has suggested that the raw materials from northern Europe were exchanged for southern manufactured goods in a system in which prime values were exchanged for added values. However, this interpretation explains only the economic value of exchanged products. The social value of northern imports in southern Europe was probably as high as the value of manufactured goods which moved to the north. Both southern and northern imports had their prestige value only outside of their areas of origin. As they travel, prestige objects change their value (from economic and artistic to social). Goods which passed out of local circles of knowledge (which united producers and consumers) start to have a special value in a practical and/or symbolic sense. This is why long-distance trade (where knowledge about foreign imports was limited, partial, highly symbolic and restricted to elites) always had a very important position in establishing, maintaining and changing social, political and economic power.

In both a technological and an ideological sense merchants covered a gap in knowledge between producers and customers (Renfrew 1993:10). The prestige value of material objects was created in this gap. Amber in the Mediterranean world had its value only because its sources were unknown; it was obtained from foreign and distance regions through a chain of indirect transactions. Amber's physical properties made it particularly attractive and this gave an extra symbolic value to this material. Throughout most of the Bronze Age amber had a high symbolic and prestige value in regions of southern Europe; from the same period amber finds have been very rarely discovered in the Baltic region, where this material probably had only an economic value. Since it was relatively easy in the North to obtain amber, it never had a prestige value in this region. An exception to this situation comes from Pomerania; in Hallstatt C and D, amber began to appear in a number of graves, in a context which suggests that this material had a prestige value. This is, however, a very specific phenomenon and will be discussed further below.

In prehistoric societies, prestige and social value was given to very select objects. For instance, local communities from the region near the mouth of the Vistula River could easily have obtained a number of different types of shells. Instead, they chose to give a high value only to a specific type of cowrie shell which had to be obtained from Mediterranean regions. These shells had to be gained through long-distance exchange. Knowledge about them was very fragmented and places of origin were unknown. The trade in such objects was easy to monopolise and control. It is also characteristic that cowrie shells (in opposition to most of the southern imports which have been found in the northern part of Europe) did not have added or technological value. Their high value was directly related to a gap in knowledge which separated their place of origin and the northern communities in which they were used.

A high value of bronze and bronze imports was created through even more complicated processes. Probably all bronze objects which have been discovered in northern Europe were made of metals which were obtained from the south or the east. As a result of this, bronze itself had an important value because it was made of metals of unknown origin. Secondly, metal objects were made via a complicated process of smelting, knowledge of which was strictly restricted and socially distributed. Finally, a number of bronze goods were obtained directly from other regions, and both geographical and technological knowledge about them was very fragmented. This fragmentation of knowledge increased the symbolic value of bronze.

As mentioned above, the high value of things is founded in their material, form, and use. Materials from which prestige goods were made could have a high value themselves, but this value usually was geographically restricted. Amber, for example had an important value only outside its area of origin, in the same way cowie shells had a particular value in the north. The social value of some manufactured goods could also be primarily associated with their material instead of their forms (e.g., Hallstatt C blue glass beads from eastern Pomerania which had their origin in the Mediterranean regions) (Fig. 2). It is rather unlikely that these finds had a distinctive value because they were made in the shape of a bead; instead, their value should be related to the rare material from which they were produced.

The situation is much more complicated for bronze products. Bronze had an important economic and symbolic value; however, only objects of particular forms could have prestige character. The value of these goods was not directly related to the quantity of material which was used for their production. In centres of bronze production, heavy bronze ingots could have a significant commercial value but they could not obtain an important prestige position. This position could only be related to the artistic value of bronze products. Prestige goods had to carry a specific social message. They had to be closely related to a person (the owner) but at the same time they had to be socially active. Prestige objects were publicly used in very defined situations (e.g., in forms of drinking or eating vessels used during feasts). In northern Europe, most imported goods which had a prestige value were weapons, ornaments and vessels.

Furthermore, in large areas north of the Alps and the Carpathian Mountains, in the late Bronze Age the forms in which bronze could be produced, stored and exchanged were tightly restricted. It is clear that these areas obtained large quantities of metal from the south and from the east; it is no accident that no ingots or any other objects of similar shape or similar use have been found. For local communities in northcentral Europe, bronze had value not only as a material in its own right, but, above all, it had to be ren-

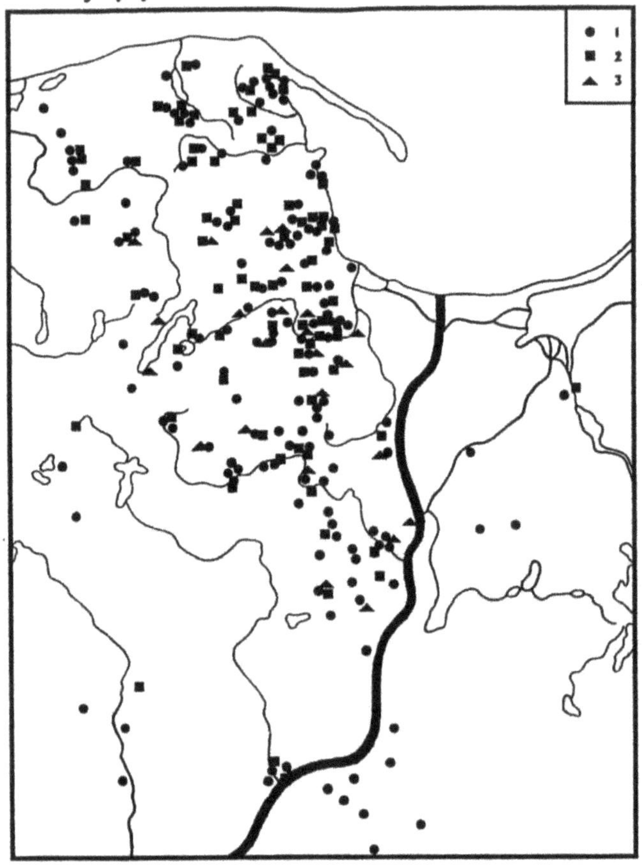

Figure 2 The distribution of cowrie shells, blue glass beads and amber beads in eastern Pomerania (based on Łuka 1963): 1 – glass beads; 2 – amber beads; 3– cowrie shells.

dered into the shapes of particular objects. Even hoards of so-called scrap bronze contained pieces of cut, but definitive, objects. Local producers developed sophisticated technologies of metal smelting. Through exchange networks they obtained tin and copper from distant areas and supplied bronzes to other regions; they always produced objects, not but the bronze itself.

In the Nordic zone, this phenomenon was clearly represented by an intensive production of different types of rings and other ornaments of similar shape which have been discovered in large quantities. Because of their size or weight many of these rings never could have been used as ornaments. Instead, they were used to store a value of bronze and thus were not used to produce other objects. At the end of the Bronze Age, when the Nordic area experienced a significant shortage of metal, some Pomeranian metallurgical centres began to make hollow bracelets; these were pure imitations of heavy bracelets which had been manufactured in the earlier period. This suggests that the value of a form was more important than the value of the bronze itself.

The social value of some objects which were made of a specific material and had a defined shape, could change in relation to how they were used. Prestige goods had their social value only if they were presented in an appropriate context. A value is not created by a secret accumulation of goods but by public consumption and use (or even waste in the modern sense). In the Baltic area, many bronze objects probably had the highest social value in the moment of their symbolic destruction and deposition in hoards or graves. Changes in the pattern of social consumption of prestige goods might suggest significant changes in a system of symbolic and social values (e.g., in the western Baltic region in the Bronze V period, a new custom of deposition of bronzes in hoards appeared on a large scale, in opposition to the previous period, when most metal objects had been placed in graves; Bradley 1990; Blajer 1992). This suggests that from the Bronze V competitive wealth-destruction took place on occasions other than the death of a chieftain. Nevertheless, both types of consumption of high value objects were social and active rather than private and passive.

In modern societies, one of the most important elements of the value of material things relate to authenticity. Objects which have a significant prestige position have to be original; their artistic or practical values have a secondary meaning. This concept of authenticity is a relatively modern idea and in prehistoric societies it did not play as important a role where the object's value was related to material, shape and use. At the same time, origins and producers of such objects were insignificant and very often unknown. Any distinction between an original import and a locally made copy was unclear and many such copies were used in exchange systems. This process was particularly characteristic for bronze production, where a good copy was as good as an original. At the same time, access to bronze production was strictly restricted and socially distributed.

In the late Bronze Age, many bronze objects from the south (together with ideas of their production) were traded to the northern parts of central Europe. In new geographic and cultural environments material things and ideas were redefined. Many of the so-called foreign objects could be produced outside an area where their concepts were first formulated (e.g., the Hallstatt painted pottery which was produced on a large scale in Silesia, in south-western Poland: Alfawicka 1970; or the north Italian imports which were copied in the Alps region: Kossack 1954). The intensive polemics between archaeologists about the possible origins of different types of material things are not only representations of different academic views, but above all, they express ambiguity in understanding concepts of imports in prehistoric communities.

What is important is that the value of imports can only be understood in relation to the aims of exchange. These aims were to provide enjoyment, excitement, economic benefits, but most of all, to win social games of preserving and exercising the power of individuals and of communities (Davis 1992). The results of exchange of archaeological finds (very often only represented by simple dots on distribution maps) can explain very little.

Transportation, maritime trade and boats

During periods of intensive long-distance intercultural contacts the means of transport had (in addition to economic value) high prestige, social, and religious value. This universal phenomenon, which took place in different periods and in separate parts of the world, was also present in the Baltic region in the late Bronze Age. Throughout most of this period, an intensive exchange of bronzes and other things was based on maritime cycles which united the separate regions of the Baltic zone. Probably in the Bronze V and VI periods, these cycles were joined in a system connecting very distant areas: between Jutland and southern Scandinavia in the west; and the eastern Baltic, and centres of metal production in the area of the middle Volga and Kama Rivers in the east.

Social systems of local communities in the Nordic world and in the whole area of the Baltic were based on a large-scale consumption of bronzes which stimulated intensive communication based on water transport. As a result boats began to play a very important role not only as vehicles (used to carry valuable goods) but also as things which had a value in themselves. A man or a community without a boat was a man or a community without power; indeed, without even the potential ability to have power. Very soon boats had the value of a symbol of power for their owners, not only during their lives but also after their deaths. The so-called boat-graves first appeared in Jutland and southern Scandinavia and then spread across the Öland and the Gotland Islands to the regions of present-day Latvia and Estonia and reached farther inland along the main rivers. The social value of boats was also manifest in the 'solar barque' representations from the same period (Fig. 3). A similar process took place in Scandinavia and in other regions of the Baltic Sea in the Viking Period when means of transport again had important social, economic and symbolic value.

The late Bronze Age and the early Iron Age were also periods of intensive contacts with other parts of Europe. Increasing influences of the nomadic world stimulated interactions between the steppe areas of the eastern Europe and the central part of the continent. The clearest representations of these contacts were the changes in funeral traditions (e.g., the introduction of inhumation on a large scale and the development of rich princely graves). In the Hallstatt culture, as well as in other parts of central Europe, a new symbolic value was given to horses and wheeled-vehicles. This was represented by a large number of graves in which horse skeletons, horse-gear and wagons were deposited. In other parts of central Europe where old traditions of cremation were still very strong, the new value of horses and wheeled-vehicles was expressed in pictorial representations (e.g., in Eastern Pomerania) (Pare 1992).

Wagon-graves in central Europe and boat-graves in northern Europe appeared as the result of the same processes of change which took place during a period of intensive interregional contacts. These contacts had manifestations in new systems of value in which ordinary means of transport achieved new prestige positions. Boats and wheeled vehicles were known and used for centuries before they began

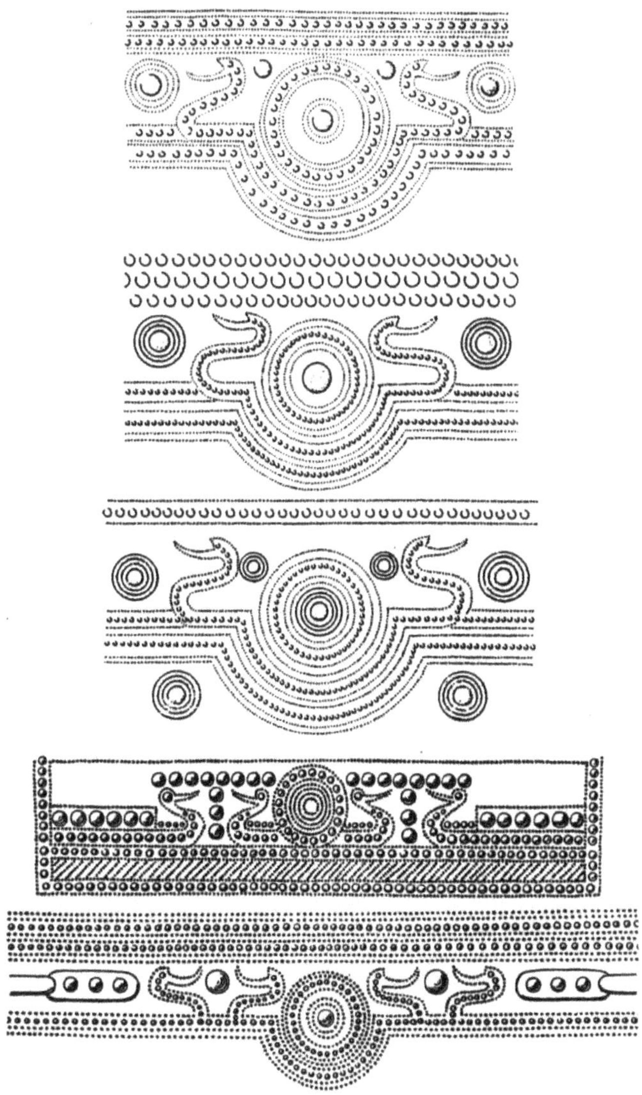

Figure 3 Examples of 'solar barque' decorations (after Kossack 1954; Jockenhövel 1974; Kristiansen 1993).

to enjoy high social value. This value of the means of transport, as for any other material thing was geographically and chronologically restricted.

Maintaining and changing systems of social and material values

In late prehistory, social and political elites used their power to preserve specific needs and values; it was a basic way to preserve their social positions. Changes in a value system were signs of creativity or decline in social, political, or economic systems while social values had to be recognised and accepted by a community. Political elites had a primary interest in their preservation; politics (power) creates links between exchange and value (Appadurai 1986: 3).

An important way to maintain the high value of prestige objects was through exclusion. On the one hand, high value goods were received through specific, restricted forms of exchange; they had to be represented by particular types of objects and be displayed publicly during particular social events. On the other hand, objects of important social value were received primarily through transactions conducted with strangers rather than with kin or neighbours. This is why, at the end of the Bronze Age, long-distance trade was so important for maintaining the social structures of local communities. Even if some high social value goods were distributed between neighbours or kin, this would have taken place in completely different social contexts and should be understood as the consumption of prestige things rather than as exchange. As a result of this consumption the power of elites and the loyalty of relatives were maintained.

The social value of material things was created and maintained not only through restrictions in exchange systems but also by strict limitations on the use of selected objects. As was discussed earlier, the Mälar axes were probably only used as objects of high social and symbolic values in opposition to other types of axes. In the same way, some types of chariots and wagons known from central Europe, had exclusively symbolic and prestige value. The best examples are those which were heavily decorated (e.g., from Eberdingen-Hochdorf, Stuttgart-Bad Cannstatt, Býí-skála Cave and many others (Pare 1992). In the regions of the Lusatian Culture and particularly the Pomeranian Culture, some types of pottery had important symbolic significance, and their production and use were strictly restricted to funeral ceremonies.

As presented earlier, the social value of particular objects was separate from the technology of their production. Wheeled-vehicles had been known in central Europe for almost 1000 years before the Cimmerian (or other generally nomadic influences) helped redefine the social value of such objects. Then, the new value of wheeled-vehicles was maintained by local elites who restricted their use to ceremonial and funeral contexts. A similar process took place in the eastern Baltic region where the practical knowledge of shipbuilding developed locally. However, as a result of contacts with the Nordic world during the late Bronze Age ships began to have new, important social and symbolic values.

At the transition from the Bronze Age to the Iron Age, the development of iron metallurgy was socially and culturally (but not technologically) limited. Many local communities from central Europe had the knowledge and technical ability necessary for the production of iron long before they began to smelt and use it on a large scale. Iron could be used for the production of much more efficient weapons and tools than could bronze. This suggests that the social value of bronze was much more important than was its practical value. Local societies from different areas of central and northern Europe (particularly from the Nordic zone) based their social structures on the large consumption of bronzes. These societies strictly controlled the trade and production of bronze objects and they were not interested in developing production of other metals. Probably they were more likely to restrict iron metallurgy as it could threaten the existing systems of value and thus destabilise the power of local elites.

This is one of the reasons why in central and northern Europe, the transition from the Bronze Age to the Iron Age took place much later than it did in Italy, or even in the Alps area. In these regions, the adoption of iron and the development of a new system of value was a result of internal changes in local societies and was primarily stimulated by political events occurring in southcentral Europe and by changes in long-distance exchange networks. With the development of the Hallstatt culture, the area of the Alps was no longer interested in supplying objects of a high social value (and, in general, bronze) to the regions farther north. To a large extent a shortage of bronze was responsible for an economic and social crisis in the Baltic region at the beginning of the Iron Age.

In Hallstatt C and the beginning of Hallstatt D, although local communities from centres of power near the mouth of the Vistula River tried to maintain the old systems of value prestige bronze objects were replaced, to a large degree, by other goods of a high social value (e.g., blue glass-beads, cowrie shells and other products of Mediterranean origin). These goods also had to be obtained through a system of long-distance exchange that connected central Italy, the western Alps and southern and central Germany, with the southern Baltic area. These new prestige objects were also associated with a new Iron Age system of value. East Pomeranian societies represented a unique example of societies in transition from the Bronze Age to the Iron Age. They adopted elements of two separate systems of value while they used new prestige objects to maintain the old Bronze Age social structures, these new imports were also representations of values characteristic for the Iron Age.

This situation allowed and stimulated the large-scale adoption of iron. Pomeranian metallurgical centres inherited a tradition of intensive bronze smelting which was characteristic of the Nordic zone. Nevertheless, during Hallstatt D, these centres developed their own substantial iron production and, very soon, Pomerania began to supply iron products to vast areas of the eastern Baltic and even further south to regions of the post-Lusatian Culture. This process could only have taken place because social demands for a new metal appeared and a previously unknown value was given to this new product.

How different were the social values of bronze and iron products or, more generally, how significant were differences in the social structures and value systems of the Bronze and Iron Age communities? This raises further questions about definitions of the Bronze and Iron Ages. The European Bronze Age, particularly in its northern version, is not simply a period in which people used bronze to produce tools, ornaments and weapons. It is more accurately described as a period in which communities had particular social structures which they expressed in a characteristic system of values. By the end of the Bronze Age these social structures had become very elaborate and in some regions (e.g., in Kujavia and a part of Great Poland) they had served to organise large groups of people. In the Bronze Age, elites played an integrating role in communities. Although they were an essential part of the social structure they could hold and exercise their power only to the degree allowed by a given society. The position of a chieftain had to be maintained through the public consumption of objects of a high social value. Prestige was associated with the function of being a chief rather than with the individuals themselves.

This situation changed in the Iron Age, when many communities experienced the progressive individualisation of their members. Leading positions in these communities came to be associated with active, powerful individuals who achieved their positions through continuous competition with other individuals, rather than through broad social acceptance. As a result, in southcentral Europe the Hallstatt culture developed with many competitive centres of local power. In northern parts of central Europe significant political and economic decentralisation took place. This is seen in the decline of large fortified settlements and the development of smaller open sites.

The production and consumption of iron was more suitable for this new social situation than was the production and use of bronzes. The European sources of tin and copper are geographically restricted and a bronze metallurgy could only have developed in relation to long-distance trade. Such trade was maintained and restricted to the Bronze Age elites. Conversely, iron ore is relatively common in Europe and was directly used by local centres of power. Bronze was used to maintain the given hierarchical structures of the Bronze Age communities, while iron was produced to increase (i.e., to take) the political and economic position of local leaders. Iron and iron-production were neither reasons nor results of changes in systems of social value and structure. It is more correct to say, after Hodder (1992), that causes and effects have an interactive character in a given context; thus the introduction of large-scale iron-production and the changes in social structures and value systems were both reasons and result. On the one hand, iron was introduced as the result of internal changes in Bronze Age societies and of shifts in patterns of long-distance exchange. On the other hand, iron and iron-production to a large extent stimulated these changes.

Progressive individualisation in the early Iron Age communities is documented in the changes in funeral traditions. In many areas of central Europe which were not directly influenced by the Hallstatt culture, new forms of the so-called house-urns and face-urns appeared. In Eastern Pomerania a large quantity of face-urns have been found. Many of them have very realistic representations of the human face. A large number of these urns were accompanied by objects of high social value (e.g., bronzes, blue-glass and amber beads, cowrie shells and other imports of Mediterranean, particularly Italian, origin (Łuka 1963). Most of these objects represented different forms of ornament (necklace, earrings) and they could be directly associated with their owners, both during their lives and after their deaths. These ornaments had a prestige value in the Bronze Age sense but at the same time they had a new value which was given to them by individuals; consumption of these products could be a public as well as a private ac.

Changes which took place in Pomerania in the transition from the Bronze to the Iron Age created an ambiguity in value systems. Important social value was given not only to new imports and materials (particularly iron) but also to amber, a material which had been known in the Baltic area for most of prehistory. With Hallstatt C, amber, which always had an economic and trade value in northern Europe, began to have an important symbolic value; in many graves from this period amber necklaces and single beads have been found. This new social value of amber appeared as a result of intensive and relatively direct contacts with northern and central Italy, where this material has been frequently discovered in contexts which suggest that it had a distinctive social and symbolic role. Thus long-distance exchange and interregional contacts were used not only to maintain the prestige value of material things and social structures of local communities, but also to create confusion in a value system in which objects of local origin could significantly change their status.

Through this long-distance exchange network a funeral tradition (in which house- and face-urns were used) was introduced in the northcentral Europe. Even if there are few formal and chronological similarities between the Etruscan canopies from Chiusi and the Pomeranian face-urns, both traditions represent a similar pattern of changes in social and symbolic values. The physical representation of a dead person was one of the most important elements of a new funeral tradition. It was also the manifestation of a process of individualisation which took place in many (even geographically distant) societies during the transition from the Bronze to the Iron Age. This transition occurred at different times in different parts of Europe and this is why changes in funeral traditions and social values in Italy occurred much earlier than they did in northern Europe.

The new position of individuals in communities also influenced art. The well-established old style of geometric and animal (particularly bird) representations which had been characteristic for the Urnfield cultures, was gradually replaced by human representations (e.g., these depicted on pottery vessels and urns) which have been found in Hungary, Pomerania and other regions.

Conclusion

In conclusion, it is possible to say that the late Bronze and early Iron Age was a time of change in value systems and that this process was clearly related to changes in social, economic and political structures. In the Bronze Age, the social value of material things was created through a process of long-distance exchange. This value could not be associated simply with the prime, added, artistic, or use (utilitarian) value of prestige objects. The social value of particular material goods was regionally geographically, culturally and temporally restricted. As these goods travelled, the nature of their value changed (e.g., from the economic to the social). Over a long period of time, different categories of material things moved in and out of having a high social value; the best examples being selected types of means of transport.

In a community, systems of value had an interactive character. On the one hand, they were created and maintained by local societies. On the other, they limited and modelled these societies. Of course all systems were flexible enough to allow individual creativity and personal choice. This probably was responsible for gradual changes in systems of value. Nevertheless, significant changes only appeared in relation to more global, interregional processes, which influenced large areas of central Europe (e.g., an increase of steppe influences in Hallstatt B3 and C, the development of the Hallstatt culture, and the broad introduction of iron metallurgy).

With the beginning of the Iron Age, a significant decline in long-distance trade systems took place in central Europe. As a result, an important social value was given to some material things which were produced by local communities and not to objects which had to be obtained from distant regions. The social value of material goods became more closely related to their utilitarian and aesthetic values. Both iron tools and weapons (as well as new forms of bronze ornaments) could be included in this process.

This phenomenon was a part of a larger process of individualisation which was characteristic of the transition from the Bronze Age to the Iron Age. In Bronze Age communities, a high social value was given to objects which had an active social role. Even if they were closely related to a particular person, their consumption had to be publicly recognisable and accepted. In the Iron Age, an important social value was also attached to products which could be produced and accumulated locally; these products were used to maintain the positions of provincial leaders. Individuals preserved their position not through public acceptance, but by continuous competition and via the accumulation of goods (e.g., exotic ornaments) which could be associated with a person during his life and after his death. Furthermore, in many societies the practical or utilitarian value of material objects (e.g., iron tools) became more important than their symbolic value.

Bibliography

Alfawicka, S. 1970. *Ceramika Malowana Okresu Halsztackiego w Polsce*. (Biblioteka Archeologiczna 22). Warszawa: Ossolineum.

Appadurai, A., 1986. Introduction: commodities and the politics of value. In *The Social Life of Things*, edited by A. Appadurai, pp. 3-63, Cambridge: Cambridge University Press.

Bailey, F.G. 1971. Gifts and Poison. In *Gifts and Poison*. edited by F.G. Bailey, pp. 1 - 26, Oxford: Basil Blackwell.

Blajer, W. 1992. Ze studiów nad skarbami okresu halsztackiego w Polsce. In *Ziemie Polskie we Wczesnej Epoce Elaza i ich Powizania z Innymi Terenami*, pp. 101-110. Rzeszów: Muzeum Okrgowe w Rzeszowie.

Bradley, R. 1990. *The Passage of Arms*. Cambridge: Cambridge University Press.

Davis, J. 1992. *Exchange*. Buckingham: Open University Press.

Hodder, I. 1992. *Reading the Past*. (second edition). Cambridge: Cambridge University Press.

Jockenhövel, A. 1974. Eine Bronzeamphore des 8. Jahrhunderts v. Chr. von Gevlinghausen, Kr. Meschede (Sauerland), mit Beiträgen von Hans Beck, Hans-Jürgen Hundt und Günter Lange. *Germania* 52(1): 16-53.

Kopytoff, I., 1986, The cultural biography of things: commoditization as process. In *The Social Life of Things*, edited by A. Appadurai, pp. 64-91. Cambridge: Cambridge University Press.

Kossack, G. 1954. *Studien zum Symbolgut der Urnenfelder- und Hallstattzeit Mitteleuropas*. (Römisch Germanische Forschungen 20). Berlin.

Kristiansen, K. 1993. From Villanova to Seddin. The reconstruction of an elite exchange network during the eight century B.C. In *Trade and Exchange in Prehistoric Europe*, edited by C. Scarre, and F. Healy, pp. 143-151. Oxford: Oxbow Books

Łuka, L.J.. 1963. Uwagi o niektórych kontaktach Pomorza Wschodniego z basenem Morza ródziemnego we wczesnej epoce elaza. *Archeologia Polski* 8(2): 274-288.

Marx, K. 1970 [1867]. *Capital: Vol. I*. London: Lawrence and Wishart.

Pare, C.F.E. 1992. *Wagons and Wagon-Graves of the Early Iron Age in Central Europe*. Oxford: Oxford University Committee for Archaeology.

Patrushev, V.S. 1971. Kelty starshego Achmylovskogo mogilnika i ich funkcjonalnoe naznanenie. *Kratkie Soobshchenija Instituta Archeologii* 128: 37-62.

Renfrew, C. 1986. Varna and the emergence of wealth in prehistoric Europe. In *The Social Life of Things*, edited by A. Appadurai, pp. 141-168. Cambridge: Cambridge University Press.

Renfrew, C., 1993. Trade beyond material. In *Trade and Exchange in Prehistoric Europe*, edited by C. Scarre and F. Healy, pp. 5-16. Oxford: Oxbow Books.

Sherratt, A. 1993. What would a Bronze-Age world system look like? Relations between temperate Europe and the Mediterranean in later prehistory. *Journal of European Archaeology* 1(2): 1-57.

Simmel, G. 1978 [1907]. *The Philosophy of Money*. London: Routledge.

Chapter 9

Objectification, embodiment and the value of places and things

John Chapman

Introduction

It is an implicit part of each person's worldview that there are some places in the world which, for them, have value. This often unstated belief is worth further exploration for, if we can identify what it is that gives places their value, we may be able to discover what gives people their value also.

There is a widespread tendency amongst anthropologists to ignore places in discussions about value. A good example is A. Weiner's (1980) consideration of the social reproduction of elements of cultural value, listed as human beings, social relations, cosmological phenomena and resources such as land, material objects, names and body decorations – i.e., almost everything of cultural value except places. Similarly, although her definition of objectification is (as we shall see) most stimulating, Marilyn Strathern (1988: 175-6) makes no mention of places in the construction of value – only persons and things. This omission is related to a more general neglect by anthropologists of the topic of 'landscape' – with the first major anthropological treatments of the subject appearing but recently (Bender 1993; Hirsch and O'Hanlon 1995; Rodman 1992).

In this chapter, an attempt is made to relate the concepts of objectification and valuation as appropriate to things to the field of landscape through a consideration of places as objectified and embodied spaces. Some insights from recent research into material culture are offered as the basis for a comparison of how places and things acquire cultural value. The aim of the chapter is to provide a theoretical framework for the analysis of place-value and its *modus operandi*. These notions will then be explored through a consideration of prehistoric settlements near the Serbian capital of Belgrade (Beograd). Let us begin with some first principles derived from the work of Bourdieu.

Habitus, fields and capital

I propose to locate the study of place-value in a framework which owes much to the work of the French sociologist, Pierre Bourdieu. For it is one of Bourdieu's achievements (through his concepts of habitus and field) to transcend the structure – agency dichotomy which has burdened much of recent archaeological theory-making. It is difficult to summarise adequately his work over two decades, for three reasons: the author has a massive *oeuvre*; the work itself has great internal complexity; and the work is defined by changing interpretative practices. What follows is an attempt at such a summary.

Bourdieu's theory of practice rests on two key concepts: habitus, on which Bourdieu grounds the production of a common-sense world endowed with an objectivity secured by consensus on the meaning of both practices and the world (Bourdieu 1977: 80); and fields, the objective domains in which power is constituted by the acquisition and use of capital (Bourdieu and Wacquant 1992: 85-97). Bourdieu relies on the habitus to provide a theoretical means of the production of tradition based on strategies rather than rules. Since the substitution of strategies for rules re-introduces time into the analysis, social practices are defined by the fact that their temporal structure, direction and rhythm are constitutive of their meaning (Bourdieu 1977: 9). Practices are located in different domains, not as sub-systems, but as loci of the practical realisation of habitus (Bourdieu 1977: 83).

Spatial relations govern practices and representations through a dialectical relationship between objectification (the institution of the social in things) and embodiment (the institution of the social in the body). Each practice is invested with an objective meaning through the magic of the world of objects, which in turn is read with the body (1977: 89-91). Bourdieu asserts that, in ancient societies, there is a quasi-perfect correspondence between objective order and subjective principles of organisation - a world of 'tradition' termed 'doxa' (1977: 164).

In societies with little economic differentiation, the dispositions of each individual (their marks of social position) are reinforced by others' practices, such as feats or ceremonies, and by institutions which constitute and express collective thought, such as art, myth and language. In such societies, systems of dominance are based not on economic capital but rather on the conversion of economic into symbolic capital, such as the reputation or the prestige of the family. In the sense that these dominance systems require endlessly renewed strategies of inter-personal exchange, 'gentle exploitation' (1977: 193) is much more costly than overt domination. Such dominance practices are concealed insofar as 'every established order tends to produce (to very different degrees and with very different means) the naturalisation of their own arbitrariness' (1977: 164).

Critics maintain that the problem with the habitus is its very coherence – whether its tendency to closure, which prevents change through the naturalisation of arbitrariness (D. Gregory 1994: 407-9) or its exclusion of history except as an add-on that is not produced by the system (Connell 1987: 44, 94). Yet others focus more than does Bourdieu on resistance to habitus in those residual and emergent arenas of practice – the sites of resistance – which are not fully articulated with the habitus (Williams 1977; cf. Dirks et al. 1994).

For Bourdieu, however, change is related first to competing

discourses, which are confronted in 'fields of opinion', while objective crisis is raised in terms of the loss of the social world's character as a natural phenomenon, at which point the natural character of social facts can be discussed and therefore de-mystified and changed. From the outset, Bourdieu complemented the concept of habitus with that of 'field', thus providing the locus for social change through the struggle for capital of various kinds. It can now be proposed that practices are not the product of the habitus but rather the product of the encounter between the habitus and social fields. In contrast to the habitus, which generates practices and attitudes in agents' bodies, the field can be defined as a network of objective relations between positions, the latter characterised by their present or potential situation in the structure of the distribution of types of capital (Bourdieu and Wacquant 1992: 97). It should be observed that the structure of a field is different from the networks through which a field manifests itself; the field is primary over the individuals, who are agents socially constituted as active in the field. Fields have sub-fields, which are not sub-systems or parts but which have their own logic, rules and regulations (e.g., the novel in the field of literature). In a more dynamic sense, the field is also the site of struggles in which individuals seek to maintain or alter the forms of capital specific to the field (whether symbolic, economic, social or cultural). Bourdieu identifies a key hermeneutic circle here (Bourdieu and Wacquant 1992: 107): to construct the field, one must identify the form of capital specific to it but to construct the forms of specific capital, one must know the specific logic of the field. Since the Medieval period, the development of Europe is seen by Bourdieu as the (Weberian) differentiation of fields of practice, each with its specific forms of capital, value and institutions (Bourdieu 1991: 25).

Bourdieu identifies two ways in which the relationship between habitus and fields operated. The first is a relationship of conditioning, in which the field structures the habitus, as the product of the embodiment of the immanent necessity of a field or set of fields. The second is a relationship of cognitive construction, in which the habitus contributes to the constitution of the field as a meaningful world full of sense and value (Bourdieu and Wacquant 1992: 126-7). This is the sense in which one can speak of Bourdieu's theory of practice as a dual theory - social reality exists twice, once in the fields and again in the habitus. Thus Bourdieu characterises the two-fold object of social science as the relationship between the two realisations of historical action – in bodies and in things – and as the double relationship between habitus and fields. The institution of the social in the body produces the stable, self-constituting habitus, while the institution of the social in things produces ever-changing fields of practice.

A critique of Bourdieu's 'social space'

While in the later version of Bourdieu's theory of practice he offers a convincing context for the production of change and continuity, and while he focuses on the importance of the temporal constitution of habitus, Bourdieu rarely examines the importance of real, concrete space and place.

Throughout his research project, Bourdieu has privileged time over place and one particular kind of place over all others. Time is held to be at the core of social analysis – at the interface between the habitus and the field (Bourdieu and Wacquant 1992: 137). The habitus temporalises itself in the very act in which it is realised (1992: 138). Bourdieu spends much effort untangling the agrarian calendar of Kabylia, acknowledging that submission to the collective agricultural rhythms so rigorously demanded is because spatial structures and temporal forms structure not only the group's representation of the world but the group itself (Bourdieu 1977: 163).

In his discussions of social space (e.g., Bourdieu 1977: 89-91; 1991: 229-251), Bourdieu identifies the house as inhabited space as the principal locus for the objectification of generative schemes (1977: 89). Other spaces tend to be treated as merely the topological grounds for objective relations within fields. Bourdieu treats social space on the abstract level of a field of forces, stressing that a sense of 'one's place' is the practical mastery of the social structure as a whole and even commenting that the space of relationships is just as real as geographical space (1991: 230-2). Fields are, after all, based upon an analytical and aspatial logic, quite distinct from social networks and even further separated from inhabited space. Although recognising that the map is one of his classic triad of substitutions (together with the calendar and the genealogy, substituting homogenous, continuous, geometric space for the discontinuous patchy space of practical paths – 1977: 105), Bourdieu rarely examines the importance of real, concrete space and place in the institution of the social. The house apart, the spatial location of practices of embodiment and objectification are rarely specified. For Bourdieu, other places, such as wells, rivers and markets, figure briefly as examples of the institution of the gendered classification of the world (1977: 159-162), without being theorised as 'occupied' – the site of dwelling – in a manner different from that pertaining to houses.

By limiting the institution of the social to things and to persons, Bourdieu's account misses an important dimension of the construction of reality through social practices, which is situated in places and the landscape. Social space is not merely a topological ground for relationships – it is itself socially constituted and, as we shall see, through differentiation, specific spaces develop properties of place-value and memory which contribute to the development of personal identities. What, then, are the processes whereby the social is instituted in the habitus and in fields of practice?

Embodiment and objectification

It is a basic part of Bourdieu's position that every historical action brings together two states of history – the embodied history that constitutes the habitus and the objectified history which is accumulated over time in things, machines, monuments, books, law, etc. (Bourdieu 1981: 305). There is a complex and multi-facetted relationship between objectification and embodiment in Bourdieu's writings but the essence of the relationship is dialectical, forming the key to how spatial relations govern practices and their representations (1977: 90).

Embodiment
If the body in the habitus is socially constructed, then the method of construction is embodiment – the incorporation of characteristics of wider relations which encompass the body. One may distinguish five characteristics which are embodied – history, fundamental cultural principles, the structures of the world and the habitus, social distances and cultural capital. The first four of these define structuring principles for practice and share the paradoxical characteristic that, as soon as they are incorporated in the body, they are internalised and forgotten, to re-emerge as naturalised, legitimate and self-evident. Embodiment triggers remembering whilst causing forgetting: while the body is treated as the memory of the fundamental principles of the arbitrary content of culture (Bourdieu 1977: 94), the body does not memorise the past – it does not even represent what it performs – it enacts the past (1990: 73). This enactment and re-enactment begins in childhood and continues as a 'structural apprenticeship' (1977: 89) which acts as the principal mechanism of cultural transmission.

In the dialectical relationship between the body and space, the body enacts its own sense of place and those of other social actors, confirming the power relationships between actors in their fields. The female body and the male body are perceived and constructed in different ways within the habitus according to its practices, as are those bodies classified according to other social divisions. In the naturalisation of the most fundamental social choices, the body is constituted as an 'analogical operator' (1990: 71), establishing practical equivalences among social divisions based on age, gender and class.

In summary, the physical body accretes to itself cultural and social meanings throughout the life-cycle, from birth to death, in a process of social construction. Insofar as the construction of society is contested through practice within fields, the body becomes a politicised body – what Bourdieu (1990: 20) terms an 'incorporated politics'. All social terms, categories and classifications are the product of a dialogue between the social actors in an ongoing drama of embodied life, the extent of disagreement and solidarity constituting the degree of social differentiation as much as being constituted by it. How are such categories and classifications expressed in objects and places?

Objectification
Let us begin by turning to things before we consider places. Recent research in material culture has produced many insights into things which may, with advantage, be related to places. A useful starting-point is the theory of culture founded on objectification, which has been developed by Danny Miller (1987). Miller characterises objectification as the dual process whereby a subject externalises itself in a creative act of differentiation and in turn re-appropriates this externalisation through sublation (1987: 28). This productive differentiation builds upon itself, leading to the development of both the subject and culture itself through a mutually constitutive process.

Importantly, Miller identifies the element of self-alienation from the subject which cultural production inevitably brings but stresses that the new form in which externalisation is returned bears the essence of the exchange relationship by which the subject develops (1987: 33, 62). He stresses too that material objects are the principal means of objectifying the sense of the past, in turn validating claims of self-development and self-created change (1987: 125). Miller also reminds us (1987: 71) of Simmel's insight that, if objectification is a precondition for culture and therefore society, then it is mediated by exchange. Finally, the case is made out for the importance of the consumption of objects, often through re-contextualisation, in the construction of individual and group identities (1987: 175).

In his study of the dialectical processes productive of culture, Wagner claims that 'in learning how to use tools, we are secretly learning how to use ourselves' (1975: 77). He quotes Rilke's dictum that tools 'use' human beings, just as toys 'play' with children. For Wagner, tool use is about the objectification of our skills as the controls which tools place on the relationship between humans and the environment. This takes us close to Bourdieu's dialectical relationship between embodiment and objectification: the embodiment of skills is inseparable from the objectification of tool manufacture – comparable to Miller's externalisation and sublation. But Wagner takes this embodiment further: he sees humans as mediators of things, as a kind of 'universal catalyst' (1975: 138); permeable to things, humans have the capability to 'become' the things around them, to make them a part of their knowing, acting being. If things are so important, it is logical to expect humans to confer value on them. Wagner argues that all things with cultural value are 'invested' with life: they partake of the self and also create it (1975: 77).

This, then, is the link between objectification and personification: valuable items take on part of the qualities of their makers, just as their makers embody qualities of skill and resourcefulness in the manufacturing process. This blurring of the human – object boundary has important consequences for our conceptualisation of production, for, just as the value pertaining to the object is validated communally, so the life qualities invested in the object are regarded as part of the creativity of the maker in relation to a wider value-laden world. Hence, producers cannot be regarded simply as agents in a technological process but rather – to use Rowlands' phrase – 'facilitators' in larger processes of natural reproduction (1993: 148). It is to these larger processes that we now turn.

In *Gifts and Commodities*, C. Gregory (1982) posited two economic polarities – clan-based gift economies former based on the predominance of methods of consumption (personification) and capitalist commodity-based economies based on the predominance of methods of production (objectification). In gift-economies, consumptive production refers to that mode of social reproduction depending upon the consumption of things for the production of persons (1982: 90). Since gift-things must be produced before they can be consumed, the methods of their production are governed by the ideology of consumption, hence production includes productions of objects as symbols.

Strathern (1988) has elaborated on consumptive production by proposing that personification in wealth objects, far from being set up against objectifications, should be seen as one way of producing objectification: for 'objects are not created in contradistinction to persons but out of persons' (1988: 171-2, 176). Strathern's use of such terms as 'creation' and 'out of persons' betokens the reproduction of objects rather than their manufacture, touched upon earlier. If so, it is a reproduction which includes the inculcation of value into objects as the basis of objectification (Strathern 1988: 176; my emphasis).

If objectification is concerned with the inculcation of value in persons and things, the question arises how may this be achieved. Amongst the enormous variability of uses to which artefacts are put, one may distinguish two general attributes which lead to the attribution of value to objects: presencing and categorisation. In view of restrictions of space, I shall focus on the first of these attributes exclusively.

Presencing

Prown (1993) has argued that artefacts constitute the only class of historical events that occurred in the past but survive into the present. As authentic, primary, historical material, objects can be re-experienced and it is in this re-experiencing that the world of the Other (other people, other objects, other values) is brought into contact with the present. It is in this sense that Weiner (1985: 210) submits that 'the object acts as a vehicle for bringing past time into the present', as a visual substitute for history, the ancestors and the immortality of human life (1985: 224).

Likewise, objects have the power to evoke images from the sub-conscious in a way that language and speech rarely do (Rowlands 1993; cf. Miller 1987: 99-100). More actively, such an evocation empowers objects to consolidate the possession of past events associated with their use or ownership (Rowlands 1993: 144). In this way, presencing acts on the self as much as on other living people, the ancestors or the deities, just as the habitus ensures the active presence of past experiences (Bourdieu 1990: 54). Inalienable objects have the power to define one's historical self-identity just as they confirm for the living the powerful connections between the group and the ancestors and deities (Weiner 1985: 210; 1992: 3, 11).

The presencing power of objects can be important in resisting or affecting change. Weiner discusses the strategy of a new hegemonic group inventing traditions plausibly linked to the past through the use of objects heavy with the authority of the past. By contrast, Bender (1989: 89) has described how objects anchor and celebrate a 'socio-moral order' where authority is passed from ancestor to senior to junior in unending process. The way in which particular objects can carry such a weight of constantly-renewed tradition is through the biographical details of each object, whose particularities are known to persons and are made known through persons (Kopytoff 1986; cf. Bender 1989; Rawson 1993). Rawson (1993: 79) throws down a challenge to archaeologists and anthropologists alike: 'All objects have an ancestry that is as important to an understanding of their roles as are their current use and function. If we do not know its ancestry, we cannot read the history from a thing'.

These examples of the multiple ways in which objects can presence the Other demonstrate why value is enshrined into material culture. Viewed in a Bourdieuesque framework, presencing becomes a key creator of objectified history; the objects which presence the Other are prototypical 'cultural objects', living social institutions – simultaneously a socially instituted material object and a particular class of habitus (Bourdieu 1986: 256, note 8). In summary, objectification – the way in which persons and things are construed as having value – is fundamental to social practice. As Yanagisako and Collier (1987) propose, social systems are, by definition, systems of inequality; if a society is a system of social relations and values, and values entail evaluation, all things and actions are not equal. Values inevitably create inequalities by ensuring rewards for those living up to valued ideals and punishments for the others. In this sense, all symbols and meanings are always evaluative (Yanagisako and Collier 1987: 39). Therefore, we can consider such a form of the differentiation of value as applying with equal force to places, in a general and a relational sense rather than a particular and substantive sense (cf. Munn 1986: 8), constituting existential rather than intrinsic relations (Weiner 1992: 15).

What is a place?

Just as the body is a house of being, with language one function of the body, so the body acts in a meaningfully constituted web of spaces, places and regions; without the body and bodily practices, a place would remain a space. Richardson (1989) compares the transformation of space into place with other kinds of work: the transformation of a stone into a tool, behaviour into conduct, sounds into words, or nature into culture. This means, in Bourdieuesque terminology, that place is space objectified and the landscape represents the objectification of wider human practices. Like the human body, space remains a site of potential which is not actualised until the institution of the social in that space turns it into a place and the institution of the social in a wider setting turns them into a landscape. One of the principal aspects of social practices is the institution of human and collective identities in places and landscapes.

One of the most insightful of humanistic geographers over the past 30 years is Yi-Fu Tuan (1973; 1977; 1978). For

Tuan, the notion of 'place' is arbitrary, elusive and protean. In general terms, spaces are transformed into places through the acquisition of definition and meaning, so that places are created by repetitive experience, comparable to Bourdieu's habitus. Tuan sees the identity of place as having two distinct forms. Places are locations in which people have long memories for the bygone generations. But places are also the centre of power as well as meaning relative to their environs, the node at which activities converge. These two qualities of place are defined as fields of care (whereby places are known from the inside through the operation of human emotions) and public symbols, which provide significance in a wider, public milieu (Tuan 1977). Importantly, Tuan argues that the power of symbols in places is dependent upon the depth of the human emotions experienced in the fields of care.

The movement from space to place which Tuan discusses is central to the process of social colonisation of an unknown landscape, in which a neutral, value-free, meaning-less physical space takes on properties of meaning and value from those who colonise it (Chapman 1988). An integral part of this process of spatial differentiation in the landscape is the matching of place-based activities with those people and groups who are empowered to be in the places that matter, to carry out significant activities and to organise the participation of others not so empowered. This process begins from Foucault's idea that the control of space lies at the heart of social power (quoted in Rabinow 1984). Since most of the social groups under study are small-scale communities with restricted hierarchical differentiation, networks of social power are most readily related to the social space which they have created. Individuals take the inherently risky step of creating and maintaining social power through their propensities to take action on their own behalf or on behalf of the group. Social activity per se produces power reflexively, just as power provides the opportunities for further action. The more varied, differentiated or specialised the activity or the place where it occurs, the greater the potential social power accruing to the individual concerned.

The term 'arena of social power' has been coined to identify those places where ideological, economic, military and political power (Mann 1986) can be spatially identified. This concept leads to a technique for identifying the differentiation of social power through time and place. Arenas of social power mark a conjunction of a specific place, with its functions and meanings, and the social actors who have the power (including knowledge) to perform the activities in that place. The appearance of new arenas of social power in a given region is always an important change and requires explanation. It has been proposed that one way to approach otherwise unmanageable contradictions within the existing social structure is a spatial displacement which allows different forms of social action, of a nature otherwise inappropriate or impossible, in traditional time-space contexts (Chapman 1993).

The proposition advanced here is that significant places objectify key generative schemes of importance for the social reproduction of the group, the mechanism for the definition of the community's identities in time/space. Given that social practices will be instituted in the form of the site or monument, it follows that changes in the form of sites and monuments should be related to changes in the underlying practices of the group. In circumstances where social change is possible or desirable for part of the group, but where it is in conflict with traditional group ideology, the question of how to renegotiate social reproduction is of particular significance.

A familiar pattern of social reproduction concerns the use of opposition to a traditional mode in order to formulate and clarify new practices of social reproduction. In this way, a cycle of ideological strategies may be set up, based on the establishment of difference from the past, which constitutes itself through spatial strategies in relation to reuse of previous monuments, abandonment or continuity of occupation. By contrast, the continued use of traditional practices at the same monument will act as the ritualised context for the maintenance of habitus, the reproduction of value and meaning.

Places, people and identity

In a stimulating discussion of modernism and postmodernism, Derek Gregory has identified a crucial change in people's lives that took place after the First World War, which meant that the truth of daily experience no longer coincided with the place where it took place (D. Gregory 1994; see also Kern 1983). These early steps in the transition towards what is now termed 'globalization' separates 'us' from 'them' in ways which we can, by definition, hardly experience. Before globalization, most communities in small-scale societies lived locally (i.e., within a network of local places and people whom they knew as insiders. The network being connected to the outer world by kinship ties which were their own long-distance specialists and by outsiders). In small-scale societies, localism is so pervasive that a generic term for 'place' is as unnecessary as it is unthinkable.

In his discussion of Pre-Colombian Amerindian place-names, Robinson (1989) has outlined a set of toponyms referring to 'kin-territories', which mean either 'people-places' or 'place-peoples'. Such toponyms record an interesting example of the interdependence of cultural form, social behaviour and place. Robinson goes on to argue (1989: 161, 167) that people and places are hard to separate because the identity of a person is tied to that of his or her place. If a person's place is not known, how is it possible to know the ethnicity, the morality, or the worth to the community of that person? If this claim is perhaps extreme, even deterministic, the core of the idea is still important; the close relationship between the identity of people and that of their places. Wilson (1988) elaborates this point by proposing that, with settled life, the anchoring of a person in a particular place results in the identification of that person with the place and vice versa. It is this reciprocal identity of person and place which is the essence of property, ownership and the right to exclude others and which leads to a sustained sense of a person's political character (1988: 70-71).

Just as Strathern (1988: 175-6) has characterised objectification as the manner in which persons and things are construed as having value, so too can places be construed as having value and meaning-in-themselves. It is the objectification of place-value and place-meaning by the users and inhabitants of those places which produces not only the places themselves but also the identity of the places and of the persons who use and inhabit the places.

Important though the self-constituting notion of places and personal identity may sound, it must be acknowledged that identities cannot emerge through the reflection of the characteristics of places, rather they emerge through negotiation between individuals in those places. Gregory claims that it is an insight due to feminist geographers that places are the sites where identities and subjectivities are negotiated (D. Gregory 1994). In this process, different individuals come to claim varied meanings and values for the places which appear to be shared as common loci of activity. The process through which such varied claims come to be enunciated is grounded in the twin contexts of the past of such places and the wider spatial contexts in which the places are set (Massey 1994). For Massey, places do not have single, pre-given identities; rather, places are shared spaces, constructed out of juxtaposed, intersecting and articulating, but always multiple, social relations (Massey 1994: 276).

It is a leitmotif in the work of the cultural analyst Raymond Williams that the landscape expressed a deep sense of the past (Williams 1973: 1984). There are two mutually reinforcing ways in which these pasts are presenced, (cf. objects): materialisation (comparable to Bourdieu's objectivisation) and rhetoric. For Williams, places were not just the sites of an event but 'the materialisation of a history which is often quite extensively retracted' (Williams 1979). Hence the form of past monuments conveys the sense of a witnessing of the deeds of the past from which the present cannot escape - a form of presencing. But this testament remains mute until the places are incorporated into the practices of their inhabitants for their own purposes and often in strikingly different ways. Places have a narrative level of their own, in which the meaning potential latent in the landscape is actualised by individuals and groups in their everyday social practices. This means that the narratives of separate places are combined and re-combined in a larger narrative told and re-told by residents, neighbours and strangers (Berdoulay 1989). It is in the course of this larger narrative that the conflicting claims for the identities of places and related people can be negotiated.

A more refined development of these processes of identity-formation has been presented by Rob Shields in his extended consideration of marginality as the major theme of western civilisation (Shields 1991). Shields begins by arguing that people use particular discourses about places as a mark of their own 'insider' status in the relevant communities. This implies that group affiliation is created through knowledge of discourses which locate places as particular types of places, in contrast to other peoples and places which can be defined as 'outsiders'. The notion that cultural knowledge is central to group affiliation is reinforced by the idea that the essential marker of a cultural activity is the process of place-identification; the naming of a place marks an insertion into a symbolic realm of a specific material space whose meaning can be discussed only in the context of that symbolic realm of discourse.

Shields' most valuable contribution is his three-level nested hierarchy of spatial identity: mythology, place-myth and place-image. At the highest level, a mythology of place identities is a type of group cosmology, comprising the overall system of relative similarities and differences between all known places. Here the uniqueness of places are set against their communalities in a relational system of overall significance. The communal mythology is formed by a set of place-myths. Place-myths represent the conflicting but often internally coherent visions of the identity of a particular place. It is often the case that different groups negotiate their own versions of a place-myth with other groups; it is also common that myths about a certain place can change with time. Such place-myths consist of a collective set of place-images.

Place-images derive from face-to-face encounters with particular places and consist of discrete meanings associated with real places regardless of their character in reality. People who visit places commonly construct their images through one or more of three processes (Shields 1991: 47): over-simplification (the reduction of the place to a single trait), stereotyping (the amplification of a particular trait of the place), and labelling (the deeming of a place to have a particular, or essential, nature). In this way, place-identities begin to be formed at the lowest level; they tend to be dominated by core images, often in the form of 'mental maps' (cf. Küchler 1993), which tend to remain embedded despite other changes.

These three levels of mythology, myth and image operate as 'insider' stories – as part of the symbolic construction of communal identities despite the poly-vocality of the images existing at the individual level (Shields 1991: 262). Rather than denying collective image-formation or consciousness, Shields opposes group myths and private behaviour, claiming that the tension between group myth and personal experience forms the basis for social action. How does this schema relate to places in the past?

Settlement

A settlement pattern thus comprises a network of settled places which were once occupied, abandoned and re-occupied. They were variously associated through a social network of ancestral traditions and historical narratives, each with its own place-values and myths. Küchler (1993) has used the notion of a 'mental map' in her discussion of the choice of settlement spaces in New Ireland. She finds that the locals used their picture of the location of old house sites, gardens and secondary forest as pointers to the new sites to be occupied (1993: 96-7). These 'forgotten places', together with the record of their inhabitants, enabled the reconstitution of social relations across time through negotiation of their dominant meanings.

It is rarely mentioned that places can have negative as well as positive connotations. On the positive side, a place may have cosmological significance, as a key location in an ancestor-myth or cosmological scheme. On a lower ritual level, another place may be the locale for ceremonies of particular significance. The death of a particularly significant individual at a certain place may provide yet a third place with distinctive associations with a past chief or big-man. Alternatively, a visit by a renowned long-distance specialist, replete with travellers' tales and exotic material culture, may give a fourth place a special flavour. This may also be achieved through celebrated subsistence successes, whether a run of bumper harvests, great hunting anecdotes or spectacular fishing expeditions. Different groups and sub-groups will emphasise one or more factors over others in the process of negotiation.

On the negative side, places may mark a defeat in battle, where members of the group were killed, captured or injured, while a renowned or dreaded act of witchcraft or spirit-possession may be remembered in another place. Negative place-values may be just as important in prohibiting future occupation of a place as the decline of any local resource. All of these accounts are, in Shields' term, 'insider stories'; possession of this knowledge is a sign of membership of the group.

Time-marks/place-marks

Competing claims to place-value are the norm of social networks and it may be that unanimous acceptance of the primacy of a single place is a comparatively rare event. But such an acceptance is, in itself, a major social decision, worthy of its own special place in the group mythology. This decision constitutes the formal recognition of a place as a timemark – the temporal equivalent of a landmark (Chapman 1997a) – not only incorporating the historical narratives of the place into a new version of the group mythology but also underlining the time at which the group decision was made. Recognition of a place as a timemark is a new step in place-formation – an important stage in the biography of a place as much as the creation of a set of new relations between this place and all other places within the settlement cluster and perhaps also special places in other clusters.

The process of group selection of a special place marks, pari passu, a new stage in terms of social integration, group formation and/or group consolidation. This process is a good example of Robinson's (1989) claim for the close identity of people and their places (or places and their people). Such a statement is also indicative of a social consensus in the present, a communal decision to stake out their history in a place that they wish to call their own. This decision marks, in Pred's (1986) terminology, the mobilisation of resources for the creation of a dominant institutional project. Whichever place is marked by this choice, the very fact that such a choice has been made at all may be construed as an act of social integration by a group sufficiently cohesive to be leaving material remains as their marker. Through this decision, the importance of place is coterminous with the importance of people, not in the sense of the 'central people' beloved of processualists in their hunt for low-level 'central places' but rather through a stable group possessed of sufficient communal resources to create a dominant institutional project that would enshrine long-lasting meaning for the group.

Hence, the selection of one place in preference to others refers to specifics of the places' mythology and myths which, though inaccessible to direct archaeological observation, do follow discernible principles. Differentiation of places already related in a network of narrative can lead to the occasionally unanimous decision amongst a group of the selection of a single special place. Once this place becomes a timemark in the settlement cluster, its place-value and place-myths dramatically change, offering an important social resource which can be activated in the future through continued site occupation or re-occupation. But it must be recalled that, at any time, good reasons can be produced for the abandonment of even a famous place. The continued occupation of a special place is a matter for negotiation and consensus, despite (or could it be because of?) the weight of ancestral tradition.

Landscapes

Counterposed to the special place, one may posit the existence of many minor places of no particular distinction – a difference emphasised by the landscape historian J.B. Jackson (1984). Jackson identifies two inter-dependent forms of landscape - the political landscape and the vernacular landscape. In contrasting these two landscapes, which are always found together, Jackson stresses that the essential function of landscape is to combine the monumental, the landmark, with the transitory. Jackson's classification is based on a distinction between humans as political animals (where the landscape is a human creation belonging to humans, a well-defined domain which gives humans a different status from other species) and humans as inhabitants (with the landscape as a habitat which is essentially pre-human, where humans belong to the landscape in the sense that they are its product and where they take responsibility for nature and other species).

The landscape of the inhabitants (the vernacular landscape) achieves its identity over the course of time, its coherence forming only after generations of unrest, confusion and conflict; when it stops evolving, we can say what it is. In an inhabited landscape, the land implicates its inhabitants as members of a working community on that land. The mobility of people, places and boundaries is typical of the inhabited landscape. If an element in the vernacular landscape is visible, it is because that element is permanent. Yet each place sees itself as the centre of the world, an oasis of order in a sea of surrounding chaos, inhabited by 'The People'. Spaces between dwellings in a vernacular landscape indicate personal relations, the involved and often contradictory traditions of the community.

This incessant re-making of the inhabited landscape is ignored or resisted by the political landscape, whose essential characteristic is a belief in the achievement of identity through the sanctity of place. In the political landscape, the function of place is to make people visible and let them put down their roots: their centrality is altogether more obviously based on social power. The political landscape is an altogether larger arena, more permanent and visible, often with a coherent and imposed design and boundaries which help to create a political or sacred identity. In the political landscape, the 'natural' environment (the land) has no inherent identity of its own but is rather a means to an essentially economic end. It is the permanence of place, in a social as much as a topographic sense, that gives people their lasting identity.

The tell of Vinča-Belo Brdo in context

The reconstruction of the occupation sequence at Vinča is complex, and yet, paradoxically, based on only the scantiest of stratigraphic evidence. For practical purposes, only one measured section and two sketch sections have been published for the early excavations (Vasić 1910: Tafel 7a; 1936: Slika 213-214) and Vasić's data on house-plans is patchy at best. A recent publication of two well-documented sections from the central part of the tell now forms the most complete basis for the interpretation of the Vinča stratigraphy (Stevanović and Jovanović 1996: Figs. 2-2a, 3-3a). In a previous study, I reconstructed a total of eleven Neolithic occupation phases – one pit-level dated to the Starčevo Period and 10 building horizons dated to the Vinča period in a total deposit of 6.15-6.50 m with each horizon lasting some 50 years (Chapman 1981: 6-10). Using the more recent data, Stevanović and Jovanović (1996: 201) propose thirteen building sub-horizons, divided into the following: six sub-horizons (I/1-2 and II/1-3 and III/1) in an Early Vinča phase covering an accumulation of 4.5 m of deposit; three sub-horizons (III/2 and IV/1-2) in a middle phase of 1 m; and four sub-horizons (V/1-2 and VI/1-2) in a late phase of 2 m of deposit (1996: Figs. 2a and 3a). The important new data concern the fixing of the excavation of Ditch Q to the middle phase, a ditch which Stevanović and Jovanović maintain was used to define the central core of the settlement (1996: 198-9). There is some confusion over the phasing of horizon III, which is placed in Phase 1 and also in Phase 2 (1996: 201). I have arbitrarily placed sub-horizon III/1 in the early phase and sub-horizon III/2 in the middle phase. Otherwise, this is a major advance over the stratigraphic documentation from the earlier excavations. It is unfortunate that the authors do not attempt to relate either Vasić's (1910) stratigraphic units, nor this author's (1981) stratigraphic sequence to the new phasing.

It is now time to explore these issues further through the consideration of one special type of place – a prehistoric tell. If there is a single site in Serbia which enshrines the values and the prestige of the Serbian Neolithic, it is most certainly the great mound of Belo Brdo (Serbo-Croat = white hill) some 12 km East of the capital Belgrade (Beograd = white town) (Fig. 1). The bulk of the Neolithic display in the National Museum of Belgrade, as well as the new Archaeological Park at Vinča itself, bear witness to the artefactual wealth and cultural value of the Belo Brdo finds – finds which merit the designation of the site as the eponymous site of the Vinča culture. The earlier excavations at Vinča were published in what was perhaps the most important Serbian Neolithic monographs before the Second World War – the four volumes of *Praistorijska Vinča* (Vasić 1932-36). Since the rise of the Socialist state of the former Yugoslavia, the fame of Vinča has been continuously reproduced in a series of prestigious conference reports and magnificently illustrated museum catalogues (Srejović et al. 1984; Srejović and Tasić 1990). The new excavations from 1979-1984 have led to further important discoveries which confirm the site as one of the dozen key sites of the European Neolithic (Čelić 1984; Stevanović and Jovanović 1996). There can be little doubt of the value of the place that is Vinča in modern archaeological research as much as recent heritage developments. But no researcher on the Vinča mound has so far attempted to define what it is about the place that made it so important for the prehistoric occupants of the white hill.

The first point about Vinča is that the settlement is a tell - not the only tell in the Vinča network but the only known tell for the region within a 100-km radius of the site itself. Before the time that Vinča emerged as a tell, settlement mounds were widespread in Thessaly, Macedonia and Bulgaria but were only beginning to appear sporadically in Slavonia (e.g., Bapska-Gradac), Bosnia (e.g., Gornja Tuzla), Transylvania (e.g., Tartăriă), Oltenia (e.g., Vădastră) and Hungary (e.g. Vésztő-magóri halom).

As currently seen from the Danube, the hill rises majestically up from the loess terrace. In prehistory, prior to severe fluvial erosion, the mound would have risen more gently from the riverbank to reach a height of over 8 metres by the end of the Neolithic period. This is higher than almost all known prehistoric tells in Macedonia, Bulgaria and Greece (with the exception of Tell Djakovo, an 18 m mound in Thrace: Todorova 1978). Without visiting the site, it is hard to capture the visual attraction of a tell in a sea of 'flat sites' – sites which were occupied over one or two generations and then abandoned. The principle of verticality is one aspect of the problem of the tell of Vinča – a unique site but one constituted in multi-dimensional relationship to the other sites of the north Šumadija. To ask how did the mound achieve such a height, we must ask what kind of architectural practices have been documented on the Vinča mound.

The earliest occupation at Vinča was a small early Neolithic (i.e., Starčevo) settlement on the loess terrace of the

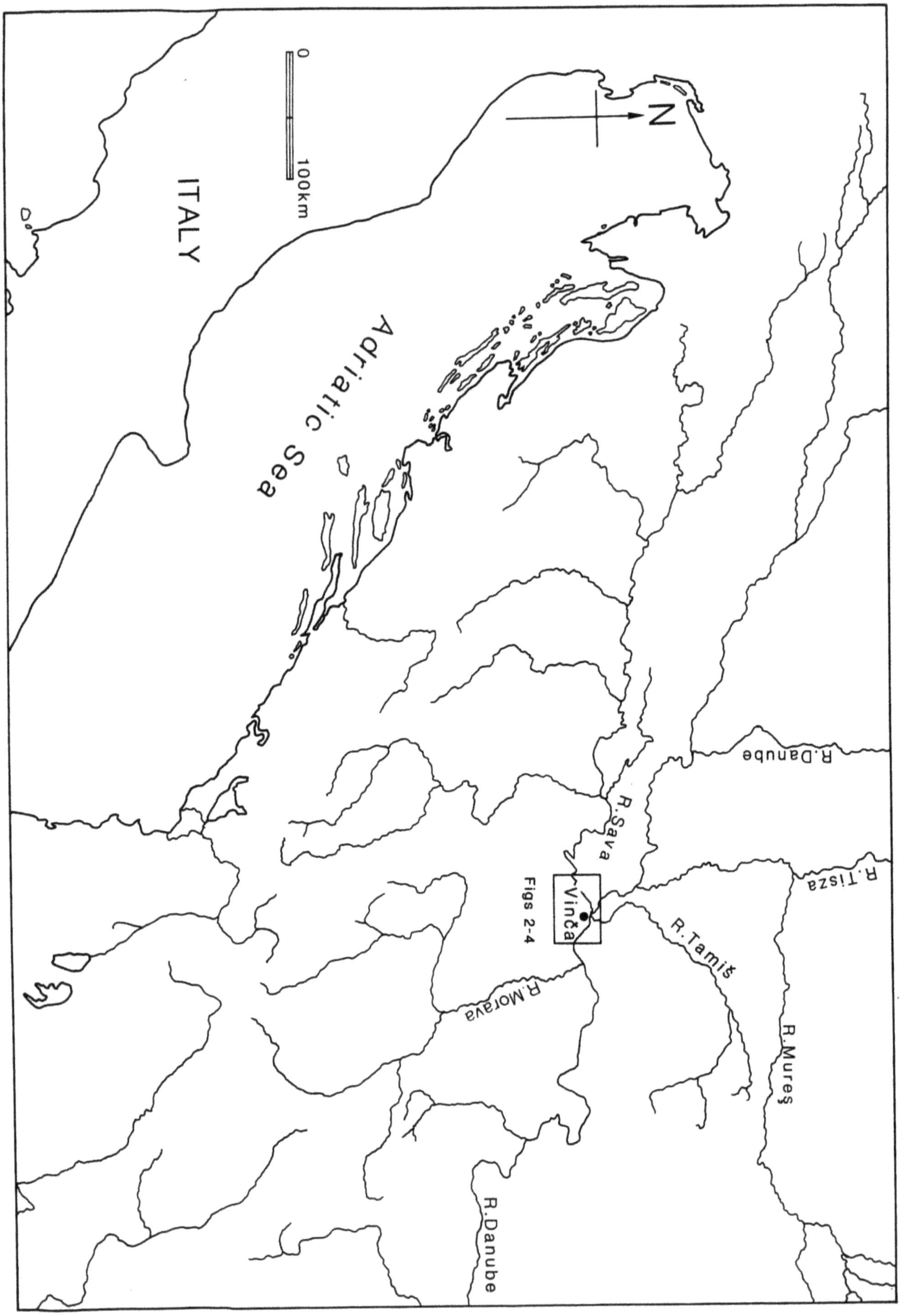

Figure 1 Location map of Vinča and its surrounds.

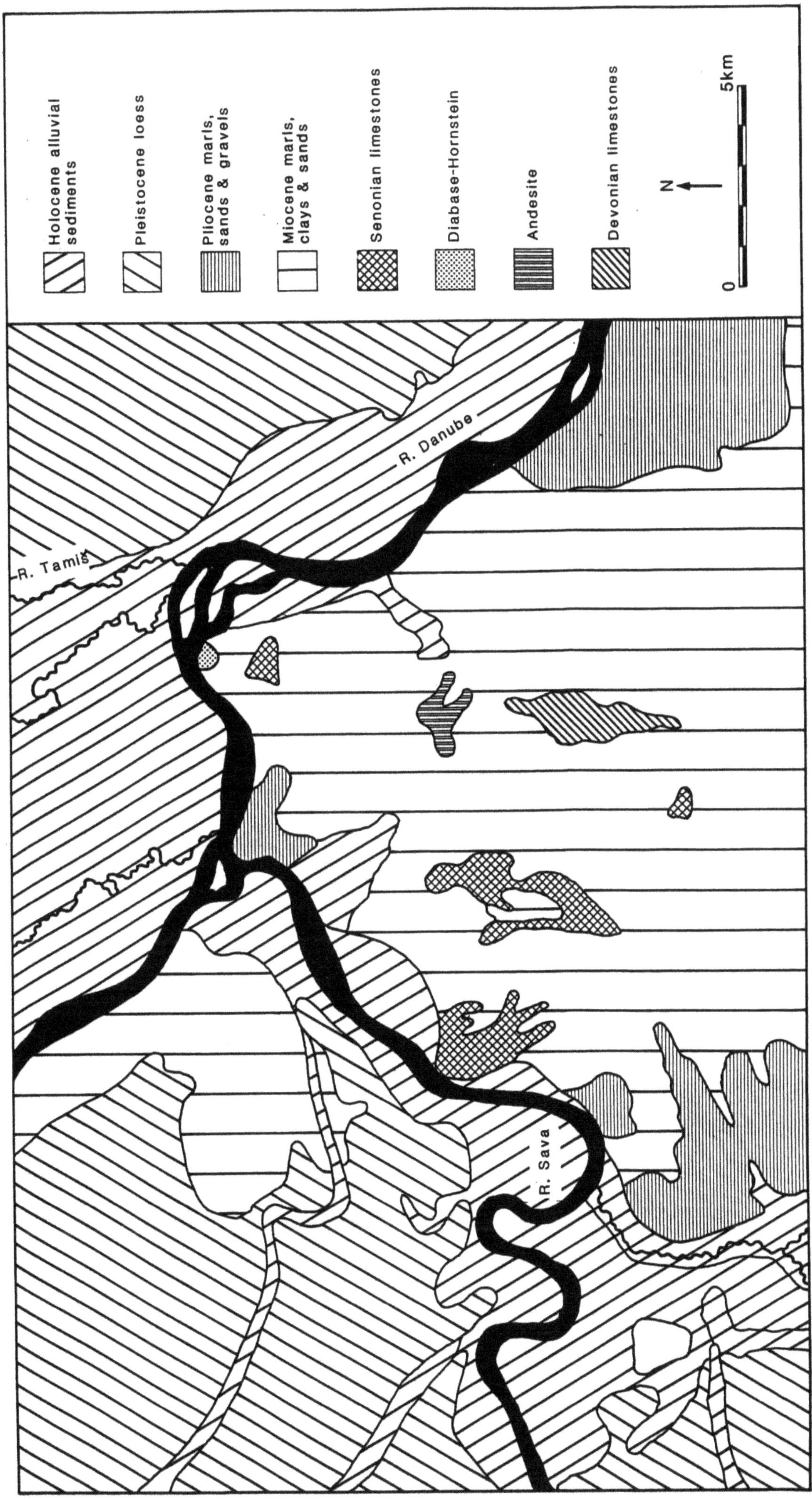

Figure 2 Geology of North Šumadija.

river Danube (Letica 1968; Garašanin 1984). Because of the later, Vinča, occupation, very few features from this earliest occupation contained only Starčevo pottery – one damaged pit and a grave with nine skeletons. Ten Vinča building horizons follow, dating to c. 4400-3900 bc. In these levels, minor conflagrations are a regular feature, as is the levelling of house debris to form a stable platform for new construction and the in-washing of sediment from other parts of the tell. An exceptional case is the floor in Profile 213, rebuilt six times after local fires. Some of the areas between the houses served as yards with stamped floors, with open ovens and clay pits common and open fireplaces frequent. In the post-Vinča period, four middle Copper Age (Bodrogkeresztúr) graves have been found, as well as a Baden occupation with open fireplaces and possibly pit-huts, and a scatter of Kostolac sherds (Tasić 1984a).

This was followed after a gap of several centuries by a short but intensive early Bronze Age (Vatin) occupation, with over 25 pit-huts, often badly damaged by the most recent phase of site use (i.e., a Medieval cemetery) (Tasić 1984b). The latest prehistoric occupation was a Celtic hilltop settlement with a defensive ditch (Čelić 1984).

There are therefore three parts of the prehistoric Vinča narrative which will provide different components of the site's place-value, each with their own significant additions (? and subtractions) to the story of the site – the early phase (Starčevo occupation 0, Vinča occupations 1-3), the main occupation (Vinča occupations 4-13) and the late, post-Vinča occupations.

The early phase

The earliest occupation of the Belo Brdo terrace is in the middle of the Starčevo period, c. 5700 CAL BC. Excavations of this phase are insufficient to give use a clear picture of the character of the settlement; however, one ritual context stands out (the multiple burial in the pit known as the Ossuary; Letica 1968) a find rare in the First Temperate Neolithic and comparable to the group burials at Mala Vrbica Ajmana (Stalio 1986; Radosavljević and Krunić 1986) and Kladovo and Velesnica (Vasić 1986).

Otherwise, the pits and pottery are no different from pits

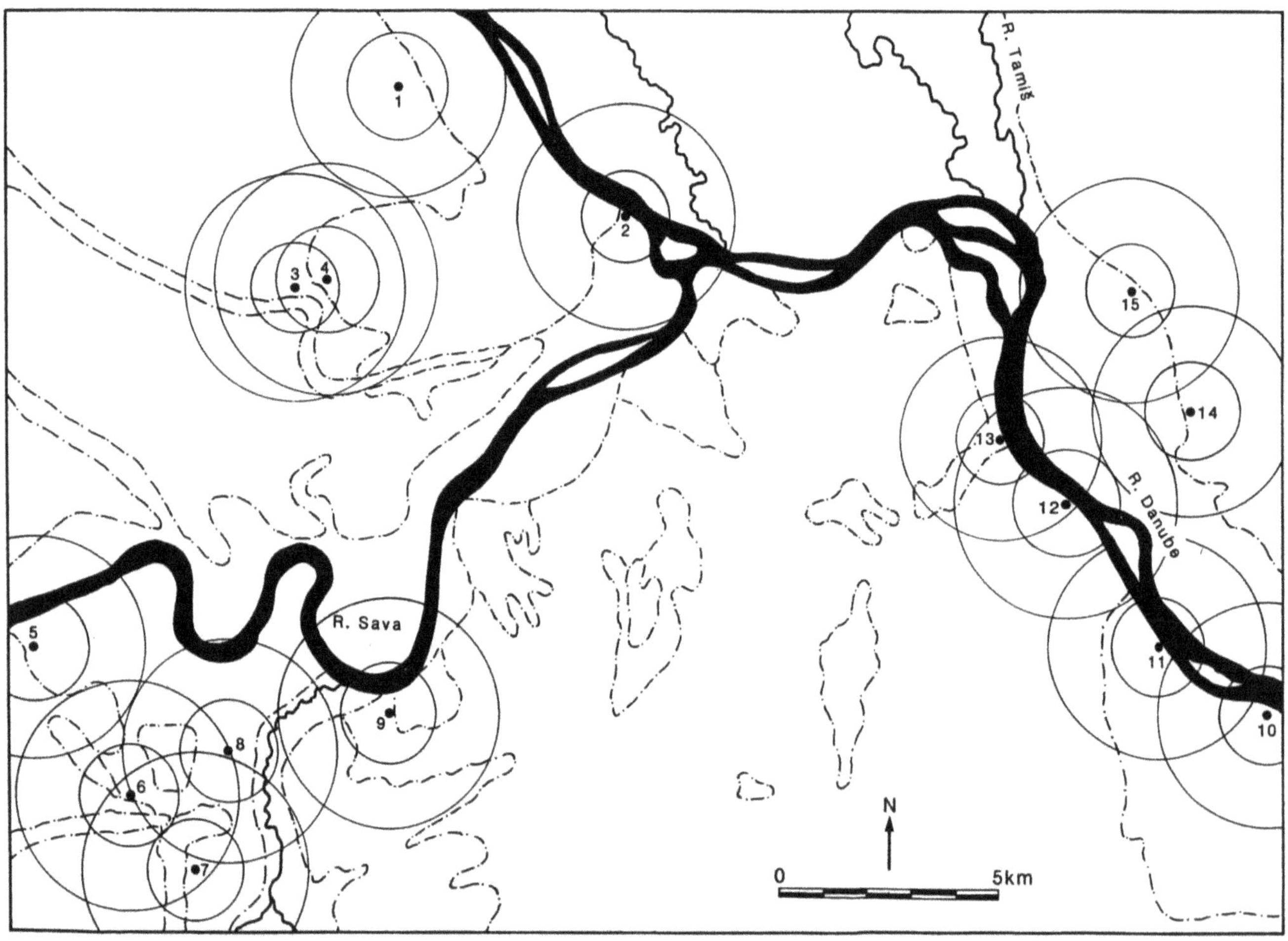

Figure 3 Location of north Šumadija Starčevo sites. 1 Batajnica-Crvenka; 2 Zemun-Gardoš; 3 Dobanovci-Ciglana; 4 Dobanovci-Selo; 5 Obrenovac-Skela; 6 Obrenovac-Grabovac; 7 Stubline; 8 Obrenovac-Zvecka; 9 Barić; 10 Brestovik; 11 Grocka; 12 Ritopek; 13 Vinča-Belo Brdo; 14 Omoljica; 15 Starčevo-Grad.

and pottery on neighbouring Starčevo sites, of which at least three are known within a radius of 10 km (Fig. 3). The most important neighbouring site – the eponymous site of the Starčevo network – lay on a similar loess terrace on the opposite bank of the Danube. At Starčevo-Grad, radiocarbon dates from the most recent excavations have yielded a date range of 4900-4600 bc (5600-5300 CAL BC), suggesting a repeated use of the terrace, rather than an occupation covering the entire length of the Starčevo sequence. It seems likely that the FTN occupation at Vinča was broadly coeval with the use of the Starčevo-Grad site.

Although the social relations between the two communities cannot currently be inferred, it is likely that the persons from both sites would have been part of the same breeding network(s) and, as kin of some kind, each would have been aware of the others' places, their subsistence strategies and preferred farming, fishing and hunting locations (for Starčevo: Clason 1980; J. Renfrew 1979: Table 5; Barker 1975). The Belo Brdo terrace took its place as one of the nodes of settlement in a network of occupied, abandoned and re-occupied places, where the memories of those ancestors kept alive those 'forgotten places' and helped to reconstitute the web of social relationships across time. A narrative of places was already well-developed before the emergence of a tell at Vinča.

After an abandonment of the Belo Brdo terrace during the Late Starčevo phase, the first remains of above-ground dwellings occur c. 5000 CAL BC, a time for which there is no evidence as yet for other site use in that stretch of the river Danube. At this time, there was no tell at Vinča. It is a paradox that a tell cannot by definition begin life as a tell - its earliest incarnation is as a flat site, like other flat sites in its vicinity. Such places did not take on the visual characteristics of tells for some generations but remained *in statu nascendi*. There is a critical time between the first re-occupation of a place and the physical manifestation of a mound – a period of generations, if not centuries – in the case of Vinča, a low mound of perhaps 2 m had been formed by the end of the early part of the Early Vinča (or Vinča-A) phase. For this reason, the phrase 'tell formation' is, I believe, inappropriate, for it carries implications of future action not present in the initial act. Such a denial of the contingent possibilities inherent in future action is, I believe, quite illegitimate.

Origins of the tell

There are, therefore, two questions framing the issue of the origins of a tell such as Vinča: why did communities stay on the same sites at all?; and why were particular places selected for this re-occupation? I shall maintain that place-value and the ancestors are deeply implicated in both questions (for an extended discussion, see Chapman 1997b).

The physical transformation of a tell-to-be into a tell depends upon two long-term physical concentrations – of people and house daub. The commitment to long-term association is part of the process of increased sedentism, recognised in the archaeological record by the construction of larger, more durable houses and the occupation of larger settlements (Tringham and Krstić 1991; Stevanović and Jovanović 1996; Stevanović 1997).

The nucleation of people in households living close to one another is the first pre-requisite of tell-becoming: it is unlikely that tells will develop on a large flat site where households live in dispersed structures (Chapman 1989). Such living conditions have their own specific advantages and disadvantages, of the kind produced by constant, intense social interaction. It is by no means certain that many communities would accept the long-term disadvantages of increased friction and conflict over the pleasures of heightened social relationships (Chapman 1988; 1993). The generation of a set of communal constraints upon behaviour is one method of maintaining long-term social cohesion in such sites (Chapman 1989; 1993). It is undoubtedly true that such long-term stability in the face of local conflict would have required social integration at the supra-household level. Perhaps the most likely reason for the acceptance of such constraints on individual and/or household behaviour is the centrality of ancestral paces in the ideology of domestic communities (Chapman 1994).

The physical concentration of house daub derives from two main processes: the slow washing of mud from house walls by the rain and the more severe act of levelling the remains of destroyed or abandoned structures. If the remains of only one house are levelled at a time (e.g., Tringham's claim for Opovo: Tringham et al. 1992: 382; Stevanović 1996) or if rain-fed deposition is the main method of accumulation, then tell-formation would indeed have been very slow. This may indeed have been the case in the early stages of the lives of tells-to-be. But new attitudes to daub would have been required to create the mounds which survive today, with their heights of several metres off the plain. The architectural practice proposed here is that daub from previous living structures was incorporated into the fabric of the new living surface as a physical way of grounding the community in ancestral values.

In both kinds of nucleation, the primacy of commitment to a communal rather than a household ideology is evident: the memory of the community of ancestors binds the living to a special place and these ties become more reticulated and complex through constant presence. In this way, the strength of the living community is related to the physical emergence of the tell-to-be as an ancestral place – a true mound.

It should be noted that staying in one place has often been associated with changes in subsistence strategies and the development of more complex farming practices, such as manuring and crop rotation. This was a tenet of Childe's differentiation between permanent tell settlements and flat sites based on shifting agriculture (Childe 1958) and the argument has been repeated later (e.g., Dennell 1978; Dennell and Webley 1975). However, adjacent flat sites in a site cluster are in practice exploiting similar territories as would be utilised by tell groups – the difference being that

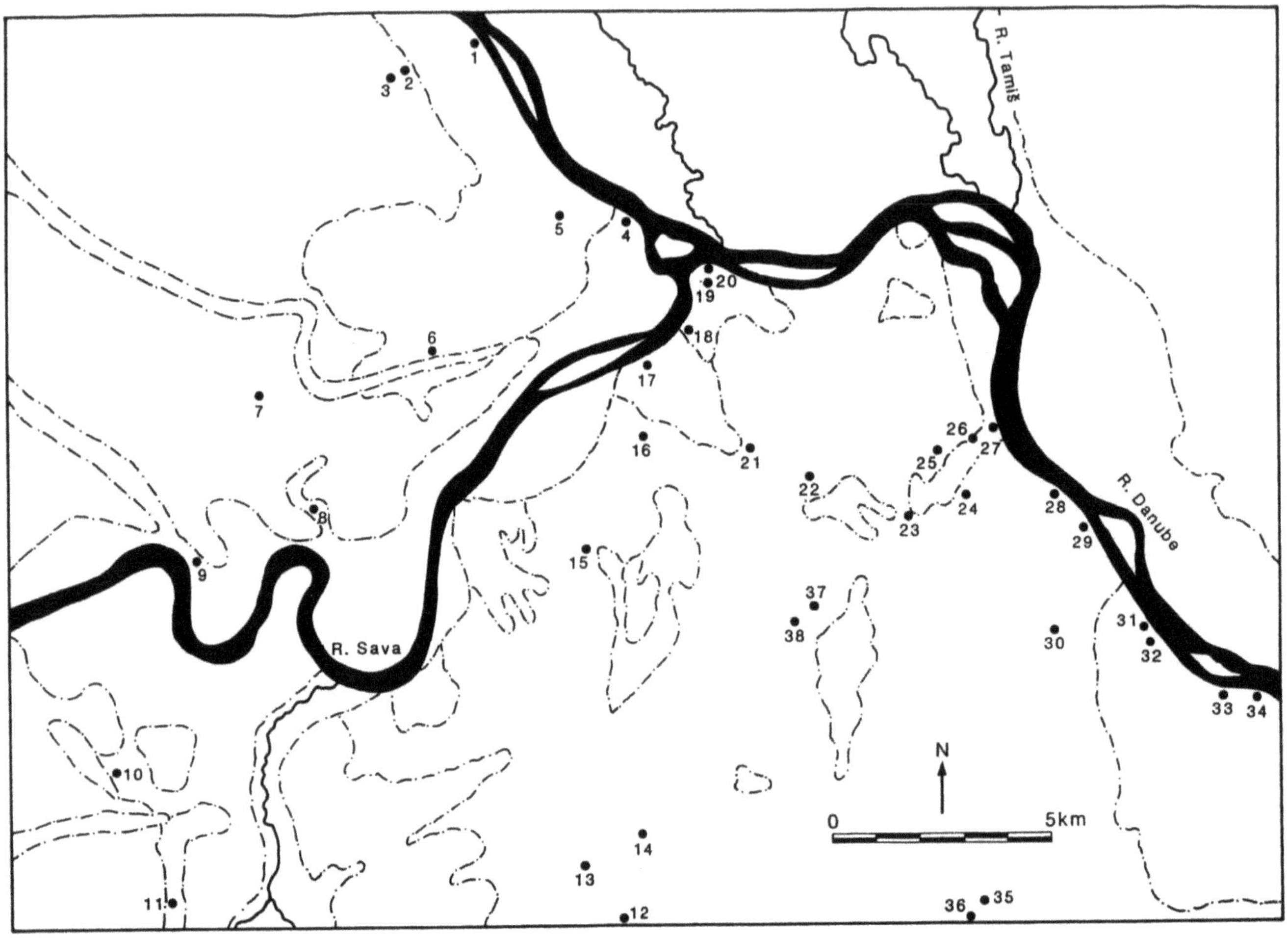

Figure 4 Location of north Šumadija early Vinča sites. 1 Batajnica-Biljarički Brod; 2 Batajnica-Kapela; 3 Batajnica-Crvenka; 4 Zemun-Gardoš; 5 Zemun-Biljarički Brod; 6 Surčin; 7 Bečmen; 8 Boljevci; 9 Progar; 10 Obrenovac-Grabovac; 11 Stubline-Crkvine; 12 Boždarevac; 13 Baćevac; 14 Barajevo; 15 Železnik-Rt; 16 Beograd-Žarkovo; 17 Beograd-Čukarica; 18 Beograd-Senjak; 19 Beograd-Studentski Trg; 20 Beograd-Gornji Grad; 21 Beograd-Banjica; 22 Kumodraz; 23 Leštane; 24 Boleč; 25 Boleč-Mlin; 26 Vinča-Raskršče; 27 Vinča-Belo Brdo; 28 Ritopek; 29 Ritopek-Plavinački Potok; 30 Zaklopača; 31 Grocka-Periferija; 32 Grocka-Agino Brdo; 33 Brestovik; 34 Brestovik; 35 Popović-Madjarsko Groblje; 36 Popović-Mali Drum.

they are living in different but nearby places. Therefore, tell-living does not necessarily and of itself indicate a more advanced form of agriculture. It is, however, likely that the stable households forming tell communities would develop longer-term patterns of land tenure or ownership than is normal on shorter-term flat sites. Such a development would also support the communal cohesion suggested by nucleated living on ancestral paces. It should also not be forgotten that the location of tells and site clusters was confined to the most productive and fertile parts of the environment, generally speaking lowland valleys and the edges of old lakes.

Thus, it is proposed here that communities stayed on the same sites long enough to initiate the formation of mounds because of the development of greater sedentism and because of ancestral relations with the places which they selected. Ancestral relations had effects on land tenure, nucleated site occupation and the use and modification of the social environment of house daub. Such practices reflexively demonstrate the emergence of cohesive, long-lasting communities and the emergence of tells-to-be. But what were the social practices which enabled the reproduction of a stable, enduring habitus on the Vinča tell?

Ritual, prestige and exotics

The early part of the Early Vinča phase at Belo Brdo is distinguished from all other known Vinča-A sites by a remarkable congeries of social practices, which could in no way be predicted from the earlier, Starčevo occupation (Fig. 4). Three types of finds occur in major concentrations at Vinča and Vinča alone in this phase: ritual finds, prestige ornaments and exotic lithics such as obsidian (Chapman 1976; 1981). Any one such concentration of valued finds would make a site significant at the beginning of a new cultural development. The combination of all three heralds an extraordinary focus of socially valuable practices, itself suggestive of multiple reasons why the Vinča settlement might assume greater-than-usual place-value.

The wealth of ritual artefacts at Vinča is one of the site's best-known characteristics; it is estimated that over 2,000 figurines, mostly fragmentary, have been excavated at the

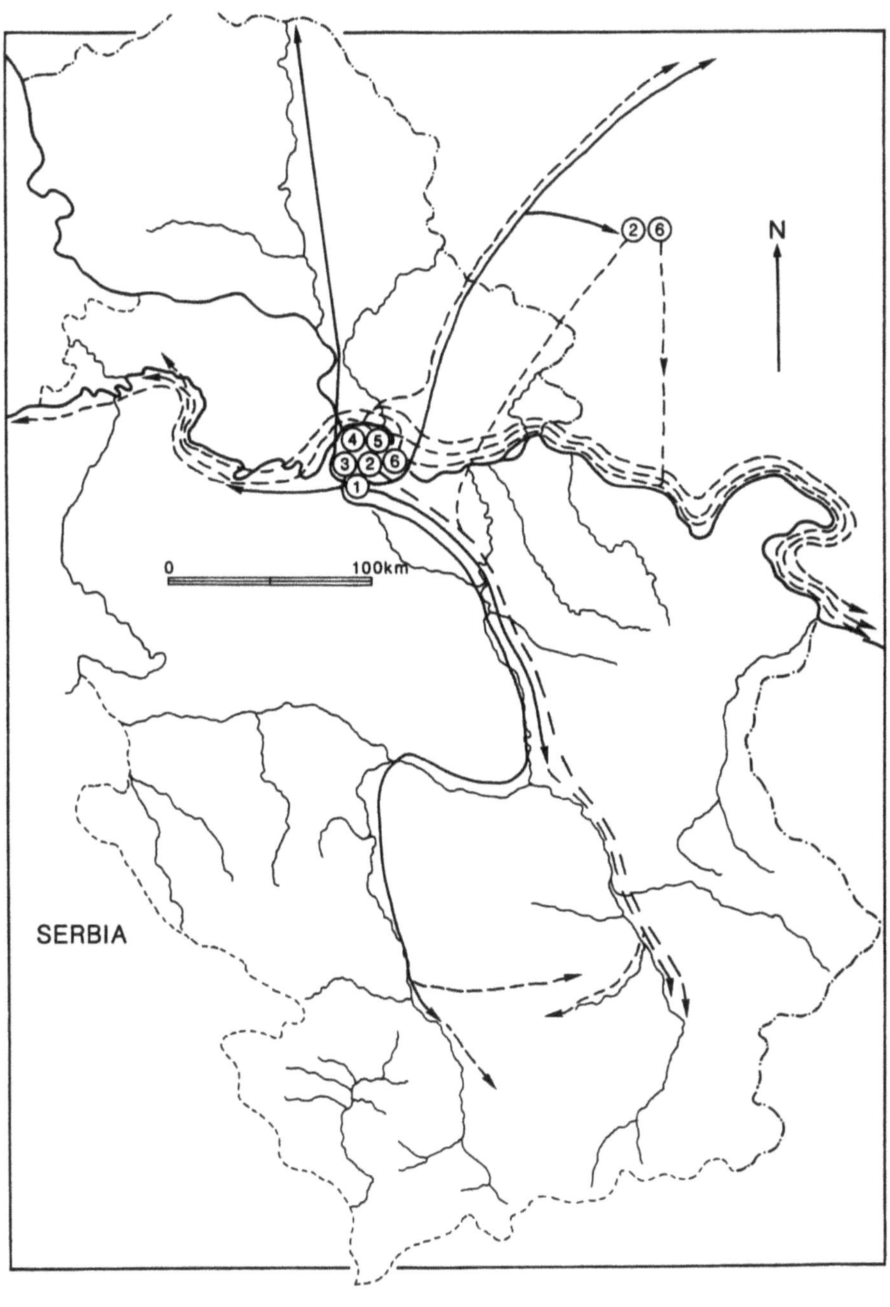

Figure 5 Diffusion of ritual artefacts in the Vinča network (after Chapman 1981: Fig. 161). 1 incised signs (44-4200); 2 tripod altar (42-4000); 3 monumental figurines (42-4000); 4 narrow-lined figurine decoration (42-4000); 5 bucranium shrines (42-4000); 6 two-headed figurines (42-4000). Key to lines: double-line - 44-4200 bc; single-line - 42-4000 bc; long dashed-line - 4000-3800 bc; short dashed-line - 38-3500 bc.

site (Letica 1964; Chapman 1981). Several hundred figurines are known from the earliest phases (my phases 1-3), in comparison to a handful at most from any other Vinča-A site (e.g., Gornea, Supska, Gornja Tuzla). Most of these fired clay figurines have five traits: they tend to be anthropomorphic; they are usually small in size; if gendered, they tend to be female; they tend to be discarded broken; and they tend to be discarded out of doors. Miloje Vasić, the excavator of the majority of these figurines, has provided little contextual evidence for specific examples. The most we can assume is that, in the earliest Vinča phase, ceremonies involving, or culminating in, the structured deposition of figurines in outdoor settings were a regular practice at the Vinča site, and a rarity elsewhere in the central Balkans. However, there are some seven types of ritual artefact which can be identified in these phases at Vinča (Fig. 5), including prosomorphic lids, bucrania, incised signs, tripod altars, two-headed figurines (Fig. 6), monumental figurines and figurines with narrow-line decoration (Fig. 7) (Chapman 1976; 1981: Fig. 161). Without more contextual information, it remains difficult to relate such find categories to those of the figurines. But it is vital to note that, according to the available dating evidence (Chapman 1981), Vinča is the place where such innovations in ritual objects were made and it was only in the later part of the Early Vinča phase (Vinča-B/C) that such innovations were incorporated into ritual practices on other Vinča sites. Both the concentration of valued ritual objects at Vinča and the pattern of their distribution at later sites supports the notion that Vinča was some kind of a ritual centre during the earliest Vinča period.

The manufacture of small objects of semi-precious stone (in particular, alabaster, marble and rock-crystal) is a charac-

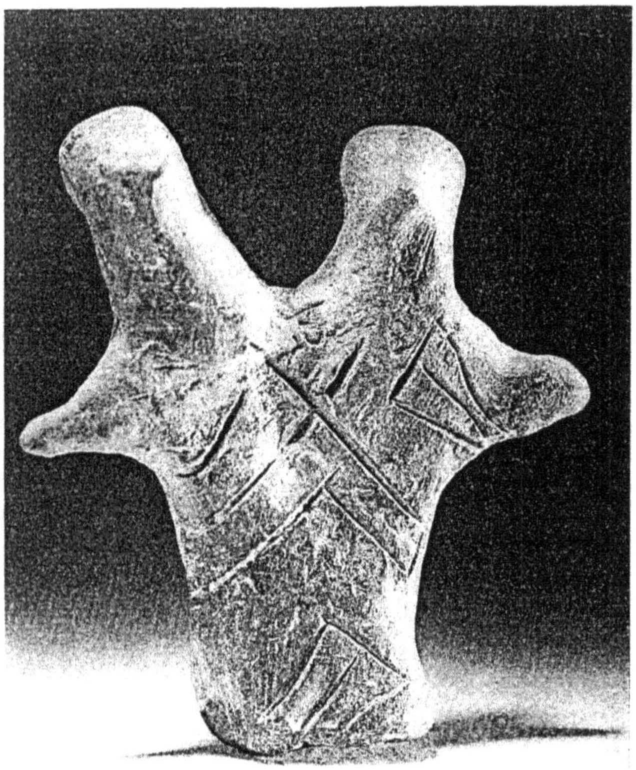

Figure 6 Double-headed figurine from Vinča-Belo-Brdo (after Srejović et al. 1984: Kat. 170). Height – 4.5 cm.

Figure 7 Figurine with narrow-line incision from Vinča-Belo-Brdo (after Srejović et al. 1984: Kat. 180). Height – 10 cm.

teristic of the Vinča network as a whole. The objects made are distinguished by their forms and the precision of their manufacture. Two forms are most frequent - the so-called 'mushroom amulet' (Fig. 8) and the so-called 'animal head' (Fig. 9). Both forms were manufactured in hard rock which was acquired from a distance: the marble presumably from sources in the Šumadija (perhaps Venčac), the rock-crystal from the Rudnik Mountains and the alabaster perhaps from the Fruška Gora (Chapman 1976). Each rock type shares a similar suite of techniques – grinding, facetting and polishing. Their small size (rarely larger than 8 cm) suggests a use as personal ornaments in some kind of costume or in a display; almost all of them have been found as complete items. The distribution of these objects is strictly limited to a small network of sites, mostly in the northern part of the Vinča network (Chapman 1981: Figs 140-141). By all criteria, these objects enshrined cultural value. Once again, there are very few occurrences of these ornaments outside Vinča in the earliest phase – and relatively few outside Vinča later on. The current dating evidence is suggestive of the notion that these ornament types were first manufactured at Vinča and that the innovation was distributed outwards to other sites in a later phase (Vinča-B/C). Unlike the fired clay figurines, the stone ornaments were durable and hard to damage and had the potential for long survivour-hood, even across several generations.

The third category of special finds at Vinča combines the more mundane quality of tools with an exotic flavour implied by remote access. Obsidian (a grey to black volcanic glass) is favoured by farming communities for its sharpness and attractive appearance in many parts of southern Eurasia. The only known sources of obsidian in southeast Europe are in the Zemplín / Zemplén Mountains of southeast Slovakia (the so-called Carpathian 1 source) and in northeast Hungary (the so-called Carpathian 2a-2b sources) (Williams-Thorpe et al. 1984; Bíró 1988). The peak period of the exchange of obsidian in eastern Europe was the period 5000-4500 CAL BC corresponding exactly to the first five hundred years of the Vinča use of Belo Brdo. Obsidian is frequent in the Early Vinča levels at Vinča, generally discarded in a broken and/or utilised state, outside of the houses. Analysis of the relative frequencies of obsidian by period at the Vinča tell (Srejović and Jovanović 1957; cf. Kaczanowska and Kozłowski 1990) portrays dwindling resource, with the peak of interest in the earliest Vinča levels – a total of 63 percent of all lithics by

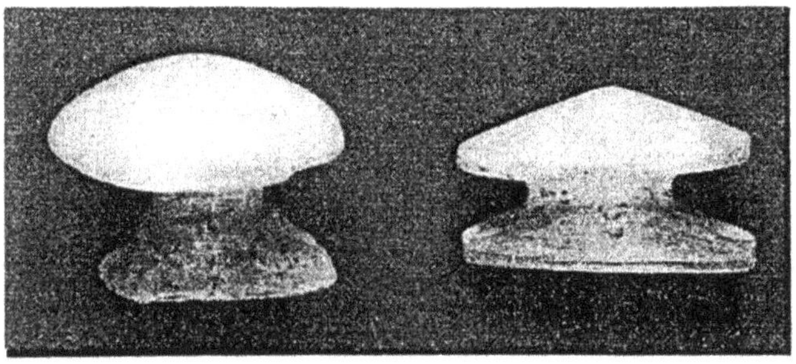

Figure 8 Polished stone 'mushroom amulets' from Vinča-Belo-Brdo (after Srejović et al. 1984: Kat. 224-5). Basal diameter of left example – 4.0 cm.

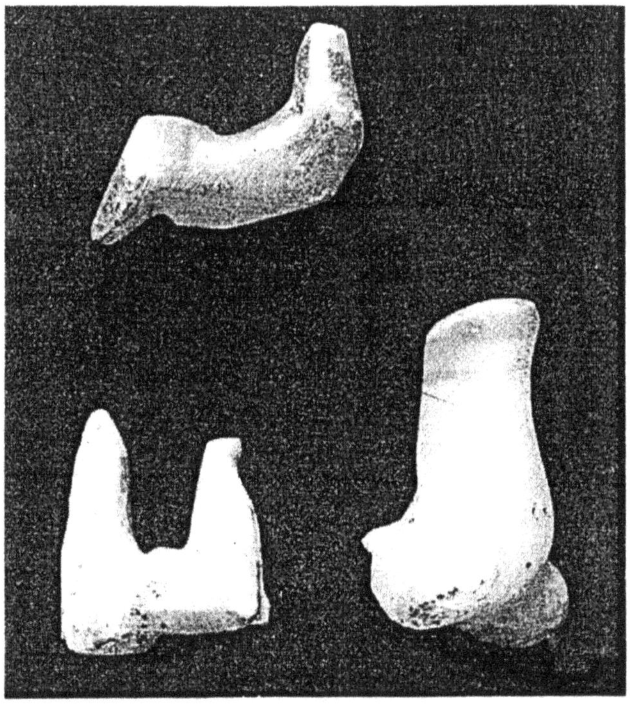

Figure 9 Polished stone 'animal heads' from Vinča-Belo-Brdo (after Srejović et al. 1984: Kat. 196-8).

number. In comparison with other earliest Vinča sites, this makes Vinča the main place for the acquisition of Zemplín obsidian (a result which I had, in an earlier synthesis, interpreted as evidence for directional trade via Vinča to the rest of the Šumadija to the south – Chapman 1981: Figs 108-110). My current view is that the quantity by weight of obsidian is so small that this reduces the likelihood of Vinča acting as a trading centre for redistribution of lithics in an inter-regional exchange system. What I now wish to emphasis vis-a-vis the obsidian in the earliest Vinča phases is its presence as a sign of long-distance relations across the middle Danube Basin – relations in which few other earliest Vinča sites appear to have participated. Once again, the valuable exchange items in this phase are concentrated in the hands of those living on the tell-to-be of Vinča .

While it is regrettable that so little contextual evidence is available for the earliest Vinča levels at Vinča, the general picture is unambiguous: the concentration of much of cultural value in one settlement in contrast to others both near and far. The wide range of valued artefacts implies an unusually large set of significant cultural activities; in the exchange field and the ritual field, both fields were reinforced by the appropriate symbolic capital. The cumulative effect of the biography of so many valued objects through their presencing of other significant social actors must have been extremely powerful contributing not only to the narrative of the place in which they became associated but also to the staging of the many and varied performances on the tell itself. The variety of artefacts conjures up the image of a community of persons with rich social identities developed not only through the objects which they used but also through the place in which they dwelt. The global and the local (in Neolithic terms) were, as ever, points of contrast. On the one side, the biographies of local ritual objects created, perhaps for the first time at Vinča, for tell ceremonial and maintained and passed on to later generations either intact as ancestral objects or indirectly through the repetition of similar rituals in similar places. The exchange items, on the other – each bringing a history of the people who mined or quarried the raw materials, those who manufactured the artefact, those through whose hands the item passed on its travel. The sheer variety of experiences amongst the tell-dwellers at Vinča would have led to different experiences of all these living aspects of material culture – producing different place-images and place-myths which were contested in the social flux which comprised

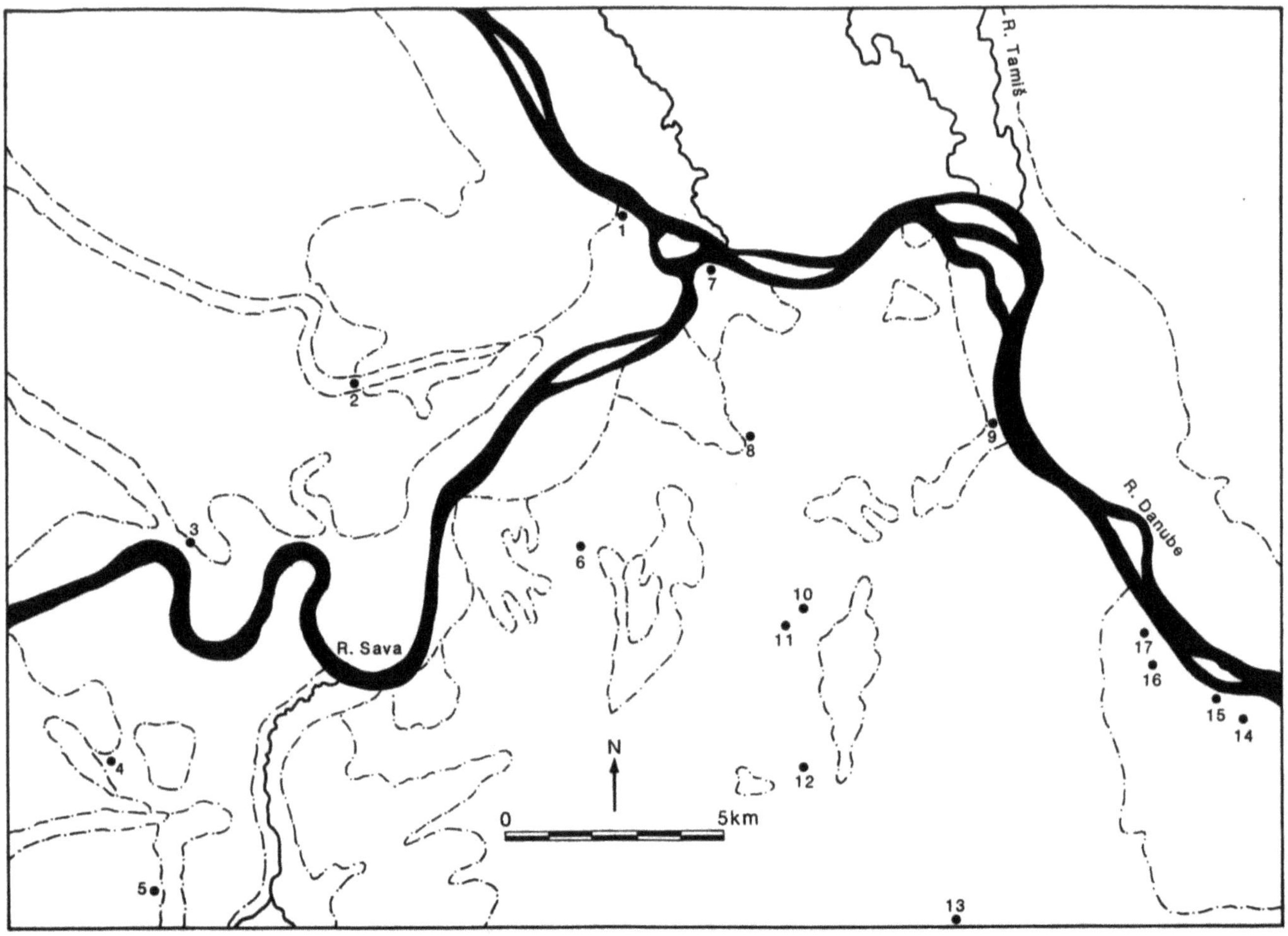

Figure 10 Location of north Šumadija late Vinča sites. 1 Zemun-Gardoš; 2 Jakovo-Kormadin; 3 Progar; 4 Obrenovac-Grabovac; 5 Stubline-Crkvine; 6 Železnik-Rt; 7 Beograd-Gornji Grad; 8 Beograd-Banjica; 9 Vinča-Belo Brdo; 10 Avala-Mala Stena; 11 Avala-Šuplja Stena; 12 Ripanj; 13 Popović-Mali Drum; 14 Brestovik; 15 Brestovik; 16 Grocka-Agino Brdo; 17 Grocka-Periferija.

the social identity of an important place. But why did the communities at Vinča choose to continue to live there rather than elsewhere?

The context of local places (those small-scale relatively undifferentiated Starčevo settlements along the banks of the Danube) is only part of the history of settling down on the Belo Brdo terrace. Nandris has demonstrated that the FTN comprised an inter-regional network of communities, whose non-ceramic material culture links are as significant as their regional ceramic differences (Nandris 1972). We may therefore assume that a network of exchange links connecting communities in the central Balkans pre-dated the establishment of the first Vinča settlement on the Belo Brdo terrace. Spatial as well as resource factors account for the location of this early centre. Lying close to the geographical centre of the Vinča network, and near the confluence of four major Danubian tributaries (the Tisza, the Tamiš, the Sava and the Morava) the area of Vinča attracted the maximum concentration of cultural interconnections. In addition, the proximity of fertile soils and rich rock and mineral resources made the Vinča area an obvious location. However, these factor are insufficient to explain why settlement continued through much, if not all, of the earliest Vinča phase when alternative village locations could have been settled nearby. There is, in the last instance, a crucial role in the ancestral location of the Vinča tell-to-be with its rich associations of place-value and object-value.

The main occupation

The main occupation at the Vinča site is defined as phases 4–10 (in traditional terms – Vinča B to D). At the beginning of this period, a low mound 2 m in height had accumulated on the Belo Brdo terrace. By the end of the period, the mound had increased to some 7.5 m in height and was the highest tell in Serbia. How was it that this gradual increase in deposition was sustained for so long and to such effect?

Vertical dominance

The creation of tells is dependent on the passing of much structured social time, experienced cyclically as the return to the start of each new settlement occupation after the completion of a full cycle. By the time a tell can be recognised as such, it is by definition a multi-occupational monument with a long history of its own. The notion to be explored here is that there is a social advantage to be gained from preference for the continued occupation of mounds in that the tell community gains vertical dominance over communities living on other flat sites. In this sense, the coming-into-being of tells does not represent the end-point of a process but rather the opening-out of a new phase in the landscape history of its settlement cluster.

Vertical competition is a direct implication of the selection of certain tells-to-be for re-occupation over other flat sites which remain abandoned or only rarely occupied. The competitive element is expressed physically, in terms of the sheer height of settlement-remains which are incorporated into the mound. In the world of established tells, monumental visibility marks the competition over the embodiment of ancestral place-values. There are two forms of competition in which tell communities participate: the competition between tell-occupants and the occupants of other, flat sites; the competition within different sub-groups of tell-occupants, each of whom may have different readings of their narrative tradition.

The mound–flat site distinctions express a vertical difference which may assume various ideological meanings. The most obvious is that the higher the mound, the longer the occupation and therefore the greater the ancestral time-depth of that site. This point may be underlined with reference to the living as much as to the dead, in terms of the longer traditions of the resident kin-group(s), the diversity of their social relations and the processes of group formation and expansion. There may also be a cosmological significance to the height of mounds, whether in terms of a distinction between the sky and the earth, a more general high – low dichotomy, or between mounds that are dry compared with surrounding land that is flooded. Whichever of these possible divergences in meaning is actualised, the tell-dwellers are at an ideological advantage over flat-site occupants, who may well need recourse to social relations with tell-dwellers for their own social reproduction.

The vertical dimension also contributes to the competition over contradictory or varying readings of group mythologies, place-myths and the place-values associated with individual tells. There is a contrast between the actual state of place-identities through time (unfixed, contested and multiple as they were) and the ideological strategy of defining special places in terms of their timeless past, an unchanging ancestral time which can be used for the purposes of social control by one group or sub-group (cf. Morphy 1993).

It is also possible that the location of individuals, houses or both at the top of high tells would have been to be significant and the individual on top of the tell would have been able to see farther than those living on flat sites. The aspect of viewing others and being viewed is perhaps more important than the potential for physical supervision of off-tell activities in the landscape opened up for tell-dwellers.

It is likely that the mound–flat site competition would have overlapped with and been reinforced by other forms of competition between limited interest groups (or LIGs, to use Taylor's helpful term: Taylor 1992). Such LIGs may well have cross-cut tell and flat site residence, as well as formed only a partial correlation with kin groups, exchange partners, age-sets, gender-based groups and other activity groups (ritual associations, hunting parties). One of the implications of tell nucleation is the increased likelihood of the occurrence of many more such LIGs on tells than on smaller, more dispersed flat sites. It is thus not surprising that there is a well-documented correlation between rich and diverse material culture and tell occupations such as that at Vinča, given the social distinctions present in the multiple social networks in which tell-occupants were embedded. Often, a history of deposition of richer and more distinctive material culture on tells compared to flat sites reinforced the advantage of tells in ritual competition and the acquisition of exotic artefacts.

The competitive ideology expressed by the vertical tell dimension and the acquisition of rich and diverse material items was an outgrowth of the continuing negotiation over the meaning of the historical narratives within which each settlement cluster was enmeshed and the rivalries generated by intensive if small-scale social interactions on nucleated settlements. These social developments were not necessarily predictable at the time when tells-to-be were emerging but themselves emerged after the apparent stabilisation of a tell mound tradition. A primary characteristic of periods of tell-occupation is the paradox between the apparently timeless tell mound tradition and the intense contestations of groups and sub-groups for the identity of both communities and their places.

The notion of timemark seems particularly appropriate to the Vinča tell (for discussion, see above) in view of the novel social practices and artefactual innovations which characterised its earliest occupations. The longer that the Vinča settlement continued as the only tell in the Šumadija, the more important its role as a timemark must have been. Yet the tradition of Vinča as a ritual centre and key place in prestige relations and exchange networks was not only maintained and built upon but was in fact also changed by the later part of the Early Vinča phase. The peak in variability of ritual paraphernalia was reached in this phase, when a wide range of often novel forms of figurine and other cult objects were deposited on the tell, increasingly within houses. The shifts away from the relatively simple figurine forms typical of the earliest Vinča phase may imply a differentiation of ritual practice in which contestation is important as tradition. Compared to other putative ritual centres in the late Early Vinča phase, it could be argued that the Vinča tell remained the most significant in terms of quality, quantity and diversity of ceremonial objects. However, it is noticeable that most of the innovations of this phase in the realm of household tools and pottery are developed not at the Vinča tell but in other regions - notably the upper Tamiš basin (for textile equipment) and the Middle Morava valley (for pottery) (Chapman 1981).

Within the region

Although the Vinča tell maintained strong exchange links

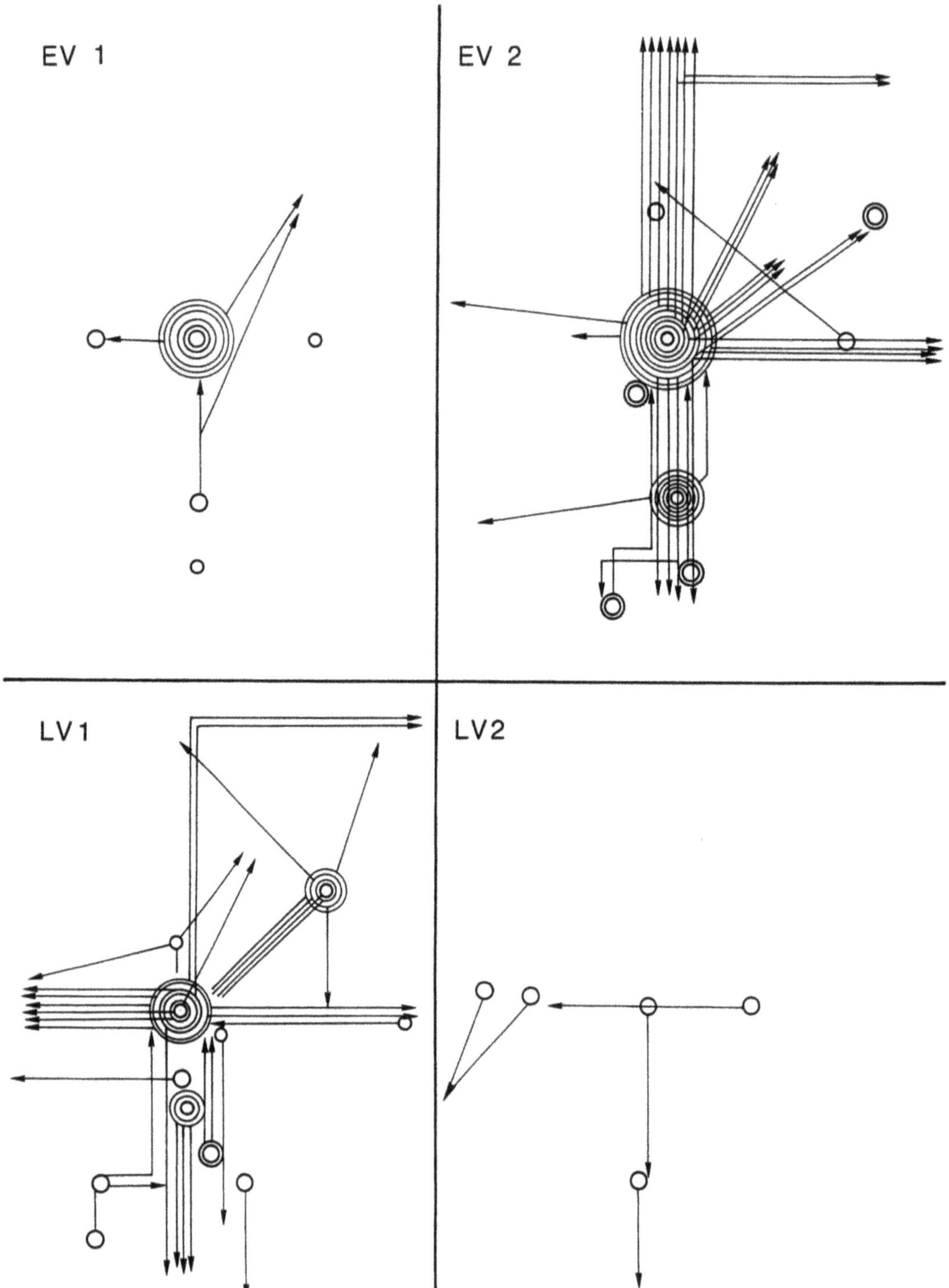

Figure 11 Schematic characterisation of exchange routes in the Vinča network with Vinča-Belo Brdo at the centre (after Chapman 1981: Fig. 165). EV 1 c. 4400-4200 bc; EV 2 c. 4200-4000 bc; LV 1 c. 4000-3800 bc; LV 2 c. 3800-3300 bc.

with all neighbouring regions, this phase is marked by the appearance of a second exchange centre (located north east of Vinča in the Vršac region) also on the edge of the plain and with good access to fertile soils and to rich rocks and minerals (Fig. 11). A whole new form of exchange good (the Mediterranean shell *Spondylus gaederopus*) is relatively rare at Vinča but was concentrated on the Vršac sites, midway between the lower Danube valley route and the middle Tisza route (Chapman 1981: Fig. 105). The *Spondylus* shell was the first raw material of long-distance exchange significance which was not primarily focussed on the community at Vinča. This is an indication of the social and cultural dynamics of this period. Nonetheless, the Vinča tell continued to receive extraordinary exchange objects (and none more surprising than two complete vessels from the south Hungarian Neolithic, the famous Szakalhát face-pot - Vasić 1936: 37, T. 33, 68 - and, in the Late Vinča phase, a complete storage-jar from the Tisza network - Vasić 1936: PV IV, Slika 151). Each vessel stands more than one metre in height and each is decorated with elaborate incised motifs highlighted with brightly coloured crusted paint. If it is hard to imagine the transport of these heavy and cumbersome pots down the Tisza on a raft, the alternative of potters from first the Szakalhát network, then later the Tisza network, travelling to the Vinča tell to make the vessels *in situ* raises intriguing questions about breeding networks or long-distance specialists.

The Szakalhát and Tisza vessels are not the only signs of long-distance exchange during the main occupation of the Vinča tell. There is convincing artefactual evidence for a series of overlapping exchange networks which linked Serbia to many different regions, including the Alföld Plain. Obsidian from southeast Slovakia and northeast Hungary reached its peak of distribution in the early fifth millennium CAL BC (Williams-Thorpe et al. 1984; Bíró 1988), with finds in Slavonia, Bosnia, Serbia, Transylvania Oltenia and even Greek Macedonia (Kilikoglou et al. 1996). Mega-distance exchange, passing vessels through many hands up to 800 km is attested by the occurrence of small quantities of decorated Szakalhát pottery from southeast Hungary as far south as Thessaly (Grundmann 1932). By the same token, Vădastră decorated sherds are known from Szakalhát contexts in Hungary, polished stone mushroom amulets are known from Szakalhát sites (Szénaszky 1976) and a Vinča prosopomorphic lid has been found in a Gumelniţa context at Petru Rareş (Berciu 1961). These fifth millennium inter-regional exchange networks are generally thought to reflect down-the-line exchange, with individuals rarely travelling farther than the next village and exchanges generally embedded in other local social transactions. However, it seems just as likely that these objects moved through the activities of what Helms (1988) has termed 'long-distance specialists' rather than through the long chain of down-the-line inter-village contacts (for a Neolithic case, see Perlès 1992).

Helms has discussed the ethnographic evidence for the high status of such specialists in their own communities, since they have witnessed far more than local people and they have lived to tell the tale. It is indeed the traveller's tale that is the main medium of information exchange. When such specialists returned home, their ideas and information held special interest and possibly even cultural significance, not least if they were conveyed in epic tales and retained in oral tradition. In this way, tells such as Vinča were the focus not only of ritual but also of long-distance specialists whose special skills at presencing the exchange objects which they brought won prestige for the objects as much as for the specialist.

Bucranium cults and incised signs

In the Late Vinča period, there were many signs that the Vinča network was in decline (Chapman 1981). The disappearance of formerly-prized materials such as obsidian from the tell indicates in microcosm what was happening to Vinča exchange networks. They were shrinking in extent and declining in both quality and quantity of artefacts. No developments of ritual innovations are recorded at the Vinča tell in the Late Vinča phase and many aspects of craft production (with the exception of metallurgy) appear to be in decline. Two aspects of ritual practices on the Vinča tell are of particular interest in the Late Vinča phase: the bucranium cult and the use of incised signs on other artefacts.

The bucranium cult is characterised by the plastering, and frequently painting, of life-size cattle skulls which are then either attached to the gable ends of Vinča houses or fixed to the interior of the house. Two classic examples from inside houses come from the Late Vinča houses at Vinča (Vasić 1936: PV II, Slika 85-86). It is interesting that, although the earliest example of a bucranium comes from the Vinča tell (one of the ritual innovations dated to the later part of the Early Vinča phase), the majority of bucrania are dated to the Late Vinča period and mostly come from inside houses. As the household gains in importance as a permanent institution in Vinča settlements (Tringham and Krstić 1991), there was a tendency to locate an increasing number of ritual practices within rather than outside the house. The notion that household wealth in cattle is somehow associated with the rise in bucrania remains to be fully evaluated (see Russell this volume).

The incised signs of the later Balkan Neolithic have been at the heart of debates between diffusionists and processualists over high-level cultural change (Vlassa 1963; C. Renfrew 1973). More interestingly, a contextual approach to these signs, which occur on pottery, figurines, loom-weights, spindle-whorls and other weaving pieces, tablets and plaques, provides insights into economic as much as ritual practices (Chapman 1981; Winn 1981). There is a marked concentration of incised signs in two of the main ritual centres: the Vinča tell and the large flat settlement of Turdaş (Makkay 1969), yet even at Vinča, only a handful of the more than 2,000 figurines have signs incised upon them. Moreover, in other settlements with little evidence for non-domestic cult practices, such as Banjica (Todorović 1969), the concentration of incised signs is more readily understood in the economic context. The occurrence at Banjica of the same incised sign in two superimposed house-floors, the second re-built after a gap of perhaps 50–100 years, suggests that these signs are related to family land ownership and traditional rights of land or property inheritance (Chapman 1981).

The important point about the incised signs from the Vinča tell is that they become common only in the Late Vinča period, precisely when figurines are becoming less common and more standardised and formalised. However, most of the figurines inscribed with signs date to this Late Vinča phase. Perhaps this is an indication of the competing groups who are attempting to control economic and ritual practices on the tell. One hypothesis worth future investigation is that, with increasing economic significance of incised signs, the guardians of traditional tell ritual practice (those who control the performance associated with figurines) attempt to re-invigorate an ailing ritual tradition with new imagery, with associations based upon the incised sign.

In any event, the changes to be found in microcosm on the Vinča tell are found on a much wider stage in the Vinča network itself, which was shrinking in the late fifth millennium CAL BC, and which had disappeared by 3800 CAL BC (Chapman 1981). It is, however, surely significant that after a broadly continuous occupation covering more than a millennium the Vinča tell (perhaps the most powerful symbol of the Vinča network) was abandoned more than 500 years before the dissolution of the Vinča network.

In summary, the millennium long occupation of the Vinča tell not only led to the accretion of a rich and extremely diverse set of place-values (which were based upon a huge range of place-myths and place-images) but also acted as the habitus for over 30 generations of tell-dwellers and as structuring structure and structured village community. When J.B. Jackson (1984) summarises the distinction between his political and vernacular landscapes by talking of the lasting identity gained through the permanence of place in the political landscape, the tell of Vinča is one of those places which Jackson would have had in mind: ancestral relations and traditions embodied in the very vertical growth of the site; competition and the contestation of identities objectified in the houses and artefacts which define the settlement. If a millennium long occupation is the very stuff of narrative, the Vinča tell has a more intricate and elaborated story to tell than most other sites in the central Balkans.

The late occupation

A particularly critical time for tells are periods of temporary abandonment, after which new residents have the opportunity to redefine a historical narrative to provide support for their own position as pre-eminent in the local settlement cluster (this is a version of the invention of traditions – Hobsbawm and Ranger 1983). In the late occupations of the Vinča tell, different groups with varying cultural traditions objectify their social relations by dwelling on the tell but this is often a short-term use of an ancestral resource.

The three episodes in the Copper Age each portray a very different character. The Bodrogkeresztúr occupation is predominantly the appropriation of a settlement domain (the domestic space par excellence) as part of their own mortuary domain. While few other Bodrogkeresztúr graves are known from Serbia, very few Bodrogkeresztúr occupations and hardly any graves are known from the tells of the Hungarian Plain (Chapman 1995). The typical Bodrogkeresztúr mortuary cluster is a group of 5-20 graves in a small cemetery (Patay 1974); the largest known cemetery (at Tiszapolgár-Basatanya) contains 87 middle Copper Age graves (Bognár-Kutzian 1963). Thus, the group of four shallow graves excavated into the surface of the Vinča Neolithic tell is a statement of ancestral claims to the settlement domain that had gone before; a statement presumably made by a newly emergent social group requiring a timemark of their own on the tell. It is noteworthy that the absence of any differentiated material culture is equally important as a statement of what the Bodrogkeresztúr group wished to say about their association with the Vinča tell.

The Baden episode appears to stand in contrast to the Bodrogkeresztúr mortuary practices, insofar as it betokens a short-lived domestic use (Tasić 1984a). Here, there is a deliberate imitation of Late Vinča houses with massive daub floors as well as an opposition to the mortuary claims advanced by the previous group. The similarity of the Baden episode with that of the previous group lies in the rarity of differentiated material culture. Here the emphasis is on continuity with the ancestors through a similar act of architectural practice rather than through the use of distinctive artefacts.

The third Copper Age episode appears to have been the most short-lived: the thin scatter of Kostolac sherds across parts of the site. The presumably short-term visits paid to the tell by people using such pottery emphasise that mobility as much as rootedness in place provides a link to the ancestors. Movement through a site carries with it the memories of previous places and experiences, some of which were actively presenced on the new site irrespective of the length of stay. Thus the claim that the Kostolac network was based upon much more mobile settlement practices (Tasić 1984b) has implications for the manner in which memory was culturally transmitted and does not imply that such transmission did not take place.

The only Bronze Age occupation was an intensive settlement episode by inhabitants in the Vatin network. This was a relatively rare occurrence, since Vatin tell occupation is poorly attested. The Vinča episode follows abandonment of the tell for some centuries, after which the tell is re-focused in the domestic arena. Tasić (1984b) hypothesises that a gold hoard from the village, culturally diagnostic to the Vatin network, may derive from the tell itself. This would form the only distinguishing feature of the Vatin appropriation of the tell's living space, together with its encoded memories and place-value.

The foundation of a hilltop settlement surrounded by a defensive ditch in the late Iron Age is as yet poorly recorded (Čelić 1984). While it may be argued that the military significance of a prominent hill such as Belo Brdo was the main reason for this Iron Age foundation, one should remember that many European Iron Age centres were located close to, if not directly on top of, previously significant places (for Celtic oppida, see Murray 1995; for British hillforts, see Sharples 1991). Hence, as details emerge of the latest prehistoric occupation on Belo Brdo, the place-value of the hill should not be ignored. The excavation of a large defensive ditch in the Iron Age echoes the long-preceding intra-mural ditch Q cut by the Neolithic community in subhorizon III/2 – equally part of an attempt to define community boundaries.

In summary, the post-Vinča episodes on the Vinča tell are varied in form and content, exhibiting differing ways in which present needs could be linked to the past. The place of the Vinča tell in each successive place-mythology is consequently likely to vary widely between the different aspects of the past which are stressed and those which are ignored. With the exception of the Baden houses with solid clay floors, there are few signs in either the Copper or the Bronze Ages of a strategy in which the past was brought into the scope of the present through a strategy of similitude.

Conclusion

The value of places and things is closely related to the value of the people who respectively dwell in them and utilise them. The embodiment of values in things and places is a potent source of identity for people, places and objects. One of the main means of bringing life to places and things is the technique of presencing, by which other people's interests in the ongoing cultural narrative is maintained despite their physical absence.

The place value of key institutional projects (timemarks in their own right) such as tells is related to three main factors: the place-mythologies which were built up around the site; the body of artefacts which is not only of immediate use in quotidian activities and ceremonies but also presenced a wide range of others; and the ancestral presence which guaranteed the ideological security of the habitus. The example of the Vinča-Belo Brdo tell is instructive as much for its convoluted life history (a narrative progressively developed over a millennium of occupation) as for its rich and varied repertoire of artefacts many of which were originally created in or near the tell. In this chapter, not only is it hoped that the value of the Vinča artefacts in the museum or heritage context has been reinforced but also that some understanding has been gained through a contextual study of how these artefacts gained value in the first place. But the key aspect of the value of the Vinča artefacts remains the place-value of the tell itself.

Bibliography

Barker, G. 1975. Early Neolithic land use in Yugoslavia. *Proceedings of the Prehistoric Society* 41: 85-104.

Bender, B. 1989. The roots of inequality. In *Domination and Resistance*, edited by D. Miller, M. Rowlands and C. Tilley, pp. 83-95. London: Routledge.

Bender, B. (ed.) 1993. *Landscape, Politics and Perspectives*. Oxford: Berg.

Berdoulay, V. 1989. Place, meaning and discourse in French language geography. In *The Power of Place. Bringing Together Geographical and Social Imaginations*, edited by J.A. Agnew and J.S. Duncan, pp. 124-135. Boston: Unwin Hyman.

Bíró, K. T. 1988. Distribution of lithic raw materials on prehistoric sites. *Acta Archaeologica Hungarica* 40: 251-274.

Bognár-Kutzian, I. 1963. *The Copper Age Cemetery of Tiszapolgár-Basatanya*. (Archaeologia Hungarica 42). Budapest: Akadémiai Kiadó.

Bourdieu, P. 1977. *Outline of a Theory of Practice*. Cambridge: Cambridge University Press.

Bourdieu, P. 1981. Men and machines. In *Advances in Social Theory and Methodology: Towards an Integration of Micro- and Macro-sociologies*, edited by K. Knorr-Cetina and A.V. Cicourel, pp. 304-317. London: Routledge Kegan Paul.

Bourdieu, P. 1986. The forms of capital. In *Handbook of Theory and Research for the Sociology of Education*, edited by J. G. Richardson, pp. 241-258. New York: Greenwood Press.

Bourdieu, P. 1990. La domination masculine. *Actes de la Recherche en Sciences Sociales* 84: 2-31.

Bourdieu, P. 1991. *Language and Symbolic Power*. Cambridge: Polity Press.

Bourdieu, P. and L.J.D. Wacquant 1992. *An Invitation to Reflexive Sociology*. Cambridge: Polity Press.

Čelić, S. (ed.) 1984. *Vinča Praistoriji i Srednjem Veku*. Beograd: Centar za Arheološka Istraživanja.

Chapman, J. 1976. *The Balkans in the Fifth and Fourth Millennia BC*. Unpublished Doctoral Dissertation, University of London.

Chapman, J. 1981 *The Vinča Culture of Southeast Europe. Studies in Chronology, Economy and Society*. Oxford: BAR.

Chapman, J. 1983. Meaning and illusion in the study of burial in Balkan prehistory. In *Ancient Bulgaria Volume 1*, edited by A. Poulter, pp. 1-45. Nottingham: University of Nottingham Press.

Chapman, J. 1988. From "space" to "place": a model of dispersed settlement and Neolithic society. In *Enclosures and Defences in the Neolithic of Western Europe*, edited by C. Burgess, P. Topping and D. Mordant, pp. 21-46. Oxford: BAR.

Chapman, J. 1989. The Early Balkan village. *Varia Archaeologica Hungarica* 2: 33-53.

Chapman, J. 1991. The creation of social arenas in the Neolithic and Copper Age of South East Europe: the case of Varna. In *Sacred and Profane*, edited by P. Garwood, P. Jennings, R. Skeates and J. Toms, pp. 152-171. (Oxford Committee for Archaeology Monograph No. 32). Oxford: Oxbow.

Chapman, J. 1992. The creation of arenas of social power in Serbian prehistory. *Zbornik Narodnog Muzeja (Beograd)* 14: 305-317.

Chapman, J. 1993. Social power in the Iron Gates Mesolithic. In *Cultural Transformations and Interactions in Eastern Europe*, edited by J.C. Chapman and P. Dolukhanov, pp. 61-106. Aldershot, Avebury.

Chapman, J. 1994. The living, the dead and the ancestors: time, life cycles and the mortuary domain in later European prehistory. In *Ritual and remembrance. Responses to Death in Human Societies*, edited by J. Davies, pp. 40-85. Sheffield: Sheffield Academic Press.

Chapman, J. 1995. Social power in the early farming communities of eastern Hungary – perspectives from the Upper Tisza region. *A Jósa András Múzeum Évkonyve* 36: 79-99.

Chapman, J. 1997a. Timemarks and placemarks - the social construction of prehistoric landscapes in eastern Hungary. In *Semiotics of Landscape: Archaeology of Mind.*, edited by G. Nash, pp. 31-45. Oxford: BAR.

Chapman, J. 1997b. The origins of tells in eastern Hungary. *Neolithic Settlements*, edited by P. Topping, pp. 139-164. Oxford: Oxbow.

Childe, V.G. 1958. *The Prehistory of European Society*. London: Cassell.

Clason, A. 1980. Padina and Starčevo: game, fish and cattle. *Palaeohistoria* 22: 14-173.

Connell, R.W. 1987. *Gender and Power. Society, the Person and Sexual Politics*. Cambridge: Polity Press.

Dennell, R.W. 1978. *Early Farming in Bulgaria from the Vth to the IIIrd Millennium B.C.* Oxford: BAR.

Dennell, R.W. and D. Webley 1975. Prehistoric settlement and land use in southern Bulgaria. In *Palaeoeconomy*, edited by E.S. Higgs, pp. 97-109. Cambridge: Cambridge University Press.

Dirks, N.B., G. Eley and S.B. Ortner 1994. Introduction. In *Culture – Power – History. A Reader in Contemporary Social Theory*, edited by N.B. Dirks, G. Eley and S.B. Ortner, pp. 3-45. Princeton: Princeton University Press.

Garašanin, D. 1984. Die Siedlung der Starčevo-Kultur. In *Vinča*, edited by Srejović, D., B. Stojanovic, N. Tasić and D. Krstić, pp. 191-194. Beograd: Srpska Akademija Nauka I Umetnosti.

Gregory, C.A. 1982. *Gifts and Commodities*. London: Academic Press.

Gregory, D. 1994. *Geographical Imaginations*. Oxford: Blackwell.

Grundmann, K. 1932. Aus neolithischen Siedlungen bei Larisa. *Archäologische Mitteilungen* 57: 102-123.

Helms, M.W. 1988. *Ulysses' Sail. An Ethnographic Odyssey of Power, Knowledge and Geographical Distance*. Princeton: Princeton University Press.

Hirsch, E. and M. O'Hanlon (eds) 1995. *The Anthropology of Landscape. Perspectives on Place and Space*. Oxford: Clarendon Press.

Hobsbawm, E. and T. Ranger (eds) 1983. *The Invention of Tradition*. Cambridge: Cambridge University Press.

Kaczanowska, M. and J.K. Kozłowski 1990. Chipped stone industry of the Vinča culture. In *Vinča i Njen Svet*, edited by D. Srejović and N. Tasić, pp. 35-48. Beograd: Srpska Akademija Nauka I Umetnosti.

Kern, S. 1983. *The Culture of Time and Place*, 1880-1918. Cambridge, Mass.: Harvard University Press.

Kopytoff, I. 1986. The cultural biography of things: commoditization as process. In *The Social Life of Things. Commodities in Cultural Perspective*, edited by A. Appadurai, pp. 64-91. Cambridge: Cambridge University Press.

Küchler, S. 1993. Landscape as memory: the mapping of process and its representation in a Melanesian society. In *Landscape, Politics and Perspectives*, edited by B. Bender, pp. 85-106. Oxford: Berg.

Letica, Z. 1964. The Neolithic figurines from Vinča. *Archaeology* 17(1): 26-32.

Letica, Z. 1968. Starčevo and Körös culture at Vinča. *Archaeologica Iugoslavica* 9:11-18.

Makkay, J. 1969. The Late Neolithic Tordos group of signs. *Alba Iulia* 10:9-49.

Mann, M. 1986. *The Sources of Social Power. Volume 1. From the Beginnings to AD 1789.* Cambridge: Cambridge University Press.

Massey, D. 1994. *Space, Place and Gender.* Cambridge: Polity Press.

Miller, D. 1987. *Material Culture and Mass Consumption.* Oxford: Blackwell.

Morphy, H. 1993. Colonialism, history and the construction of place: the politics of landscape in Northern Australia. In *Landscape, Politics and Perspectives,* edited by B. Bender, pp. 205-244. Oxford: Berg.

Munn, N.D. 1986. *The Fame of Gawa. A Symbolic Study of Value Transformation in a Massim (Papua New Guinea) Society.* London: Duke University Press.

Murray, M. 1995. Viereckschanzen and feasting: socio-political ritual in Iron Age central Europe. *Journal of European Archaeology* 5(2): 125-151.

Nandris, J. 1972. Relations between the Mesolithic, the First Temperate Neolithic and the Bankeramik: the nature of the problem. *Alba Iulia* 6: 61-70.

Patay, P. 1974. Die hochkupferzeitliche Bodrog-keresztúr-Kultur. *Bericht der Römanisch-Germanisch Kommission* 55: 1-71.

Perlès, C. 1992. Systems of exchange and organisation of production in Neolithic Greece. *Journal of Mediterranean Archaeology* 5(2): 115-164.

Pred, A. 1986. *Place, Practice and Structure. Social and Spatial Transformations in South Sweden: 1750 - 1850.* Totowa, N.J.: Barnes and Noble.

Prown, J.D. 1993. The truth of material culture: history or fiction? In *History from Things. Essays on Material Culture,* edited by S. Lubar and W.D. Kingery, pp. 1-19. Washington: Smithsonian Institution.

Rabinow, P. (ed.) 1984. *The Foucault Reader.* Harmondsworth: Penguin.

Radosavljević-Krunić, S. 1986. Résultats de l'étude anthropologique des squelettes provenant du site Ajmana. *Djerdapske Sveske* 3:51-58.

Rawson, J. 1993. The ancestry of Chinese bronze vessels. In *History from Things. Essays on Material Culture,* edited by S. Lubar and W.D. Kingery, pp. 51-73. Washington: Smithsonian Institution.

Renfrew, C. 1973. *Before Civilisation.* London: Academic.

Renfrew, J. 1979. The first farmers in south east Europe. *Archaeophysika* 8: 243-265.

Richardson, M. 1989. Place and culture: two disciplines, two concepts, two images of Christ and a single goal. In *The Power of Place. Bringing Together Geographical and Social Imaginations,* edited by J.A. Agnew and J.S. Duncan, pp. 140-156. Boston: Unwin Hyman.

Robinson, D. 1989. The language and significance of place in Latin America. In *The Power of Place. Bringing Together Geographical and Social Imaginations,* edited by J.A. Agnew and J.S. Duncan, pp. 157-184. Boston: Unwin Hyman.

Rodman, M.C. 1992. Empowering place: multilocality and multivocality. *American Anthropologist* 94: 640-656.

Rowlands, M. 1993. The role of memory in the transmission of culture. *World Archaeology* 25(2): 141-151.

Schwidetsky, I. 1971-72. Menschliche Skelettresten von Vinča. *Glasnik Antropološkog Društva Jugoslavije* 8-9: 101-112.

Sharples, N. 1991. *Maiden Castle.* London: Batsford/ English Heritage.

Shields, R. 1991. *Places on the Margin. Alternative Geographies of Modernity.* London: Routledge.

Srejović, D. and B. Jovanović 1957. Pregled kamenog orudja i oružja iz Vinče. *Arheološki Vestnik* 8: 256-296.

Srejović, D., B. Stojanović, N. Tasić and D. Krstić (eds) 1984. *Vinča.* Beograd: Srpska Akademija Nauka I Umetnosti.

Srejović, D. and N. Tasić (eds) 1990. *Vinča i Njen Svet.* Beograd: Srpska Akademija Nauka I Umetnosti.

Stalio, B. 1986. Le site préhistorique Ajmana à Mala Vrbica. *Djerdapske Sveske* 3: 27-43.

Strathern, M. 1988. *The Gender of the Gift.* Berkeley: University of California Press.

Szénaszky, G. 1976. *Újabb Ásatasok Békés Mégyeben.* Békéscasaba: Múnkacsy Mihaly Múzeum.

Tasić, N. 1984a. Die Siedlung und Gräber aus der Kupferzeit. In Srejović et al., pp. 211-214.

Tasić, N. 1984b. Die Siedlung der Vatin-Kultur. In Srejović et al., pp. 214-216.

Taylor, T. 1992. The Gundestrup cauldron. *Scientific American* 266(3) : 84-89.

Todorova, H. 1978. *The Eneolithic Period in Bulgaria in the 5th millennium BC.* Oxford: BAR.

Todorović, J. 1969. Written signs in the Neolithic cultures of southeastern Europe. *Archaeologica Iugoslavica* 10: 77-84.

Tringham, R., B. Brukner, T. Kaiser, K. Borojević, Lj. Bukvić, P. Steli, N. Russell, M. Stevanović and B. Voytek, B. 1992. Excavations at Opovo, 1985-1987: socioeconomic change in the Balkan Neolithic. *Journal of Field Archaeology* 19(3): 351-386.

Tringham, R. and D. Krstić 1991. Conclusion: Selevac in the wider context of European prehistory. In *Selevac - a Neolithic Village in Yugoslavia*, edited by R. Tringham and D. Krstić, pp. 567-615. Los Angeles: University of California Press.

Tuan, Yi-Fu.1973. Space and place: humanistic perspective. *Progress in Geography* 6: 211-252.

Tuan, Yi-Fu. 1977. *Space and Place. The Perspective of Experience*. London: Arnold.

Tuan, Yi-Fu. 1978. Space, time, place: a humanistic frame. In *Timing Space and Spacing Time. Volume 1: Making Sense of Time*, edited by T. Carlstein, D. Parkes and N. Thrift, pp. 7-16. London:Arnold.

Vasić, M.M. 1910. Die Hauptergebnisse der prähistorischen Ausgrabung in Vinča im J. 1908. *Prähistorisches Zeitschrift* 2: 23-39.

Vasić, M.M. 1932-6. *Praistoriska Vinča I-IV.* Beograd: Universiteta Beograda.

Vasić, R. 1986. Compte-rendu des fouilles du site préhistorique à Velesnica. *Djerdapske Sveske* 3: 264-285.

Wagner, R. 1975. *The Invention of Culture*. Englewood Cliffs, N.J.: Prentice-Hall.

Weiner, A. 1980. Reproduction: a replacement for reciprocity. *American Ethnologist* 7: 71-85.

Weiner, A. 1985. Inalienable wealth. *American Ethnologist* 12: 210-227.

Weiner, A. 1992. *Inalienable Possessions. The Paradox of Keeping-while-Giving*. Berkeley: University of California Press.

Williams, R. 1973. *The Country and the City.* London: Chatto and Windus.

Williams, R. 1977. *Politics and Letters.* London: New Left Books.

Williams, R. 1984. Between country and city. In *Second Nature*, edited by R. Mabey, pp. 209-219. London: Jonathan Cape.

Williams-Thorpe, O., S.E. Warren and J. Nandris 1984. The distribution and provenance of archaeological obsidian in central and eastern Europe. *Journal of Archaeological Science* 11: 183-212.

Wilson, P.J. 1988. *The Domestication of the Human Species.* New Haven: Yale University Press.

Winn, S. 1981. *Pre-writing in Southeastern Europe: the Sign System of the Vinča Culture ca. 4000 BC.* Calgary: Western Publishers.

Yanagisako, S.J. and J.F. Collier 1987. Toward a unified analysis of kinship and gender. In *Gender and Kinship. Essays Towards a Unified Analysis,* edited by J.F. Collier and S.J. Yanagisako, pp. 14-50. Stanford: Stanford University Press.

Živanović, S. 1986. Restes des ossements humains à Velesnica. *Djerdapske Sveske* 3: 286-288.

Chapter 10

The social life of Italian Neolithic painted pottery

Robin Skeates

The social life of prehistoric pots

The premises with which I begin this paper are that artefacts are social things and that material culture plays an active part in the cultural process through which human groups construct and transform themselves (Miller 1994). The many qualities of artefacts (e.g., their size, technical appearance, decorative style, instrumental function, provenance, rarity, age, and relationships with individuals or social groups) have a vast potential which can be exploited, particularly in non-literate societies. Often these potentials are exploited and artefacts act as signs which invite or repulse action and which facilitate, inhibit and reinforce patterns of social life. Artefacts, then, are something practical through which people can express themselves and come to an understanding of themselves, of others and of abstract concepts. They can even be treated as belonging inalienably to persons or as if they were persons themselves. Artefacts' effectiveness stems from the subtle way in which they work. They form part of the taken-for-granted but culturally-constructed environment within which people live; they form a frame and express concepts often on an almost sub-conscious level. Such concepts are sometimes only brought out by oratories and actions in special performative contexts.

This social perspective on material culture has only gradually been adopted in archaeological pottery studies since the late 1970s when scholars such as Ian Hodder highlighted the way in which the production and use of different styles of pottery decoration can participate in the creation of social identities (Hodder 1979). However, more recent studies (especially those by anthropologists and ethnoarchaeologists) have developed this theme and have also begun to interpret changes in ceramic traditions as results of deliberate actions, related to social innovation and in which potters can play an important role (e.g., Graves 1991; Babcock 1993; Barley 1994). The concept of social identity has also been reconsidered and is now seen not as a fixed entity but as one which varies according to context. It is to themes such as these that I wish to contribute in this paper on the social life of Italian Neolithic painted pottery.

From the outset, however, it is important to recognise the limitations of archaeological inference, particularly considering that we are dealing with prehistory. The issue of generalisation presents a serious dilemma. On the one hand, cross-cultural generalisations and ethnographic analogies are unhelpful to the prehistorian. Meanings and values of artefacts are not only culturally-specific, they are also potentially multivalent. On the other hand, to a certain extent due to a lack of sufficiently detailed archaeological information we are forced to look at prehistoric societies in general terms and to rely upon ethnographic analogies to broaden our interpretative horizons.

Lack of detailed information concerning the production process also presents a serious limitation to our understanding of Italian Neolithic pottery. For example, it is almost impossible to establish the age, gender and status of the potters; the ethnographic record is of little help, for general statements such as '88.9% of potters around the world are female' (Arnold 1985) conceal a multitude of local variations (e.g., Herbert 1993; Barley 1994). Another problem is that by focussing attention upon pottery (and in particular painted pottery) there is the risk of isolating pottery as an artificial category of analysis. In fact, pottery is likely to have comprised but one of a number of container technologies that could also have included vessels made of less archaeologically visible materials such as wood, basketry and leather (De Boer 1991). In Neolithic central Italy, it seems clear that painted pottery's distinctiveness as a category changes over time and in relation to other categories of material culture.

The use of a contextual approach by archaeologists comprises an attempt to recognise (if not overcome) some of these problems. In a contextual approach, the changing meanings and values of artefacts are considered in relation to their dynamic historical, spatial, social and material contexts (Hodder 1982). It is this approach that I shall adopt in my study of Italian Neolithic painted pottery.

The recent life-history of Italian Neolithic painted pottery

Surprisingly, perhaps, a contextual study needs to start with the relatively recent life-history of Italian Neolithic painted pottery because, in retrospect, it now seems clear that traditional archaeologists' strategies of display and interpretation have distanced this pottery from its original prehistoric contexts.

Here is an example. In 1934, Ugo Rellini published a book which brought together all of the Neolithic painted pottery found in Italy since about 1865 and which, since that date, had been dispersed to numerous museums both in Italy and abroad. The title of his book translates as *The Oldest Painted Pottery in Italy* (Rellini 1934). This is significant in that it refers to the already well-known and valuable Greek and Mycenean painted pottery and in that it defines Rellini's Neolithic painted pottery as a distinct (chronologically antecedent) 'Italian' and equally valuable archaeological category. In the text, Rellini praises the pottery in terms of its beauty and elegance and the skill with which it was made. Thus from an early stage in its archaeological life-history, Italian Neolithci painted pottery was rapidly transformed into a museum commodity that was used by museum curators to win prestige through their collection, display and exchange of the material remains of the past.

In addition, decorated pottery has traditionally been used by archaeologists in Italy as a tool to help establish chronological sequences and to chart the relations between different groups of prehistoric peoples. This is the so-called typological approach in which stylistic groupings of decorated pottery were assumed, on the one hand, to have a precise chronological significance, and on the other hand, to correspond to postulated ethnic groups. Like the museological tradition, this has bound the pots closely to contemporary discourses amongst archaeologists; it has surely contributed to its distancing from its original prehistoric social uses, values and meanings. At the risk of making them the hostages of a new archaeological discourse which prioritises the study of social relations, it is the original uses, values and meanings which I now want to consider.

A social history of Neolithic painted pottery in Abruzzo

In this study, I want to examine the rise and fall of Neolithic painted pottery, particularly in the Abruzzo region of east-central Italy. Drawing upon the theoretical and methodological framework above, this study attempts to develop models proposed over the last decade by Caroline Malone, John Chapman and myself (Malone 1985; Chapman 1988; Skeates 1993). I shall focus upon interpretations; the relevant data are summarised in Appendix 1 and are described in some detail in my doctoral thesis (Skeates 1992).

5500-4850 BC

The first pottery appeared at sites throughout the Abruzzo region at about 5500 BC[1]. It was initially represented by quite coarse fabrics with fairly simple impressed and incised decoration (Fig. 1). This pottery appeared as part of a wide-ranging package of Neolithic innovations that were gradually adopted by hunter-gatherer groups throughout Europe and which included new ways of producing, storing and consuming food and drink. According to radiocarbon dates, this package spread northwards up the Adriatic coast from southeast Italy to Abruzzo (Skeates 1994).

Along with the rest of the Neolithic package a previously established potting tradition could well have been introduced in the coastal lowlands of southern Abruzzo by small groups of immigrant agriculturalists coming from the densely settled northern Tavoliere Plain. This suggestion is based upon the close similarities in the more complex techniques and motifs of pottery decoration found in both of these areas as well as similarities in settlement and subsistence patterns. An alternative suggestion is that connections could have been strengthened between groups already settled on the coastal lowlands of southern Abruzzo and those in northern Puglia. Either way, long-distance exchange relations appear to have been maintained and strengthened over time between these coastal groups and their friends or relatives in the northern Tavoliere. This is suggested, after about 150 years, by the expansion of the ceramic repertoire with the addition of more complex impressed and incised decorative motifs and simple painted decoration (again which appear to have stemmed from southeast Italy). An example of a coastal lowland immigrant site is Fontanelle. Its decorated ceramic repertoire includes fairly distinctive southeast Italian Guadone-style elements such as incised slashes combined with brown painted lines and incised triangles filled with red paint and stab-and-drag impressions (Fig. 2). Potters working at sites such as Fontanelle originally may have brought or obtained their potting skills and decorative styles from groups in southeast Italy and then maintained and transformed them as part of social strategies to maintain their social identity and, above all, their social connections with their ancestral heartland.

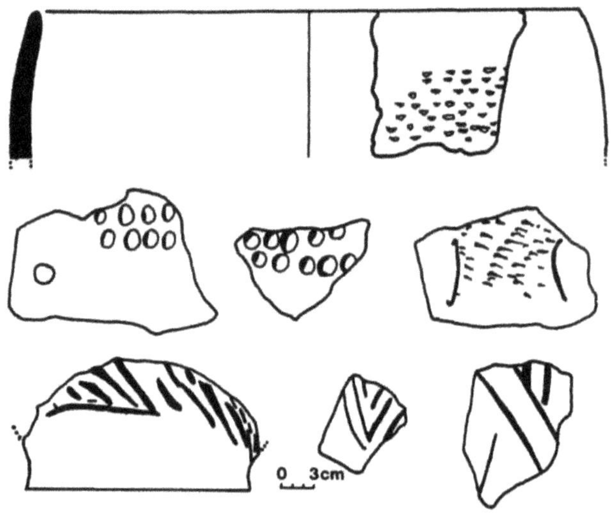

Figure 1 Simple impressed and incised ware from Villaggio Rossi (after Geniola 1982).

In Abruzzo (further to the north and further inland) indigenous groups of hunter-gatherers seem to have readily adopted and adapted the Neolithic package from the coastal groups. Early pottery and domestic animals, for example, which were commonly deposited by the indigenous groups

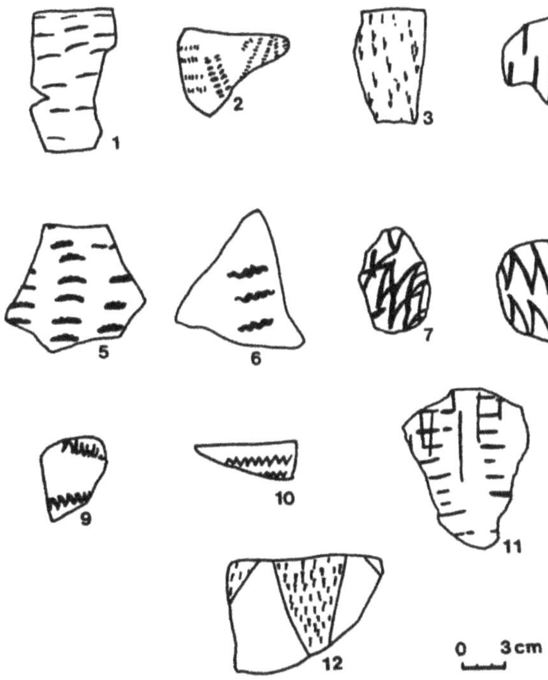

Figure 2 More complex Guadone style impressed and incised ware from Fontanelle (after Ducci et al. 1986-7).

Figure 3 Painted fineware from Catignano (after Tozzi 1978; 1982).

in their ritual caves alongside the bones of their ancestors, might have been adopted as novel goods which were valued both socially and symbolically and which were used to service increasingly numerous and elaborate rituals which probably involved an element of feasting and which were performed within a context of increasing sedentism and social complexity. A good example is Grotta Continenza which is located in the inland Fucino Lake basin. Here, in a low chamber filled with stalactites, a group of four pottery vessels (placed in a niche in the cave wall) were used as containers for the cremated human remains of a woman and two children and for some ground red ochre. They were deposited alongside numerous other human remains and the mainly articulated remains of domestic animals (including six sheep, two dogs and one pig) which may have been left as sacrificial offerings.

However, in the quantity and range of pottery found exhibiting special southeast Italian elements (such as shell impressions and red-filled and red-painted decoration) there is a progressive fall-off with distance from the coast. This might be interpreted in terms of differing degrees of social and geographical access to the important long-distance networks of exchange (which were established along the Adriatic coast and controlled by groups based in the coastal lowlands) and to the socially valued commodities and knowledge which flowed along them.

4850-4700 BC

From about 4850 BC, the treatment of ceramics in the Abruzzo region underwent significant changes. From a typological point of view, technologically and stylistically more distinct categories of ceramics were produced. The increasingly abundant figulina category stands out in particular as a fine, well fired, yellow and polished fabric that was often decorated in a regionally distinctive style of painting (named by local archaeologists as the Catignano style). This is characterised by the common use of red bichrome painted decoration and by a few examples of red and brown or black trichrome. It is especially represented by bowls and flasks and this suggests that they were used for the storage and serving of liquids (Fig. 3). Other categories of fineware were also decorated with increasing elaboration: with two eyes and a mouth being incised around a protruding lug handle (the nose) to form a face on the side of at least one vessel and others being decorated by red- or white-filled incisions. Changes also occurred in the ways in which pots, and especially painted pots, found their way into archaeological deposits. Many pots were now intentionally and permanently removed from further use and circulation by being broken and buried in explicitly ritual contexts. At the lowland site of Villa Badessa, for example, painted vessels were deposited in the graves of two adult women. In the settlement of Catignano, a great quantity of painted pottery was found in the fill of a crop-storage silo that had been re-used for the burial of an old adult woman who during her life-time had had her skull trepanned. In another burial at Catignano, a broken and undecorated grey bowl was placed next to the head of a child a few years old. In the interior of the region, painted pottery was also deposited in caves which were traditionally used as repositories for socially valued objects and as liminal places for the performance of rituals during the Neolithic (Malone 1985; Skeates 1991; Whitehouse 1992). One of these caves, Grotta Oscura, also has wall paintings which could date to this period.

We still have little information about the potters and their relatives who were ultimately responsible for these changes in the production and consumption of pottery. It seems likely, however, that they worked at lowland aggregation sites which stand out in the archaeological record as centres of production, accumulation and ceremonial consumption and where the pots are likely to have been embedded in both daily and ceremonial routines. These developments in the treatment of ceramics can be interpreted in a number of ways.

On an inter-regional scale, the Catignano painted style exhibits a certain degree of continuity with earlier potting traditions in the Abruzzo region; above all it appears as a regional variant of a previously established tradition of red painted ware found in the Tavoliere region of northern Puglia (the so-called Passo di Corvo style). This is the same area from which knowledge of potting and later stylistic developments spread during the early Neolithic and it ties in with evidence of increasing quantities of south Italian Lipari obsidian being imported into Abruzzo at this time. The change in ceramic tradition can perhaps, in part, be interpreted as a further strengthening of long-distance social and exchange relations between the people of lowland Abruzzo and their ancestral heartland to the south. More specifically it can be interpreted in terms of the establishment of a degree of stylistic and cultural dependency in which potters in the north emulated their more innovative, well-connected and prestigious neighbours to the south. In turn, the Catignano style appears to have stimulated the local development of early painted pottery to the west of the Apennines as is found, for example, at roughly contemporary (perhaps slightly more recent) sites such as Pozzi della Piana in Umbria and Grotta di Monte Venere in Lazio (Passeri 1970:238; Delpino and Fugazzola Delpino 1987). In this case, the Abruzzo potters could have gained prestige for their cultural exports.

On a local scale, the changes in ceramic use (in particular in the use of the increasingly distinctive painted fineware) during both daily and special occasions may have been bound up with a process of re-defining the social identity of members of the community. At a time when larger and more sedentary agricultural communities were being formed, the local production and use of a regionally distinctive style of painted fineware may have contributed to enhancing the identity, legitimacy and cohesion of new social groups. Also, the deposition of painted vessels (possibly filled with drinks) in graves, as gifts for selected deceased people to take with them to the afterlife, may have contributed symbolically to social and ritual discourses concerning on the one hand, the common dichotomy between fertility and the threat of death and, on the other hand, the age- and gender-based social definition of important but possibly anomalous members of society (in this case including older women and young children). The pots (and in particular those decorated with anthropomorphic features) may also have served to contain and locate spiritual forces (whether they were perceived as ancestors, nature spirits, deities, or diseases) (cf. David et al. 1988; Berns 1990; Herbert 1993; Barley 1994).

4700-4400 BC

About 150 years later (i.e., from about 4700 BC) the treatment of ceramics in the Abruzzo region again underwent a process of transformation. A new style of painted pottery (which has been named the Ripoli style) was developed in northern Abruzzo. The range of decorative motifs employed (as well as some of the vessel forms) is completely different to that of the preceding Catignano style. The Ripoli painted decoration is broadly characterised by the use of trichrome zones (generally comprising parallel lines or filled triangles) bordered first by a narrow band containing a row of dots and then by a broad red band (Figs. 4-5). However, each individual vessel seems to have been decorated slightly differently. They also seem to have been painted skilfully; the slender lines always maintain their parallelism. The painted pottery belongs to a restricted range of vessel forms: 1) necked flasks, often with small lug-handles placed around the rim which were probably used in sealing the mouth of the flasks; 2) single-handled carinated cups, some of which have elaborate handles including anthropomorphic and zoomorphic ones; and 3) large hemispherical vessels with four small ring-handles placed around the body and occasionally set on pedestal bases. Like earlier painted vessels, all of these are forms which seem best suited to the storage and serving of liquids. Great quantities of this painted pottery were found at the aggregation site of Ripoli (situated in the lowlands of northern Abruzzo) which was quite probably the centre in which it was produced. Early excavations by Messina apparently led to the discovery of a simple kiln at this site but investigations of it were apparently limited and no details have been published (Rellini 1934:42). This pottery could have been produced without kilns (e.g., in bonfires). The painted pottery was deposited at the site mainly in cavities (the function of which remains unclear) which might have been filled during the course of ceremonies (rather than as during the removal of domestic refuse).

Small quantities of this pottery were also exported to other sites in Abruzzo and further afield (e.g., to southern and

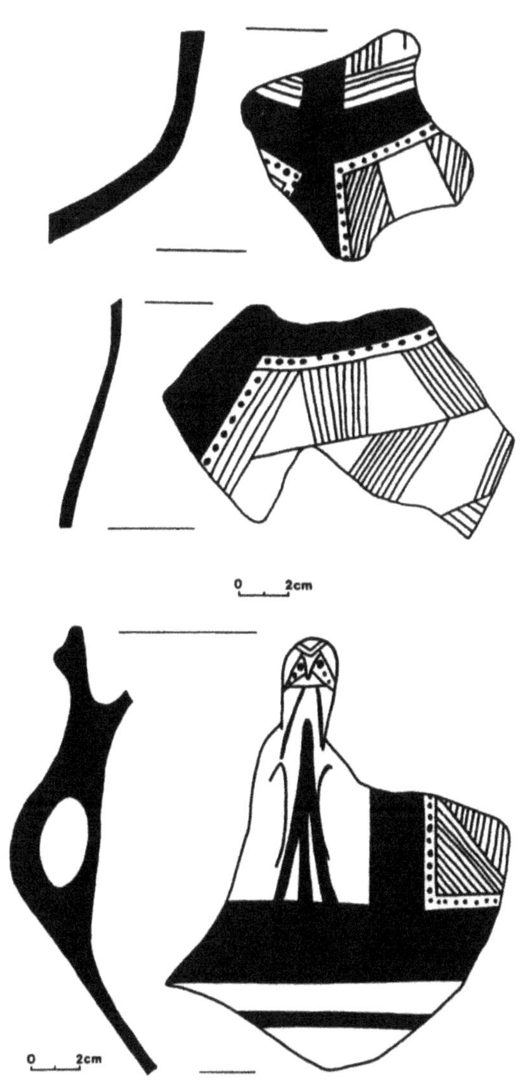

Figure 4 Painted fineware from Ripoli (drawn from the originals in the Atri museum deposit).

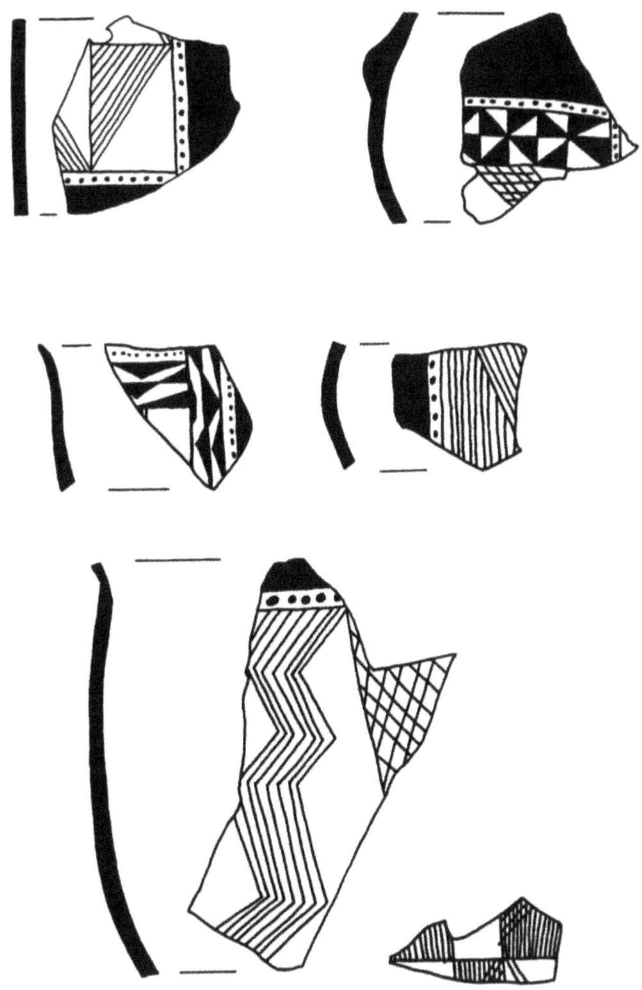

Figure 5 Painted fineware from Ripoli (drawn from the originals in the Atri museum deposit).

west-central Italy and even Liguria in north-west Italy over 450 kilometres away)[2] (Appendix 2). Half of these sites were caves in which the painted pots appear to have been ritually deposited alongside an increasingly wide range of other special objects. In Grotta dei Piccioni in Abruzzo, for example, Ripoli painted pottery was found in the same deposits as other styles of imported pottery, disarticulated human remains, animal meat bones, personal ornaments (made of sea shells and coral), a red painted shell trumpet, a group of intentionally deposited whole pottery vessels, and a concentration of possibly intentionally smashed pots (Skeates 1991). In Grotta Scaloria Alta (in northern Puglia) local and imported pottery vessels (including some from Ripoli) were left with great care in order that they collect stilicide water; over the course of thousands of years they have become completely embedded in the stalactites (Tinè and Isetti 1975-80).

The Ripoli style was one of a number of regional variants within a broadly shared inter-regional style of trichrome painted fineware that was produced and exchanged by various later Neolithic groups in central and southern Italy and Dalmatia. Chronological precedence can be given to the Danilo and Scaloria Alta styles of Dalmatia and northern Puglia which appear, in part, to have influenced the local development of the Ripoli style (Skeates 1992). On such vessels, regional variation is exhibited by the specific decorative motifs and their organisation; inter-regional uniformity is exhibited by the broader decorative style which organised the motifs into panels filled with dark geometric linear patterns and was bordered by black or brown bands. It has been suggested that the specific motifs only had local significance whereas the general style was read and transferred between distant communities (Chapman 1988).

This general stylistic uniformity seems explicable with reference to the broader context of the long-distance inter-regional exchange networks which expanded significantly throughout the central Mediterranean region at this time (Skeates 1993). The networks are clearly represented in the archaeological record by the long-distance movement of valuable commodities. These included not only regional styles of painted fineware but also obsidian bladelets, greenstone axes and sea-shell ornaments. It is also possible that less archaeologically visible things (such as special foods and drinks, marriage partners, and special skills and knowledge – including those relating to potting), circulated alongside these objects. On the basis of analogies with the work of social anthropologists stretching back to that of Marcel Mauss (1967), it is tempting to suggest that such exchanges took place as part of a large-scale system of alliance and ceremony within which compacts of peace, friendship, marriage and kinship (or of revenge and war) were made between members of different communities and were marked by ceremonial and reciprocal exchanges of valuable gifts. Such systems ensure not only the sharing of geographically localised commodities and cultural information but also can enhance or diminish the prestige, authority and status of groups and individuals, particularly through the creation of dependency and debt.

Assuming that such a context is appropriate to the Neolithic of the central Mediterranean region, it is tempting to pull together all these different lines of enquiry concerning the Ripoli painted pottery (including the study of its form, function, decoration, exchange and final deposition) and to propose a more detailed model of its social meaning and value. On a local scale, the production and use (both daily and on special occasions) of the regionally distinctive Ripoli style of painted fineware may (like the previous Catignano style) have contributed to enhancing the identity, legitimacy and cohesion of a newly established social group at a time of continuing agricultural settlement, social aggregation and growing competition between lowland communities over resources. On an inter-community and inter-regional scale, such pots (painted in regionally distinctive but overlapping styles) could have contributed to a process of social integration and differentiation, particularly when used and displayed on ceremonial occasions in which socially distant groups came together to form alliances and exchange gifts. More specifically, the pots (including their decoration and contents) could have contributed to heightening the social effect of such ceremonial activities. By displaying a recognisably shared decorative style (and perhaps also by serving potent drinks, such as stilicide water or early alcoholic beverages such as mead or beer which could have acted as social lubricants and agents of hospitality) the pots could have contributed to reducing the stress inherent in encounters and to helping turn foreigners into friends. On the other hand, through their dazzling beauty and their stylistic influence and through the potency and generosity of their contents, the pots could have contained an element of rivalry and could have been manipulated to win prestige on such occasions.

4400-3400 BC

From about 4400 BC, the ceramics of the Abruzzo region underwent further changes. Potters produced increasing quantities of relatively indistinguishable fine black and red burnished ware which was often plain or minimally decorated with simple incised motifs or by the application of plastic features. Also, there was a corresponding decrease in the production of the fine yellow figulina fabric and in its painted decoration. In fact trichrome painting was abandoned and was replaced (at sites such as Fonti di San Callisto) by the limited use of a new black paint which exhibited some new motifs such as the checkerboard and the wavy line placed around the rim of vessels (Fig. 6). By about 4200 BC pottery painting had been abandoned entirely. That is not to say that fineware in itself became de-

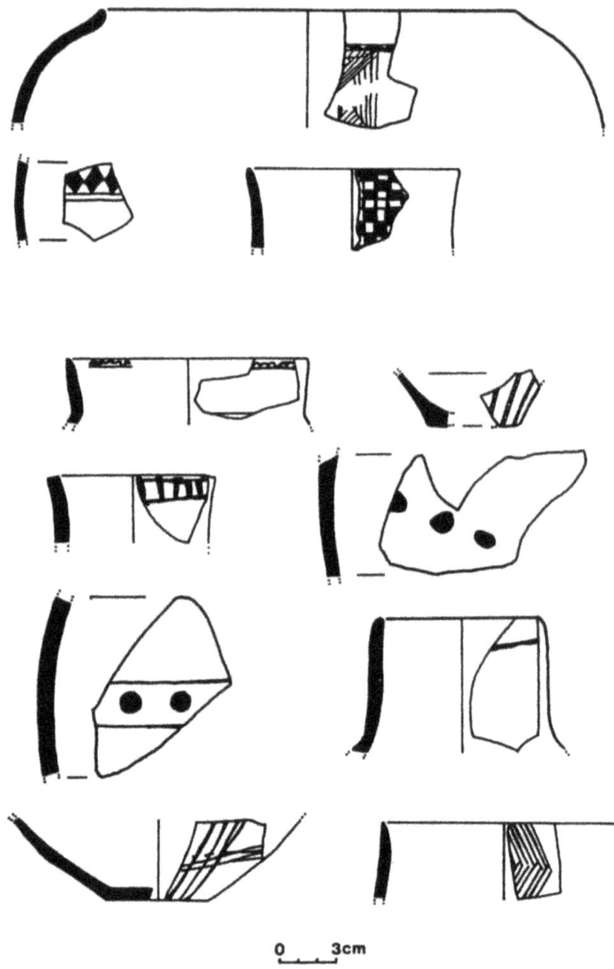

Figure 6 Painted pottery from Fonti di S. Callisto (after Radi 1986-7).

valued at this time; a black fineware cup was placed near to some bodies in one of the burial cavities which made up the new cemetery established in the middle of the Ripoli site. Inland at Grotta la Punta there are some examples of monochrome fineware that look like long-distance imports from southern and northern Italy.

This ties in more broadly with evidence concerning the inter-regional exchange network which now appears to have reached a peak of stability and extent in the central Mediterranean region. This is reflected by the increase in the quantity and range of exotic commodities flowing into the Abruzzo region (including a new range of stone weapons and the first copper tools) which were accompanied by broader cultural changes (e.g., in subsistence and mortuary practices). Within this system, the origins of the stylistic changes in Abruzzo can be clearly traced to influential ceramic traditions previously established in southern and northern Italy (the late Serra d'Alto and Diana-Bellavista styles and the Lagozza style respectively). As in earlier periods, this suggests that potters in Abruzzo were somewhat culturally dependent upon their more innovative and influential neighbours whose ceramic styles they again emulated. However, the impact of these external stylistic influences was felt throughout much of the central Mediterranean region at this time. The widespread result was that elaborately decorated and regionally distinguishable styles of painted fineware were abandoned in favour of equally fine (but increasing plain and uniform) finewares which conformed to more inter-regionally recognisable styles. By masking traditional regional differences (which were bound up with traditional forms of material culture and ritual practice) and by emphasising similarities in the style of their finewares (which were displayed, used and exchanged on public occasions), potters may have participated in a widespread strategy adopted by local groups to maintain and strengthen their social access to the increasingly important long-distance ceremonial exchange networks. This was essentially the same strategy that was pursued by social groups in Abruzzo throughout the Neolithic and which led not only to the adoption and development but also the abandonment of Neolithic painted pottery in peninsular Italy.

Endnotes

1. All dates are in calibrated years BC.

2. The scale of the export of Ripoli style painted pottery to sites outside Abruzzo has been commonly over-estimated in previous studies. This is due to an inappropriately broad definition of the Ripoli style and also because Ripoli was one of the first sites with Neolithic painted pottery to be discovered and excavated in Italy (e.g., Bray 1966; Barfield 1981; Malone 1986). Therefore, in order to distinguish it from other Italian painted pottery styles, I favour a strict and narrow definition of the Ripoli style: pottery with a figulina fabric and a decoration of trichrome painted zones generally comprising parallel lines or filled triangles bordered first by a narrow band containing a row of dots and then by a broad red band.

Acknowledgements

I would like to thank my colleagues in the School of World Art Studies and Museology at the University of East Anglia (and Cesare Poppi in particular) for their comments on an earlier draft of this paper.

Bibliography

Amerano, G. B. 1891. Dei vasi colorati e dipinti a disegni geometrici delle caverne del Finale (Liguria). *Bulletino di Paletnologia Italiana* 17: 91-103.

Arnold, D. 1985. *Ceramic Theory and Cultural Process.* Cambridge: Cambridge University Press.

Babcock, B.A. 1993. At home, no womens are storytellers: ceramic creativity and the politics of discourse in Cochiti Pueblo. In *Creativity/anthropology*, edited by S. Lavie, K. Narayan, K. and R. Rosaldo, R., pp. 70-99. Ithaca: Cornell University Press.

Barfield, L. H. 1981. Patterns of north Italian trade 5000-2000 b.c. In *Archaeology and Italian Society. Prehistoric, Roman and Medieval Studies*, edited by G. Barker and R. Hodges, pp. 215-223. Oxford: BAR.

Barley, N. 1994. *Smashing Pots: Feats of Clay from Africa.* London: British Museum Press.

Barra, A., R. Grifoni Cremonesi, F. Mallegni, M. Poancastelli, A. Vitello, A. and B. Wilkens 1989-90. La Grotta Continenza di Trasacco. I livelli a ceramiche. *Rivista di Scienze Preistoriche* 42: 32-100.

Berns, M.C. 1990. Pots as people: Yungur ancestral portraits. *African Arts* 23(3): 50-60.

Bianco, S. and M. Cipolloni Sampò 1987. Il neolitico della Basilicata. *Atti della XXVI Riunione Scientifica, Istituto Italiano di Preistoria e Protostoria. Il Neolitico in Italia.* Firenze: IIPP: 301-320.

Bonuccelli, G. and Faedo, L. 1968. Il villaggio a Ceramica Impressa di Capo d'Acqua. *Atti della Società Toscana di Scienze Naturali* 75: 87-101.

Borzatti von Löwenstern, E. 1962b. Scavi nella Grotta S. Nicola nel bacino del Fucino. *Rivista di Scienze Preistoriche* 17: 205-222.

Bray, W. 1966. Neolithic painted ware in the Adriatic. *Antiquity* 40: 100-106.

Burri, E. 1977. Pitture rupestri nella Valle del fiume Orta (Abruzzo). (Nota preliminare). *Bollettino del Centro Camuno di Studi Preistorici* 16: 141-147.

Chapman, J.C. 1988. Ceramic production and social differentiation: the Dalmatian Neolithic and the western Mediterranean. *Journal of Mediterranean Archaeology* 1: 3-25.

Cremonesi, G. 1965. Il villaggio di Ripoli alla luce dei recenti scavi. *Rivista di Scienze Preistoriche* 20: 85-155.

Cremonesi, G. 1968. Contributo alla conoscenza della preistoria del Fucino: la grotta di Ortucchio e la Grotta la Punta. *Rivista di Scienze Preistoriche* 23: 145-204.

Cremonesi, G. 1973. Il villaggio neolitico di Fossacesia (Chieti). Nota preliminare. *Bollettino del Centro Camuno di Studi Preistorici* 10: 79-88.

Cremonesi, G. 1976. *La Grotta dei Piccioni di Bolognano nel Quadro delle Culture dal Neolitico all'Età del*

Bronzo in Abruzzo. Pisa: Giardini.

Cremonesi, G. 1985. Note su nuovi insediamenti dell'Età dei Metalli nella piana del Fucino. In *Studi di paletnologia in onore di Salvatore M. Puglisi*, edited by M. Liverani, A. Palmieri and R. Peroni, R, pp. 791-804. Roma: Dipartimento di Scienze Storiche, Archeologiche e Antropologiche dell l'Antichità, Università di Roma 'La Sapienza'.

Dall'Osso, I. 1915. *Guida illustrata del Museo Nazionale di Ancona*. Ancona: Museo Nazionale di Ancona.

David, N., J. Sterner and K. Gavua 1988. Why pots are decorated. *Current Anthropology* 29(3): 365-389.

DeBoer, W.R. 1991. The decorative burden: design, medium, and change. In *Ceramic Ethnoarchaeology*, edited by W. Longacre, pp. 144-161. Tucson: The University of Arizona Press.

Delpino, F. and M.A. Fugazzola Delpino 1987. La di Monte Venere nell'ambito della cultura del Sasso. *Atti della XXVI riunione Scientifica, Istituto Italiano di Preistoria e Protostoria. Il Neolitico in Italia*. Firenze: IIPP: 671-679.

De Pompeis, C. 1978. Resti di un villaggio della cultura di Ripoli a Città Sant'Angelo (Abruzzo). *Atti della Società Toscana di Scienze Naturali* 85: 161-170.

D'Ercole, V. 1988. L'Abruzzo dalle comunità di villaggio alle società urbane. Unpublished MS.

Ducci, S., Perazzi, P. and Ronchitelli, A. 1986-7. Gli insediamenti neolitici Abruzzesi con Ceramica Impressa di Tricalle (CH) e Fontanelle (PE). *Rassegna di Archeologia* 1986-7: 65-128.

Fugazzola Delpino, M. A. 1987. Il Neolitico nel Lazio settentrionale. *Atti della XXVI riunione scientifica, Istituto Italiano di Preistoria e Protostoria. Il Neolitico in Italia*. Firenze: IIPP: pp. 253-271.

Geniola, A. 1982. *Marcianese. Il Villaggio Rossi. Entità del Neolitico Medio Arcaico Abruzzese*. Lanciano: Itinerari.

Graves, M.W. 1991. Pottery production and distribution among the Kalinga: a study of household and regional organization and differentiation. In *Ceramic Ethnoarchaeology*, edited by W. Longacre, 112-143. Tucson: The University of Arizona Press.

Graziosi, P. 1944. La Grotta all'Onda. *Archivio per l'Antropologia e la Etnologia*, 72: 73-100.

Grifoni Cremonesi, R. 1988. L'area del parco nazionale d'Abruzzo a del pre-parco dal Paleolitico all'Età del Bronzo. *Atti del 1ø Convegno Nazionale di Archeologia. Villetta Barrea, 1/2/3 Maggio 1987*: 19-26.

Grifoni, R. and A.M. Radmilli 1964. La Grotta Maritza e il Fucino prima dell'età Romana. *Rivista di Scienze Preistoriche* 19: 53-127.

Herbert, E.W. 1993. *Iron, Gender and Power. Rituals of Transformation in African Societies*. Bloomington: Indiana University Press.

Hodder, I. 1979. Pottery distributions: service and tribal areas. In *Pottery and the Archaeologist*, edited by M. Millett, pp. 7-23. London: Institute of Archaeology.

Hodder, I. 1982. *Symbols in Action: Ethnoarchaeological Studies of Material Culture*. Cambridge: Cambridge University Press.

Malone, C. 1985. Pots, prestige and ritual in Neolithic southern Italy. In *Papers in Italian Archaeology IV. The Cambridge Conference. Part II. Prehistory* edited by C. Malone and S. Stoddart, pp. 118-151. Oxford: BAR.

Malone, C. 1986. *Exchange Systems and Style in the Central Mediterranean 4500 - 1700 B.C.* Unpublished doctoral dissertation, University of Cambridge.

Mattiocco, E. 1981. *Centri Fortificati Preromani nella Conca di Sulmona*. Chieti: Soprintendenza Archeologica dell'Abruzzo.

Mattiocco, E. 1986. *Centri fortificati Vestini*. Sulmona: Soprintendenza Archeologica dell'Abruzzo, Museo Civico di Sulmona.

Mauss, M. 1967. *The Gift: Forms and Functions of Exchange in Archaic Societies*. London: Norton.

Miller, D. 1994. Artefacts and the meaning of things. In *Companion Encyclopedia of Anthropology*, edited bt T. Ingold, pp. 396-419. London: Routledge.

Palma di Cesnola, A. 1967. Il Neolitico medio e superiore di San Domino (Arcipelago delle Tremiti). *Rivista di Scienze Preistoriche* 22: 349-392.

Passeri, L. 1970. Ritrovamenti preistorici nei Pozzi della Piana (Umbria). *Rivista di Scienze Preistoriche* 25: 225-251.

Radi, G. 1979. Resti di un villaggio neolitico a Villa Badessa (Pescara). *Atti della Società Toscana di Scienze Naturali* 86: 405-414.

Radmilli, A. M. 1981. *Storia dell'Abruzzo dalle Origini all'Età del Bronzo*. (Second edition). Pisa: Giardini.

Rellini, U. 1934. *La Più Antica Ceramica Dipinta in Italia.* Roma: Meridionale.

Rozzi, R. and A.M. Radmilli 1951-2. Tortoreto di Abruzzo (Teramo). Villaggio eneolitico del Pianaccio. *Bullettino di Paletnologia Italiana* 8: 112-115.

Russi, V. 1981. Puglia. Notiziario. *Rivista di Scienze Preistoriche* 36: 343.

Skeates, R. 1991 Caves, cult and children in Neolithic Abruzzo, central Italy. In *Sacred and Profane*, edited by P. Garwood, D. Jennings, R. Skeates and J. Toms, pp. 122-134. Oxford: Oxford University Committee for Archaeology.

Skeates, R. 1992. *The Neolithic and Copper Age of the Abruzzo-Marche Region, Central Italy.* Unpublished doctoral dissertation, University of Oxford.

Skeates, R. 1993. Neolithic exchange in central and southern Italy. In *Trade and Exchange in Prehistoric Europe*, edited by C. Scarre and F. Healy, pp. 109-114. Oxford: Oxbow Books.

Skeates, R. 1994. Towards an absolute chronology for the Neolithic in central Italy. In *Radiocarbon Dating and Italian Prehistory*, edited by R. Skeates and R. Whitehouse, pp. 61-72. London: Accordia Research Centre and The British School at Rome.

Tinè, S. and E. Isetti 1975-80. Culto neolitico delle acque e recenti scavi nella Grotta Scaloria. *Bullettino di Paletnologia Italiana* 82: 31-70.

Tozzi, C. 1978. Un aspetto della corrente culturale della ceramica dipinta in Abruzzo: il villaggio di Catignano (Pescara). *Quaderni de la Ricerca Scientifica* 100: 95-111.

Tozzi, C. 1982. La transition du Néolithique ancien au Néolithique moyen dans la côté Adriatique (Abruzzo-Marche). Le Néolithique ancien Méditerranéen. *Actes du colloque international de préhistoire. Montpellier 1981. Archéologie en Languedoc*: 319-324.

Whitehouse, R.D. 1992. *Underground Religion: Cult and Culture in Prehistoric Italy.* London: Accordia Research Centre.

Winn, S. M. M. and D.M. Shimabuku 1980. *The Heritage of Two Subsistence Strategies: Preliminary Report on the Excavations at Grotta Scaloria, Southeastern Italy, 1978.* (Occasional Papers in Anthropology 9) Halifax, Nova Scotia: Department of Anthropology, St. Mary's University,.

Appendix 1

Sites in Abruzzo with Neolithic painted pottery. Provinces: CH - Chieti; PE - Pescara; AQ - L'Aquila; TE - Teramo.

Period	Site	Prov	Coloured decoration	References
5500-4850 BC	Villagio Rossi	CH	Red-filled incisions	Geniola 1982
	Fontanelle	PE	Brown painted lines, red-filled incisions & a ? red coloured surface	Ducci et al. 1986-7
	Grotta dei Piccioni, spits 22-21	PE	2 sherds with traces of red colouring	Cremonesi 1976
	Capo d'Acqua	AQ	1 sherd simple red band	Bonuccelli & Faedo 1968
	Cellitto	AQ	Red painted	Cremenosi 1985
	Grotta S. Angelo, stratum IV	TE	Red painted bands	Radmilli 1981
4850-4600 BC: Catignano style	Catignano	PE	Red & white filled incised, bichrome red paint, trichrome red & brown/black paint	Tozzi 1978, 1982
	Grotta Oscura	PE	Simple red band paint	Burri 1977
	Grotta di Pescosansonesco	PE	Catignano red band paint	Radmilli 1981
	Grotta dei Piccioni, spits 20-18	PE	Red and black paint	Cremonesi 1976
	Villa Badessa	PE	Bichrome red painted	Radi 1979
	Grotta Continenza	AQ	3 sherds simple red band	Barra et al. 1989-90
	Grotta S. Nicola	AQ	2 sherds red painted	Borzatti von Lowenstern 1962
	Grotta S. Angelo, stratum V	TE	Catignano red band paint	Radmilli 1981
4600-4400 BC: Ripoli style	Grotta di Pescosansonesco	PE	Ripoli painted	Radmilli 1981
	Grotta dei Piccioni, spits 17-16	PE	Red and brown bichrome paint	Cremonesi 1976
	S. Agnese	PE	Red paint	De Pompeis 1978
	Cellitto	AQ	Ripoli painted	Grifoni Cremonesi 1988:23
	Grotta Maritza, spits 28-24	AQ	Red & brown bichrome paint	Grifoni & Radmilli 1964
	Settefonti	TE	Ripoli painted	Mattiocco 1986
	Grotta S. Angelo, stratum V	TE	Ripoli painted	Radmilli 1981
	Pianaccio	TE	Red & yellow paint	Rozzi & Radmilli 1951-2
	Ripoli, eg. cavity 12	TE	Red & brown bichrome & trichrome paint	Dall'Osso 1915; Rellini 1934; Cremonesi 1965
	S. Domenico	TE	Ripoli painted	D'Ercole 1988
	S. Mario a Vico	TE	Ripoli painted	D'Ercole 1988
4400-3400 BC	Fossacesia	CH	Red-filled incised, red tinted	Cremonesi 1973
	Fonti di S. Callisto, lower level	PE	Red, brown & black bichrome, 1 sherd red & black bichrome paint	Mattiocco 1981
	Grotta dei Piccioni, spits 15-12	PE	Red & brown bichrome & trichrome paint, 1 red coloured	Cremonesi 1976
	Grotta la Punta, spits 9-8	AQ	Bichrome & trichrome paint	Cremonesi 1968

Appendix 2

Sites outside Abruzzo with Ripoli painted pottery

Site	Italian region	Pottery references
Cala Tramontana	S. Domino	12+ sherds from flask. Palma di Cesnola 1967: Figs. 15.1, 10.4
Contrada Ciccalento	N. Puglia	1 sherd. Russi 1981: 343
Grotta Scaloria Alta	N. Puglia	3+ sherds. Tine & Isetti 1975-80: Tav. B. 1-2; Winn & Shimabulu 1980: Pl. VIII. A-B
Loenessa di Melfi	N. Basilicata	1 sherd. Bianco & Cipololli Sampo 1987: 311, Fig. 3.3
Il Fosso dei Due	Ponti Lazio	1 sherd. Fugazzola Delpino 1987: 261, Fig. 4
Grotta Lattaia	Toscana	1 sherd. Cremonesi 1965: 129
Grotta all'Onda	Toscana	? 1 sherd. Graziosi 1944
Grotta delle Felci	Capri	1 sherd: cup. Rellini 1923: 328-9, Tav. II.6
Caverna dell'Acqua	Liguria	1 sherd: cup. Amerano 1891: Tav. IX.1

Index

(**bold** page numbers refer to figures, maps or tables)

www.ingramcontent.com/pod-product-compliance
Lightning Source LLC
LaVergne TN
LVHW071217210926
848482LV00015B/835